Asia's W9-BCN-530 Giant

Asia's Next Giant

South Korea and Late Industrialization

Alice H. Amsden

OXFORD UNIVERSITY PRESS
New York Oxford

Oxford University Press

Oxford   New York   Toronto
Delhi   Bombay   Calcutta   Madras   Karachi
Petaling Jaya   Singapore   Hong Kong   Tokyo
Nairobi   Dar es Salaam   Cape Town
Melbourne   Auckland

and associated companies in
Berlin   Ibadan

Library of Congress Cataloging-in-Publication Data

Amsden, Alice H.
Asia's next giant.
Bibliography: p.
Includes index.
1. Korea (South)—Industries. 2. Industry and
state—Korea (South) 3. Korea (South)—Economic
conditions—1960–   . 4. Korea (South)–Economic
policy—1960–   . I. Title.
HC467.A629   1989   338.09519′5   88-36231
ISBN 0-19-505852-6
ISBN 0-19-507603-6 (PBK.)

4 6 8 10 7 5 3

Printed in the United States of America

Preface

This book seeks an answer to the puzzle of why South Korea has grown so much faster than most developing countries, even those that have gone through what is called "late industrialization." Late industrialization applies to a subset of developing countries that began the twentieth century in an economically backward state based on raw materials, and dramatically raised national income per capita by selectively investing in industry. Included are South Korea, Taiwan, Brazil, Turkey, India, and Mexico. This book also treats Japan as a late-industrializing country, which makes the list all the more heterogeneous. Diversity notwithstanding, *all late industrializers have in common industrialization on the basis of learning,* which has conditioned how they have behaved. These countries industrialized by borrowing foreign technology rather than by generating new products or processes, the hallmark of earlier industrializing nations.

South Korea's growth is a classic example of late industrialization, and embodies all of the elements common to these countries. It has involved a high degree of state intervention to get relative prices "wrong" in order to overcome the penalties of lateness, the growth of large diversified business groups (even in Taiwan) to transcend the hardships of having to compete without the advantages of novel technology, the emergence of salaried managers responsible for exploiting the borrowed technology (the private entrepreneur in large companies playing a much reduced role compared to earlier times), and a focus on shopfloor management to optimize technology transfer. All these factors allowed Korea to be among the first countries to penetrate world markets on the basis of low wages rather than a technological edge. England succeeded during the First Industrial Revolution on the basis of invention, and leading firms in Germany and the United States at a later time captured market share from England on the basis of innovation.

But Korea has succeeded far beyond the non-East Asian late industrializers. This book will examine in detail the factors that contributed to its success. It will analyze the crucial role of government not only in subsidizing certain industries to stimulate growth, but in setting stringent performance standards in exchange for the subsidies. In other countries—in Turkey and India, for example—subsidies have been dispensed primarily as giveaways. In Korea the "wrong" prices have been right because government discipline over business has enabled subsidies and protection to be less than elsewhere and more effective. If the big business groups of Korea have been loaned long term capital at negative real interest rates, the government has demanded that they use the borrowed capital productively, not speculatively. If they have been allowed to sell in protected domestic markets, they have had to produce and sell in the export market. Discipline over business as well as labor provided the starting point for high growth rates of productivity, which allowed Korea to borrow extensively in international capital markets without overextending itself financially. The Big Push into heavy industry was financed primarily with overseas loans, but at the beginning and end of the period 1973 to 1979, the ratio of foreign debt to GNP was virtually unchanged.

The book will also examine why the power of the state to discipline big business was greater in Korea—and Japan and Taiwan as well—than in other late-industrializing countries. Although the historical and cultural factors that, in turn, drove the Korean state to act in a relatively disciplined fashion are too complex to be considered in detail, they include meritocracy in the civil service, militarism, raw material scarcity, and not least of all, a hyperactive student movement that mobilized popular support to keep the government honest. Appropriately enough in an industrialization based on learning, the role of students should not be minimized, either as conscience of the industrialization process or as key resource.

A country like Korea can serve as a useful model from which other aspiring industrializing countries can learn. What is required, however, is an empirically relevant theory of both the general paradigm of late industrialization and its special variants—particularly as found in South Korea. It is toward the development of such a theory that this book is dedicated.

Company-level research for the present volume was undertaken initially in conjunction with a project sponsored by the Productivity Division, Department of Economic Development, of the World Bank, entitled "The Acquisition of Technological Capability in Newly Industrializing Countries." I am indebted to the bank for financial assistance. I also benefited from discussions with participants on the project, and the following people were particularly helpful: Carl Dahlman, Linsu Kim, Sanjaya Lall, Francisco Sercovich, Simon Teitel, and Larry Westphal. Linsu Kim and I were collaborators on this project and to him I owe an especially large debt of gratitude for his insights into Korean management, and to the distinction between learning through copying and imitating and learning through apprenticing with foreign firms.

Additional financial support was provided by the Division of Research of the Harvard Business School. I am grateful to Dean John McArthur, Jay Lorsch, and Ray Corey for their consistent help. I also wish to thank the following people at the school for stimulating discussions: the late William Abernathy, Kim Clark, Therese Flaherty, Jai Jaikumar, George Lodge, Earl Sasser, Bruce Scott, Richard Rosenbloom, and Lou Wells. Alfred D. Chandler, Jr. provided unstinting guidance and personal encouragement.

My field work in Korea benefited from the assistance and cooperation of many individuals in different capacities. Mong Joon Chung was particularly helpful in facilitating my research at the Hyundai group. I am especially indebted to the following people for helping me to understand the dynamics of shopfloor management: K. S. Choi, Shipbuilding Division, Hyundai Heavy Industries, and S. B. Hong and Y. S. Chough, Pohang Iron and Steel Company. Sun Shik Min of Harvard Business School provided excellent research assistance, as did Choon Heng Leong for an earlier draft. Young-Ki Kim Renaud taught me the basics of the Korean language at Harvard College.

This book benefited from initial editing by Marilyn Shephard, and was also improved by helpful comments from Herbert J. Addison. Jean Smith and Aehyung Kim oversaw final efforts in completing the manuscript. The people in the Word Processing Center at Harvard Business School, some of the world's best typists, bore the brunt of the work.

Finally, I am deeply indebted to the following people for intellectual as well as personal support: Richard Bensel, David Cole, Takashi Hikino, Richard R. Nelson, Myra Strober, Lance Taylor, and Raymond Vernon. The book is dedicated to my mother, Regina Scharer Hoffenberg, and to the memory of my father, the late Julius William Hoffenberg.

Contents

    Back-Door Competition   319
    From Learner to Teacher   320
    Labor Relations   324

    Epilogue   327

    Bibliography   331

    Name Index   353

    Subject Index   359

Tables and Figures

Figures

Asia's Next Giant

CHAPTER ONE

Industrializing through Learning

THE CASE OF KOREA

This is a book about Korea and how it came to be a major factor in the world economy. But it is also a book about the industrialization process that Korea followed. This process, which will hereafter be referred to as *late industrialization,* has profound implications for a range of other countries that are also struggling to compete in the world of international business. Korea's success in this struggle can thus be seen both as a fascinating story in itself and as an example from which others may learn. It is also an example of a new way of industrializing that challenges long-held assumptions of generations of economic thinkers.

LEARNING: A NEW MODE OF INDUSTRIALIZATION

The First Industrial Revolution in Britain, toward the end of the eighteenth century, and the Second Industrial Revolution in Germany and the United States, approximately 100 years later, shared the distinction of generating new products and processes. By contrast, economies that did not begin industrialization until about the twentieth century tended to generate neither, their products and processes being based on older technology. Economies commencing industrialization in the twentieth century transformed their productive structures and raised their incomes per capita on the basis of borrowed technology. They produced using processes conceived by unallied economic and political units. The means by which they managed to compete will be referred to here as *learning.*[1]

The nature and role played by technical knowledge, therefore, separates the industrial revolutions in England, Germany, and the United States, on the one hand, from the industrialization that oc-

[1] Gerschenkron (1962) explored the costs and benefits of backwardness, but he did not systematically examine catching up as a process of learning how to compete.

curred in twentieth-century agrarian societies. If industrialization first occurred in England on the basis of invention, and if it occurred in Germany and the United States on the basis of innovation, then it occurs now among "backward" countries on the basis of learning.

The paradigm of late industrialization through learning generalizes to a diverse assortment of countries with different growth records: Japan (although in many respects it is unique among late-industrializing countries), South Korea, Taiwan, Brazil, India, possibly Mexico, and Turkey. (This list might be expanded, but one cannot add to it the city-states of Singapore and Hong Kong, because neither began from the agrarian or raw material base that is typically taken to be the starting point of industrial transformation.) Growth rates differ among late-industrializing countries, but in all cases industrialization has come about as a process of learning rather than of generation of inventions or innovations. Learning, moreover, has been based on a similar set of institutions. This book explores the nature of these institutions in general and suggests why Korea has performed so successfully. The conventional explanation for why countries like Korea, Japan, and Taiwan have grown relatively fast is that they have conformed to free-market principles. In fact, the fundamentals of their industrial policies are the same as those of other late industrializers. In all cases key prices do not reflect true scarcities. Instead, it is argued in the chapters that follow, Korea has had an outstanding growth record because the institutions on which late industrialization is based have been managed differently.

Industrialization on the basis of learning rather than of invention or innovation is not unique to the twentieth century. The global process of industrialization has always tended to be combined and uneven, with leaders and laggards, forerunners and followers. If England pioneered on the basis of invention in the eighteenth century, Continental Europe and the United States pursued on the basis of learning in the nineteenth. If Germany were itself an innovator in the nineteenth century, it also studied the examples of early England and other emulators such as France and the Netherlands. The United States in the nineteenth century has been described as both borrower and initiator (Rosenberg, 1972). While many American and German firms were innovative leaders, most were followers.

Nevertheless, a process of industrialization whose central tendency among leading firms is learning rather than invention or innovation of significantly novel technology is a distinct phenomenon and deserves treatment as such. For individual firms the absence or presence of new technology generation is decisive in determining the basis on which they compete internationally. Innovators are aided in the conquest of markets by novel products or processes. Learners do not innovate (by definition) and must compete initially on the combined basis of low wages, state subsidies (broadly construed to include a wide variety of government supports), and incremental productivity and quality improvements related to existing products. In turn, different modes of competing are associated with differences in firms' *strategic focus*.

The corporate office, inclusive of research and development functions, tends to be the strategic focus of companies that compete on the basis of innovation. This is because it is at the administrative level that new technology gets developed and marketed. Critical significance is attached to the organization and operation of research and development because here are created the profit-making opportunities that drive the entire company.

The shopfloor tends to be the strategic focus of firms that compete on the basis of borrowed technology. The shopfloor is the focus because it is here that borrowed technology is first made operational and later optimized. Because products similar to those that the company produces are internationally available, the strategic focus is necessarily found on the shopfloor, where the achievement of incremental, yet cumulative, improvements in productivity and product specification are essential to enhance price and quality competitiveness.

Beginning in the 1960s, learners have moved rapidly into the mature markets developed by innovators. The high *level* of productivity of long-established innovators has been contested by learners' lower wages, higher subsidies, as well as intense efforts to raise productivity incrementally. Total costs in many industries appear to have run neck and neck (see the discussions of cotton textiles, ships, and steel in later chapters). International competition has heated to a degree that may be unprecedented.

THE RELATIVE SPEEDS OF INDUSTRIALIZATIONS

While the most successful twentieth-century industrializers have invited inquiry about their rapid growth and structural change, the nineteenth-century European emulators have drawn attention to their slowness. In the words of David Landes,

> In this effort to study and emulate British techniques, the nations of western Europe were favored by a number of advantages. To begin with, they had behind them an experience of organized and increasingly effective political behavior. . . . Similarly, their supply of capital and standard of living were sub-

stantially higher than in the "backward" lands of today. And with this went a level of technical skill that, if not immediately adequate to the task of sustaining an industrial revolution, was right at the margin. . . . In short, if they were in their day "underdeveloped," the word must be understood quite differently from the way it is today. . . . Nevertheless, their Industrial Revolution was substantially slower than the British.

Why the delay? Surely, the hardest task would seem to have been the original creative acts that produced coke smelting, the mule, and the steam engine. In view of the enormous economic superiority of these innovations, one would expect the rest to have followed automatically. (Landes, 1969, pp. 125–6)

Why indeed the delay? And why was it that industrialization beginning in the late nineteenth century and then following World War II appears to have progressed far faster than that of the Napoleonic War period?[2] Part of the answer lies in the advancement of science, which is worth discussing here briefly. The advancement of science underlies the distinction between industrializing by invention in the First Industrial Revolution and industrializing by innovation in the Second. Scientific advancement also had an electrifying effect on the growth rates of twentieth-century latecomers.

As the terms are typically used, *invention* and *innovation* are intimately connected, because innovation presupposes invention in a logical sense. In textbook treatments of new technological developments, invention is associated with the idea and comes first, followed by innovation or the application of the idea to commercial uses. Invention and innovation are regarded here, however, not as abstract stages, one preceding the other in new technological discoveries, but rather as descriptions of particular historical periods, invention preceding innovation in an intergenerational sense. As characteristics of two distinct time periods, one key difference between the two lies in their degree of scientific content.

The scientific content of the inventions of the First Industrial Revolution moved the world far beyond the mysticism of the Middle Ages toward a transparent understanding of how mechanical devices worked, but discoveries occurred primarily by observation, trial, and error. The Second Industrial Revolution, however, represented a discrete giant step forward insofar as technological change began to occur, far more than previously, on the basis of theory and experimentation (Bernal, 1965).

---

[2] Maddison (1982) provided time series data on trends in output and per capita income. His research suggests that both variables grew faster in sequentially later industrializers.

The application of science to production provided the basis for the stream of German and American innovations that lowered the British flag. For three interrelated reasons, the advancement of science also made it far easier for technology to be transferred, and so science had a profound effect on the "backward" countries: (1) Although technology remained (and still remains) idiosyncratic even in basic industries, higher scientific content increased its codifiedness or explicitness, making it more of a commodity and hence more technically and commercially accessible and diffusible from country to country.[3] (2) The application of science in the fields of transportation, communications, and management improved the *means* of technology transfer. Technical assistance, not being dependent on the know-how of a particular person, can now be dispatched over longer distances to larger numbers of people more quickly and anonymously. (3) The crowding out of art by science on the shop floor has dealt a blow to the skilled craftsworker.[4] The rise in the scientific content of technology has made operations far easier to transfer to a group of latter-day learners among whom all-around mechanical skills are scarce.

The impact of the advancement of science on the "backward" regions was ambiguous, however. Despite the benefits, it created a far wider gap in relative income levels and technological capabilities than existed previously between nations, and it also strengthened the hand of the stronger nations over the weaker. In any event, taking all factors into consideration, the speed with which late learners in the twentieth century have industrialized may not be any greater than that of the European emulators in the early nineteenth century. What is decisive is how one dates the onset of industrialization and how one decides when a country can legitimately be described as industrialized.

If one dates the start of industrialization in the European emulators from, say, 1776, when the new economic order in Britain was given theoretical recognition by Adam Smith; and if one dates the closing of the gap between Europe and England from, say, 1850 to 1873—or about ninety years later—after which England began to be overtaken; then Korean industrialization, dating from the time Korea was opened by foreign imperialists, does not appear especially fast. Korea's industrialization can be said to have begun in the 1870s, when the 1,000-year-old Yi dynasty began to shatter as a conse-

[3] A view of technology as idiosyncratic is developed at length by R. R. Nelson and Winter (1982). See also a piece by R. R. Nelson (1987) specifically related to "backward" countries.

[4] That technological change deskills workers (below the management level) is argued by Braverman (1974). For a critique of his argument, see Kelley (1986).

quence of Japanese intrusion, much as the Tokugawa regime in Japan had been shaken by the appearance of Admiral Perry only two decades earlier. Then followed a delay in the onset of industrialization in Korea of about ninety years, until the 1960s, when Korea's growth rate accelerated. Moreover, the revolutionary period of Korean industrialization continues, in that rapid growth and structural change are still in full swing and Korea has not yet come anywhere close to catching up with the most advanced countries. Even in mature industries, labor hours required per unit of output in the late 1970s were far higher in Korea than in Japan, by a scalar that averaged roughly 2.8.[5] In the mid-1980s, Korea's share of industrial activity arising from its own R&D laboratories was minuscule. In any event, Korea's growth rates only surpass all records if industrialization's start is assumed to be the point of acceleration in the 1960s.

Nevertheless, why late industrialization was slow in starting in Korea can be explained by the same set of factors that explain why late-industrializing countries progressed faster than the European emulators once their industrialization got under way. The institutions of late industrialization that underscore its success, and whose absence is responsible for delay, are the following: an interventionist state, large diversified business groups, an abundant supply of competent salaried managers, and an abundant supply of low-cost, well-educated labor. These institutions are the focal point of later chapters.

KOREA AS A SPECIAL CASE OF LATE INDUSTRIALIZATION

In late-industrializing countries, *the state intervenes with subsidies deliberately to distort relative prices in order to stimulate economic activity*. This has been as true in Korea, Japan, and Taiwan as it has been in Brazil, India, and Turkey. In Korea, Japan, and Taiwan, however, the state has exercised discipline over subsidy recipients. *In exchange for subsidies, the state has imposed performance standards on private firms*. Subsidies have not been giveaways, but instead have been dispensed on the principle of reciprocity. With more disciplined firms, subsidies and protection have been lower and more effective than otherwise.

Below the level of the state, *the agent of expansion in all late-indus-*

---

[5] The industries included in this calculation are cotton textiles, paper, rubber tires, caustic soda, cement, iron castings, and ball bearings. The engineering method was used to calculate productivity, which involves computing required labor hours per unit of output. The study was undertaken by Han'guk Saengsansong Cent'a (Korea Productivity Center, 1985). For a comparison of productivity levels and growth rates in Korea and Japan, calculated as output divided by employment, see C. K. Kim, Yoo, and Whang (1984).

trializing countries is the modern industrial enterprise, a type of enterprise
that Chandler (1977) described as large in scale, multidivisional in
scope, and administered by hierarchies of salaried managers. Even
in Taiwan, an economy with a reputation for small-scale enterprise,
the large-size firm (often a government enterprise) spearheaded industrialization in the early stages of growth (as will be discussed in
Chapter 7). In Korea, the modern industrial enterprise takes the
form of diversified business groups, or *chaebol,* whose size and diversity are similar to those of the *zaibatsu,* Japan's prewar big business groups. Diversified business groups are common to all late-
industrializing countries, but those in Korea are especially large. The
Fortune list of 500 international private non-oil-producing firms in
1986 included ten from Korea and only seven from all other developing countries combined (*Fortune,* 1987). The size of the chaebol
and their broad diversification into nonrelated products have allowed them to survive the hardships of late industrialization, to penetrate the lower end of numerous foreign markets, and to supplant
the need for multinational firms to undertake major investments in
targeted industries. Whereas Korea has depended heavily on foreign
loans, it has entertained almost no direct foreign investment outside
the labor-intensive sectors.[6]

*Salaried engineers are a key figure in late industrialization because they
are the gatekeepers of foreign technology transfers.* The protagonist of industrialization has shifted from the entrepreneur in the late eighteenth century, to the corporate manager in the late nineteenth, to
the salaried engineer in the late twentieth. Squeezed between the
state on the one hand and the salaried engineer on the other, the
private entrepreneur's usefulness in the multidivisional enterprises
of late industrialization appears much reduced when measured by
the standards of the entrepreneurial histories of advanced countries.

Salaried engineers have performed especially well in Korea because society has invested heavily in education, from the primary
level on up. In terms of sheer quantity, enough engineers have been
trained to ensure that sufficient numbers pursue the career intended
by their education. A large number of engineers has meant competition among them for the best jobs and the fastest promotions, thereby
driving up productivity.

While a strategic focus on the shopfloor may be a *tendency* in late

---

[6] The chaebol themselves have already begun to invest overseas as a way to jump
over foreign tariffs, provide parts for their exports (in, for example, the case of automobiles), tap into high technology (in, for example, the case of electronics), and
obtain raw materials (see *Maeil Kyŏngje Sinmun,* 1986e, 1986h). According to data
from the Ministry of Finance, investments overseas by Koreans totaled $738.5 million
as of March 31, 1987, 43% of which was in North America.

industrialization, this tendency may be stronger, depending on the country. Chapter 7 highlights three outstanding points in Korea's case. First, Korean firms have shown a preference for hiring engineers over administrators. Beginning in the early 1960s, while the number of managers of all types increased modestly, the number of engineers grew far more quickly. Second, even as managerial capitalism in Korea has spread, overhead has been kept in check. The ratio of white-collar workers (excluding clerks) to blue-collar workers remained constant between 1960 and 1980, even declining slightly. Korean firms have not created huge overheads; instead they have appointed managers to production positions on the shop floor, which is where the competitive advantage of late-industrializing countries lies. Third, the number of layers of management has been kept quite small in Korea. Engineers at the plant level keep in close contact with the ranks.

Turning now to production workers, *late industrializations have exceptionally well-educated work forces by comparison with earlier industrializations.* Moreover, the wages of these workers have generally been prevented from rising rapidly by a conspiracy of forces: political repression, an unlimited labor supply at the onset of growth, an absence of international opportunities to migrate, and the insignificance of a class of skilled crafts-persons, who were the organizers of trade unions in earlier periods. Korea, however, like Japan before it, has set a number of world records in the area of labor, which has made its work force unusually productive.

On the one hand, Korea appears to have the longest work week in the world, a throwback to the work week in effect in the harsh factory system under Japanese colonialism. On the other hand, *Korea's real-wage growth rate may exceed that of any previous industrial revolution (with Japan's a close second) and that of any contemporary one.* High average real-wage increases have acted as an inducement to workers to produce, and to managers to acquire more technological capability. In addition, Korea's work force is highly segmented, which has energized a new labor aristocracy. Korea has the dubious distinction of having one of the highest gender wage gaps, an honor shared by Japan. On average, Korean women earn less than half of what men earn. Korea, like Japan, also has one of the largest manufacturing wage dispersions between light and heavy industry, allowing both types of manufacturing activity to coexist.

All of these institutions are discussed in detail in later chapters. In each case there is a common thread that binds Korea, Japan, and Taiwan with other late-industrializing countries. In contrast, there is a distinct pattern in all three cases that makes their relatively fast growth rates more comprehensible. Rather than introducing each institution of late industrialization in more detail, however, a further introduction to the institution of the state only is presented here because the state's role in late industrialization is especially controversial.

THE STATE

The first step toward understanding how "backward" countries in the twentieth century eventually expanded is to ask how they fell behind relative to the industrialized world in the first place. The development process is enormously complex, but one can say as a first approximation that (1) the onset of economic expansion has tended to be delayed by weaknesses in a state's ability to act and (2) if and when industrialization has accelerated, it has done so at the initiative of a strengthened state authority.

The reasons why some countries in the twentieth century have found themselves behind others in income and wealth can be grouped tentatively into four categories: natural resource endowment, population, market forces, and institutional factors. The natural resource explanation for backwardness can be dismissed out of hand. The association between resource endowment and per capita income is visibly weak, Korea and Japan being cases in point. The attribution of underdevelopment to excess population is now also pretty well discredited. Population explosions are currently believed not to have led to failure to industrialize but rather to have emerged as a consequence of such failure.[7]

There remain, therefore, two major contending views—the market and the institutional. The market explanation for economic development poses as the grand mover and shaker of the past 200 years of economic progress. Nevertheless, whereas no one could possibly deny the overreaching role that the market has played in speeding growth, one must distinguish between the market and the market *mechanism*. The former refers to the means to satisfy supply and demand. The latter refers to rules for allocating resources. All industrializations have made use of the market. However, defiance of the market mechanism does not explain why late industrializers delayed so long in starting to expand, nor can adherence explain why they eventually succeeded in growing.

The economic histories of "backward" countries are quite varied,

[7] The argument that rapid rates of population increase are the consequence of failure to develop was most cogently put by Myint (1964).

yet the archetypal late industrializer in the twentieth century was at one time or another a colony of one of the Great Powers (Japan is unique as a learner among the potentates). Colonial histories differ, but the typical economic regime of a colony was quite exemplary from the viewpoint of competitive theory. Basically, colonies followed policies of free trade and exploited their comparative advantage in the agricultural commodities markets. Their growth, therefore, could not be said to have been stunted by failure to be guided by the market mechanism.[8] Indeed, it could be said to have been stunted by failure to follow interventionist policies, namely, throwing up trade barriers and providing subsidies to promote local industry.

This leads to the final explanation, one related to institutions, not least of all the state. Quite simply, industrialization was late in coming to "backward" countries because they were too weak to mobilize forces to inaugurate economic development and to fend off a wave of foreign aggression begun in the second half of the nineteenth century. Their weakness, moreover, arose from internal social conflict—ethnic, racial, regional, or class. Such conflict precluded arrogating enough power to a central authority to prevent foreign intervention, invasion, or the catastrophic loss of statehood altogether.

States in modern history have always intervened to spur economic activity. Even the First Industrial Revolution, whose guiding principle was laissez-faire, is now being reassessed by historians with this axiom in view.[9] The British government intervened to maintain law and order and to minimize the flight of technological capability to foreign lands, albeit flat-footedly (Henderson, 1954). In the second phase of intervention, that associated with the Second Industrial Revolution in Germany and the United States, state intervention intensified because the economies of Germany and the United States were required not merely to industrialize but also to catch up. We can think of infant industry protection as the primary characteristic

---

[8] Reynolds argued that under colonial regimes of free trade, the "backward" regions grew at a fairly rapid clip, although to be sure, there were exceptions to the rule. According to Reynolds, "Against the view that 'life began in 1950,' . . . the Third World has a rich record of prior growth, beginning for most countries in the 1850–1914 era." (Reynolds, 1985, p. 4). In anticipation of the obvious objection, that developing countries are still desperately poor, Reynolds wrote, "Certainly people in Western Europe and the United States are much better off than people in Sri Lanka [the example he used], though not as much better off as the World Bank Table suggests . . . conversion from the local currencies to U.S. dollars at official exchange rates exaggerates the actual difference in consumption levels" (p. 40).

[9] See, for example, Taylor (1972).

of this era. Analytical coherence has been provided by writers like List (1856) and Sombart (1933).[10]

To catch up in the twentieth century has required still heavier doses of government support because backwardness has been relatively greater. The instruments of intervention have been cumulative. Not only have states in late-industrializing countries intervened by protecting infant industries. They also have intervened by providing private investors with a battery of incentives that, simplified, boil down to subsidies. The tariff epitomizes the age of infant industry protection. The subsidy, which includes tariff protection and financial incentives, epitomizes the struggle to industrialize after the Second World War.

As Gerschenkron (1962) has pointed out, backward countries are fortunate to have a backlog of technologies to draw upon. Yet Gerschenkron failed to give equal weight to the proposition that the more backward the country, the harsher the justice meted out by market forces. The inherent conflicts of the market apply to all users, rich and poor alike. But the conflicts are sharpest among the least well endowed. Countries with low productivity require low interest rates to stimulate investment, and high interest rates to induce people to save. They need undervalued exchange rates to boost exports, and overvalued exchange rates to minimize the cost of foreign debt repayment and of imports—not just imports of raw materials, which rich and poor countries alike require, but also of intermediates and capital goods, which poor countries alone are unable to produce. They must protect their new industries from foreign competition, but they require free trade to meet their import needs. They crave stability to grow, to keep their capital at home, and to direct their investment toward long-term ventures. Yet the prerequisite of stability is growth.

Under such disequilibrating conditions, the state's role in late industrialization is to mediate market forces. The state in late industrialization has intervened to address the needs of both savers and investors, and of both exporters and importers, by creating multiple prices. Some interest rates are higher than others. Importers and exporters face different prices for foreign currency. Insofar as the state in late industrialization has intervened to establish multiple prices in the same market, the state cannot be said to have gotten relative prices "right," as dictated by supply and demand. In fact, the state

[10] The extent of tariff protection in the United States is the least appreciated. McCraw (1986), however, argued that protection rather than free trade tends to be the rule in American history.

in late industrialization has set relative prices deliberately "wrong" in order to create profitable investment opportunities.

Korea is no exception to this general rule. Chapter 3 examines accumulation in Korea at the industry level, a departure from typical practice because most studies of government intervention in late-industrializing countries tend to be highly aggregative. The industry focus of Chapter 3 is cotton spinning and weaving, Korea's leading sector in the 1960s. Even in a relatively labor-intensive sector like cotton textiles, the government intervened to protect local industry from Japanese competition, intervention taking the form of tariffs, quotas, export subsidies, subsidized credit, and so forth. As later chapters indicate, subsidization rose further in the heavy industries.

Korea, therefore, provides supporting evidence for the proposition that economic expansion depends on state intervention to create price distortions that direct economic activity toward greater investment. State intervention is necessary even in the most plausible cases of comparative advantage, because the chief asset of backwardness—low wages—is counterbalanced by heavy liabilities. *Where Korea differs from most other late industrializing countries is in the discipline its state exercises over private firms.*

Discipline by the state over private enterprise was part and parcel of the vision that drove the state to industrialize. Park Chung Hee, who presided over Korean industrialization from 1961 until his assassination in 1979, revealed the vision in 1963 in a book modestly entitled *The Country, the Revolution, and I.* Park's ideas were influenced by the "revolutionaries" Sun Yat Sen, Kemal Pasha, Nasser, and the Meiji rulers. From the Meiji, the only unreservedly successful of the revolutionaries, Park learned the importance of indigenizing foreign ideas, of crowning a political hierarchy with an emperor (the *I* of the Revolution), and of allowing "millionaires who promoted the reform" to enter the central stage, "thus encouraging national capitalism" (Park, 1963, p. 120). The millionaires were envisioned by Park to have created large-size plants to realize economies of scale. He saw the government's role as one of overseeing the millionaires to avoid any abuse of power.

The discipline exerted by the state, and the rise of big business, were interactive. Big business consolidated its power in response to the government's performance-based incentives. In exchange for stunning performance in the areas of exports, R&D, or new product introduction, leading firms were rewarded with further licenses to expand, thus enlarging the scale of big business in general. In exchange for entering especially risky industries, the government rewarded entrants with other industrial licenses in more lucrative sectors, thus furthering the development of the diversified business group in particular.

Discipline may be thought of as comprising two interrelated dimensions: (a) penalizing poor performers; and (b) rewarding only good ones. Evidence of the former has taken two guises in Korea. First, in industries weakened at various times by over-expansion (some heavy industries, construction, shipping), firms have been subject to rationalization, as discussed in Chapter 5. Second, discipline has taken the form of refusal on the part of the government to bail out relatively large scale, badly managed, bankrupt firms in otherwise healthy industries. The bail-out process has been highly politicized insofar as the government has typically chosen close friends to do the taking over of troubled enterprises (the production facilities of troubled enterprises are never allowed to rot). This corruption notwithstanding, when the victim of bankruptcy has appeared to be poorly managed, the government has deserted it.

One finds evidence of the government's cold-bloodedness towards poorly managed firms in distress in a variety of otherwise prosperous industries. For example, a company named Shinjin had a larger market share in the Korean automobile industry in the 1960s than Hyundai Motors. Shinjin's owner, however, could not survive competition from Hyundai's "Pony" and the oil shock in the 1970s. The company went bankrupt and the government, as banker, transferred Shinjin's holdings to Daewoo Motors. Another early automobile manufacturer, Asia Motors, was also abandoned (Amsden and Kim, 1985). In the cement industry, the largest producer in the 1970s went bankrupt because it tried to optimize an old technology rather than switch to a new one. Its production facilities were transferred by the government to a *chaebol*, the Ssangyong group, owned by one of the ruling party's elders. The Taihan group, a pioneer in the electronics industry, had an ailing consumer electronics division which failed. Eventually the government oversaw its transfer to Daewoo Electronics. Construction firms such as Kyungnam (merged into the Daewoo group) and Samho (acquired by Daelim Engineering) are typical cases of firms that although they once enjoyed government support, were abandoned after going bankrupt—when other firms in their industry were prospering—for reasons which observers generally agree were related to incompetence. A badly managed *chaebol* of considerable size that the government recently punished with dismemberment was the Korea Shipbuilding and Engineering Company. The Kukje-ICC group has also been pilloried.

Of greater importance to the credibility of the disciplinary process in Korea than punishing poor performers, however, has been insuring that the government's friends—most of whom have undoubtedly been bailed out on at least one occasion—have generally performed well. This dimension of discipline has been critical because so much of Korean industrialization has involved rewarding the same small set of government friends with favors for expansion. The chapters that follow, therefore, concentrate on providing evidence that repeated support by the government to a small set of big business groups was exchanged, *de facto*, for good performance. Good performance is evaluated in terms of production and operations management rather than financial indicators. Evidence comes from fairly detailed case studies of approximately thirty-five enterprises in the textile, cement, paper, steel, shipbuilding, general machinery, automobile, and construction industries. Several subsidiaries within a business group were studied (five in the case of Hyundai, three in the case of Samsung) to analyze, among other issues, whether repeated patronage by the government was justified on efficiency grounds.

The sternest discipline imposed by the Korean government on virtually all large size firms—no matter how politically well connected—related to export targets. There was constant pressure from government bureaucrats on corporate leaders to sell more abroad—with obvious implications for efficiency. Pressure to meet ambitious export targets gave the Big Push into heavy industry its frenetic character. Additionally, firms have been subject to five general controls in exchange for government support.

First, the government has owned and controlled all commercial banks. One of the first acts of the government of Park Chung Hee was to nationalize the banking system. (The government of Syngman Rhee had denationalized it a decade earlier to appease American pressures.) Although pressures to liberalize in the 1980s led the government to privatize commercial banks, thereby strengthening aggregate economic concentration and income inequality, the government maintained its control over commercial banking.[11] Government

---

[11] Korea has a reputation for relatively equitable income distribution; yet the statistics on income distribution published by the Korean government and the Korea Development Institute in the 1980s are improbable. (See for example, the figures contained in a paper by Suh and Y. H. S. Cheong, 1986.) They purport to suggest that the size distribution of income in Korea is still highly equitable by comparison with the developing countries. (For early results on income distribution in Korea, see Chenery and Ahluwalia, 1974.) Yet these findings are counterintuitive, because Korea's rate of aggregate economic concentration and wage inequalities are among the highest in the world (suggested in later chapters). Official measures of income distribution also ignore the "informal sector," which is huge. (See an unpublished paper prepared for the World Bank by Bhalla, 1979.) The statistical findings by the Korean government and Korea Development Institute of relatively equitable income distribution partly arise from the fact that income is fairly equitably distributed in agriculture, and even

control of the purse has helped orient the chaebol toward accumulating capital rather than toward seeking rents.

Second, in luring firms to enter new industries with the plums of
protection and subsidies, the government has imposed discipline by
limiting the number it has allowed to enter (although usually to not
fewer than two firms per industry). This has ensured the realization
of scale economies and the rise of the mammoth business groups
that the government foresaw as necessary to build basic industry. In
the 1960s and 1970s, the government became premier entrepreneur
by using its industrial licensing policies to determine what, when,
and how much to produce in milestone investment decisions.[12]

Third, discipline has been imposed on "market-dominating enterprises" through yearly negotiated price controls, in the name of
curbing of monopoly power. At the end of 1986, as many as 110
commodities were controlled, including flour, sugar, coffee, red
pepper, electricity, gas, steel, chemicals, synthetic fibers, paper, drugs,
nylon stockings, automobiles, and televisions.[13]

Fourth, investors have been subject to controls on capital flight, or
the remittance of liquid capital overseas. Legislation passed in the
1960s (T'ŭkpyŏl pojen kaching chŏbŏlpŏp) stipulated that any illegal
overseas transfer of $1 million or more was punishable with a *mini-
mum* sentence of ten years' imprisonment and a maximum sentence
of death. In the 1980s, the degree of compliance with the law has
fallen into doubt.[14] Nevertheless, in the two preceding decades, its
harsh terms are believed to have been a credible deterrent to private

in the 1980s agriculture accounted for about 30% of employment. A study by Choo
(1987) indicated that income distribution is more equitable for agricultural households than for nonagricultural households (both workers and self-employed). See also
the discussion in Chapter 2 on the distribution of wealth.

[12] In the 1980s the government "liberalized" industrial licensing but still exerted
control over who could enter new or old industries, or expand capacity, by means of
the following measures: (1) the Korean Antitrust Law, which prohibits firms from
controlling more than 40% of the assets of their subsidiaries (this measure is designed
to control the chaebol's ability to expand/diversify); (2) credit controls, which set ceilings on debt-equity ratios and/or debt-sales ratios (to control further the chaebol's
ability to expand/diversify); (3) a ban on large firm's entry into industries designated
for small- and medium-size firms; (4) a ban on large firm's entry into industries which
supply large firms; and (5) a ban on expansion in, or entry into, industries subject to
government "rationalization."

[13] Kyŏngje Kihoekwŏn (1986).

[14] Still, a bankrupt shipping magnate was believed to have committed suicide in
1987 for fear of being prosecuted under the law's terms. See *BK* (1987a). K. M. Kim
(1987) discussed the extent of capital flight and legislation to control it. Kim said
Morgan Guarantee figures on capital flight are exaggerated because they include direct foreign investments by Koreans, but that it is unthinkable that capital flight does
not exist.

investors who might otherwise have used public subsidies to build personal fortunes abroad.

Fifth, the middle classes have been taxed, and the lower classes have received almost nothing in the way of social services. This has enabled a persistent deficit in the government account to reflect long-term investments.

It is unclear whether the strong economic measures taken by the Korean state could have been taken under political democracy, although Japan, the etatist European countries, and recent events in Korea all suggest that such measures and political democracy are compatible. What is clear is that, without a strong central authority, a necessary although not sufficient condition, little industrialization may be expected in "backward" countries. Even getting relative prices "right" according to textbook theory would require a state strong enough to battle whoever stood to suffer from a loss of government support.

THE PROCESS OF CATCHING UP

Landes (1969) mentioned labor supply only briefly in his analysis of catching up, and he certainly did not view abundant labor as Europe's competitive asset in industrialization. To the contrary, he saw the attainment of competitiveness by learners in the nineteenth century as being burdened by low labor costs. He argued that after industrialization gained momentum in Britain, the same abundant supply of impoverished rural laborers that had made possible Europe's prefactory industry began to act as "a deterrent to mechanization and concentration" (p. 139). For Gerschenkron (1962) as well, labor did not lend a competitive advantage to late developers because a suitable labor force did not exist: ". . . industrial labor, in the sense of a stable, reliable, and disciplined group that has cut the umbilical cord connecting it with the land and has become suitable for utilization in factories, is not abundant but extremely scarce in a backward country" (p. 9).

The creation of competitiveness on the basis of an abundant, relatively well-educated labor supply is the key difference of latter-day twentieth-century learning. In the nineteenth century, the United States and Germany caught up with Britain on the basis of innovation, not on that of cheaper labor. As we shall see in a later chapter, even when Japan penetrated deeper into world markets after the turn of the century, its cheap labor was but one of several assets it used to gain market share. Therefore, the conquest of world markets, beginning in the mid 1960s, by late-industrializing countries on the *almost* exclusive basis of low wage rates represents a new phenomenon, a truly new international division of labor. Nevertheless, firms have still had to be subsidized in order to compete, even before any attempts to move beyond the light manufactures, and certainly after.

After a country invests in labor-intensive manufactures, the next logical step, from both a technical and demand-side point of view, is to invest in heavy industry. Subbranches of heavy industry prosper even in small countries, as evidenced by the composition of industry in Austria, Belgium, and Switzerland. (The only advanced country that does not appear to have some heavy industry is Denmark.) Yet the heavy industries have drawn criticism from economic historians and advisors alike for being an irrational symbol of liberation from backwardness and a violation of comparative advantage.

Symbolism apart, the real significance of the heavy industries for late industrialization lies in the turning point they represent for the unit of production and the basis on which this unit competes. First, with the heavy industry sector comes the modern industrial enterprise, and hence salaried management. The salaried management of the cotton spinning and weaving industry in Korea is far less professional than that of the heavy industries. Second, with the heavy industry sector comes a new mode of competition—oligopoly. Of equal significance, the transition from light to heavy industry involves a transition from competing on the basis of cheap labor to competing on the basis of modern facilities and skills, given whatever labor costs made entry possible. It usually follows that the target of competition is directed away from low-wage firms to firms that are also competing on the basis of modern facilities and skills, whatever their initial entry costs. Such firms tend to be found mainly in advanced countries. For late industrializers, therefore, the transition from light to heavy industry involves a transition from competing against firms from other low-wage countries to competing against firms from high-wage ones that have access to vastly more experience and technical expertise.

Complicating the process of catching up for late-industrializing countries is the fact that the progression from light to heavy industry has not been undertaken by the same set of firms. In Korea, leading firms in the light industries did not become the leading firms in the more technically complex industries, with the exception of electronics. The production of black-and-white television sets allowed big chaebol like the Samsung and Lucky-Goldstar groups to advance from assembly to higher value-added activities in consumer electronics, and from there to computer electronics. Nevertheless, electronics products accounted for a small share of total exports—only 10% in 1976 (before the rise of heavy manufactured exports) and only 11% in

1984, afterward (Bank of Korea, various years [a]). Korea's major exports from 1965 to 1975 were apparel, cotton textiles, and miscellaneous manufactures. In the case of cotton spinning and weaving, there were almost no technical or managerial linkages to newer industries. The cotton textiles firms that benefited internally from international competition in the form of exposure to better management techniques and improved production processes did not serve as the organizational building blocks for the economy's more skill- and capital-intensive pursuits. None of the leading chaebol evolved from a base in cotton textiles (although one had a base in worsteds). With profit-maximizing horizons that were short term, entrepreneurs who were conservative, and managers who were oriented more toward the art than the science of production, cotton textiles firms did not become the agents of further industrialization.

Catching up, therefore, was an involuted process, as discussed in Part III of this book. The dynamic driving comparative advantage involved a discontinuity, the leading sector of the 1960s not providing the initiative for diversification in the 1970s. It was also the diversified business group that tended to penetrate new industries, not the specialized single-product firm, making the dynamics of dynamic comparative advantage all the more different from the textbook case (see Chapter 10).

OVERCOMING TECHNOLOGICAL IGNORANCE: FROM RENT-SEEKING TO INVESTING

Whatever the time period and whatever the firm structure, learners rely heavily on foreign know-how to narrow the gap. If they are to be at all successful at learning, they visit international expositions, attend conferences and lectures, read technical journals, hire experienced workers, visit overseas plants, engage foreign technical assistants, consult machinery suppliers, and buy, borrow, beg, and steal foreign designs. The form of technology acquisition has tended to change, however, as technology itself has become more science-based and as the firm has come to be viewed less as a means to earn a livelihood and more as a means to earn a profit. The central tendency has shifted from the absorption of foreign technology through copying and self-teaching to the adoption of foreign technology through investing in foreign licenses and technical assistance. The former mode of technology acquisition may be called *imitation,* and the latter, *apprenticeship* (see Amsden and Kim, 1985b).

In Korea, massive imports of foreign licenses and assistance have been viewed as a means to attain technological independence, and thus as part of a larger effort, in both the public and private spheres, to avoid foreign control. Industrialization has occurred almost exclusively on the basis of nationally owned rather than foreign-owned enterprise. Foreign technical assistance has been purchased in preference to depending on foreigners to run Korean plants. Whether in Korea's shipyards, steel mills, machinery works, automobile plants, or electronics factories, the credo has become, "Invest now in in-house technological capability—even if outside expertise is cheaper—to reap the rewards of self reliance later."

To understand how Korea attained competitiveness, it is necessary to understand the nature of the technological backlog that Korea, and other late learners like it, borrowed. This is most easily accomplished by drawing a comparison between Korea and a still earlier industrializer, Germany, during the stage of its catching up. Veblen has written on imperial Germany, the forerunner not just of Korea but also of Japan. He drew a comparison between Germany's assimilation of foreign technology and England's borrowing from Continental Europe during the period of Tudor rule. According to Veblen,

> The necessary technological proficiency of Germany was of a kind to be readily acquired; much more so than the corresponding technological proficiency acquired by the English in Tudor times by borrowing from the Continent. In this earlier English case what had to be borrowed and assimilated was not only a theoretical knowledge and practical insight into the industrial arts to be so taken over, but a personal habituation and the acquisition of manual skill on the part of the workmen employed; a matter that requires not only insight but long-continued training of large numbers of individuals—apprenticeship. . . . (1915, p. 187)[15]

By contrast, Veblen also argued,

> The technology which Germany borrowed in the nineteenth century is a different affair in respect of the demands which it makes on the capacities and attention of the community into which it is introduced. It is primarily an affair of theoretical knowledge, backed by such practical insight into its working conditions as may be necessary to the installation of the mechanical equipment. In all this there is little of an obscure, abstruse or difficult kind, except for such detailed working out of technological applications of theory as call for the attention of expert specialists. (p. 188)

---

[15] In the next four paragraphs, all page references are to Veblen.

Like the Germans before them, Korean firms were generally not taxed by the need for their operatives to acquire manual skills. Few worker apprenticeships existed in Korea, and formal vocational training did not commence immediately even in some of the largest firms. Although the chaebol sent vast numbers of employees abroad for training, the incidence was greatest at the upper end of the job hierarchy—although inclusive of foremen. And whereas large numbers of technical assistants from abroad consulted in Korea, including operatives with specialized skills, little effort was made to have them settle in Korea. A far graver problem for Korea than for Germany, however, was the acquisition of theoretical knowledge. The problem for Germany, according to Veblen, was minor, and was soon manifested by Germany's success at innovating. Korea, on the other hand, lacked theoretical knowledge at the world frontier, not only in the machinery-building sector, which Veblen dwelt on, but also in the continuous-process industries and, to an acute degree, in electronics. The benefits of backwardness notwithstanding, therefore, the shift of the world technological frontier in the century after Germany industrialized left Korea relatively further behind, and made it more difficult for Korea to solve what even for Germany was the most intransigent problem of technology transfer: the detailed working out of technological applications of theory.

The problem of technology transfer, however, cannot be seen merely in technical terms. Socially, it touched on the tribulation common to all early capitalist development: of getting adventurers in the field of business to take technology seriously. According to Veblen, what contributed to the triumph of manufacturing over finance as the dominant mode of profit-making in Germany was that, "These German adventurers in the field of business, being captains of industry rather than of finance, were also free to choose their associates and staff with a view to their industrial insight and capacity rather than their astuteness in ambushing the community's loose change" (p. 194). The German production engineers who were hired advanced the notion that industrialization depended on technical competence. Veblen stated,

The responsible staff and corps in these industries, being men who had come through the schools instead of through the country store and the pettifogger's law office, were not incapable of appreciating that range of theoretical and technical knowledge that is indispensable to the efficient conduct of modern industry; and so the German industrial community was as surely and unresistingly drawn in under the rule of the technological expert as the American at about the same period [the late nineteenth century] was drawn in under the rule of the financial strategist. (pp. 195–6)

It would be an exaggeration to say that the industrial community in Korea became "surely and unresistingly" drawn in under the rule of the technological expert, because, by world standards, there were no experts in Korea. Nevertheless, like their German counterparts, the production engineers who were the gatekeepers of technology transfer came through the schools. And in a society hungry to catch up, with a steadfast faith in the value of education, the practical knowledge that these professionals wielded went a long way toward winning them influence and esteem. The industrial community in Korea, therefore, became "surely and unresistingly" drawn in under the rule, if not of the expert, then of the technological trainee. Once the entrepreneurs recognized that government subsidies could make manufacturing activity profitable, and that Korean engineers could build ships that floated and steel that bore weight, they increasingly turned their attention away from speculating toward accumulating capital.

Symptomatic of the passionate desire to organize and hasten the process of catching up, the Koreans pushed ahead with forming a native cadre of engineers and technicians. The number of schools in both Germany and Korea was large, unusually so by contemporary standards. The plain fact of the matter is that Korea was a successful learner partly because it invested heavily in education, both formal and foreign technical assistance (see Chapter 9).

The preponderance of foreign technical assistance came from Japan, a fact that gave Korea an edge over other late-industrializing countries that were culturally and geographically further afield than Korea from Japan. Japan may not have been as close to the world technological frontier as the United States, or as generous in transferring its proprietary know-how, but it emerged as the world's premier producer, and communicated to Korea both the most efficient production techniques and a seriousness about the manufacturing function.

PLAN OF THE BOOK

This book is divided into three parts. Part 1 surveys Korean history and the origins of state policies that led to the successes of Korean late industrialization. Part 2 examines the ways that Korean management and the work force were transformed into major factors in the growth of Korean industry. Part 3 discusses the creation of comparative advantage in several industries and the reasons why one only kept pace with expansion while the others drove it.

PART I

The State and Business: History and Policies

CHAPTER TWO

A History of
Backwardness

THE RETARDING EFFECTS OF A WEAK STATE

This chapter examines how late industrialization in Korea was retarded by a state too weak to intervene and stimulate capital expenditures. It also takes the position that when industrialization began to accelerate, it did so in response to government initiatives and not to the forces of the free market. Finally, it will argue that these processes can be thought of as general propositions applicable to similar countries.

From 1876, when Japan coerced Korea to open its doors to foreign trade, until 1961, when Korean army officers seized control in a coup d'état, the question of state power overarched Korean history.[1] In the interregnum, Korea had to debate its destiny with not just one but two occupying powers, Japan and the United States. It swallowed a heavy dose of the bitter pill of foreign domination, the realpolitik of all latter-day twentieth-century learning. Therefore, in this and the next chapter the concern is with the friction that enabled Korea to emerge after ninety years of so-called "modernization" with at least some of its skin still intact, though only half its original size and not yet possessed of a full stomach.

This chapter generally follows a chronological order, one objective being to provide a summary of modern Korean history. Within each discrete historical episode, however, the organizing theme is the state. The period of rule under the late Yi dynasty is discussed first to establish a benchmark for later contrast with strong centralized rule. Then the two occupations are considered for the purpose of assessing what has come to be called "modernization," which took place in the period of statehood denied. Finally, the regimes of Syngman Rhee and General Park Chung Hee are introduced in relation to their two major antagonists, the student movement and the U.S. AID administration.

[1] In the 1980s, the *legitimacy* of state power had become the burning issue.

Little in this history is in any way premonitory of Korea's later
success, except that resistance to foreign domination in Korea beginning in the 1870s was immediate and unusually obstreperous, and
the country's hyperactive student movement maintains this tradition
a century later.[2] The years 1876–1910 were memorable for the spectrum of reform movements they stirred.[3] At the beginning of the
period, the Yi dynasty gave its last gasps of repentance, and at the
end of the period, there was outright insurrection. Of a population
of roughly 12 million, the number of insurgents killed in, say, 1907–
1908, was estimated by Japan at over 14,000 (C. I. E. Kim, 1962).
Betwixt and between, some movements expressed themselves as
peasant rebellions, demanding egalitarianism as well as liberation from
foreign influence. Other movements were led by Western-educated
intellectuals who called for the withdrawal of foreign concessions,
the scrutiny of royal accounts, the creation of schools, and freedom
of speech and press. To be sure, visions about statehood were con-
voluted by class. Though the foreign aggressor was universally hated,
the privileged elites collaborated with it to avoid social change, and
the impoverished rural masses tolerated it in the absence of better
alternatives. Nevertheless, in Korea, nationalism found an ideal climate in which to grow. Whereas many other colonies were pieced
together from geographical units that were racially, tribally, or religiously distinct, Korea had existed for centuries as a nation with an
unusual homogeneity of language, ethnicity, and culture. Although
it took almost a century before the idea of the nation-state was to
triumph over the previous reality, these early reform movements are
noteworthy—in spite of their short-term failure—for a vision of Korea that was ultimately responsible for pushing industrialization
through.

An abortive attempt by Japan to invade Korea had occurred in

[2] For an account by Korean authors of Korean resistance to Japanese rule, see Ahn
et al. (1980). W. K. Han (1977) analyzed the rise of Korean nationalism as a response
to foreign invasion.

[3] Comparing student militance in two Japanese colonies, Korea and Taiwan, Tsurumi wrote,

> In Taiwan, student demonstrations against favoritism toward Japanese classmates
> had also surfaced from time to time, but although serious incidents occurred in
> individual schools, these never became a stepping stone to city-wide student pro-
> test, and anti-Japanese defiance in Taiwan never knew the country-wide solidarity
> shown by Korean students. (1984, p. 307–8)

For some accounts of the period 1876–1910, see Conroy (1960), who argued that
Japanese colonialism was not motivated by economics; and Shoichi (1970) who argued
that it was. See also Chen (1968), Duus (1984), Juhn (1965), H. H. Kim (1980), C. S.
Lee (1963), B. B. Weems (1964), and C. N. Weems Jr. (1954). Koh (1966) presented
an historical comparison of the cotton industry in Japan and Korea.

1592–1598. Just two years later, in 1600, the Tokugawa regime came
to power in Japan. For the next 276 years, Japan witnessed the rise
of commerce and a more productive agrarian system, while Korea
celebrated its victory over Japan in relative quiescence. When Japan
reappeared on Korean shores in 1876, less than a decade after the
imperialist had itself become the unwitting host of foreign intruders,
Korea encountered a much more formidable foe. Hastily, Japan assumed the role of precocious colonialist, extorting trade treaties from
Korea even before either country had a central bank, despite the
fact that the Meiji had to suppress the Satsuma rebellion at about
the same time it had to suppress a rebellion in the Korean army.[4]
Consequently, a decisive difference would determine the subsequent
course of Korean history—the greater degree of centralized state
power.

THE YI DYNASTY

According to Pallais, an historian of the period,

> Although prime responsibility for Korea's eventual subjugation
> to Japan must be attributed to foreign imperialism, Korea's ca-
> pacity to adapt to the demands of the modern world in the late
> nineteenth century was hindered by those factors responsible
> for the extraordinary stability of the Yi dynasty (1392–1910).
> This stability was in large measure the result of a state of equi-
> librium produced by the interrelationships between a monarchi-
> cal, bureaucratic, and centralized government structure and an
> aristocratic and hierarchical social system. The *yangban* elite, which
> had many of the attributes of an aristocracy, maintained itself
> by legal and de facto inherited status, privileges, landholding,
> officeholding (in the central bureaucracy), and utilization of
> Confucian orthodoxy for the legitimization of status and eco-
> nomic interests. King and aristocrat were both mutually antag-
> onistic and mutually supporting; each was dependent on the other
> for the continuation of his place in the political and social struc-
> ture. (1975, pp. 4–5)

Typically law and order are extolled as preconditions for growth,
and what Pallais called attention to is the precondition of a strong
state for law and order:

> The balance of power between monarchy and aristocracy was
> an asset for the maintenance of stability, but it was a liability

---

[4] Kublim (1959) presented an early overview of the context in which Japan colo-
nized.

when Korea was faced with the need to expand central power
to mobilize resources for defense and development. . . . One of
the main problems for the traditional Korean state as it moved
toward the twentieth century was, therefore, overcoming the
limitations on central authority in order to build national strength
in the face of threatening challenges from the outside world.
(1975, p. 5)

Pallais went on to say that later peasant rebellions and threats of
foreign invasion in the 1860s created a sense of urgency about the
need for reform, but the traditional system was incapable of allowing
a major shift in the balance of power toward strong central and mo-
narchical leadership. Furthermore, the challenge to the privileges of
the upper classes gave rise to a reaction of the privileged against
reform, and thus a reversion to limited monarchy.

The balance of power between state and aristocracy pirouetted on
an impoverished peasantry, the state empowering the landlords to
tax the peasantry, and the landlords protecting the state and providing it with a share of its revenues—but not a large enough share to
accumulate a surplus.[5] The upshot was entropy:

In the late Yi dynasty, the problems of revenue shortage and
peasant unrest were both caused primarily by the aristocratic
landowning class's monopoly over the land and free-floating resources of the country. One of the main reasons for the weakness of the central government was its inability to tax land effectively to meet its needs in a time of domestic crisis and foreign
challenge. . . . The existence of a centralized bureaucratic
structure—as opposed to a decentralized or feudal political order—was no guarantee of greater centralized control over land
and the tax revenues accruing therefrom. (Pallais, 1975, p. 58)

So weak was Korea's state in the Asian context that it had maintained a tributary relationship with the Ming dynasty of China since
1392. One result was the decline of local industry. The needs of the
royal household were increasingly met with the imports of luxury
goods that were obtained in exchange for tribute in China. Production in government factories declined as a consequence and then
declined still further as a result of the employment of slaves or
handicraft workers who were required to render compulsory services without adequate compensation. Farmers maintained household industries solely to meet their own needs and to fulfill tributary
obligations to landlords. Although independent artisans produced

[5] W. K. Han (1977) examined the relationship between the state, the yangban system, and the "exploited classes."

handicrafts for other's use, the high degree of subsistence that characterized the economy meant little market activity. When Japan arrived to trade in the 1870s, a money economy had not yet spread throughout Korea. Soon the Japanese yen became the accepted currency, replacing barley and rice as the medium of exchange.[6]

Another result of subjugation was the adoption of a Confucian system of class relations and beliefs, which, if rich in its own terms, was a deterrent to capitalist enterprise. Koreans may not have been drawn into capitalist enterprise kicking and screaming, but they were conditioned by Confucianism to accord it low status. Further, the ability of Korean manufacturers to compete against Japanese goods was complicated by a primitive distribution system. Internal trade was carried on by itinerant peddlers, since there were few retail stores in small villages and towns.

The itinerant merchants used advanced accounting methods, yet bulls or humans provided the only means of conveyance by which they could transport goods. They were outcompeted when the Japanese began using more modern transport. In the cities proper, merchants were granted monopoly rights by officials in return for an agreement to supply needed merchandise at nominal prices. Consequently, merchants grew accustomed to monopoly rights to trade certain categories of goods in certain geographical areas. They sought to preserve their local monopolies to counter the threat of foreign competition, rather than to study the new methods of merchandising introduced by foreign traders. Because the opening of ports was forced upon the Korean government, it could not impose its own protective duties. "At any rate, it is doubtful whether any high ranking government official was aware of the implications of tariff duties on domestic commerce and industry" (Juhn, 1965, p. 46).

First unable to compete against Japanese goods, Korea lost more and more ground to its interloper. The monarchy was forced to rely on China to suppress a peasant uprising in 1894, which gave Japan a pretext under which to increase its military presence. Japan declared Korea a protectorate after routing Russia in war in 1905. Finally, with the defeat of insurgents and the dissolution of the Korean army, Japan formally annexed Korea amidst American indifference in 1910.

THE CONTRADICTIONS OF MODERNIZATION

The judgment on Japan's contribution to Korea's subsequent success has gone through several iterations, although the facts have by and

[6] Cole and Park (1983) gave a brief history of Korean financial development under Japan.

large remained the same. The accounts of colonialism written before 1920 are enthusiastically favorable, praising Japan for uplifting a population that lacked "dignity, intelligence, and force."[7] This image of enlightenment was tarnished, however, by stormy demands of an estimated 2 million Koreans for independence in 1919, inspired by President Wilson's "Fourteen Points" (Baldwin, 1969). Whatever glint remained in the image was altogether obliterated in the 1930s when Japan engulfed Korea in its war efforts. However, the critiques of colonialism by Korean scholars in the early postwar period tend to be overdrawn, the whole detestable episode swathed in the blackest of colors. After the Korean economy began to expand in the 1960s, the verdict was handed down in English-language publications that Japanese colonialism had been a "modernizing" force:[8]

> Japanese colonial rule cannot be seen as an unrelieved disaster. It is true that, during the period of colonial rule, . . . many Koreans experienced an absolute, not just a relative, decline in their standard of living. And yet, for all the hardships imposed on the Korean people, Japanese colonial rule laid some of the key foundations for Korea's later entrance into modern economic growth. (Mason et al., 1980, p. 75)

The Japanese dismantled the institutions of 1,000 years of dynastic rule and accomplished overnight, in 1910, what the dynastic rulers had failed or neglected to achieve in centuries: the abolition of slavery, the codification of civil law, and more.[9] The Japanese also created a modern infrastructure in the areas of finance, transportation, and commerce. Nevertheless, Japanese colonialism was far more successful in smashing old foundations than in establishing new ones.

[7] These were the views of George Kennan, confidante of Theodore Roosevelt, as quoted in Grajdanzev (1944). Grajdanzev puzzled over why the early views of Japanese colonialism were so favorable. For the period 1910–1945, see Y. Chang (1971), de Brunner (1928), H. Kim (1971), H. K. Lee (1936), Y. K. Lee et al (1971), Mizoguchi (1979), Nakamura (1974), and E. Kim and Mortimore (1977). For overviews see S. P.-S. Ho (1984) and Toshiyuki and Yuzo (1984). For statistical approaches, see S.-C. Suh (1978) and Ban (1971). Amsden (1987a) provided an overview on theories of imperialism.

[8] The general literature on modernization is voluminous. From an economic perspective, the classic work is that by Rostow (1960). For a critique, see Baran and Hobsbawm (1961) and Fishlow (1965). From a sociological perspective see Levy (1966). For a critique, see A. G. Frank (1969).

[9] Other reforms included separation of the royal household from affairs of state, outlaw of all forms of discrimination against commoners, abolition of the Confucian-oriented national exams, the adoption of a new tax system based on payments in cash rather than kind, separation of judicial functions from the executive departments, institution of an independent court system, legalization of remarriage by widows, and removal of a ban on early marriage. Juhn (1965) presented a brief summary.

Paradoxically, in a late industrializer like Korea, colonialism re-
moved the old blockages to industrialization but created new ones in
its wake.

Korea's intrinsic weakness first manifested itself as a failure to
compete against foreign goods. After Japan withdrew in 1945, Korea was no more able to compete on the basis of its manufactures
than it had been before. Indeed, a quantum shift in the world technological frontier had left Korea relatively further behind. The Japanese had followed in the footsteps of Korean intellectuals and
Christian missionaries in emphasizing formal education. In fact, investments in education, even at the university level, were unusually
high by colonial standards, but they were motivated by policies designed to assimilate Koreans into Japanese society as the lower elements, policies that lent the colonial interlude its nasty character.
Education at the higher levels was altogether lacking in the technical
fields, except in agronomy and medicine, and because of discrimination in hiring, Korean academia had few productive outlets.[10] Japanese corporations in Korea discriminated against Koreans at the
managerial and even at the supervisory level. If, therefore, as is
sometimes contended, the technical and managerial literacy rate rose
as a consequence of Japanese manufacturing enterprise, it must have
levitated.[11] As for Korean capitalists, they existed at the fringes, unable for the most part to compete against Japanese goods.

Between 1910 and 1920, industry in Korea was altogether discriminated against by Japan in favor of agriculture. Then, after the 1919
uprising, a wafer-thin stratum of Korean capitalists was deliberately
cultivated to further collaboration. With minimal assistance, an entrepreneurial class emerged, drawing its members from the yangban
and from the commoner class. The new entrepreneurs were numerous enough to increase the variety of the indigenous elite, from
landlord and scholar before the occupation to landlord, business-
man, and intellectual after it.[12] In 1938, however, Korean paid-up
capital as a share of total paid-up capital in industry equaled only
12.3%. Moreover, the paid-up capital of the average Japanese corporation was more than six times as large as that of the average

[10] For an overview of colonial education in Korea, see Tsurumi (1984).

[11] Mason et al. (1980) suggested a process of "learning-by-watching," but this seems
a farfetched notion of modernization. Moreover, in the area of technical and managerial skills, it would have been difficult even to "watch," since many cognitive skills,
particularly in large-scale organizations, are not practiced out in the open. However,
Koreans may have learned more in the banking sector at the managerial level than
they did in manufacturing. See Moskowitz (1979).

[12] Eckert (1986) presented the interesting case of a large-scale Korean enterprise in
textiles that survived into the period of postcolonial rule.

Korean firm (Grajdanzev, 1944). This size distribution reflected the fact that when, in the 1930s, Japan roared into heavy industry in Korea in preparation for war, it did so on the basis of zaibatsu capital. By 1941 70% of total Japanese investment in industry in Korea was accounted for by six zaibatsu groups (Ewing, 1973). Korean managers were altogether excluded from such enterprises, and with few exceptions, large-scale enterprise was not under Korean ownership. Therefore, when the Korean economy was resuscitated in the 1950s, it bore some unique features but many familiar marks of colonial distortion. There was overcapacity in textiles and light manufactures and undercapacity in basic industry. There were a large number of small-size firms but a hiatus in the large-size category. The skeletons of Japanese-owned corporations in basic industry, which the Korean government inherited, were plentiful but ill managed and technically problematic to operate.

The contradictory quality of modernization under Japanese colonialism was especially vivid in agriculture, which, being both the object of Japanese aggression and the heart of Korean economy and society, became a battleground. The Japanese colonial government's objective was to raise land-tax revenues. Toward this end, it had created a ponderous bureaucracy and carried out a land reform after 1910. The bureaucracy, while highly centralized, reached down to every village in the form of a police force and an agricultural extension service. As for the land reform, it replicated the agrarian structure existing in Japan in the late-nineteenth century. The state collected taxes from a landlord class, and landlords collected rents from their tenants. On the one hand, this reform represented a giant step forward insofar as it substituted the market for brute force as a mechanism by which to induce higher productivity. On the other hand, the establishment of property rights and the dispossession of the peasantry created acute distress. The same system in Japan was less exploitative because an urban labor market imposed a ceiling on rural rents. In Korea, however, with no urban alternative the peasantry was squeezed to the bone (see the appendix to this chapter).

During World War II, an estimated 10% or more of the Korean population was earning its bread abroad. More than 1 million Koreans were working in Japan, about 1 million were settled in Manchuria, some 200,000 were in the Russian Far East, and about 100,000 were in other countries, primarily China (Grajdanzev, 1944). Both hunger and politics were responsible for emigration. Koreans had lived in the frontier area of Manchuria and in the Russian Far East for centuries, but after 1905 many more had fled there as rebels. By 1945, more politically conscious by far, the insurgents were key figures in the postwar struggle for the state.[13] The Korean population in China was divided between Japanese camp followers and resisters trying to reach the Chinese army to fight against Japan. The Koreans who were living in Japan proper were chiefly unskilled workers, miners, and agricultural laborers who had been drafted for employment in wartime Japan.

The end result of Japanese colonialism in Korea was a society that was unable to support itself and totally at odds. Peasant opposed landlord, and those who resisted Japanese colonialism opposed those who collaborated. Under these conditions, the machinery of modern government that Japan had bequested was a useless inheritance. With a distended police force accustomed to domestic repression, and a minuscule army incapable of national defense, Korea once again fell victim to the Great Powers.

THE COLD WAR

The events that transpired between August 1945, when Japan retreated from Korea, and June 1950, when the Korean War began, were as complex as the underlying issues. The power and ideological struggles of the Cold War were visited upon a nation that was itself divided, although political polarities at the national and international levels were often not synonymous. According to B. Cumings, who looked under a microscope at the period 1945–1947,

> Communism in Korea in 1945 did not signify a deeply held world view, or adherence to an authority residing in the Kremlin, or commitment to Marxist internationalism. It was a specifically Korean communism. Its adherents could scarcely be distinguished from nationalists and conservatives in their belief in the uniqueness of the Korean race and its traditions and the necessity to preserve both, or in their understanding that a unique Korea required unique solutions. What did distinguish Left from Right was (1) a commitment to a thoroughgoing extirpation of

[13] B. Cumings (1981) wrote:

By 1945 as much as 11.6% of the Korean population was outside Korea, most of it in Japan and Manchukuo, and that fully 20% of all Koreans were either residing abroad or in a province other than their native one. This massive redeployment of population produced severe dislocations of Korean society because population mobility had historically been very low. In this period, Korean peasants first became uprooted from their villages and entered industry or urban life, or both, in Japan, Manchukuo, and northern Korea. As mentioned earlier, much of this uprooted population returned to their native homes after liberation to participate in the politics of postwar Korea. (p. 490)

Japanese influences in Korea, with all that this implied for Korean society and for Koreans who had profited from colonial rule; (2) a commitment to mass politics and mass organization and to the social equality that this implied; (3) a commitment to the reform of Korea's "feudal" legacy, feudalism being a code for gross inequalities in the allocation of resources, particularly land. (1981, p. 86)

These were the politics of the Korean People's Republic, with a network of affiliated trade union, peasant, student, and people's committees spread throughout the Korean peninsula. It was the government of the People's Republic that both the Russian and American armies confronted when their occupation of Korea began.

Both superpowers responded ultimately by establishing political outposts in Korea, but their initial reactions to the new government were opposite. Russia recognized the Republic almost immediately and within nine months of the liberation from Japan in the North, "landlordism had disappeared, the land had been redistributed, major industries had been nationalized, radical reform had eliminated the worst abuses of the colonial factory system and had established formal equality for women" (B. Cumings, 1981, p. 382). Thereafter Russian policy was oriented toward ensuring that the political faction in power in the North was amenable to Russian influence, although that faction was perhaps the least distinguished and capable of all the possible political groupings. The United States did not recognize the People's Republic, causing it to be destroyed amidst a bloody uprising in 1946, after which point an American alliance was formed with political sympathizers. The rest, as they say, is history. Cold War politics played themselves out, ending irrevocably in war (1950–1953) and the division of Korea into two geographically and ideologically separate parts. If, however, one is to understand the ensuing course of industrialization in what is now South Korea, one must understand three key American policies.

First, the American occupation forces chose to work through the most conservative political faction, the Korea Democratic Party (KDP). Insofar as the KDP had little grassroots support in its organization, the American forces also relied on Korean civil servants and police who had served under the Japanese.[14] The KDP was self-described as a party of "patriots, notables, and various circles of the intellectual stratum." It stood for the promotion of world peace and national culture, the enhancement of the livelihood of the working masses, and rational reorganization of the land system. According to

[14] This point is stressed in a critical account of the United States' policy in Korea in the 1940s and 1950s by H. C. Park (1986).

B. Cumings, "the reason for this befogged and cryptic agenda for Korea's future is not hard to find: a group did not win popularity in Korea in 1945 by urging the maintenance of landlordism, private ownership of industry, little or no punishment for collaborators, and the continuation in power of those Koreans who had influence under Japanese" (1981, p. 97).

Although the KDP subsequently lost power, its significance lies in the fact that it safeguarded the last survivors of the yangban class, who resurfaced after the convulsions of war as the elite of the new order. Although, for the most part, the landlord class vanished by the end of the 1950s, some of the same individuals who were privileged yangban became privileged politicians, government bureaucrats, educators, and industrialists. This lent a continuity to postwar change. The weak Korean state of the 1870s was supplanted by the strong one of the 1960s, and the art of statehood may have been rooted in a class culture transmitted without interruption across generations. Moreover, the anticommunism of the KDP set the standard for future regimes. When the military junta took power in May 1961, it claimed that Korea was on the "verge of subversion by the communists," that only the Korean armed forces were capable of preventing communism from taking root among the people, and that only through their timely action was the country saved from a communist coup (S. Han, 1974, p. 178). Notwithstanding the military junta's pervasive intervention in the economy, an act that might otherwise be associated with socialistic tendencies, anticommunism has been the dominant political ideology guiding Korean industrialization.

Second, the American occupation forces groped toward land reform in response to violent peasant demands, to the Soviet example in the North, and to the need to build commitment to a war that pitted kith and kin against one another (M. H. Choi, 1960). The agrarian reform of the Japanese was pushed one stage further, and land was redistributed to the tiller. Although land-to-the-tiller in Korea never enriched the peasantry or overflowed the state tax coffers, its long-run effects were major. Reform redirected idle capital away from land speculation to manufacturing and uprooted a class that had not proved itself progressive. It relieved the bottleneck in food supply, which in turn dampened inflationary pressures.[15] It created a far more equitable income distribution. Finally, it cleared the field for strong centralized state power.

[15] Although land reform caused temporary dislocations in agricultural production, it begat a highly productive system once peasants were provided with capital, fertilizer, and other inputs to pursue scientific farming (see Ban, Moon, and Perkins, 1980).

As a consequence of land reform, Korea has enjoyed a reputation among developing countries as one with a relatively equitable income distribution (World Bank, 1983). This reputation has become increasingly undeserved as industrialization has advanced. Korea has unusually high levels of aggregate economic concentration and of wage inequality by international standards.[16] Land reform fell far short of the demands of the People's Republic for an "act of destruction willed against a whole ruling class," (B. Cumings, 1981, p. 69), and anticommunism alone did not amount to much of an agenda for Korea's future. Nevertheless, land reform did respond to the ancient cry for egalitarianism.[17] When Korea was an overwhelmingly agrarian country, land reform undoubtedly contributed to greater equity in the size distribution of income. In the late 1930s, 3% of all farm households had owned over two thirds of all land, whereas ten years later, fewer than 7% of all households were landless (Ban et al., 1980). In conjunction with an expanding education system, growing urban employment, and the rags-to-riches fables of a few hard-driving industrialists, land reform provided industrialization with a plausible vision, a Korea of equal opportunity.

Third, to fight the Korean War, the Americans buttressed the Korean army. At the beginning of the war, the Korean military was not much more than a small constabulary. At the war's end, it numbered 600,000 men—the fourth largest army outside the Soviet bloc. It had modern heavy equipment and an officer corps of significant proportions (H. B. Lee, 1968). After biding its time in the 1950s and blinking at the student revolution that brought a decade of political incompetence to a close, the military would open a new chapter on both growth and state power in the 1961 coup. Here was the ultimate Spite from Pandora's box.

AID AND THE ORIGINS OF THE DIVERSIFIED BUSINESS GROUP

The 1950s paralleled the millennium of dynastic rule that ended in 1876 in that more energy was spent plundering the existing surplus

[16] The process of measuring equality in Korea is vexed by institutional factors. Inequality in Korea is likely to be understated for three reasons: (1) The value of real estate and other assets, which tends to appreciate with inflation, rose more rapidly in the 1970s than wages. Because this value is excluded from income and these assets tend to be owned by higher income earners, the treatment of such assets is likely to result in the understatement of inequality. (2) The equivalent of the United States' Internal Revenue Service in Korea sometimes includes and sometimes excludes from the calculation of personal income, capital gains, rent, and interest payments. Such income is also taxed differently from wage income. (3) It was possible until 1988 to open bank accounts in Korea under an assumed name.

[17] Brandt (1986) has a discussion of egalitarianism in postwar Korea.

than producing more, the surplus itself arriving in the alluring form
of U.S. foreign aid for war reconstruction. The average annual inflow of aid from 1953 through 1958 was $270 million excluding mil-
itary assistance, or roughly $12 per capita per year. This was nearly
15% of the average annual gross national product (GNP) and over
80% of foreign exchange (Cole and Lyman, 1971). To maximize aid
inflow, macroeconomic policies featured low interest rates, an overvalued exchange rate, a deficit budget financed by borrowing from
the Central Bank when taxes and aid-generated revenues were insufficient, and Central Bank financing of commercial bank credit to
the private sector. Such policies inevitably produced an internal financial gap between government transactions and private transactions, and an external financial gap between import demand and
foreign exchange supply. The state, under the leadership of Syngman Rhee and other "patriots, notables, and various circles of the
intellectual stratum," then allocated aid entitlements in exchange for
political campaign contributions. When campaign contributions ran
into diminishing returns with respect to votes (at one time the number of political parties was estimated at 344), elections were rigged
or the constitution was amended.

The windfall gains from aid provided a basis for the emergence
of an altogether new entrepreneurial element, less conservative in
outlook than Korea's older textiles industry and far more growth
oriented than its small-scale sector. During the period when venality
was pervasive (the First Republic, 1948–1960), political connections
led to an uneven distribution of the spoils. Fortunes, therefore, were
amassed, the "gravy train" starting with sales of Japanese property
at below-market prices. Favored firms, whatever their origins, were
allocated hard currency to import scarce materials—grains and fertilizers—that they then resold on the domestic market at monopoly
prices. They were given loans at subsidized interest rates. They were
granted tax exemptions, and they were awarded preferential contracts for large-scale government projects (K. D. Kim, 1976). The
magnitude of fraud is indicated by the size of the loans that the most
favored firms received, "loans" on which they paid neither interest
nor principal. A Government Audit Report, prepared in 1961 after
the First Republic's fall, suggests that total outstanding loans equaled
about $140 million (or about half of the average yearly grant aid in
the 1950s).[18]

According to the Government Audit Report on Illicit Wealth, the

---

[18] According to the Government Audit Report, quoted in C. H. Park (1963), total
outstanding principal on loans in 1961 was W48,574,122,000, and interest was
W10,271,000,000. Using the real effective exchange rate for 1962 (because the won
was devalued twice in 1961), as calculated by Y. C. Park (1985), the interest and
principal on these loans in dollars was about $140 million.

industries to which these enterprises thriving on venality belonged included textiles, paper, housing, mining, fertilizer, flour, alcohol, glass, pottery, livestock, construction, warehousing, and trade. This is a wide range of industries, and while textiles is represented, it is underrepresented in proportion to its weight in total output (the textiles industry accounted for approximately 20% of manufacturing value added in the 1950s).[19] The point is that the cradling of enterprises in illicit wealth was not industry specific. These subsidized entrepreneurs were generalists, devoted to moneymaking in whatever industry the opportunity arose. They drew their members from all social classes, although they tended to be better educated and much more likely to have descended from the gentry than were their social peers (Jones and Sakong, 1980). In this respect they provided a link with the past. Their novelty lay in the fact that they skated over the stage of incremental growth that was characteristic of small-scale enterprise, operated with a different logic of investment from that of traditional cotton spinning and weaving firms, and formed crack troops to penetrate new industries.

Thus, as the high-aid era drew to a close, the embryo of a new social, economic, and political force had been conceived. The 1950s had witnessed a decrease in the size of agricultural enterprises and the death knell of the nobility, along with an increase in the size of industrial enterprises and the tentative groping toward a symbiotic relationship between the state and the progenitors of large diversified business groups (chaebol). The rise of the chaebol, moreover, relit some of the glimmer of economic activity that had been characteristic of the 1930s. By international comparison, the growth rates Korea attained during the high-aid era were superlative. As indicated in Figure 2.1, between 1953 and 1958 the average annual rate of change in the volume of production of both heavy and light manufactures was the highest in Korea of all 36 countries for which U.N. data were available.[20]

U.N. data, however, exclude North Korea, which was growing roughly three times faster than the South (Cole and Lyman, 1971). What's more, the growth rates that the South chalked up were unsustainable. By 1959 the economy was deeply depressed, partly the effect of conservative macroeconomic policies and partly the effect of the winding down of aid and of the reconstruction boom. With

[19] This represents value in 1975 constant market prices, as reported by the Korea Development Bank (1984).

[20] The data are in real, rather than nominal, terms but are bound to contain substantial margins of error, since they are among the earliest attempts of the United Nations at international growth comparisons.

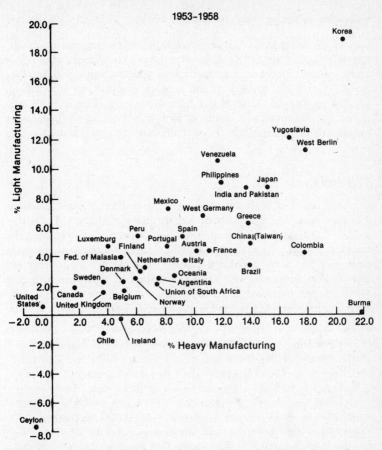

Figure 2.1 Average Percent Annual Rate of Change in the Volume of Production, Heavy and Light Manufacturing, 1953–1958. *Source:* United Nations (1960).

tariff protection and subsidized credit, the textiles industry had achieved in half a decade what it had failed to achieve in half a century of political discrimination—modern plants of international scale to undertake integrated spinning and weaving. The growth rate of textiles output, however, turned negative at the end of the 1950s as firms added to their capacity to take advantage of cheap U.S. credit (Y. B. Kim, 1980). "Thus, by the early 1960s, U.S. officials had become extremely gloomy about the prospects of Korean development" (Mason et al., 1980, p. 195).

THREE CONTENDING VIEWS

Out of the corruption, paralysis, underachievement, and bitter disappointment of the 1950s came three conflicting views about how Korea should proceed, one associated with students and intellectuals, one articulated by U.S. aid advisors, and the one that was ultimately to prevail—that of the Korean military. The issue of economic development was foremost and, although submerged under politics, its failure underly the turmoil that brought the decade to a close.

The Students

In April 1960, a high-school student protesting crooked elections was slain by police and his body was thrown into the sea. The atrocity provoked youth- and student-led demonstrations throughout the country. The president, Syngman Rhee, called on the army to intervene, but the army remained passive. The American government did likewise, disgusted with Rhee and disturbed by his intransigence toward Japan that obstructed the formation of a greater Pacific alliance. Within days, the Second Republic fell. According to H. B. Lee,

> The April Revolution was a giant social revolt. The suffering and revolting self that had been emerging in the latter part of the decade of the 1950s was now given its full play. The students began revolting against the Liberal Government, but their success touched off a general revolt in the society. The people revolted against the government. The young revolted against the old. In many schools, students revolted against their teachers. In some government ministries, junior civil servants revolted against senior civil servants. In a more serious vein, some eight lieutenant colonels openly revolted against some generals, requesting that the army be cleared of corrupt elements. (1968, p. 119)

There was nothing revolutionary about the outcome of the April events, though. They provoked an election that voted into power a party little different in outlook, age, and background from the previous regime. Thus the protests continued. Among the protesters, however, were radical reformists who had been silenced under Rhee—trade unionists, whose activities had been circumscribed by a state-run labor federation (Ewing, 1973); socialists, teachers, and unemployed intellectuals, whose ranks had been decimated during the Korean War; and students, spearheaded by the Student League for National Unification (*Minjok T'ongil Yongmaeng*) of Seoul National

University. Although the alliance of radicals and moderate reformists could trace its antecedents back to the early reform movements of the late nineteenth century, its vision of economic development was still undefined, consisting of little more than vague demands for full employment and more aggressive policies to eliminate poverty. The radical view of how Korea should proceed, however, focused its attack on imperialism. The radicals, in particular, opposed a blanket technical agreement, in the offing between South Korea and the United States, that gave the United States the right to "continuous observation and review" of the way U.S. financial and technical assistance was being administered. The radicals were joined in their opposition to this agreement by nonreformist politicians who termed it "shameful" and organized mass demonstrations against it (S. Han, 1974, p. 183).

The United States

The economic policies that the United States espoused in Korea showed consistency over time, the tumultuous events of the 1940s and 1950s merely reinforcing that central tendency. The lesson that the United States drew from the upheavals in Korea was the need for stability before growth, and this lesson was at the heart of American short- and medium-term macroeconomic policies toward Korea. Long-term goals were perceived in terms of the law of comparative advantage, the objective being to reduce Korea's dependence on aid. For the purpose of developing a sound economy, aid was dispensed on the principle of static efficiency, that is, building infrastructure, natural resource-processing facilities, and light industry on the basis of small-scale enterprise. This policy reflected little of the Keynesian revolution then sweeping American universities. Economic advisors in Korea, for the most part, were not academics; rather they were affiliated with the U.S. military and with international aid organizations. The policies that the United States advocated were based on traditional market theory and were precursors to those of the World Bank and of the International Monetary Fund (IMF).

The immersion of international organizations like the IMF and the World Bank in the industrialization of latter-day twentieth-century learners is unique in the history of emulation. So, too, is the amount of foreign aid to which Korea has had access. Therefore, it is of interest to explore the extent to which, if at all, these policies and aid shaped Korean industrialization, one of the more successful cases to emerge from the Cold War era.

By and large, the Rhee administration staunchly opposed the U.S. policy package. The rancor between the two countries exceeded what could reasonably be expected from a corrupt aid recipient, a frugal aid donor, and the inherent indignity of the aid relationship. According to one observer, "The most touchy subjects of controversy between the two governments, among many less crucial that cannot all be cited, were Rhee's insistence on an unrealistic exchange rate and the pleading by the United States for a comprehensive stabilization program with proper budgetary methods and restrictive monetary and credit policies" (Reeve, 1963, p. 122). Corruption apart, Rhee's position was that a stabilization package comprising devaluation, a balanced budget, tight money, and high interest rates would make growth all but impossible.

The U.S. fear of inflation flared at the time of occupation, although there was no reversion to the hyperinflation of the war years after a sharp increase in prices during the first quarter of 1946 (Bloomfield and Jensen, 1951). Nevertheless, as the Korean War approached, the U.S. Secretary of State, Dean Acheson, fired off a "missile" to the Korean Ambassador that read:

> It is the judgment of this government that the financial situation in Korea has already reached critical proportions and that, unless this progressive inflation is curbed in the none-too-distant future, it cannot but seriously impair Korea's ability to utilize effectively the economic assistance provided. . . . Government expenditures have been vastly expanded by bank overdrafts without reference to limits set by an approved budget. Tax collections have not been increased, aid goods have been underpriced, and governmental subsidies have been expanded . . .
>
> Unless the Korean Government is able to take satisfactory and effective measures to counter these inflationary forces, it will be necessary to reexamine, and perhaps to make adjustments in, the . . . Administration's assistance program in Korea. (April 7, 1950)[21]

Nevertheless, hyperinflation did not materialize during the Korean War either. Price increases slowed with good harvests, and "the relative movements of prices and money supply from mid-1950 to mid-1953 support the proposition that money was used mainly for transaction purposes . . ." (Cole and Park, 1983, p. 222). Between 1953–1955 and 1960–1962, the GNP deflator averaged only 16.7%, despite an unbalanced budget and heavy lending by the Central Bank. However, the United States had engineered a massive devaluation of 300% immediately after the Korean War, another devaluation in 1955, and two devaluations in 1961 (Cole and Park, 1983; Krueger, 1979). The

[21] This document is reproduced in Tewksbury (1950).

U.S. government's concern with fiscal and monetary restraint was ingrained, spilling over to long-run measures beginning in the early 1950s. In the words of two advisors from the Federal Reserve,

> The fact that the sizable long-term investment program being currently carried on by Government Agencies . . . has been financed by bank credit expansion has contributed very materially to the present inflation. . . . At the present moment . . . everything must be done to discourage further long-term lending until the budgetary situation is normalized. (Bloomfield and Jensen, 1951, pp. 49–50)

The casus belli became Rhee's contention that U.S. aid did little to promote long-run growth. In fact, if aid-financed imports of food, beverages, and manufactures are classified as consumer goods; if crude materials, fuels, and chemicals are classified as intermediate goods and raw materials; and if machinery and transport equipment are classified as capital goods, then capital goods accounted for a very small share of total imports—3.4% in 1953 and 11.7% in 1960. Even though consumer goods, during the same period, declined in importance—from 70.4% of total imports in 1953 to 35% in 1960—this was only because the share of intermediate goods and raw materials had risen to 50% of the total (Krueger, 1979), and the Rhee government protested that intermediate goods and fuels were largely designated for light industry.

In the half decade following the end of World War II, the aim of project aid had been to develop capital projects

> which would ultimately make the provision of further assistance unnecessary. Emphasis was given in planning to the expansion of electric power-generating facilities, expanded tungsten production, the development of new anthracite coal fields, rehabilitation of the fishing industry, the production of chemical fertilizers and the expansion of the railway system. (U.S. House of Representatives, 1954, p. 12)

This is a quotation from an invaluable report of a U.S. congressional subcommittee that took the trouble to visit Korea and conduct field interviews on the eve of a new development program, with only six years to go before the Korean military coup. What did the subcommittee discover about postwar Korea?

In terms of physical capital, the subcommittee discovered the evidence of Japan's unassailable contribution to growth, and yet a dearth of large-scale enterprise:

> Manufacturing activity is more highly developed than is generally appreciated. With the exception of Japan, the proportion of

total Korean output derived from manufacturing, prior to the invasion in 1950, was higher than in any other Asian country, and a considerable variety of fabricated products was produced, although the scale of enterprise was in general, quite limited. (p. 196)[22]

In terms of human capital, however, "there is a serious deficiency in technical and supervisory personnel"; although in the business community "managerial skills appear to be available, but far too much [sic] of these skills is diverted to unproductive trading and speculation" (p. 38). As for the contribution of U.S. aid to skill formation,

It was apparent that not sufficient attention has been given under the aid program to training Korean personnel in various technical and managerial fields vital to the rehabilitation program. Experience gained in the military training program under United States supervision indicates that the Koreans are quick to absorb and apply technological knowledge if they are given the opportunity. . . . The need for greatly expanded civilian training programs for Korean personnel is particularly pressing when the reluctance of the Japanese to train Koreans for jobs above the most menial level is considered. (pp. 38–9)

Nevertheless, technical backwardness is not likely to have diminished greatly under the new U.S. aid development program initiated in 1954–1955. Of fifty-one new projects, most focused on small-scale enterprise in light manufacturing (Mason et al., 1980); furthermore, of the few large-scale projects attempted in basic industry, most ran into snags. U.S. influence on technical and managerial literacy in the civilian sector, therefore, was bipolar. In the area of quality control, and particularly in the construction industry, it had an unambiguously positive effect on civilian subcontractors, as discussed in Chapter 9. Technology transfer, however, was problematic in large-scale projects and served as a bad example for local managers.

Confounding the problem of corruption in technology transfer on the part of aid recipients was a lack of unified administration among aid donors. The Audit Report to the U.S. Congress described the administrative arrangements of aid projects as "complex and confusing" and contrary to "sound management principles." The consequence was delay and technical bungling. Following are three examples:

In telecommunications,

---

[22] Page references in this and the next paragraph are to U.S. House of Representatives (1954).

A primary cause for these planning difficulties was the rapid rotation of supervisory personnel without adequate overlap of replacements. A contributory cause was . . . the use of military personnel inexperienced in domestic communication systems. (98)[23]

In a large machinery shop (the Pusan Iron Works),

A considerable portion of the machinery ordered for this project had been delivered . . . but . . . was in storage at the plant site and in customs warehouses. The delay in releasing the equipment was attributed to financial difficulties of the plant and to the need for technical assistance in layout and installation. (p. 112)

In a waste-silk processing plant, a small-scale project,

This project illustrates the lack of thorough technical studies resulting in the omission of several features essential for competent plant construction. (p. 113)

On net, *the impact of U.S. occupation on Korean industrialization was probably similar to that of Japan, as characterized by the U.S. congressional subcommittee: "modernizing but distorted and unbalanced."* The difference between them was that the Japanese colonial administration had enacted a model of centralized state management in Korea that was in tune with the historical stage of development in which both Japan and Korea found themselves, whereas the liturgy of U.S. economic advisors was private ownership and decentralized control. The corruption of the Rhee regime had strongly reinforced the conviction supporting the latter approach.

The U.S. authorities argued forcefully for privatization of the banking sector (although that sector later proved the most powerful tool for shaping the course of industrial activity after subsequent nationalization by the military). The U.S. authorities contended that private ownership would subject banks to fewer political pressures and induce them to act more responsibly. A report prepared by consultants from the Federal Reserve Bank of New York emphasized this viewpoint:

The importance for Korean economic and financial welfare of getting the ownership and control of these banks into private hands is so great . . . that it is to be hoped that special efforts will be made by those in charge of vested property disposal to

[23] Page references are to the 1957 Audit Report.

> seek out responsible private interests who would be willing to purchase these shares. (Bloomfield and Jensen, 1951, p. 73)

The government initiated action in 1954 to divest itself of shareholdings in commercial banks that it had acquired from former Japanese owners, but it was unsuccessful in several auction attempts.

In 1957, however, the government succeeded in selling its shares to a relatively small number of large stockholders, "mainly wealthy businessmen who were prospering from high profits on government-controlled import licenses" (Cole and Park, 1983, p. 53). The government also introduced strong deflationary measures. By 1960 unemployment was estimated at one fifth the total labor force. Per capita income, according to U.N. estimates, was less than $100, roughly the same as that in India, one quarter that of Japan, and two thirds that of Taiwan (United Nations, 1961). Furthermore,

> Delays [amounting to six years] in putting [an] admittedly costly domestic fertilizer plant into production contributed significantly to the chronically large excess of imports over exports, since long-established intensive cultivation in South Korea demand[ed] huge quantities of chemical fertilizer to maintain the fertility of the soil. The value of exports remained exceedingly low. (Reeve, 1963, p. 126)

Despite all these failures of the U.S. aid administration, the agreement giving the United States wide latitude to "observe" and "review" Korea's economic policies was overwhelmingly approved by the National Assembly on the deathbed of the Second Republic (S. Han, 1974).

The Military

Over twenty-five years after the coup d'état of May 1961, the U.S. government was still a powerful force in Korean affairs, as was the military, although General Park Chung Hee, who had presided over the coup and over the Golden Age of growth, had been assassinated in 1979. Moreover, the student movement remained hyperactive. Therefore, while the military's view about how Korea should proceed was the one that prevailed, the other two poles of dissent had survived. On the one hand, the student movement kept afire demands for democracy, civil rights, higher wages, egalitarianism, eradication of poverty, and protection of the small-scale firm. On the other hand, the United States continued to stand in relation to Korea the way water stands in relation to fish.

The U.S. government and the Korean military shared a fundamental obsession with anticommunism and a commitment to private enterprise. Thus, when 5,000 troops crossed the Han River and entered Seoul on May 16, 1961, the United States looked on blankly. Both countries needed one another in the geopolitical vortex of the postwar period, yet the United States decidedly held the upper hand. Although Korea could threaten to withhold payments on the huge foreign debt that it would soon amass, the U.S. government could threaten to close world markets to Korea's exports, the lifeblood of its economy; to reduce subsidies to Korea's defense budget; and to subject Korea and its statesmen to all the pressures that were at the disposal of the global hegemonic power. Nevertheless, as will be discussed in the next chapter, in the mealy matter of economic growth, Korea charted an independent course.

The military's only claim to government was its ability to create a sustainable mechanism to raise national income. In the general election immediately after the coup, Park Chung Hee had defeated the opposition candidate only by a slim margin. In the general election two years later, the last for at least another two decades, he won a landslide victory because growth had accelerated in the intervening years. Growth, therefore, took precedence over other claims, income distribution most certainly included. In Park's words,

> The economic, social and political goals we set after the revolution are: promotion of the public welfare, freedom from exploitation, and the fair distribution of an income among the people. It is obvious that these goals cannot be reached overnight. They are, nevertheless, the fundamental aims of the economic order towards which we must move.
>
> Before these goals can be achieved, we must see to it that after more than a decade of stagnation, our poor economic power is greatly strengthened and that the heretofore shrunken or undeveloped power of productivity is fully utilized. We must take a great leap forward toward economic growth. . . . It is urgently necessary to have an economic plan or a long-range development program through which reasonable allocation of all our resources is feasible. (C. H. Park, 1962, p. 224)

If the lesson that the United States learned from the Korean upheavals was the need for stability before growth, then the military learned that causality ran in the opposite direction, from growth to stability. Inflation in Korea during the period 1962–1979 averaged 18.4%—lower than that in Latin America but higher than that in India, China, Taiwan, Hong Kong, Singapore, Japan in its fast-growth phase, or still earlier learners in theirs.[24] This is not to suggest that government policy in Korea during the high-growth period was reckless; after all, the government was not unaware that hyperinflation and bankruptcy of foreign exchange reserves are the ingredients of countercoups. Rather, the policy was risky. As will be argued in the following chapters, however, risk was mitigated by leaving as little as possible to chance and the vagaries of the market.

Within the first 100 days of its assumption of power, the military had announced its intention to launch the first five-year development plan. By the time Park's book, *Our Nation's Path*, was sent to press in February 1962 and still another of his books, *The Country, The Revolution and I*, was published one and a half years later, the twin pillars of the military's strategy to industrialize had been devised. The scaffold was still missing, little mention being made of exports, but there was clarity on the critical roles of both large-scale enterprise and long-range planning. However, apologies and rationales for supplanting market forces by state power were put forth in terms of both roles. In the case of large-scale enterprise,

> One of the essential characteristics of a modern economy is its strong tendency towards centralization. Mammoth enterprise—considered indispensable, at the moment, to our country—plays not only a decisive role in the economic development and elevation of living standards, but further, brings about changes in the structure of society and the economy. . . . Where the appalling power of mammoth enterprise is concerned, only with private profit under a self-assumed assertion of contribution to national development, there is no free competition. . . . Therefore, the key problems facing a free economic policy are coordination and supervisory guidance, by the state, of mammoth economic strength. (C. H. Park, 1962, pp. 228–229)

In the case of planning,

> The economic planning or long-range development program must not be allowed to stifle creativity or spontaneity of private enterprise. The overall national development program may necessitate, for the rational operation of the economy, reluctantly imposed administrative controls over the regional relocation of various industries and planning for investment. Yet we should

[24] Data on inflation in Korea are presented in Table 3.1. Data on inflation in other countries are from International Monetary Fund, *International Financial Statistics*, various years. For data on inflation in Japan, 1905–1970, see Ohkawa and Rosovsky, 1973. Learners in the nineteenth century for the most part experienced mild price declines (see, for example, Landes, 1969).

utilize to the maximum extent the merits usually introduced by
the price machinery of free competition, thus avoiding the possible damages accompanying a monopoly system. (C. H. Park,
1963, pp. 224–5)

Although the U.S. aid advisors in Korea had tried earlier to formulate their own development plan—a task they subcontracted to a
private Washington-based consulting firm—the plan's object, to ter-
minate aid, led to its rejection by the Rhee forces. In 1958, however,
Rhee had established an Economic Development Council, staffed by
many "young foreign-educated intellectuals," fed on the ideas of
planning that were then sweeping the economic development
profession from the universities (H. B. Lee, 1968, p. 90). It was this
concept of national planning, if not the identical plan, that later inspired the military rulers.

Park, whose principal hobby was said to be the study of Korean
and world history, compared the Korean "revolution" under his
leadership in 1963 to the Meiji reform, the modernization of China
under Sun Yat-Sen, Kemal Pasha's development of Turkey, and
Nasser's revolution in Egypt. Park's discussion of Japanese modernization is interesting both for what it says and for what it does not
say. What it omits, even elliptically, is any reference to the nuts and
bolts of the Japanese model—export strategy, investment policy, exchange rate regime, and so on. That these influenced Korean policymakers is indisputable, but they came later. What Park's discussion
includes is an analysis of Japan's industrialization, not as a matter of
policy but as a matter of relations between the state, social classes,
and ideology. According to Park's reading of history, the causes of
the modernization of Japan were as follows:

1. The Meiji reform had as its ideological basis a nationalistic patri-
   otism.
2. Thereby they succeeded in Japanizing foreign thoughts that came
   in volume, and guarding the reform tasks undergoing then-
   repeated domestic ordeals from foreign invasion.
3. By eliminating the influence of feudal lords and directly connecting the emperor with the energetic middle class, a progressive
   atmosphere to overcome feudalism was created.
4. Millionaires who promoted the reform were allowed to enter the
   central stage, both politically and economically, thus encouraging
   national capitalism. An imperial system was thus established with
   the emperor at the apex of the pyramid of political and economic
   forces, and with the nobility serving as elder statesmen of the
   nation.

Park concluded by saying, "The case of the Meiji imperial restoration will be of great help to the performance of our own revolution. My interest in this direction remains strong and constant" (C. H. Park, 1963, pp. 120–1).

This, then, may be said to have been Park's vision for Korea's industrialization when he marched across the Han, no doubt casting himself in the role of emperor. The vision could not be implemented in the absence of a strong state. In 1961, however, the field was clear for the assumption of state power. The landed nobility had been destroyed; the peasantry was less rebellious as a result of a land reform; and the "captains of industry" were beholden to the state for their regeneration. Only workers and students remained as opponents to military rule. Industrial workers, however, were still only a small portion of the population. As for the students, their role in an industrialization based on learning became pivotal. The *Hangul* generation, the first generation of students since the nineteenth century to escape education under the Japanese, came off the streets and into the modern factories of the 1970s as managers. In Chapter 3, attention turns to the model of accumulation that bound these social forces together.

CONCLUSION

The Korean state was able to consolidate its power in the 1960s because of the weakness of the social classes. Workers were a small percentage of the population, capitalists were dependent on state largesse, the aristocracy was dissolved by land reform, and the peasantry was atomized into smallholders. The behavior of the Korean state became influenced by two forces outside the class structure: the student movement and the American occupation forces (first the U.S. army, then the U.S. aid administration). The student movement kept the new government relatively honest. The American occupation forces drove the Korean military toward developmentalism, the only realistic course to reduce dependence on American support.

It is to industrialization policies that attention is now turned.

APPENDIX 2-1

Colonial Agriculture

From Japan's perspective, Korea was a valuable asset by dint of its agricultural resources. This is not to say that a food supply was the only motive for Japanese aggression. Raw materials in the northern part of Korea, geopolitics, nationalism, and the Korean market were also contributory factors. Moreover, Japanese imperialist policy shifted over time. Rice riots in Japan led to an emphasis on agriculture in Korea, while protests by Japanese farmers over declining farm prices prompted a policy reversal (Duus, 1984). After 1930, industrialization in Korea was stressed as Japan began its conquest of Manchuria. Nevertheless, the exploitation of agriculture was the major endeavor of the Japanese colonial administration, and Korea was even singled out for a special role in this regard: to serve as a colony for Japanese settlers. Japanese settlers were slated not only to supervise and guide the improvement of Korean agriculture, they were also to set up farms and work the land with their own hands. This added dimension of imperialism was absent in Taiwan, where the mosquito frustrated foreign settlement, and in fact, "the differences between Taiwan and Korea cannot be overemphasized" (Moskowitz, 1974, p. 78). However, Japanese farmers never became a significant proportion of total Japanese settlers. The myth of a sparsely populated Korea dissipated, and the Japanese population as a percent of the total population in Korea never amounted to as much as 3% (T. H. Kwon et al., 1975). Nevertheless, the settler mentality endured and created far fewer opportunities for Koreans in business and the civil service and far more abusive race relations than might otherwise have been the case.

In the first year of annexation, Japan initiated a cadastral survey to determine the size, value, and ownership status of every plot of land. By 1919 the survey had been completed and a new, less regressive tax system had taken effect. The new agrarian structure implanted in Korea in the interim was very similar not only to the one that existed in late nineteenth-century Japan but also to the one that Japan instilled in early twentieth-century Taiwan (see Amsden, 1985). Superficially, it resembled the one that had been in effect for a thousand years, whereby the state collected taxes from landlords and landlords collected rents from tenants. Moreover, although Korean specialists are divided on this point, the same individuals who were last landlords under the old system most likely became landlords under the new one; now, however, the landlords worked in conjunction with former bureaucrats, Confucian scholars, and the Japanese (Cumings, 1974). Japanese landlords—both corporate and individual—may have possessed as much as 50% of Korea's total available land (see the estimates of Ho, 1984, and of Grajdanzev, 1944). Nevertheless, in key respects, the new agrarian structure was quite distinct.

Under the precapitalist system, peasants had traditional rights to their land and were unlikely to lose it. Under the new system, they had no rights at all. On the other hand, under the precapitalist system, landlords lived by virtue of their political domination, and the resolution of disputes between landlord and peasant depended directly on force. Under the new system, landlords lived by virtue of their property rights; their land was alienable, and disputes, in theory, were resolvable by law.

Some appreciation of the differences between these two agrarian systems is gained by looking at the major problems associated with the dynastic agrarian structure and the advantages of tenancy. Formerly, the economic surplus largely went to a parasitic landlord class. Taxes were paid by the landlords to the monarchy, but only enough to sustain it, not enough to allow it to invest. By and large, the landlords used the surplus for political consumption—to buy patronage and to build their military strength. The peasantry, moreover, was not dependent on the market, and therefore was not forced to be efficient. If peasants were lucky enough to accumulate a surplus, they were not driven to invest it in improvements. By contrast, the new system represented a radical improvement insofar as it introduced the market as a stimulant for increased productivity. Tenants were exploited to the maximum. In the presence of population pressures there was competition to acquire tenants' leases, and rents escalated. Neither did Korean peasants enjoy the alternative open to Japanese peasants—industrial employment—an alternative that might otherwise have set a ceiling on rents and acted as a further stimulant to efficiency. Instead, exploitation of the Korean peasantry increased, while the colonial administration's cadastral survey expanded tax collections and discouraged landlords from investing in tax evasion.

In light of the foregoing, one would expect Japan's agricultural policies in Korea to have resulted in a decline in the welfare of the masses, a deterioration in income distribution, and a rise in output; in fact, this is what occurred. The index of rice consumption fell from 100 in 1915–1919 to only 56 in 1934–1938. A similar decrease in consumption index characterized millet, barley, and beans. In 1932 the rice available per member of a landlords' family was 11.43 koku; the comparable figure for tenants was only 0.41. Meanwhile, between 1910 and 1941, agricultural output rose at an average annual rate of 2.3% (S. C. Suh, 1978). Over time, the social composition of the agricultural population shifted toward tenancy. Tenants accounted for 37.7% of the agricultural population in 1918 but for as much as 53.8% in 1932. In the late 1930s, less than 3% of farm households owned about two thirds of the cultivated land area (Grajdanzev, 1944; see also references in footnote 5).

There appears to be general agreement that from the perspective of economic development, Japanese imperialism was less effective in Korea than in Taiwan. For comparisons in agriculture and in education, see Ho (1984) and Tsurumi (1984), respectively.

CHAPTER THREE

The ABCs of Japanese and Korean Accumulation

COMPETITIVE ADVANTAGE IN KOREA VERSUS IN JAPAN

This chapter is concerned with how acceleration in Korean investments and exports was activated. Exploiting its low-wage advantage to gain entry to international trade, Korea scored breathtakingly rapid increases in output. Table 3.1 shows that during the first two five-year plans, 1962–1966 and 1967–1971, the real growth rate of GNP averaged 9% per annum. In the period 1972–1979, growth was still higher, 10% on average each year. A decomposition of GNP growth rates is presented in Table 3.2. It is evident that exports and investment, the subjects of this chapter, led overall economic activity. Consumption grew only modestly. The real growth rate of exports, deflated by the U.S. wholesale price index, averaged a phenomenal 40% in the period of the first two five-year plans (Table 3.1). Between 1972 and 1979 (the year of Park's assassination), the export growth rate averaged 28%, all the more remarkable because during this period the industrial composition of output and exports in Korea was radically transformed. In 1971 the share in merchandise exports of heavy manufactures was only about 14%. The share had increased to 38% by 1979, and by 1984 to 60%, roughly the same share as heavy manufactures in total merchandise output (Table 3.3).

Korea is evidence for the proposition that if and when late industrialization arrives, the driving force behind it is a strong interventionist state. The need to intervene is greater than in the past because the curses of backwardness are greater. The relativity of this proposition is illustrated by examining Japan's foray into world trade in cotton textiles (spinning and weaving) in the first third of the twentieth century. Cotton textiles continue to serve as the illustrative

Table 3.1   Basic Macro Indicators, 1962–1984

Year	GNP Growth Rate (%)	Change in GNP Deflator	Export Growth Rate[a]	Export Growth Rate[b]	Real Effective Exchange Rate[c]	Ratio, Current Account/GNP	Terms of Trade[c]
1962	2.2	13.5	31.7	31.0	112.0	−2.0	NA
1963	9.1	28.3	61.1	61.6	134.4	−3.7	111.3
1964	9.6	30.0	37.9	37.6	106.3	−0.8	112.5
1965	5.8	6.3	45.8	43.0	91.6	0.3	114.3
1966	12.7	14.2	42.9	38.3	96.1	−2.7	127.7
1967	6.6	15.8	34.0	33.7	107.9	−4.1	132.2
1968	11.3	15.9	45.1	41.5	115.2	−7.4	137.7
1969	13.8	14.6	35.4	30.3	120.1	−7.3	132.6
1970	7.6	15.7	34.0	29.3	124.2	−7.1	133.8
1971	8.8	13.4	28.5	24.3	120.7	−8.7	132.7
1972	5.7	16.4	47.9	41.7	109.4	−3.5	132.1
1973	14.1	13.4	95.9	73.2	92.4	−2.3	125.4
1974	7.7	29.5	37.5	15.7	93.6	−10.9	102.1
1975	6.9	25.8	10.8	1.4	93.5	−9.0	92.1
1976	14.1	20.5	56.2	49.2	103.4	−1.1	105.1
1977	12.7	15.8	28.6	21.1	103.9	0.0	112.4
1978	9.7	21.9	26.5	17.4	101.0	−2.2	117.8
1979	6.5	21.1	15.7	2.8	110.7	−6.4	115.3
1980	−5.2	25.6	17.1	2.6	100.0	−8.7	100.0
1981	6.2	15.9	20.1	10.0	103.1	−6.9	97.9
1982	5.6	7.1	1.0	−1.0	106.9	−3.7	102.2
1983	9.5	3.0	11.1	9.8	100.2	−2.1	103.1
1984	7.6	4.0	13.5	10.9	97.8	−1.7	105.3

[a]GNP, gross national product; NA, not available. In nominal U.S. dollars.
[b]Export value deflated by U.S. wholesale price index.
[c]1980 = 100.
Sources: Bank of Korea and International Monetary Fund.

case when discussion turns to the Korean economy in the 1950s and
1960s. Cotton textiles accounted for over 20% of manufacturing value-
added and became Korea's major export item.

Unlike Korea, Japan as a colonizer had been able to rely on more
competitive weapons than merely low wages to capture market share
in cotton textiles from Lancashire during the 1900–1930 period.[1]
Korea, twenty years later, had only low wages with which to compete
against Japan, and low wages in the absence of government support
proved insufficient to stimulate export activity. In the 1950s Washington actually thwarted Korea's efforts to export by prohibiting U.S.

---

[1] Lancashire was the home of cotton textiles manufacture in what was then the
world's leading producer, Great Britain.

Table 3.2 Decomposition of Gross National Product Growth Rate, 1962–1984 (Real Growth Rates[a])

Year	GNP	C	I	G	X	M	NFI
1962	2.2	5.7	6.9	0.9	12.5	32.0	11.9
1963	9.1	3.3	76.0	4.8	7.4	27.4	4.8
1964	9.6	5.6	−16.7	−3.6	23.6	−25.6	−3.8
1965	5.8	7.8	3.6	6.8	40.7	13.1	17.2
1966	12.7	7.2	75.0	11.5	52.3	57.7	71.0
1967	6.6	9.3	16.6	10.2	35.7	34.8	64.6
1968	11.3	11.4	42.4	13.1	41.6	45.9	3.3
1969	13.8	11.0	31.2	12.2	31.9	24.7	3.6
1970	7.6	11.1	0.9	6.7	22.9	10.0	−55.9
1971	8.8	10.4	6.3	10.7	20.5	20.4	−117.0
1972	5.7	5.1	−10.2	2.9	36.6	0.9	−164.4
1973	14.1	9.2	31.5	1.7	55.3	36.7	336.7
1974	7.7	7.6	29.9	10.1	−2.8	16.9	69.3
1975	6.9	5.6	1.7	4.3	15.9	0.1	127.4
1976	14.1	8.3	16.3	5.9	41.6	27.0	−114.7
1977	12.7	6.8	23.2	9.1	22.6	23.4	1,310.4
1978	9.7	9.9	22.8	13.0	19.9	29.0	−13.0
1979	6.5	8.9	19.7	0.1	−3.8	8.6	−49.8
1980	−5.2	−0.8	−23.7	6.8	9.7	−7.3	−334.0
1981	6.2	3.4	2.2	2.2	17.3	5.3	50.9
1982	5.6	4.6	5.0	2.2	6.2	2.3	0.7
1983	9.5	6.6	13.7	4.7	13.8	11.1	6.9
1984	7.6	5.7	11.9	2.3	8.1	6.8	25.8

[a]Growth rates are calculated from data in won and corrected by the GNP deflator: C, consumption; I, investment; G, government spending; X, exports; M, imports; NFI, net factor income.
Source: Bank of Korea.

imports of Korean-made textiles that embodied American aid-financed raw cotton. By the conclusion of this chapter we begin to understand better why investment and exports in Korea rose so fast beginning in the 1960s, their acceleration a function of strong state support as well as of discipline.

THE EMERGENCE OF AN INTERNATIONAL DIVISION OF LABOR

As the basis of industrialization in the world has shifted over time from invention to innovation to learning, what has also shifted is the basis on which less industrialized countries have entered world markets to compete. What we have come to take for granted as the international division of labor—in which low-wage countries hold a commanding position in products characterized by labor-intensive

Table 3.3 Percent Share of Heavy and Chemical Industry and of Light Industry in Manufacturing Output and Merchandise Exports, 1971–1984

Industry	Share	1971	1972	1973	1974	1975	1976	1977	1978	1979	1980	1981	1982	1983	1984
Heavy and chemical industry	a	40.5	39.7	42.6	49.9	47.5	49.5	50.7	53.0	54.9	56.3	57.7	58.3	59.3	61.9
	b	13.7	21.1	23.6	33.2	25.9	28.8	31.6	33.2	37.7	39.9	42.1	49.2	54.3	59.7
Chemical	c	56.2	52.2	44.8	46.9	54.3	48.1	43.8	39.6	41.0	49.3	46.9	45.0	42.2	39.2
	d	14.2	14.7	10.2	12.9	13.2	11.1	10.2	8.5	9.8	11.6	9.5	9.5	9.8	10.7
Basic Metal	c	14.5	15.4	19.7	18.1	13.3	14.5	15.2	14.7	16.0	16.6	16.7	16.4	16.2	17.0
(iron, steel, non-ferrous metals)	d	26.5	34.2	33.4	38.8	28.1	27.4	31.3	27.1	31.8	36.6	34.9	30.5	26.9	22.8
Mach. and trans. equipment	c	29.4	32.4	35.5	34.9	32.4	37.4	41.1	45.7	43.0	34.1	36.4	38.6	41.6	43.8
	d	59.4	51.1	56.4	48.3	58.8	61.5	58.4	64.3	58.4	51.8	55.6	59.9	63.4	66.5
Light industry	a	59.5	60.3	57.4	50.1	52.5	50.5	49.3	47.0	45.1	43.7	42.3	41.7	40.7	38.1
	b	86.3	78.9	76.4	66.8	74.1	71.2	68.4	66.8	62.3	60.1	57.9	50.8	45.7	40.3

[a]In total manufacturing output.
[b]In total merchandise export.
[c]Of output in heavy and chemical industry.
[d]Of export in heavy and chemical industry. Heavy includes consumer electronics.
Source: Economic Planning Board.

production techniques, and high-wage countries dominate in the remainder of industry—is a recent phenomenon, dating approximately from the end of World War II.[2] Obviously, other things being equal, low wages contribute to profitability. Yet in few industries before World War II did low wages confer a decisive lead. Since this war, moreover, low wages have given a decisive lead only to a limited number of countries.

It is clear that lower wages were not responsible for England's emergence as the first industrialized nation. For roughly a century Britain sustained a lead over European countries, which had decidedly lower living standards, because of its higher productivity. At one level a product of the social climacteric, higher productivity in Britain derived directly from the inventions that gave the First Industrial Revolution its character and established the direction of the long wave of technological change that ensued. Labor-saving processes in Britain outcompeted less mechanized techniques in lower-wage countries that failed to import the superior but costly techniques. When, moreover, the United States and Germany caught up with Britain and then overtook it, they did not do so on the basis of lower wages in conjunction with parity in "best practice" technique. In fact, wages in the United States were higher than in Britain, and at the end of the nineteenth century even Germany did not have access to as abundant labor reserves as did Britain. Moreover, Germany was not especially efficient in those industries that were most labor intensive. Dispersed home production and low productivity were common in clothing and textiles even after the turn of the century (Landes, 1969). Therefore it was neither in the area of textiles nor in the area of the least mechanized trades that Germany and the United States developed strength. Rather they contrived to overtake England as innovators, by operating in a new set of "basic" industries, employing a new set of firm structures, and, interrelatedly, utilizing a new set of production methods.

The international division of labor as we know it began at the turn of the twentieth century with improvements in communications, transportation, and technology transfer. The shape it took, however, was decided not by the United States or by Germany but rather by Japan, whose state underwrote large-scale investments in foreign technology by private firms. Writing in 1935, Hubbard expressed sentiments that might have applied to the world economy thirty years later:

[2] Little appears to have been written directly on the pre-World War II international division of labor, but there are empirical studies of changes in trade patterns over time. See, for example, Amsden (1986) and Maizels (1963); for the period 1700–1914 see Woodruff (1973); for the period 1850–1950 see Ashworth (1952).

The emergence of Eastern countries as large-scale industrial producers, their entrance into international markets, the loss of these markets to the manufacturing countries of the West, and the reaction of the latter in the form of trade restrictions in colonial territories have caused a substantial addition to the world's economic problems of today.

The more immediate problems relate to the progress of Japan, who, by reducing her costs of production to a level hitherto unknown, has extended her trading operations in every quarter of the globe and invaded and captured markets, which, in the past, had been the cherished preserves of the exporting countries of the West. (1938, p. xvii)

The Japanese thrust came largely in cotton textiles and with catastrophic effect. From 1885 to 1913, British annual sales of yarn in China fell from 20 million to 2 million pounds. In 1913 Japan sold 156 million pounds of yarn to China, and Japan's total exports of yarn and thread were worth well over twice Germany's and about 40% of England's (Great Britain, 1928; Orchard, 1930). By 1929, Japan's share of world exports of cotton piece goods was 22%; by 1935, it was 44% (Hubbard, 1938).

In the study just cited, Hubbard was at pains to demonstrate that Britain's woes were not attributable simply and solely to Japan's lower wages. Instead, Japan's rise as an international competitor was shown as reflecting its status as a young industrial power—a colonizer, not a colony. Consequently, the penetration of world markets by Japan circa the 1920s differed from that of other Asian late-industrializing countries forty years hence, which ploughed into world markets having only just shed their colonial skins.

Hubbard did concede that unskilled female cotton operatives in Japan earned one sixth the British rate, and at the other extreme, skilled male metal workers earned one half. With regard to the former class, however, "it must be noted that the female workers in Japan are mainly young girls under 20, and that if their wage rates are compared with those of young learners in the British cotton trade, the discrepancy between the two rates is not very marked" (1938, p. 113).[3] As for productivity, the difference between Japan and the United Kingdom was unclear, although cotton mills in the United States used one third the labor used in Japan. Together with other evidence, from a parliamentary investigation into global competitiveness, Hubbard was led to argue that Britain's loss of market share

[3] Page references in this paragraph and the next are to Hubbard (1938). See also Pearse (1929).

was not attributable to a low-wage interloper. Rather, Japan's strength lay in the following:

1. Group control over the industry by the Japan Cotton Spinners' Association and various other trade associations in order to check overproduction and uneconomic competition.
2. Large [and integrated] manufacturing units, working two shifts a day and equipped with ring spindles [the most modern technology] and, to a considerable extent, also with automatic looms.
3. Shipping subsidies and low shipping costs.
4. Concentration of raw-cotton imports in the hands of a few large trading concerns, and the system of bulk purchase, whereby the spinner is often able to obtain his raw cotton at the lowest possible cost.
5. Great efficiency in marketing the finished product resulting from maintenance of closer contact with customers, and from intimate cooperation between the manufacturing and mercantile sections of the industry. (p. 81)

To Hubbard's list must be added the quality of Japanese management. The proportion of university graduates in total employment was far higher in the Japanese than in the Lancashire textile industry. Ironically, Japan even sent large numbers of managers for training in the Manchester Technical School (Yonekawa, 1984).

Centralized purchase of cotton during World War I had allowed the zaibatsu to reap windfall gains. They used these to purchase modern machinery such as ring spindles. "Lancashire, with 27% of all spindles in the world has . . . only 10% of the rings and Japan, with 7% of the total has also 10% of the rings" (Hubbard, 1938, p. 109). Once the zaibatsu had reequipped their factories with the best machinery and had rationalized the process flow, "Japan's vast reservoir of cheap labour could be converted from a potential into a real asset and Japanese competition in world markets became a factor to be reckoned with" (Hubbard, 1938, p. 109).

There is no evidence that Korea challenged the advanced countries, particularly Japan, on any basis other than lower wage rates when it began exporting textiles in the 1960s. This is true even though, as will be suggested in Chapter 10, it would be simplistic to ignore the managerial setting in Korea that made lower wages operationally meaningful. Nevertheless, of the five strengths of Japan vis-a-vis Britain cited above, Korea may have achieved parity with Japan on only the first, the least developmental—cartelization. Moreover, Japan's penetration of foreign markets benefited from three additional factors to which only advanced, not backward, learners have been privileged. These factors made Japan a privileged twentieth-century learner.

1. The preponderance of Japanese manufactured exports was destined not for more but for still less industrialized countries. Before World War I, China took 90% of Japan's exports of cotton manufactures, mostly yarn, while Korea took Japan's inefficiently produced piece goods (Koh, 1966; Mitsubishi Economic Research Bureau, 1936). Then the crippling effect of war on shipping gave Japan the greater Asian market. In 1929 as much as 82% of Japan's manufactured exports was sold to its poorer neighbors. By 1957 this percentage had fallen only modestly, to 71% (Amsden, 1986). Japan, therefore, entered world markets through a back door, so to speak. Exporting to the colonies, its own and Europe's, was a downhill struggle compared with exporting to the metropolitan heartlands, which Korea and the other Asian late-industrializing countries were forced to do. As the colonies industrialized, Japan stayed one giant step ahead of them and provided sequentially more of their sophisticated imports. By contrast, Korea exported progressively more sophisticated manufactures to the metropolitan heartlands and posed an ever greater threat to their established industries and employment.

2. Japan was sufficiently industrialized in the 1920s and 1930s to pursue a "beggar-thy-neighbor" exchange rate policy to expand its exports, against the wishes of the advanced countries, which wanted an appreciated yen. On the other hand, the Korean government in the 1950s and 1960s was hard pressed to keep its currency overvalued in order to lower the costs of machinery imports, against the wishes of the advanced countries, which wanted a depreciated won. Both learners, being resource poor, were highly dependent on imported raw materials to sustain their industries, not least of all cotton spinning and weaving. But Japan was freer than Korea to depreciate and to give its exports a boost, because it was almost self-sufficient in intermediate inputs and capital goods, including textiles machinery. Imports of machinery by Japan accounted for 8.3% of its total imports in 1929, down to 6.4% six years later (Mitsubishi Economic Research Bureau, 1936, p. 537). Imports of machinery by Korea, on the other hand, accounted for 16% of its total imports in 1965, up to 29% six years later (Bank of Korea, various years [a]).

3. Japan's penetration of world markets before World War II differed from that of latter-day learners insofar as Japan's economy was sui generis, none other like it at the time combining quite the same size and degree of backwardness and modernity. At one

time it looked like Japan might encounter serious competition from China and India, but for various reasons this never materialized. In 1899 the value of India's total manufactured exports exceeded that of Japan's; by 1913 export values were equal; by 1929 Japan's manufactured exports exceeded those of India and the margin widened thereafter (Amsden, 1986). By contrast, Korea was one of a large set of postcolonial exporters with roughly the same factor endowments. As Korea industrialized and as its wages rose, countries with still lower wages provided more of a threat than a market.[4] The market environment of the international division of labor had grown more competitive.

From this perspective, low wages were an ambiguous blessing. They helped a learner like Korea to enter world markets, but they went hand in hand with backwardness. Backwardness, moreover, imposed heavy costs in the form of low domestic purchasing power, low productivity, an almost total reliance on imports for inputs, low savings, and high interest rates. These costs made it harder both to enter world markets in the initial instance and to progress up the ladder of technological complexity, realizing value less on the basis of cheap labor and more on the basis of skills.

Attention is now turned to the hodgepodge of policies that the military regime of Park Chung Hee constructed to offset these costs of backwardness, and to mediate the conflicting demands of interest groups inside Korea.

THE MODEL OF ACCUMULATION

Just as a strong state in Korea was the outcome not of policy choice but of a long process of social change, so too were the particular policies that the military regime pasted together in the early 1960s to form a model of accumulation that was rooted in the past. At the heart of the model were subsidies offered by the state to private enterprise in exchange for higher output of exports and import substitutes. The wheeling and dealing, horsetrading, and trafficking that characterized this process were reminiscent of the reciprocity that characterized relations between the state and the privileged classes under dynastic rule. The critical difference lay in the tip of the bal-

---

[4] Some newly industrializing countries, particularly Brazil, Argentina, and India, have exported large shares of their manufactured exports downstream, to developing countries. This has not been true of Korea, however, although it is trying to export more to Asian countries, and it exported as much as 10% of its manufactured exports to the Middle East during the oil boom. For a discussion of South-South trade, see Amsden (1986).

ance of power toward the state. However clumsy at first, the state used its power to discipline not just workers but the owners and managers of capital as well. A larger surplus was extracted, and this was invested rather than consumed.

Another tradition, which carried over from the 1950s to the 1960s, was the extraordinary degree to which a supposedly sovereign state was subject to intervention by the international aid establishment in its economic policymaking. While those European allies of the United States that reindustrialized after World War II were also the bene-factors not merely of aid but also of advice from American aid ad-ministrators, none was as politically unstable as Korea, nor was any other the locus of still another shooting war. These coincidences in Korea prolonged and intensified intervention accompanied by aid through the mid-1960s. Even after aid ceased, intervention contin-ued in tandem with military support. In the 1960s, the United States placed enormous pressure on Korea to accord diplomatic recogni-tion to Japan. This was viewed at the time, by businessmen and stu-dents in Korea, as suicidal both for infant industry and for cultural integrity (Cole and Lyman, 1971). In desperation, the Park regime turned to the World Bank and to the IMF as a way to multilateralize its international dependence. Yet these Bretton Woods institutions also advocated policies that put stability before growth, if somewhat less forcefully than had U.S. aid advisors during the period in ques-tion.

At the time of the military coup, inflation was down momentarily due to a strong stabilization package adopted in 1957, but GNP was stagnant. The military regime divided its attention to minister to two influential groups: cotton textiles firms, which like their Japanese counterparts had organized themselves into a powerful lobby—the Spinners' and Weavers' Association of Korea—demanding relief from excess capacity; and the progressive "millionaires," or chaebol, in disfavor with the public and press for having accumulated illicit wealth. Out of ministrations to influential groups, and insistence of U.S. aid advisors on stability before growth and fiscal conservatism, came Ko-rea's accumulation model. Attention is focused below on the trade and investment policies that emerged from this model.

TRADE POLICIES

Cotton spinning and weaving is one of Korea's oldest industries. The Kyongsong Spinning and Weaving Company, founded in October 1919, was possibly Korea's first major national capitalist enterprise (Eckert, 1986). After the Korean War, cotton spinning and weaving received the "lion's share" of foreign aid to all industry in Korea.

Considering aid as having financed both productive facilities and raw cotton, spinning and weaving may have accounted for over 10% of total aid (J. B. Kim, 1966).

The cotton textile industry was represented by a cartel, the Spinners' and Weavers' Association of Korea. According to J. B. Kim in his 1966 doctoral thesis, "the Korean cotton-manufacturing industry belongs to the category of *oligopoly* in the conventional sense." Roughly 15 integrated cotton spinners and weavers dominated the industry and recognized "mutual interdependence" with respect to pricing (p. 13). By 1957 the industry had achieved "complete import substitution," allowing the government to prohibit textile imports (Y. B. Kim, 1980, p. 208).

The performance of the industry was mixed. In terms of efficiency, performance was high. Labor productivity increased sharply in the period 1954–1963, almost trebling in the spinning sector and nearly doubling in the weaving sector (J. B. Kim, 1966). Business, however, was problematic. By the early 1960s, the industry was suffering from excess capacity. The operating rate in 1961 was 66% in cotton yarn and 50% in cotton cloth (Bank of Korea, 1963). According to J. B. Kim, textiles firms took advantage of subsidized loans from the aid establishment in the 1950s and created capacity ahead of demand. Capacity was still in excess supply in the early 1960s. There was little export activity, however, despite excess capacity and despite the provision of export incentives, which had begun in the early 1950s.[5] Nor did it prove possible to increase exports merely by devaluing the won against foreign currencies. The major effect of devaluation was worsening of the business climate by the increase in price of imported inputs, which fueled inflation.

The Korean won was devalued by 50% in 1961, from 65 to 100 won for the dollar in January and from 100 to 130 won for the dollar in February (Frank et al., 1975). The result was disastrous. According to the Economic Planning Board,

> The textile industry, as were many others, was also hard hit by the revisions in the exchange rate, as well as overproduction capacity. This can be illustrated by observing the cotton textile industry, representing the largest portion of the entire industry, which is 99% dependent upon industry imports for the necessary supply of raw cotton. . . . The price index of raw cotton increased by 11.5% in January of 1961 from the level of December 1960; reached 287.9 in February 1961, a 29.5% increase

[5] One is now led to think that export incentives were part of a "liberalization" package in the mid-1960s. This is clearly incorrect insofar as export incentives started much sooner, although they started small. (Frank et al., 1975).

over the level of the previous month; and pressed even higher
to 292.0 in March and to 299.8 in April, a level which was generally maintained throughout the remainder of the year. These
increases in the price of raw cotton affected in turn the production costs of all cotton products and the price of cotton yarn.
(1962, p. 49)

The crisis precipitated by devaluation provoked the military government to intervene with an expansionary economic package, which
exacerbated inflation even further.

In addition to business problems due to devaluation, there were
further impediments to exporting. According to a survey of members of the Spinners' and Weavers' Association, two of the more serious impediments were old plants and equipment and weak marketing channels. U.S. export restrictions presented a third obstacle:
"Before 1960 the Korean cotton-manufacturing industry could not
export manufactured cotton products, with a few exceptional cases;
and after 1960, the industry could not earn *free* foreign exchange to
the extent that it exported" (J. B. Kim, 1966, p. 48).[6] This was stipulated in an agreement between the Korean and U.S. governments
under Title I of the (U.S.) Agriculture Trade Development and Assistance Act, renewable yearly. The agreement prohibited "the resale
of transshipment to other countries or the use for other than domestic purposes" of agricultural commodities supplied as U.S. aid
(J. B. Kim, 1966, p. 48).[7] *Thus, while the U.S. aid administration in
Korea preached the theory of free trade, in practice Washington frustrated
the adoption of competitive exporting.*

The volume of exports from Korea barely budged in 1960–1962,
but bounded in 1963, 1964, and thereafter (see Table 3.4). What
seems to have turned the tide was a sharp rise in subsidies to exporters. These were Park's answer to the textile industry's woes. The
relative magnitude of subsidies is shown in Table 3.4 as part of the
export-effective exchange rate. This exchange rate reflects how liberally a government wishes to reward exporters, *although it is biased
downward because it does not include subsidized long-term loans, and long-
term capital subsidies were extremely important in Korea in certain industries
and firms.* The value of manufactured exports was higher in 1963–

---

[6] One exceptional case was noted by the Cotton Spinners' and Weavers' Association
in a book on its forty-year history. In it the United States is reported to have allowed
one of the Association's members to export cotton products to Hong Kong in 1957,
but only if their value did not exceed $2 million (Taehan Pangjik Hyŏphoe, 1987, p.
251).

[7] Textiles firms became able to export only after they procured raw cotton with
freely earned foreign exchange, around 1965.

Table 3.4 Exports of Manufactures[a] and the Exchange Rate, 1960–1965

Variable	1960	1961	1962	1963	1964	1965
Exports (mil. U.S. $)	4.1	5.7	9.6	38.6	57.7	106.4
Manufactured exports as percent of total export	12.5	13.9	17.5	44.5	48.4	60.8
Official exchange rate (won/dollar)	62.5	127.5	130.0	130.0	214.3	265.4
Export effective exchange rate[b]	147.6	150.6	151.5	189.4	281.4	304.6
Individual items as percent of total manufactured exports						
Processed food		36		21		14
Textiles		25		29		41
Lumber and plywood		07		10		14
Metal and steel products		10		21		13
Other		22		19		18

[a]Manufactures are defined as Standard Industrial Trade Classification codes 6, 7, and 8.

[b]The number of units of local currency actually paid or received for a $1.00 international transaction. Surcharges, tariffs, the implicit interest foregone on guarantee deposits, and any other charges against purchases of goods and services abroad are included, as are rebates, the value of import replenishment rights, and other incentives to earn foreign exchange for sales of goods and services abroad.

Source: For exports, Economic Planning Board, 1967. For exchange rates, Frank, Kim, and Westphal, 1975. For product breakdown, Hong, 1975.

1964 than in all previous years combined since the Japanese defeat in 1945, notwithstanding the increasing overvaluation of the won in 1963–1964 amidst high inflation. The export effective exchange rate rose from 151.5 won per dollar in 1962 to 189.4 in 1963, at the same time as exports rose. The government again devalued the won by 50% in May 1964 (after the United States made the release of food aid contingent on devaluation). Exports increased further, but so did subsidies, as indicated by the gap between the official and export-effective exchange rates. The gap between the two would have been even wider if subsidies to capital had been included.

Overvalued exchange rates were favored by the textile industry because the disadvantage of higher export prices (and presumably lower export demand) was dwarfed by the advantage of reduced input costs, since even an export-oriented industry like textiles still catered primarily to the domestic market. The share of exports to total demand in textiles production was 4.8% in 1963, 15.0% in 1966, and 47.2% in 1973 during the golden age of Korean cotton spinning and weaving (Y. B. Kim, 1980, p. 108). The subsidy, however, addressed both the supply- and demand-side issues. According to a history of the Korean textile industry,

> The government implemented numerous export promotion measures including preferential loans for operation and facility expansion, tax and tariff exemptions, wastage allowances, and other social overhead and administrative supports. It could be said that the textile industry was more effective in taking advantage of such benefits, since it had strong business organizations and more large-scale enterprises than other [light] industries. (Y. B. Kim, 1980, p. 232)

Underlying the competitiveness and dependence on subsidies of cotton spinners and weavers is their labor cost position, which has been analyzed by Woo (1978). Woo compared labor costs per bale of cotton in Japan and Korea in the late 1960s. Although his findings are sensitive to the exchange rate and also to the accuracy of data on wages and productivity, he found that labor costs in Japan and Korea ran neck and neck in the late 1960s. Had other costs been considered, the overall position of Korean producers would probably have appeared even less favorable. Subsidies to exporters in late industrializing countries have often been seen as a necessary evil to offset the higher-than-world-price that exporters have to pay for their imported inputs as a consequence of exchange rate "distortion." In fact, however, international cost comparisons such as the one undertaken by Woo (1978) suggest that *subsidies in Korea were necessary not because of "distortions" but because the Koreans could not, initially, compete against the Japanese,* even in industries such as cotton spinning and weaving in which the least developed, most labor-intensive countries supposedly have a comparative advantage. (Appendix 3–1 suggests how the Korean cotton textiles industry ultimately weaned itself from subsidies.)

By January 1965, exports had become a fixed idea for Park, and he had already begun to talk in terms of global competitiveness. He explained in his "State of the Nation Message" on January 16, 1965:

> To go with increased production, the government has set as another major target—increased exports. . . . In a country which depends heavily on imported raw materials for its industries, export is the economic lifeline. . . . For many years, Korea exported only $20 million to $30 million worth of goods a year . . . [mostly] tungsten. But in the past few years, the government and people awoke from sleep and strove. Exports began to expand rapidly. . . . Last year, our exports exceeded the $120,000,000 mark. Although there is still a gap in the balance of payments, this much is true: that we have acquired the self-

confidence that we, too, can successfully compete with others in the international export race. (Bum-shik, 1970, pp. 305–6)

Thereafter, the Park regime increasingly made exports a compulsion rather than a choice for the private sector. In addition to subsidization, a strong element of coercion underlay Korea's phenomenal export performance. The extent to which exports were a reaction to pressure rather than to subsidies, let alone the "right" relative prices, may be gauged from the survey responses of exporters to the question, What has been the effect of export targets fixed for your firm? As Table 3.5 indicates, in the year, say, 1976, 37% of respondents said the effect of export targets on their firm was positive, 10% said these targets had no effect, and as many as 53% listed negative effects.

If overseas sales were not always profitable, however, as suggested

Table 3.5 The Coerciveness of Export Targeting: Responses to question, What has been the effect of export targets fixed for your firm?, 1974–1976

Reponse	1974		1975		1976	
	Number of Firms	Percent	Number of Firms	Percent	Number of Firms	Percent
Contributed to a more rapid increase of production	48	42	48	32	58	37
Made no difference to the growth of production	16	14	24	16	15	10
Caused the firm to divert sales from the domestic to export markets	23	20	22	15	28	18
Reduced the profitability of the firm	8	7	17	12	14	9
Led to price cutting, unprofitable sales condition, and other forms of competition adverse to the firm	6	5	16	11	15	10
Led to some unprofitable exports	5	4	12	8	8	5
Raised unit costs due to the employment of inexperienced personnel or for other reasons	8	7	11	7	16	10
Led to some deterioration of product quality	1	1	2	1	1	1
Total number of responses[a]	115	100	152	100	155	100

[a]One-hundred and five firms replied to this question, some more than once, and some only for one or two years.

Source: Adapted from Rhee, Ross-Larson, and Pursell (1984).

by the negative responses of exporters, then the government compensated the losers by inflating the returns on domestic sales. It did
so by imposing trade barriers on imports. The existence of trade
barriers has been demonstrated in some detail by Luedde-Neurath:

> For almost two decades now Korea has attempted to promote
> its image as a market economy with a relatively liberal attitude
> towards imports. This stands in marked contrast, however, with
> the views held by most foreign businessmen who attempt ac-
> tually to penetrate the Korean market. Their familiarity with
> the "nuts and bolts" of the Korean import regime leads them to
> characterize it as essentially restrictive and full of hidden obsta-
> cles. (1986, p. 89)

Krueger, a student of the Korean economy who did much to promote Korea's image as a market economy, has observed,

> One final aspect of the import regime deserves mention—the
> tariff structure and attempts to alter it. One of the remarkable
> aspects of Korea's trade-and-payments regime over the period
> since 1953 has been the remarkable stability of the tariff struc-
> ture. (1979, p. 140)

Thus, together with quantitative import restrictions and government
export incentives, tariffs provided Korean business with abundant
government support. At the same time the labor-intensive industries
especially came under intense pressure for immediate export grati-
fication.

Export Dependence

Exports as a percent of GNP rose steadily from less than 5% in the
1950s to approximately 35% in the 1980s. In tandem, imports as a
percent of GNP rose, although at a slower rate. By international
standards, Korea became ultradependent on foreign trade. Table 3.6
presents the proportions of foreign trade (exports plus imports) to
national product during the course of economic development in seven
European countries, the United States, Canada, Japan, and Korea.
The evidence suggests that none of the Great Powers, whatever their
stage of development, ever had anywhere near as high a dependence on trade as did Korea. Imports and exports of commodities
as a percent of gross domestic product in Japan were never more
than 35.5%, and they were much lower in the nineteenth century
and in the 1950s.

Korea's high trade coefficient is quite similar to that of three relatively small economies—Hong Kong, Singapore, and Taiwan (World

Table 3.6 Proportions of Foreign Trade (Exports Plus Imports) to National Product (Commodities at Current Prices)

Country	Early Phase Date	%	Pre-World War I Date	%	1920s Date	%	1950s Date	%	1980s Date	%[a]	Population[b]	GNP per Capita $1984	GNP Billion $1984
United Kingdom (GNP)	1837–45	21.6	1909–13	43.5	1924–28	38.1	1957–63	30.4	1981–85	43.1	56.5	$ 8,570	484.1
France (physical product)[c]	1845–54	18.0	1905–13	53.7	1920–24	51.3	1957–63	41.2	1981–85	39.8	54.9	9,760	536.3
Germany (net total uses)[d]	1872–79	36.7	1910–13	38.3	1925–29	31.4	1955–59	35.1	1981–85	51.2	61.2	11,130	680.9
Italy (GNP)	1861–70	20.6	1911–13	28.1	1925–29	26.3	1957–63	25.0	1981–84	45.7	5.0	6,420	365.8
Denmark (GDP)	1870–79	45.6	1910–14	61.6	1921–29	57.3	1957–63	52.6	1981–85	56.2	5.1	11,170	57.1
Norway (GDP)	1865–74	55.5	1905–14	69.2	1920–29	63.5	1947–56	77.4	1981–85	66.7	4.1	12,940	57.5
Sweden (GDP)	1861–70	27.7	1911–13	40.3	1921–30	31.9	1957–63	36.5	1981–85	57.5	8.3	11,860	98.9
United States (GDP)	1834–43	12.9	1904–13	11.0	1919–28	10.8	1954–63	7.9	1981–85	14.9	236.7	15,380	3642.5
Canada (GNP)	1870–80	30.9	1911–13	32.2	1926–29	41.5	1956–60	31.2	1981–85	48.7	25.1	13,280	333.7
Japan (GDP)	1878–87	10.3	1908–13	29.5	1918–27	35.5	1950–56	18.8	1981–85	24.0	120.0	10,630	1275.8

Country	Japanese Occupation[e] Date	%	1950s Date	%	1960s Date	%	1970s Date	%	1980s Date	%[a]	Population[b]	GNP per Capita $1984	GNP Billion $1984
Korea (GNP)	1929	69.6	1955	8.8	1961–70	23.6	1971–80	53.9	1981–84	69.2	40.6	2,110	85.6
	1936–38	75.0	1958–60	9.0									

[a] All with respect to GNP except for France, which is with respect to GDP.

[b] In millions, 1980 for most countries.

[c] Value-added in agriculture and manufacturing.

[d] Sum of expenditures on private consumption, government consumption, and net domestic capital formation.

[e] Sum of agricultural and industrial production only, as adapted from data in the appendix of Grajdanzev, 1944.

GNP, gross national product.

Source: Trade figures excluding the 1980s: United Kingdom through Japan, Kuznets (1966); Korea, Grajdanzev (1944) for the Japanese Occupation and IMF (1986) for other years. Population and trade figures for the 1980s from IMF (1986). GNP and GNP per capita from World Bank (1986).

Bank, 1986). Yet Korea's high trade ratio cannot be understood as merely a response to its small domestic market. By world standards, Korea is not a small country. In the 1980s its population exceeded 40 million people and its GNP exceeded $80 billion. (Norway is a far smaller country, yet Norway's dependence on foreign trade was slightly lower than Korea's.) Rather, Korea's high trade dependence is a matter of history and politics. Under Japanese rule, Korea had been a highly export-oriented country, although exports were overwhelmingly agricultural. According to Table 3.6, in 1936–1938 imports and exports as a share of national product amounted to as much as 75%. Ironically, in the 1960s exports were viewed by the military regime as a deliverance. Park's speeches are full of references to rising self-sufficiency with every extra dollar of export earnings, and the antithesis of self-sufficiency was implicitly defined as continued reliance on U.S. largesse. Once exports got under way, moreover, their benefits became addictive. Exports of labor-intensive manufactures began to eat away at the cancer of underemployment, transforming Korea's domestic political environment. In the five years from 1965 through 1969, employment in the manufacturing sector expanded by 50%. In 1971 the industrial sector employed 100% more people than it had in 1963 (Bank of Korea, various years). And ultimately, exports opened the floodgates to foreign credit, to which attention is now turned.

INVESTMENT POLICY

Out of Park's remonstrations with millionaires came the crux of Korea's investment policies. One month after the 1961 coup, the military regime passed the Law for Dealing with Illicit Wealth Accumulation, and with great theatrics, arrested profiteers under the First Republic and threatened them with confiscation of their assets. Instead of becoming victims of martial emasculation, however, the millionaires were "allowed to enter the central stage" like the Meiji millionaires before them, albeit in a kneeling position. The government exempted most businessmen from criminal prosecution and eschewed confiscating their property. In exchange, businessmen were required to pay off their assessed obligation by establishing new industrial firms in basic industries and by donating the shares to the government, the latter condition rarely being fulfilled (Jones and SaKong, 1980). Within days, however, an alliance had been formed between business and government that laid the basis for subsequent industrialization.

There was one exception to the new government's decision to eschew confiscation: Five months after the coup, the military nationalized the banks. This proved a critical move in the long run, allowing the government to determine where, when, and how much to invest in which industries. Nationalization, however, was a hollow gesture at the time. The banks were almost bankrupt, and the question of how they were to raise funds became a paralyzing source of conflict between officials of Korea and the United States.

The military was in favor of borrowing from abroad and keeping domestic interest rates low in order to increase investment. To stimulate lending to Korea, the government amended the Foreign Capital Inducement Law in 1962 and provided government guarantees to lenders, which eliminated the risks of default and of exchange rate depreciation. Control over credit guarantees, together with nationalization of the banks, extended the government's reign over all capital flows with the exception of the unofficial "curb" market. Credit was then allocated on a discretionary basis.

Whereas subsidized credit for working capital was available to any exporter, long-term capital at favorable interest rates was allocated only to targeted firms and industries. For example, in the industries examined in detail in later chapters (i.e., cement, steel, shipbuilding, machinery), the government favored certain firms over others to become industry leaders through industrial licensing-cum-subsidized credit allocation. In the cement industry, the chaebol belonging to a party elder, the Ssangyong group, was allowed to acquire nearly half of cement-making capacity by the 1980s, and was then blessed with licenses for capacity expansions despite the existence of a more experienced cement company (the Tongyang Corporation) dating to the Japanese colonial period. In the steel industry the small mini-mills of Japanese colonial vintage were discriminated against in credit allocation in favor of a newly created state-owned integrated enterprise, the Pohang Iron and Steel Company (POSCO). In shipbuilding, seven small experienced shipbuilders were dwarfed and in some cases bankrupted by the government's assistance to the Hyundai group. In the machinery building sector, all three leading chaebol—the Hyundai, Samsung, and Daewoo groups—were favored over a slew of smaller long-standing firms.

Nevertheless, total foreign debt to underwrite long-term domestic investment grew by only 15% in 1963 and 1964[8] as the International Monetary Fund and the U.S. government, on the one hand, and the military regime, on the other, attempted to smooth their ideological differences over interest rates.

The foreign contingent was in favor of keeping domestic interest rates high in order to mobilize private savings and thus to minimize

[8] See Bank of Korea, various years (b).

Korea's foreign debt exposure. The military partly conceded to these demands. After "being pressed strongly by the United States government as well as the International Monetary Fund," the military obtained approval from the National Assembly for higher interest rate ceilings in August 1965 and pushed through an approximate doubling of interest rates at the end of September (Cole and Lyman, 1971, p. 179). Korean business groups strongly opposed the move, but the response of private savers was wildly enthusiastic. Total time and savings deposits increased by 25% in one month, tripled in one year, and doubled again the following year (K. S. Kim, 1967). Household savings as a percent of GNP increased from 0.18% in 1965 to 4.15% in 1966 (see Table 3.7). Nevertheless, household savings as a percent of GNP declined sharply in the following year, as Table 3.7 also indicates, and behaved unsystematically with respect to the interest rate thereafter. Moreover, domestic savings were never anywhere near sufficient to satisfy investment demand. Therefore, interest rate "liberalization" (it lasted for only seven years) did not do much to finance industrial expansion. What it did do was increase government liquidity and placate aid advisors, which gave Korea the green light to borrow abroad.

A regime of multiple interest rates arose, therefore, quite similar in principle to the multiple exchange-rate regime that export subsidies created. The cost of borrowing at home far exceeded the cost of borrowing abroad. This afforded the government the opportunity to discriminate in favor of particular industries and firms. As Table 3.8 illustrates, the real cost of borrowing abroad was negative (in most of the 1960s and 1970s). To qualify as a regular customer of the government for long-term subsidized credit, objectively necessary, if not sufficient, conditions had to be met even in new import-substitution industries: Big firms and small firms, young firms and old firms, chaebol and nonchaebol had to export.[9] Investment and trade policies became intimately bound.

Finally, one may note that, in addition to tariff protection, Korea reinforced its defenses against Japan as a further form of support. Once Korea had accorded Japan diplomatic recognition, it made it more difficult for Japanese companies to invest in Korean industry. Since the end of the Japanese occupation, direct foreign investment in the form of equity ownership by foreigners of production facilities in Korea has been minimal. Foreign direct investors have been welcomed to enter the light manufacturing export sector, whereas

[9] Not all import-substitution industries had to begin exporting at once. In some, the government took a long-range view. For automobiles, see, for example, Amsden and Kim, 1985a.

Table 3.7 Savings, Investment, and Consumption, as Percent of Gross National Product, 1962–1984

Year	Gross Fixed Capital Formation (1)	Increase in Stocks (2)	Total Investment (3) = (1) + (2)	General Government Savings (4)	Public and Private Corporations' Savings (5)	Household and Private Nonprofit Institutions' Savings (6)	Total Savings (7) = (4) + (5) + (6)	Deficit of the Nation on Current Account (8)	Difference Between Investment (1) and Savings (4) (9) = (7) − (3)
1962	13.95	−0.90	13.04	4.63	7.91	−0.97	11.58	1.86	−1.47
1963	13.94	4.43	18.38	4.41	7.76	3.45	15.63	4.05	−2.75
1964	11.56	2.97	14.53	4.61	7.00	3.61	15.22	0.84	0.69
1965	14.60	0.10	14.70	5.83	8.07	0.18	14.09	−0.16ᵃ	−0.61
1966	19.96	1.66	21.62	5.68	7.72	4.15	17.56	2.72	−4.06
1967	21.25	0.66	21.91	6.83	8.16	1.38	16.36	4.18	−5.55
1968	25.54	1.20	26.74	8.17	8.19	3.06	19.43	7.73	−7.31
1969	26.74	3.29	30.02	7.36	7.97	7.45	22.78	7.73	−7.25
1970	25.60	2.39	27.98	7.62	7.67	3.51	18.80	7.59	−9.18
1971	21.52	3.61	25.13	5.57	7.53	3.17	16.27	8.73	−8.86
1972	20.00	2.22	22.22	3.64	8.72	5.70	18.06	3.48	−4.16
1973	23.38	2.30	25.68	3.99	11.17	8.98	24.14	2.29	−1.54
1974	25.31	6.34	31.65	2.25	11.36	7.04	20.65	10.93	−11.00
1975	25.50	4.53	30.02	3.76	9.81	6.61	20.18	9.05	−9.84
1976	24.09	1.54	25.62	6.05	10.21	8.81	25.07	1.09	−0.55
1977	26.66	1.08	27.75	5.11	10.68	12.30	28.09	−0.03	0.34
1978	30.81	0.38	31.19	6.17	9.94	13.28	29.40	2.17	−1.78
1979	32.77	2.88	35.65	6.74	9.75	12.29	28.78	6.43	−6.87
1980	31.91	−0.66	31.26	5.67	10.29	6.63	22.59	8.67	−8.67
1981	28.85	0.29	29.15	6.12	9.34	6.96	22.42	6.91	−6.73
1982	30.27	−3.27	27.00	6.18	9.69	7.23	23.09	3.77	−3.90
1983	31.84	−4.07	27.77	7.46	10.28	7.89	25.63	2.09	−2.14
1984	30.95	−0.97	29.98	7.64	10.43	9.93	28.00	1.68	−1.98

ᵃNegative value equals surplus.
Source: Bank of Korea.

Table 3.8 Cost of Foreign Capital, 1966–1983 (Annual Averages)

	1966–1970	1971–1975	1976–1980	Unit: % 1981–1983
I Domestic bank lending rate[a]	24.4	17.0	18.0	12.5
(curb market interest rate)	(54.2)	(40.1)	(41.3)	(30.6)
II Foreign interest rate[b]	6.4	7.9	11.5	11.1
III Foreign inflation rate (GNP deflator)[c]	4.9	8.4	5.9	4.1
IV Exchange rate depreciation[d]	5.1	7.8	5.5	10.1
GDP deflator (rate of change): Korea[e]	14.6	18.7	19.7	9.9
V Real foreign interest rate (II − III)	1.5	−0.5	5.6	7.0
Interest rate differential between home and foreign markets (I − II − IV)	12.9	1.3	1.0	−8.7
Real private cost of borrowing abroad (II + IV − V)	−3.1	−3.0	−2.7	11.3

GNP, gross national product.

[a] Discounts on bills on deposit money banks (three-year moving averages).

[b] LIBOR (90 days). London Inter-Bank Offered Rate

[c] Average of Japan and United States.

[d] Bank of Korea standard concentration rate (three-year moving averages).

[e] Three-year moving averages.

Source: Bank of Korea, *Monthly Bulletin,* various issues, as cited by Y. C. Park (1985).

they have been discouraged from investing in import-substitution sectors such as pharmaceuticals and heavy industry (B. Y. Koo, 1981). In the late 1970s, direct foreign investment as a percent of gross domestic product was lower by almost half in Korea than in Argentina, Brazil, and Mexico—approximating 3% (Westphal, Kim, and Dahlman, 1985). In the 1980s, the government began to encourage direct foreign investment in the high-technology industries, but even as the absolute quantity of direct foreign investment increased, it amounted to a lower percentage of GNP in 1985 than in 1965 (see Table 3.9). Korea has industrialized on the basis of national enterprise, and in almost all years since 1965, direct foreign investment as a percent of total foreign capital inflow has fallen below 5% (Amsden, 1988).

CONCLUSION

The success of Japan, South Korea, and Taiwan has been attributed by many economists to "liberalization," or the freeing of markets from

Table 3.9 Direct Foreign Investment
(DFI), 1965–1985

Year	DFI[a]	Percent of GNP
1965	20,671	0.73
1970	13,642	0.16
1975	169,398	0.81
1976	72,160	0.25
1977	65,915	0.18
1979	107,312	0.17
1980	140,751	0.25
1981	145,327	0.23
1982	187,791	0.28
1983	267,753	0.36
1984	419,049	0.52
1985	531,720	0.65

[a]Approval basis. Unit = current $1,000.

Source: Ministry of Finance.

government control. From what we have just read, however, this view must be seriously qualified. Liberalization did indeed occur in Korea circa 1965 insofar as the exchange rate was devalued, commercial lending rates were raised, and certain imports were decontrolled. As Fischer (1970) observed, however, while we expect "big events" to have "big impacts," this reasoning is fallacious. The effect of liberalization on the economies of Japan, South Korea, and Taiwan may be likened to the effect of the Spanish Armada on European history. At one time the Armada's defeat was believed to have turned the tide of world history. Now its overall effect is recognized as minor. It neither divided Christendom (this having already been accomplished) nor prevented the flow of species to Spain (the flow reaching its peak after the Armada's defeat) nor shifted colonial supremacy to England (whose colonial efforts slumped immediately after 1588) (Mattingly, 1959, as cited by Fischer, 1970).

To be sure, liberalization in its political guise forced Korea to extend diplomatic relations to Japan, thereby raising the tempo of competition. But in exchange for greater competition, the Korean government fortified the domestic market with tariffs and quantitative restrictions and enacted legislation to protect domestic industry from direct foreign investment. Certainly liberalization also resulted in an increase in real commercial lending rates for at least seven years (1965–1972). But in exchange for higher domestic interest rates, the exchange rate and domestic inflation were allowed to render the real cost of borrowing abroad negative. Finally, liberalization probably exerted upward pressure on the price of foreign exchange. But in return for devaluation, exporters were rewarded with handsome subsidies.

In all, liberalization amounted to nothing more than a footnote to the basic text of Korean expansion. To attribute the role of equilibrator in such expansion to the market mechanism rather than to the government's dual policy of discipline and support is to misrepresent a fundamental property of the most successful cases of late industrialization.

APPENDIX

The Competitiveness of Cotton Spinning and Weaving

Exports of cotton textiles spearheaded Korea's export drive. Yet such exports appear to have been dependent on subsidies, unable to stand alone without government support. Under these circumstances they were unsustainable. The government could not forever use foreign aid or borrow abroad to underwrite them. Four developments put the textile industry in the black: (1) Foreign loans helped finance investments in modern plant and equipment, which raised productivity, (2) productivity increased through learning-by-doing, as will be discussed in Chapter 10, (3) dependence on imported raw materials declined due to a technological breakthrough overseas, the discovery of synthetic fibers, and (4) wages rose rapidly in Japan, which reduced Japan's competitiveness in textile exports (Statistics Bureau, various years). As early as August 1962, a nylon-manufacturing plant came on-stream in Korea with capacity to supply domestic manufacturers. The Hanguk Nylon Factory (now Kolon Nylon) was the first of several companies in the synthetic fiber industry. Like the others, it was privately owned but the recipient of government support in the form of subsidized credit and tariff protection. The import substitution of synthetic fibers made the textile industry more productive and less vulnerable to devaluations of the exchange rate. According to Y. B. Kim, "During the period from 1962 to 1970, the production structure of Korea's textile industry was altered to more closely resemble that of developed countries" (1980, p. 236). The industry accomplished this by import substituting chemical fibers, and by reducing the ratio of natural fiber yarns and fabrics in total textile production. "Cheaper manmade fibers resulted in improved productivity and quality, which in turn increased the demand both in home and overseas markets" (1980, p. 226).

What is noteworthy is that government intervention to make even cotton spinning and weaving profitable far exceeded what usually qualifies as "infant industry protection."

CHAPTER FOUR

The Dynamics
of Growth

THE THREE FACETS OF GROWTH

Late industrialization is characterized by three facets of growth, as Korea exemplifies. The first relates to diversification, or entrepreneurial decisions concerning penetration of new industries—which ones to penetrate, when, and with what size investment. The second relates to stabilization, or short-run macroeconomic policies to maintain the level of economic activity. The third relates to the growth momentum itself. Once under way, growth gains a momentum whose properties are distinct, depending on the presence or absence of new technological discoveries. This chapter is divided into three parts, each devoted to one of these facets of growth.

THE GOVERNMENT AS ENTREPRENEUR

The Government as Planner

The defining characteristic of entrepreneurship is planning, or deciding what, when, and how much to produce. Entrepreneurship becomes especially meaningful from a social standpoint when planning involves a new product or process. In Schumpeter's often-quoted conception (1938), the fundamental function of the entrepreneur is innovation. Innovation, in its classic definition, is absent in late-industrializing countries, yet entrepreneurship is present: Entrepreneurs in late-industrializing countries introduce products or processes that, while not path breaking, are novel in the context of the learning environment.

According to this definition, entrepreneurship in Korea has had two identities, one associated with the small firm, the other with the large one. In the case of the former, the entrepreneurial function of planning still remains privatized. The initiative to undertake minor investment projects with relatively small capital requirements appears to rest with the private entrepreneur. In such cases, the private entrepreneur is also responsible for the coordinating function, or for arranging all necessary inputs for the completion of a project, including the capital. In the contrasting case of big business, the entrepreneurial function of planning has primarily fallen to the state. So, too, has the coordinating function, insofar as the state has controlled all capital other than short- or medium-term credit available at high interest rates in the "curb" market.

Virtually every study bearing on the subject of industrialization in Korea has in some sense recognized that big businesses have had to come to terms with the expanded role of the state. Thus, Jones and Sakong (1980) argued that the crowning function of the private entrepreneur is "lenticular," meaning "the pure Schumpeterian function of combination," and the functions the entrepreneur must combine or coordinate include that of dealing with the government. All in all, Jones and Sakong explained, the functions of entrepreneurship include the following:

1. Perception of a new economic opportunity, including
   a. new products
   b. new processes of production
   c. new markets
2. Evaluation of the profitability of a new opportunity
3. Gaining command of financial resources
4. Plant design, technology, and construction supervision
5. Recruiting and training of new personnel
6. Relationship with government
7. Relationship with suppliers and purchasers (1980, p. 81)

The point, however, is not that the entrepreneur in Korea must spend a great deal of time "dealing" with the government, among other important tasks. Rather, it is that almost all important tasks are themselves transformed as a consequence of government intervention.

The initiative to enter new manufacturing branches has come primarily from the public sphere. Ignoring the 1950s, when economic policy in Korea was for all practical purposes under foreign control (see the discussion in Chapter 2), every major shift in industrial diversification in the decades of the 1960s and 1970s was instigated by the state. The state masterminded the early import-substitution projects in cement, fertilizers, oil refining, and synthetic fibers—the last greatly improving the profitability of the overexpanded textiles industry. The government also kept alive some unprofitable factories inherited from the colonial period, factories that eventually provided key personnel to the modern general machinery and shipbuilding industries, which the state also promoted. The transformation from light to heavy industry came at the state's behest, in the form of an integrated iron and steel mill, which the state pushed for in the early 1960s (too early, it seems) and then presided over from the late 1960s onward (see Chapter 12). The government played the part of visionary in the case of Korea's first colossal shipyard (see Chapter 11), and it was responsible for the Big Push into heavy machinery and chemicals in the late 1970s. It also laid the groundwork for the new wave of import substitution that followed heavy industrialization and that carried the electronics and automobile industries beyond the simple stage of assembly. The government enacted the automobile industry protection law as far back as 1962, as part of its first five-year economic development plan. In conjunction with this decision, it promoted the oil-refining industry. Thus, major milestones in Korea's industrialization have been decided by the state.

Unilateralism on the part of the government probably reached its apex at the time of the second five-year plan, in 1967, after which government and business gradually worked more closely together. The second five-year plan was prepared by the government amidst exuberance over the economy's good performance and confidence in the government's planning function. The Economic Planning Board (EPB) used an input-output planning model, supplemented by industry studies. These industry studies really amounted to project studies that provided profiles on projects in the manufacturing sector for the government to promote by using its industrial, trade, and credit policies. The fact that initiative, at the time, lay almost exclusively with the government is indicated by the finding that when businessmen began to come to the EPB for approval of projects that were *not* on the list, there was debate in the EPB about whether to consider them, even those that complemented social objectives.[1]

The Example of Electronics

The driving force of the government behind industrial change was still apparent in the mid-1970s, and for that matter, in the mid-1980s. Even in the case of the electronics industry, where developments were wholly contingent on acquisition by the private sector of technical skills, the fourth five-year plan of 1977–1981 set the pace of progress.

The government had been promoting the domestic electronics in-

[1] This view of the Economic Planning Board was expressed by Larry Westphal, an advisor to the Board at the time, in a lecture in February 1987 at the Harvard Institute for International Development.

dustry as one of the nation's key sectors for almost two decades. As early as January 28, 1969, the Electronics Industry Promotion Law was enacted to stimulate investments in assembly operations of black-and-white televisions. The intent of the fourth five-year plan was to push this activity forward, beyond the assembly stage. According to the plan,[2]

> The electronics industry will change structurally from assembly-type production to one which mainly produces the basic components and parts. In the meantime, product quality will be improved.
>
> The electronics industry will be promoted as a major export industry through the development of new technology products and the expansion of overseas sales activities.
>
> On the basis of product life cycles and *comparative advantage,* 57 items including semiconductors, computers, and related items have been selected as strategic products. [italics added]

As traditionally defined, semiconductors and computers hardly fell within Korea's area of comparative advantage, certainly not in 1976, when per-capita income in Korea was only $459, about the same as Guatemala's (World Bank, 1978). The fourth five-year plan, therefore, accelerated the import substitution of such goods.[3]

To promote higher value-added products embodying a greater level of skill and technology, the government took the following steps, above and beyond its usual incentive measures, which included arranging foreign loans totaling $221.6 million:

1. It established an industrial estate for the production of semiconductors and computers.
2. To promote "the importation of advanced technology and to accelerate technical progress," it established a research institute in this industrial estate for product development, the Electronics and Telecommunication Research Institute (ETRI). A fund of $60 million was created for the purpose.
3. It protected the domestic market against foreign competition. In the computer field, it passed legislation in 1983 to restrict imports of computers and peripherals in both the low and medium ends of the market. The law prohibited the import of most microcomputers, some minicomputers, and selected models of disk drives,

---

[2] References to the Plan are from Chungbu (1976).

[3] The government gave the same type of support to the development of color TVs in the late 1970s that it had given to the development of black-and-white TVs in the late 1960s. See Y. B. Kim (1979).

printers, terminals, and tape drives (Harvard Business School, 1985).[4]

4. It restricted direct foreign investment in electronics. It did, however, view joint ventures favorably, and most of the major business groups in the computer field—Hyundai, Daewoo, Lucky-Goldstar, and Samsung—formed them.

In the field of semiconductors, the government was still taking the lead in the 1980s (for better or worse). According to *Electronics,* an American trade magazine,

> In South Korea, people in the industry call it the Blue House Project, after the official residence of President Chun Doo Hwan whose advisers convinced him two years ago that the only way to crack the world semiconductor market would be to orchestrate a massive development project involving every important Korean company in the business.
>
> That's just what is happening now, and the goal is to position Korean chip-makers as major players in the world industry by 1991. . . . The impetus came from the president, and the muscle behind the program—called the VLSI Project—is coming from commitments by three of the largest Korean conglomerates [Hyundai, Goldstar, and Samsung]. (1987)

This VLSI project is one of many high-priority "national projects" involving collaboration between private sector R&D labs and public sector research institutes, to which the government allocates organizational capability and subsidized credit. In 1983 some 182 research projects of 131 industrial firms were selected as national R&D projects, and the government contributed about $28 million to these projects. In addition, seven special projects in semiconductors and bioengineering were funded with an additional $40 million (World Bank, 1987). To stimulate R&D generally, the government sets a lower tariff rate on equipment imported for R&D purposes. This provision is important for technology-intensive firms, and tells something about the extent to which the machinery sector is protected in general (fairly well). The government also allows firms to set aside a percentage of profits in a reserve fund that is exempt from taxation for a fixed period, for eventual investment in R&D. Venture capital corporations have been established by the government to lend to technology-oriented start-up firms. Through its procurement policy,

[4] In 1987 the government abolished import tariffs on personal computers. Nevertheless, like automobiles, imported computers appear to be subject to other taxes.

the government has also promoted the development of an indigenous electronic switching system for eventual incorporation in the
domestic public telecommunications network.

Given that the quintessential function of the entrepreneur is to
decide what and when to produce, as well as how much, the government's leadership, even in an industry like electronics, makes it necessary to redefine the entrepreneurial concept as affected by government influence in the private sphere.

The Locus of Initiative

In late-industrializing countries, the developmental state may be expected to take more initiative to diversify than the private sector does
for two reasons:

First, such a state tends to get involved with national as well as
corporate planning. If the formulation of development plans is undertaken fairly regularly, as more than a token exercise, the state
can gain an overview of the economy that the individual entrepreneur lacks.[5] This overview, and the ability to plan projects with
external linkages simultaneously, places the government in a more
advantageous position to diversify than the private sector. The five-
year plan is practically a general property of late industrialization. It
became characteristic of Indian economic development in the 1950s.
With the exit of U.S. aid advisors in 1960, Japan adopted its "Growth-
Doubling Plan." Korea's first five-year plan was inaugurated in 1962,
just after the military coup (see Chapter 2).

Planning in Korea is taken fairly seriously and formulated in a
"top-down" fashion. According to one observer,

In the preparation of the five-year development plans, which
are the most crucial skeletons of midterm policies, the EPB takes
the initial step by preparing and issuing preliminary guidelines
in terms of major policy targets and directions, together with
macroeconomic projections for both the international and domestic environment of the economy during the plan period and
beyond. . . . Individual ministries then formulate their own sec-
toral plans in accordance with the guidelines. . . . It is noteworthy . . . that policy proposals prepared by the ministries are
seldom open to the public for discussion and popular reaction.
. . . The lack of consensus-building in the policy-making pro-

---

[5] Nath (1962) argued that the government is in a better position to plan than the
private sector not because it is better at planning but because it has an overview of
the economy.

cess reflects a "top-down" approach to government policy formulation. (Whang, 1986, pp. 5–9)

Second, the initiative to diversify, particularly into more capital-
intensive investment projects, tends to fall to the state because these
projects require more comprehensive incentive packages to make them
financially attractive to private firms. Private firms in Korea contributed very little of their own capital to most investment projects.
By law, 30% of a plant's total costs had to be self-financed. In practice, however, internal financing in 1963–1973 accounted on average for only 20% of total financing (compared with 32.5% for Japan
[1954–1967] and 65% for the United States [1947–1963]) (Lim, 1981).
In 1983 the manufacturing sector in Korea is said to have financed
only 9.9% of its business through retained earnings and capital increases (*BK,* 1984). The remainder of capital was highly subsidized
and was greater the more capital intensive the industry. Differences
in subsidization by industry are suggested in Table 4.1. The loan to
value-added ratio tends to be much higher in the more capital-
intensive pursuits.

Finally, initiative tends to fall to the state because of the structure
of profit rates. The interindustry structure of profit rates is less favorable the more capital intensive the industry. One may expect,
therefore, a reluctance on the part of private investors to rush into
capital-intensive industries without strong government direction and
support.

Profitability in Different Industries

Table 4.1 presents data for Korea on gross rates of return. Gross
rate of return is defined as the ratio of nonlabor share in value-
added to capital stock, the capital stock being defined as physical
assets plus net working capital. Manufacturing is broken down into
four areas, two labor intensive, two capital intensive. The data support three interrelated conclusions. First, the most labor-intensive
industries have the highest profit rates. Second, the youngest industries (group II) have the lowest profit rates. Capital-intensive industries are subdivided into two groups. Group I comprises those capital-
intensive industries that underwent import substitution in the 1950s
(or early 1960s). Group II comprises those that underwent import
substitution later. Group II industries have the lowest rates of return. Third, the capital-intensive industries have the highest export
growth rates, besides having the highest overall rates of subsidization
(measured by the loan to value-added ratio).

Table 4.1 Gross Profits, Export Expansion, and Loans by Industry, 1971–1982

Industry	Per-Worker Fixed Assets[a]		Gross Rate of Return on Capital			Loan/Value-Added (VA) Ratio			Rate of Increase During 1971–1982		
	1971	1982	1963–71	1972–78	1979–82	1963–71	1972–78	1979–82	VA	pwFA	Exports
All manufacturing	1.14	9.27	32.3%	37.5%	37.4%	1.9	1.5	1.4	37.2	8.1	24.6
					Ratio to All-Manufacturing Average						
Very labor intensive											
Clothing and footwear	0.3	0.2	1.5	1.6	3.6	0.6	0.7	0.7	1.3	0.7	0.7
Electronic and telecommunications[b]	0.4	0.4	1.4	1.3	1.2	0.5	0.4	0.7	2.3	1.0	1.9
Miscellaneous manufactures[c]	0.4	0.4	1.3	1.3	1.1	0.4	0.6	0.6	1.0	1.2	0.5
Nonmetallic minerals[d]	0.9	0.4	0.6	1.1	1.2	0.7	0.6	0.5	3.0	0.5	6.9
Moderately labor intensive											
Machinery (medium)	0.4	0.4	0.8	1.1	1.0	0.3	0.4	0.6	7.3	1.1	—
Miscellaneous chemicals	0.5	0.6	1.7	1.7	1.3	0.3	0.4	0.5	0.6	1.0	1.4
Metal products	0.4	0.6	1.1	1.3	0.9	0.4	0.5	0.8	2.2	1.5	3.5
Electrical machinery	0.8	0.7	1.3	1.2	1.1	0.6	0.6	0.7	1.2	0.9	1.8
Textiles	1.0	0.7	0.9	0.8	0.9	1.0	1.2	1.1	0.9	0.7	1.0
Wood products	0.7	0.9	1.1	1.0	1.0	1.4	1.9	2.0	0.5	1.3	0.2

Capital intensive

Group I[f]

Synthetic fibers	1.8	1.9	1.1	1.0	1.4	1.1	1.4	1.3	0.5	1.0	3.5
Rubber tires	1.1	1.1	1.2	1.2	1.2	0.9	1.1	0.9	1.8	1.0	6.5
Glass and products	2.5	1.2	0.7	1.3	0.8	1.0	0.6	0.9	0.6	0.5	1.3
Pulp and paper	1.6	1.5	1.2	1.1	0.9	0.7	1.0	1.1	0.8	1.0	5.7
Sugar refining	3.7	3.3	1.5	1.8	1.9	0.9	0.8	1.1	1.1	0.9	8.7
Petroleum products	11.6	6.1	1.0	1.1	1.5	1.6	0.7	0.9	0.7	0.5	0.4
Cement	5.1	5.8	1.0	0.9	0.7	1.8	1.3	1.2	0.4	1.2	2.2

Group II[g]

Shipbuilding	1.5	1.3	—	0.4	0.6	2.7	1.6	1.1	9.6	0.9	8.4
Automobiles and parts	1.4	1.3	—	0.7	0.7	1.3	1.2	1.6	0.9	1.0	4.9
Machinery (large)	0.7	1.7	—	0.9	0.4	0.8	1.0	2.9	2.9	2.7	2.0
Nonferrous metals	0.8	1.8	—	1.0	0.8	1.2	1.2	1.6	0.7	2.3	0.6
Industrial chemicals	4.7	1.9	—	1.0	0.9	1.4	1.1	1.2	0.7	0.4	2.7
Iron and steel products	1.5	4.1	—	0.8	0.7	1.7	2.0	2.0	3.8	2.8	5.0

[a] Per worker fixed assets (pwFA) in million won.

[b] Radios and TVs, phonographs and tape recorders, other telecommunications equipment, household electrical appliances, and electronic parts and components for 1982 data. Data for 1971 exclude electronic parts and components.

[c] Includes precision instruments (watches and optical instruments), leather products, plastic products, and furniture.

[d] Includes glass and cement.

[e] Excludes synthetic fiber yarns.

[f] Capital-intensive industries are divided into groups, depending on their age. Group I industries tended to be established, or "import-substituted," before Group II industries.

[g] Gross rates of return for 1971–1973 are not presented because the industries in question were for the most part nonexistent. The available data refer to small firms and are not comparable with data for the later periods.

Source: Bank of Korea, Financial Statements Analysis; Korea Traders Association, Foreign Trade Statistics, as quoted in Hong and Park (1986).

These general findings are lent support by data in Table 4.2, on return on investment (ROI) over time for light and heavy industry. Between 1972 and 1984, the light industries had higher profitability than the heavy industries in almost every year.

One may infer from all this that as the capital-intensive industries showed themselves increasingly capable of exporting, they became more attractive for the government to promote. Their long gestation periods and relatively low profitability through adolescence, however, rendered them relatively less desirable investments to the private firm. The initiative to diversify, therefore, fell to the state. In the 1960s and 1970s, the government was obsessed with the question of how fast Korea could grow. Private investors were preoccupied with the question of how much money they could make. Although profit maximization and growth maximization are not, in theory, antithetical, neither are they necessarily synonymous.

Cooperation and the Overall Profit Rate

Over time, entrepreneurship has become less a monopoly of the state and more a joint venture between the state and big business. Evidence is provided by a series of anecdotes in a thesis on the chaebol (S. K. Kim, 1987). Two factors strengthened the willingness and ability of big business to be a more active partner with the state in the diversification effort: (1) The modern industrial enterprises acquired more technical and business experience. Their opinions then gained more respect in terms of decisions about which industries to enter, when, and on what scale. (2) The modern industrial enterprises came to appreciate not just the high risks of entering the heavy industries but also the high rewards.

Tables 4.1 and 4.2 indicate a convergence in profitability between the light and heavy industries as well as a *high overall level of profitability*. Inclusive of subsidies, high profitability has been a key characteristic of Korean industrialization—even if profitability does not appear initially as high as in the advanced countries. The high profit rates eventually earned in the import-substitution heavy industries created great hopes of substantial profit rates in later projects. Thus, the diversified business groups were animated to be first-movers in new industries, bringing them slightly closer to being true entrepreneurs. Chapters 10, 11, and 12 examine just how they moved.

The Government as Investor

Not just in Korea but also in Japan and Taiwan, it has been alleged that "government budgets have generally been maintained near bal-

Table 4.2 Profitability of Light and Heavy Industry: Average Rate of Return on Investment, 1972–1984

	1972	1973	1974	1975	1976	1977	1978	1979	1980	1981	1982	1983	1984
Heavy industry	7.92	10.06	12.45	9.34	9.41	8.96	9.69	9.32	7.36	9.11	8.56	9.20	9.75
Light industry	11.00	15.30	9.45	9.65	11.50	11.57	13.80	12.50	11.40	11.28	9.13	10.15	9.52

Source: Bank of Korea, various years.

Table 4.3 Public Sector Resource Balance, 1977–1981 (% of Gross National Product)

	Central Government,[a] 1977–1981 (actual)
Current revenue[b]	21.0
Tax revenue	16.3
Transfer from other levels of government	—
Current expenditures[b]	16.3
Current balance	4.1
Gross fixed investment	1.8
Overall balance (− deficit)	3.0

[a] Includes nonfinancial public enterprises other than communications.

[b] Plan figures for current revenues and expenditures are not strictly comparable owing to differences in the consolidation of subaccounts in the budget.

Source: Economic Planning Board.

ance, often with large surpluses on the current account . . ." (Sachs, 1987, p. 8). Evidence in Table 4.3 substantiates this claim. Table 4.3 shows a surplus in the "public sector resource balance." Nevertheless, the numbers in Table 4.3 are inconsistent with other numbers that indicate *a persistent deficit in government accounts.* Surplus or balance in the public sector budget appears to reflect not thriftiness on the part of the government, but discretion over how the public sector budget is defined.[6] Table 4.4, however, provides unambiguous evidence that the Korean government's investment in and operation of public-sector enterprises have tended to outstrip its saving. In other words, the government has spent far more than it has collected, and the deficit has been financed by borrowing. Table 4.4 presents data on the public sector's current account imbalances as a percentage of GNP. In sixteen of the twenty years spanning 1963 through 1982, public sector investment exceeded public sector saving. In eight of eleven years in the period 1972 through 1982, the government's deficit/GNP ratio exceeded that of the private sector. Heavy public borrowing is suggested in Table 4.5. Between 1967 and 1979, the public sector accounted for about one third of all foreign loans. Then, in

[6] Even public sector resource balance data are often inconsistent and highly sensitive to decisions about which items are or are not to be included in the accounts. For example, the source that Sachs cited on the public sector budget for 1982 is the *World Development Report,* Table 5.26, 1986. According to this source, the budget showed a deficit of as much as 4.3% for the same year (Aghevli and Marquez-Ruarte, 1985).

Table 4.4 Sources of Current Account Imbalances in Current Market Prices, 1963–1982 (Unit: Billion Won)

Year	Private Sector (A)[a]	Government (B)[a]	Government-Invested Corporations (C)[a]	Subtotal (D = B+C)	A/GNP (%)	D/GNP (%)
1963–1971						
1963	−11.67	14.34	−16.06	−2.02	−2.4	−0.4
1964	−3.39	23.26	−13.79	9.47	−0.5	1.3
1965	−27.88	36.49	−16.15	20.34	−3.5	2.5
1966	−65.20	38.82	−15.14	23.68	−6.3	2.3
1967	−70.89	51.26	−54.39	−3.13	−5.5	−0.2
1968	−136.63	57.03	−36.19	20.84	−8.3	1.3
1969	−110.80	29.98	−63.73	−33.75	−5.1	−1.6
1970	−195.55	60.91	−63.12	−2.21	−7.3	−0.1
1971	−179.19	42.81	−130.31	−87.50	−5.4	−2.7
1972–1978						
1972	35.80	−9.16	−200.51	−209.67	0.9	−5.2
1973	51.31	24.86	−107.94	−83.08	1.0	−1.6
1974	−422.54	−36.09	−223.50	−259.59	−5.8	−3.5
1975	−337.19	−129.29	−482.24	−611.53	−3.4	−6.2
1976	−20.73	329.49	−455.95	−126.46	−0.2	−1.0
1977	472.45	18.08	−749.27	−731.19	2.8	−4.3
1978	−281.57	448.27	−1,031.84	−583.57	−1.2	−2.5
1979–1982						
1979	−1,675.45	493.31	−1,170.45	−677.14	−5.8	−2.3
1980	−2,381.04	20.81	−1,344.91	−1,324.10	−6.9	−3.9
1981	−1,513.67	5.89	−1,869.06	−1,863.17	−3.6	−4.4
1982	489.47	−124.05	−2,260.19	−2,384.24	1.0	−5.0

[a]A, B, and C refer to balance after investment from savings is subtracted in each sector.

Source: Bank of Korea, *Economic Statistics Yearbook*, various years, as cited by Y. C. Park, 1985. Figures for savings and investment of government-invested corporations, which include nonfinancial operations of Federations of Agricultural and Fisheries Cooperatives, obtained from Bank of Korea's flow of funds tables.

the economic contraction of 1980–1983, its share rose to over half of the total. Nevertheless, the dividing line between a public and private loan is not always clear-cut, particularly in large-scale projects where the government and the chaebol closely interact. Thus, the government's share of foreign borrowing may be understated.

Most of the government's deficit has been accounted for by public corporations. This is in spite of the fact that almost all major investments in heavy industry with the exception of integrated ironmaking and steelmaking are in private corporations. Public corporations, however, have been important in infrastructure projects—electricity,

Table 4.5 Foreign Loans and Investment, 1959–1983 (Unit: Million U.S. Dollars)

Period	Loans (I)[a] Public	Commercial	Direct Foreign Investment (II)[a]	Total III = I + II
1959–1961	4.4	—	—	4.4
1962–1966	115.6	175.6	16.7	307.9
	(37.5)	(57.0)	(5.4)	
1967–1971	810.8	1,354.7	96.4	2,261.8
	(35.8)	(59.9)	(4.3)	
1972–1976	2,388.9	3,043.9	556.0	5,988.8
	(39.9)	(50.8)	(9.3)	
1977–1979	2,529.5	4,793.7	328.8	7,652.0
	(33.1)	(62.6)	(4.3)	
1980–1983	6,246.5	4,434.1	404.1	11,084.7
	(56.4)	(40.0)	(3.6)	

[a] Actual basis. Figures in parenthesis are percent of total.

Source: Economic Planning Board, *Handbook of Korean Economy*, 1983, as quoted in Y. C. Park (1985).

gas, railroads, highways, irrigation, and the Seoul and Pusan subway systems—and investments in infrastructure have been massive.

A balanced budget suggests that a government spends relatively little on social services. It should not be thought, however, that because the Korean government has persistently spent more than it has collected, it has spent a lot on social services.[7] *It has spent on long-term investment, not on short-term consumption.* The propensity of the Korean government to invest rather than to consume is clearly perceived when international comparisons of government spending are drawn. Table 4.6 provides data on government spending for Korea and for other East Asian and Latin American countries. The first column of Table 4.6 presents data on the government's share of total expenditures relative to GNP. The second shows its share as a percentage of fixed investment only. The Korean government is noteworthy for its relatively low share of total expenditures and high share of fixed investment; most countries demonstrate the reverse pattern.

[7] According to D. G. Kim (1986), the government spends only 20% of its budget on social services and as much as 35% on defense. Yoo (1983, p. 133) stated that in the 1970s, the Korean government spent approximately 6% of GNP on defense, the highest figure for any country outside the socialist bloc.

Table 4.6 International Comparison of Government Expenditures

Country	Government Expenditures as Percent of GNP, 1982	Government Expenditures as Percent of Fixed Investment [year(s)]
Latin America		
Argentina	21.6	19.6 (1978–1980)
Brazil	21.8	22.8 (1980)
Chile	37.6	12.9 (1978–1980)
Mexico	31.7	29.4 (1978)
Peru	18.0	14.8 (1978–1979)
Venezuela	29.6	36.3 (1978–1980)
Colombia	14.0	8.9 (1978–1980)
East Asia		
Korea	19.5	22.8 (1978–1980)
Taiwan	—	32.4 (1978–1980)
Thailand	19.9	12.8 (1978–1979)
Philippines	12.2	10.9 (1978)

GNP, gross national product.

Sources: Expenditures as percent of GNP are from *World Development Report*, various years. Expenditures as percent of fixed investment are from Short (1984).

GOVERNMENT SHORT-RUN ECONOMIC POLICIES

If the Korean economy has outperformed the late learners of Latin America, the reason cannot be said to lie in short-term austerity measures to manage external shock, because the response of the Korean government to external shock was not to batten down the hatches. During the twenty-five years after the 1961 coup, the growth of the Korean economy, though spectacular, was regularly interrupted by internal and external shocks. What with two oil crises, global depression, and an intensification of international competition, the 1970s were difficult years in which to industrialize. Nevertheless, external shocks did not derail the Korean economy from its fast-growth track. *The government borrowed its way out of balance-of-payments difficulties and sustained fast growth.* Aggressive borrowing coupled with bailouts of financially troubled firms created a supportive environment for big business. The tack most often taken by the economy after economic downturns was a resurgence of exports and rapidly resumed expansion.

Here, three stabilization exercises in response to threats of growth interruption are discussed.[8] The account builds to the stabilization

[8] The following discussion of stabilization is based on a longer study of Korea's short-run macroeconomic policies and attempts at liberalization. See Amsden (1987b) or, in the Korean language, Amsden (1988).

exercise of 1979–1984, formulated as a Comprehensive Stabilization Plan (CSP) by the military dictatorship that came to power in 1980. In all three stabilization exercises, the Korean government can be described as having accommodated the private sector rather than having been austere, austerity typically being the mood of the stabilization exercises recommended by the Bretton Woods institutions. In studies sponsored by the World Bank (1987 and Leipziger, 1988), liberalization in Korea in the 1980s is rationalized as a medicine for the economic diseases supposedly caused by government intervention in the 1970s. *Yet the premise of economic disaster is nowhere substantiated.* An impartial reading of Korea's history in this period suggests that some of the country's state bureaucracies were suffering from wear and tear as the volume of transactions increased. But *most economic indicators, including the current account and debt/GNP ratio, imply that just before the second energy crisis, the economy was performing rather well, a Big Push into heavy industry notwithstanding.*

Debt Financing

Korea has used foreign credit for two purposes: to finance its long-term investments and to borrow its way out of balance-of-payments crises in order to maintain its long-term growth trend. Korea's external debt position from 1961 to 1984 is shown in Table 4.7.

Throughout the period of the first two five-year plans, the debt/GNP ratio rose rapidly. As discussed in Chapter 3, the Foreign Capital Inducement Law was amended in 1962 to provide guarantees that eliminated the risks of default and of exchange rate depreciation. The foreign debt/GNP ratio rose from 40% in 1963 to 7% in 1965. In September 1965, a monetary reform was undertaken in which deposit and lending rates at banking institutions were more than doubled, increasing the attractiveness of lending to Korea. The foreign debt/GNP ratio rose to 14% in 1967. Then it more than doubled in four years, reaching 30% in 1971.

Among other effects of the monetary reform, Korean borrowers were encouraged by the cost differentials between domestic and foreign interest rates. The divergence between domestic and foreign borrowing rates ranged from 4.4% to 18% during 1965–1970 (Y. C. Park, 1985). Because the real private cost of borrowing abroad was typically negative (see Table 3.8), investment as a share of GNP rose from 15% in 1965 to 30% in 1969. The share of savings rose at a faster rate as income expanded and as domestic interest rates increased, but reached its peak at a lower level than investment in the same period, 23% in 1969 (see Table 3.7).

As in Latin America in the 1970s, no limits on foreign borrowing

Table 4.7 External Debt and Debt Service, 1963–1984

Year	Total Foreign Debt (million U.S. $)	Long-Term Debt as % of Total	Total Debt as % of GNP	Debt Service as % of GNP	Debt Service as % of Exports[a]	Debt Service as % of Current Transactions Receipts[b]
1963–1971						
1963	157	85.99	4.06	0.05	2.30	1.1
1964	177	94.35	5.29	0.15	4.17	2.4
1965	206	98.54	6.81	0.46	8.00	4.8
1966	392	98.21	10.26	0.34	5.20	2.9
1967	645	89.77	13.62	0.72	10.15	5.3
1968	1,199	92.58	20.07	0.77	9.47	5.2
1969	1,800	89.22	24.07	1.20	13.68	7.8
1970	2,245	83.39	25.48	2.84	28.34	18.1
1971	2,922	83.61	30.06	3.28	28.16	19.7
1972–1978						
1972	3,589	82.17	33.95	3.87	24.40	18.4
1973	4,260	83.54	31.55	4.35	17.87	14.2
1974	5,937	79.13	32.01	3.25	13.33	11.2
1975	8,456	71.51	40.55	3.38	14.01	12.0
1976	10,533	71.09	36.73	3.50	12.85	10.6
1977	12,648	70.63	33.79	3.58	13.33	10.2
1978	14,871	74.08	29.71	4.16	16.38	12.1
1979–1984						
1979	20,500	67.80	31.75	4.03	17.68	13.3
1980	27,365	61.22	44.68	4.81	17.13	13.1
1981	32,490	63.80	48.34	5.53	17.98	13.8
1982	37,295	61.94	52.65	6.23	21.15	15.5
1983	40,094	70.58	53.23	6.18	20.07	15.0
1984	43,100	73.55	53.16	6.74	20.75	17.3

GNP, gross national product.

[a] Merchandise exports.

[b] Receipts from visible and invisible foreign transactions.

Sources: Bank of Korea and Economic Planning Board.

were enforced by the government, and a rapid increase in debt service resulted, exports notwithstanding. The debt service ratio (as a percent of merchandise exports) rose from 14% in 1969 to 28% in 1970 (see Table 4.7). It was in the period 1966–1971, and later during two stabilization periods, that the big buildup of foreign debt occurred, and not as a consequence of government investment in heavy industry during the 1970s. Foreign debt in 1966–1971 was used to finance exports, to finance imports of capital goods in the light-manufacturing sector, to finance the beginning of import substitution in heavy industry (fertilizers and cement), and to finance investments in infrastructure (the share in GNP of transportation, communications, electricity, gas, and water more than doubled between 1964 and 1970) (Economic Planning Board, 1984).

The First Stabilization

The increase in the debt service ratio prompted the IMF, in a standby agreement, to require the Korean government to issue a letter of intent to limit foreign capital movements to one- to three-year loans (Frank et al., 1975). Consequently, the growth rate of foreign debt slowed by 25% and 30% in 1970 and 1971, respectively, and investment fell. There was also a lull in the growth rate of exports, stability in the real effective exchange rate notwithstanding. Whereas the real growth rate of exports averaged 36% in 1968–1969, it averaged 27% in 1970–1971. Simultaneously, there was a sharp contraction in monetary expansion (Table 4.8). The growth rate of M2 declined from 61% in 1969 to 27% in 1970. All these factors contributed to a decrease in the growth rate of GNP—from 13.8% in 1969 to 7.6% in 1970 (see Table 3.1).

To stimulate exports, the government introduced a devaluation of 12% in 1971. The immediate effect was a sharp increase in the won cost of debt financing. This created severe short-term financial problems for firms that had borrowed abroad. Rather than allow troubled enterprises to go bankrupt (the borrowers tended to be the more progressive as well as the politically best connected firms), the government bailed them out.

The bailout was specified in a Presidential Emergency Decree announced on August 3, 1972. This Decree had two immediate objectives: to revive economic activity by stimulating investment demand and to relieve the interest burden of overextended firms (Cole and Park, 1983). To stimulate investment, the government reduced overall interest rates of banking institutions. The time deposit rate was lowered from 17.4% to 12.6% and the rate on loans up to one year fell from 19% to 15.5%. To alleviate the interest burden of overextended companies, the government redistributed income from lenders to borrowers in the unofficial capital market, or curb market. All loan agreements between licensed business firms and lenders in the curb market were nullified and replaced by new agreements as of August 2, 1972. These allowed lenders the option to switch their loans into shares of the borrowing firms. By 1973 the economy was more than back on track. GNP recorded an unprecedented increase of 14.1%. The main factor behind the recovery was exports. They grew by an astounding 73%.

Table 4.8 Monetary Indicators, 1961–1984

Year	M1[a] % Increase	Broad Money M2[b] % Increase	Domestic Credit[c] % Increase	Discount Rate[d]	Inflation Rate in CPI[e]
1961–1971					
1961	14.5	27.2	41.6	10.22	6.1
1963	6.3	8.8	19.7	10.22	20.0
1964	16.7	14.3	8.8	10.50	29.8
1965	34.2	52.7	40.1	28.00	14.7
1966	29.7	61.0	30.5	28.00	11.2
1967	44.5	61.7	78.2	28.00	10.8
1968	44.6	72.0	84.8	23.00	10.4
1969	41.7	61.4	59.2	22.00	12.4
1970	22.1	27.3	26.5	19.00	16.2
1971	16.4	20.8	31.1	16.00	13.5
1972–1978					
1972	45.1	33.8	30.4	11.00	11.5
1973	40.6	35.9	31.7	11.00	3.2
1974	29.5	24.5	54.2	11.00	24.5
1975	25.0	28.2	32.2	14.00	25.2
1976	30.6	33.5	21.7	14.00	15.3
1977	40.7	39.7	23.6	14.00	10.2
1978	24.9	35.0	45.9	15.00	14.5
1979–1984					
1979	20.7	24.6	35.6	15.00	18.3
1980	16.3	26.9	41.9	16.00	28.7
1981	4.6	25.0	31.2	11.00	21.3
1982	45.6	27.0	25.0	5.00	7.3
1983	17.0	15.2	15.7	5.00	3.4
1984	0.5	7.7	13.2	5.00	2.3

[a] M1 = currency in circulation + deposit money.

[b] M2 = M1 + quasi-money (time and savings deposits).

[c] Defined as the Bank of Korea's claims on government, on government agencies, and on the private sector.

[d] The rate of discount for commercial bills of prime enterprises.

[e] CPI, consumer price index.

Source: Bank of Korea.

The stabilization of 1971–1972, unlike the two stabilizations that followed it, was not triggered by an external shock. Rather, it was precipitated by the IMF's concern about Korea's debt buildup and credit worthiness—call it external interference. Consequently, it differed from succeeding stabilizations in that it did not involve a sharp increase in foreign borrowing. Nevertheless, three characteristics of the 1971–1972 stabilization were later to repeat themselves: a devaluation, a cut in domestic interest rates, and a bailout of financially troubled firms.

Although maxi-devaluations came to characterize later stabilizations, the midi-devaluation (neither large nor small) of 1971 was unusual insofar as it led to a year-on-year depreciation of the real effective exchange rate, which depreciated still further in 1972 and 1973. One effect of the exchange rate depreciation seems to have been a rise in prices through the import of foreign inflation. The GNP deflator in 1972 was 16.4% (see Table 3.1). Therefore, although informal price controls had been in effect throughout the 1960s, the August 3, 1972 Decree called for an across-the-board price freeze, in emulation of the Nixon price freeze of a year earlier. After the freeze was lifted, fewer blanket controls over prices remained in effect, and in 1975 the declared purpose for price controls became to restrain monopoly power, as noted in Chapter 1.

The Second Stabilization

Not only was the economy back on track by 1973, but investments to diversify the economy were in full swing. Nevertheless, steel had just begun to be poured, and the first very large crude carrier had just begun to be constructed when the price of oil began to rise sharply. The first oil crisis presented a severe threat to growth because the economy was wholly dependent on oil imports, had recently diversified into energy-intensive industries, and was highly vulnerable to fluctuations in world demand. The oil price increase caused a 26% deterioration in the terms of trade.

The government responded in January 1974 with measures to maintain overall growth. A policy decision was taken to absorb fully the oil price increase, and that decision contributed in 1974 to a 62% rise in imports (Economic Planning Board, 1984). Domestic credit was expanded by over 40%. Investment as a share of GNP increased from 26% to 32% between 1973 and 1974, while the savings share of GNP declined by only 3.5%. The current account deficit jumped by a factor of 5 to 11%, an historical high, despite a growth in exports of 16% (see Table 3.1). To finance the deficit, the government both borrowed abroad and depleted its foreign reserve holdings, which fell by 3.5% in a year. Between 1973 and 1974, Korea's total foreign debt rose by 42%. Total debt as a percent of GNP rose from 32% in 1974 to 40% in 1975 (see Table 4.7).[9]

[9] In both 1973 and 1974, foreign loans as a percent of total capital inflow were lower than usual because of a temporary surge in direct foreign investment. In 1973 and 1974, direct foreign investment in total capital inflow averaged 14.8% compared with 7% for the period 1964–1972 and 4.3% for the period 1975–1983 (Economic Planning Board, 1984). With respect to loans, in 1974 and 1975 commercial loans grew in importance relative to public loans. This differed from the borrowing behavior of the preceding stabilization in 1971–1972 and the succeeding one in 1979–1982.

The country reaped the rewards of borrowing and of running down its reserves in the form of positive growth—7.7% in 1974 and 6.9% in 1975—at a time when most other non-oil-producing countries were plunged into depression. By 1976 fast growth had resumed, and GNP grew by 14.4%. Although investment as a share of GNP declined, exports grew by a staggering 49.2% (see Table 3.1).

Output continued to soar after 1976–1977, buoyed by domestic investment in heavy industry and in related infrastructure. The growth rate of output reached 12.7% in 1977. In 1978, the year before the second energy crisis struck, it equaled 9.7%, a rate just above the average for 1964–1972. The current account deficit, moreover, remained healthy until oil prices again began their ascent. As a percent of GNP it equaled only −1.1 in 1976 and −2.2 in 1978. In 1977 the current account even showed a small surplus, the first in Korea's recorded history, as remittances from the Middle East increased (see Table 3.1). Thus, *amidst the Big Push into heavy industry in 1977–1979 and just before the second energy crisis in July 1979, the Korean economy was in good shape.*

Determination of the Pace of Industrialization

We may pause here to make a general observation about the pace of industrialization in Korea (industrialization involving both the growth rate and the diversification of output). It may be said that to whatever extent possible, the government controlled the pace of industrialization, rather than allowing market forces to do so. The incentives it offered private firms had a decisive influence on both the timing of new investments and their scope. Nor is there any reason on theoretical grounds to believe that the market mechanism is a better arbiter than the state of the critical decision of how rapidly to grow, especially in the presence of unemployment and of the possibility of foreign borrowing. The idea of letting the market mechanism, rather than the government, decide the pace of industrialization is not particularly compelling from the point of view of efficiency.

In competitive theory, the market is recognized as the supreme arbiter of the rate of capital accumulation and hence of growth.[10] If the rate of savings exceeds the rate at which firms are willing to invest, interest rates are predicted to fall, thereby stimulating more investment. Even ignoring the Keynesian criticisms of this "investment" behavior, ultimately the rate of investment abstracted from its most immediate determinants depends on the capability of entrepre-

[10] The best critic of this view is Gerschenkron (1962). Gerschenkron gave careful historical examples of credit mobilization at the national level that suggested that the rate of investment is an institutionally determined variable.

neurs to assume risk. This capability combines both willingness and ability to do so, including the willingness and ability to borrow. As such, there is nothing sacrosanct about a market-determined investment rate, because it will depend on the tastes of whoever is responsible for investment decisions. Efficiency considerations do not necessarily enter the question. In the long run, the investment rate is a social variable. Other things being equal, a rate of return of, say, 15% may be considered inadequate compensation for risk in one country but adequate compensation in another.

Relying on the market mechanism to determine the pace of industrialization presumably has one merit over state intervention: The rate of inflation *may* be lower. In theory, rising prices are expected to discourage investment, either by reducing profits or by increasing risk. Whatever the relationship between inflation and investment in theory, in practice inflation *did* accompany Korea's push into heavy industry under government leadership in the late 1970s. The following discussion examines its effect.

Inflation

Although inflation in the late 1970s was below the 1974–1975 level, it was high by post-Korean-War standards. It was up from 16% in 1977 to 22% in 1978 and 1979 (see Table 3.1). The average rate of inflation in Korea in the period 1962–1969 was 17.3%. In the period 1970–1979 it was 19.3%. *The pursuit of fast growth was not restrained in the interest of price stability.* In fact, a relatively high rate of inflation was tolerated by the standards of most backward countries, save those in Latin America.

Table 4.9 suggests some of the determinants of inflation in the late 1970s. One was agricultural prices, which accelerated due to exceptionally poor harvests. Another was monetary policy, which was fairly accommodating of the high level of economic activity. M2 grew at a faster rate than in 1974–1975, although both M2 and bank credit grew less than in the period 1965–1973. The most significant rate of change, however, was that of manufacturing wages (see Table 4.10).

Manufacturing wages rose especially rapidly in 1976–1978 due to an unusual circumstance. The Middle East boom drained the most energetic able-bodied men from the labor force in unprecedented numbers. According to data from the Ministry of Labor, between 1977 and 1979 roughly 292,600 male workers migrated overseas, equaling almost 27% of the male manufacturing work force. The rate of wage increase of managerial, technical, and administrative workers also began to rise (although throughout Korea's high growth period, wage increases of production workers on the average ex-

Table 4.9 Average Periodic Rates of Change in Inflation and in Its Determinants, 1964–1984 (Percent) (Arithmetic Averages)

	1965–1973	1974–1975	1976–1977	1978–1979	1980–1981	1982	1983	1984
Inflation								
Consumer price index	11.55	24.77	12.70	16.41	25.01	7.19	3.42	2.27
Wholesale price index	8.78	34.30	10.60	15.21	29.64	4.65	0.24	0.71
PVI[a]	14.35	27.20	18.13	21.29	22.02	8.49	3.13	2.99
Determinants								
Manufacturing wages	20.45	31.16	35.25	31.48	21.39	14.86	12.00	8.32
Agriculture prices	12.56	34.86	22.22	22.57	26.07	0.31	3.36	−0.08
Price of imported materials (won)	11.98	27.92	1.58	16.35	37.55	1.33	1.22	4.01
Price of imported oil	18.84	135.18	6.05	21.91	72.16	2.51	−6.56	0.40
Price of non-oil materials	11.60	18.10	0.40	14.77	25.55	0.68	5.72	5.85
M2[b]	46.44	26.55	33.07	33.04	26.61	28.15	19.52	10.74
Bank credit	42.99	42.54	23.34	40.54	35.82	25.11	15.99	13.08

[a] Denotes the nonagriculture GNP deflator.

[b] M2 = currency in circulation + deposit money + quasi-money (time and savings deposits).

Source: Corbo and Nam, 1986.

ceeded those of higher level employees, as Chapter 8 indicates). For the first time, the rate at which nominal wages was rising exceeded the rate at which productivity was rising, and therefore, income was being redistributed to labor.

Institutional Wear and Tear

Inflation in 1976–1978, although high, coincided with fast growth, historically high savings rates, high *real* wage increases, and a low current account deficit. Yet it coincided with institutional wear and tear that was socially destabilizing.

The expression of discontent was greatest among the educated classes, the period of the Big Push of 1977–1979 having been relatively free of protest action by labor. The lowest paid workers may have been unconvinced by the government's constant reminders that they had never had it so good. The highest paid workers may have been oppressed by long work hours and the chaebol's interference in almost every aspect of their lives. But the wave of strikes that swept over Korea in 1979 occurred only after, not before, the second oil price increase, when wages in some firms fell into arrears. Moreover, the strikes occurred during the breakdown of state power in the months between the assassination of President Park Chung

Table 4.10 Inflation, Productivity, and Wages in Manufacturing, 1965–1984 (Rates of Change in Percent) (Arithmetic Averages)

		1965–1973	1974–1975	1976–1977	1978	1979	1980	1981	1982	1983	1984
Consumer price index		11.6	24.8	12.7	14.5	18.3	28.7	21.3	7.2	3.4	2.3
Wholesale price index		8.8	34.3	10.6	11.6	18.8	38.9	20.4	4.7	0.2	0.7
Total wage	N^a	21.6	31.2	34.3	34.7	36.6	19.1	20.0	14.7	11.3	8.2
	R^b	9.8	5.1	19.5	20.2	18.3	−9.6	−1.3	7.5	7.9	5.9
Production workers	N	18.3^c	27.7	29.1	35.3	38.9	18.2	21.7	14.1	10.8	10.0
	R	12.5^c	2.9	16.4	20.8	20.6	−10.5	0.4	6.9	7.4	7.7
Technicians	N	24.1^c	30.8	31.4	34.5	30.3	13.9	13.8	20.0	8.5	7.4
	R	18.3^c	6.0	18.7	20.0	12.0	−14.8	−7.5	12.8	5.1	5.1
Managers	N	22.5^c	35.4	26.9	33.0	38.2	8.6	12.5	8.4	10.5	7.1
	R	16.7^c	10.6	14.2	18.5	19.9	−20.1	−8.8	1.2	7.1	4.8
Labor productivity		13.0	10.5	10.6	11.5	15.4	10.5	16.9	7.2	13.0	10.0
Unit labor cost^d		7.7	18.8	21.4	20.5	11.4	11.1	10.0	−0.8	−1.5	−1.7

^{a}Nominal.

^{b}Real (nominal minus CPI).

^{c}1973 and 1974 only.

^{d}Rate of increase of nominal wage index/labor productivity index.

Source: Office of Labor Affairs (until 1980) and Ministry of Labor; Bank of Korea.

Hee in October 1979 and the assumption of power by General Chun Doo Whan in May 1980.

For the educated classes, the final years of the Big Push meant inflation, which reduced real returns to moonlighting, and escalating real estate prices, which disappointed dreams of home ownership in a housing market with few rental properties. With their own interests in jeopardy, the educated classes' criticisms of the government grew more vocal. The speculation that underlay escalating real estate prices was interpreted as one of several signs of misfiring of state policy. Land speculation was read as one manifestation of the misuse of subsidized loans for unproductive rather than for productive ends. A much-publicized crash program that improved rural housing but disrupted urban construction and cement exports was taken as being indicative of arbitrary and undisciplined government. The financial structure of firms was also believed to have become precarious due to high debt equity ratios.[11]

Disaffection with economic policy among the educated classes focused on the machinery branch of the heavy industries, although that branch accounted for no more than 10% of total loans to the manufacturing sector in the period 1975–1982 (Y. C. Park, 1985). However, it was in this machinery sector that the government–business recipe for entering heavy industry became distorted. In some machinery subbranches, particularly electrical generating equipment, excess capacity emerged because building to achieve economies of scale went to extremes, and too many firms were licensed to enter each manufacturing subbranch.

Indiscriminate licensing in some machinery subbranches had several possible explanations: (1) the government indulged in multiple licensing in the interests of national defense, (2) the government's administrative machinery was in need of revision to handle a larger and more complex volume of transactions, or (3) the government lost control to the chaebol, could not refuse them licenses, and abused its disciplinary device of credit allocation. For their part, the chaebol were drawn into the machinery sector by oligopolistic rivalry, subsidized credit, and the lure of riches. Either the government had to revamp its licensing procedures and regain control over the chaebol or it had to renounce control over credit allocation, thereby losing

[11] Behind-the-scenes bailouts make the reported bankruptcy rate an unreliable indicator of insolvency. Debt/equity ratios, however, have been taken as evidence of financial cliffhanging (Cho and Cole, 1986). Yet, debt/equity ratios in the manufacturing sector rose by only 13.5% between 1974–1975 and 1976–1977. In the period of accelerated investments in heavy industry, 1977–1979, debt/equity ratios remained almost constant at around 370, well below the level prevailing in Japan, 466 (Table 4.11 shows Korea's average debt/equity ratios during 1961–1984).

Table 4.11   Average Debt/Equity Ratio in
Manufacturing, 1961–1984

Year	Ratio	Year	Ratio
1961	136	1973	272
1962	154	1974	316
1963	92	1975	339
1964	101	1976	365
1965	94	1977	367
1966	118	1978	367
1967	151	1979	377
1968	201	1980	488
1969	270	1981	451
1971	328	1982	386
1972	313	1983	360
		1984	340

Source: Bank of Korea, *Financial Statement Analysis,* various
years.

an effective means by which to achieve economies of scale and competitive firm performance simultaneously.

In April 1979, the Park government itself set machinery in motion to reduce inflation and to reform administrative procedures by announcing the Comprehensive Stabilization Plan. The plan, however, was postponed by the second round of oil price increases in July and by assassination in October. Commodity price increases had led to a 13% deterioration in the terms of trade between 1979 and 1980. The deficit in the current account jumped from −2.2% of GNP in 1978 to −8.7% of GNP two years later. In 1980 the growth rate of GNP turned negative for the first time since the end of the Korean War.

The Third Stabilization

Both short-term and long-term factors appear to have been responsible for recovery, which was fairly rapid. In 1980 the GNP growth rate had been −5.2; by 1981 it was 6.2, below Korea's previous trend but above the growth rates of the Latin American late-industrializing countries and that of India. In 1980 the GNP deflator had been 25.6%; by 1982 it had fallen to 7.1% (see Table 3.1). The international environment became favorable, and the global economy began to grow faster, inflation falling sharply. Korea's terms of trade improved even at a time when the terms of trade of other late-industrializing countries continued to deteriorate.

Nevertheless, stabilization policy between mid-1979 and the end of 1982 exhibited no major departure from past practice. When private investment fell, and private savings fell even more, the tasks of borrowing and beefing up investment were assumed by the government. The deficit of state enterprises nearly doubled between 1980 and 1982 (see Table 4.4). Korea's total external debt grew by 59% from 1979 to 1981. Total external debt as a percent of GNP had been 32% in 1979, the last year of the Big Push, and increased to 48% in 1981 (Table 4.7). The stance of monetary policy varied from contractionary to expansionary, depending on whether inflation or the decline in economic activity was momentarily worse. The monetary authorities, however, acted to *lower* interest rates and hence the cost of borrowing. The intention was to avert insolvency and to mitigate inflation by reducing the cost of working capital (see Table 4.8). Many firms faced financial crises, and their debt/equity ratios rose sharply (see Table 4.11). Only one major chaebol, however, went bankrupt, *suggesting massive behind-the-scenes bailouts.*

Exchange rate policy in all three stabilizations was one of fairly sharp devaluation. In the stabilizations associated with the two energy crises, however, the exchange rate quickly appreciated after being devalued. It will be recalled that the exchange rate was a source of intense conflict between the Korean government and the United States aid administration in the 1950s and the 1960s, the former favoring depreciation of its real value, the latter, like the Bretton Woods institutions, arguing in favor of nominal devaluation. Figure 4.1 suggests its relative opaqueness, exports and the real effective exchange rate showing little relationship to one another. The real effective exchange rate and exports move together systematically in either direction in only four time periods: 1966–1968, 1971–1974, 1978–1979, and 1982–1983, although these years do not share any distinct characteristics. The rest of the time between 1966 and 1983 the growth rate of exports appears to have been influenced by other factors.

The second type of growth policies discussed thus far, relating to stabilization, may be summarized as follows: *To the extent that other growth policies favoring heavy state subsidization of new industries have been successful, they have enabled the government to act vigorously within the context of short-term macroeconomic policies to maintain the growth momentum in the face of external shocks.* This the government has done by borrowing abroad and by resorting to fairly unorthodox measures: driving down interest rates, allowing the exchange rate to appreciate after devaluation, and *not* allowing all but a trivial number of leading enterprises to go bankrupt. The Korean government may discipline private firms more than other governments in late-industrializing countries. But it also provides them with staunch support.

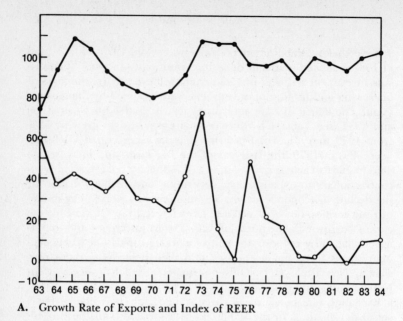

A. Growth Rate of Exports and Index of REER

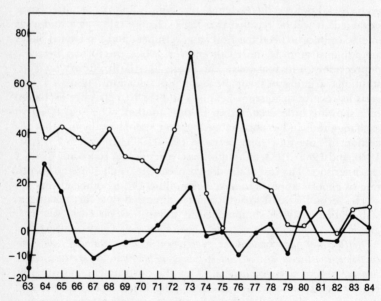

B. Growth Rate of Exports and Rate of Change of REER

THE KEY TO RECOVERY: HIGH PRODUCTIVITY

Despite a rapid appreciation of the exchange rate after 1980, exports rebounded and led the economy back to prosperity. Exports grew by 17% in 1980 and by 20% in 1981 (see Table 3.1). Behind the rise in exports lay a highly productive manufacturing sector. Ultimately, rising productivity was the critical factor in a rapid return to growth. *A stunning fact about Korean industrialization is that at the beginning and end of the period of massive foreign borrowing to finance heavy industry, the debt/GNP ratio remained more or less constant, falling slightly from 34% in 1972 to 32% in 1979 (see Table 4.7).* Evidently, the economy was using its credit productively to generate high levels of output.

The growth rate of labor productivity in manufacturing averaged 13.5% in 1978–1979, 13.7% in 1980–1981, and 11.5% in 1983–1984 (Table 4.10). The rise in output per worker had more to do with an increase in productivity than with changes in the employment rate. Although the nonfarm unemployment rate rose to a peak of 7.5% in 1980 (up from 4.7% in 1978), it fell steadily thereafter, to 4.9% in 1985. The average annual growth of nonfarm employment, moreover, although slower than it had been previously, was nonetheless substantial: 4.9% in 1979–1985 compared with 8.5% in 1976–1978 and 6.9% in 1970–1975 (Economic Planning Board, various years).[12]

In part productivity increased as exports rose and as excess capacity became utilized, allowing exports to rise still further. In part it increased as capital-intensive investments in heavy industry began to fructify, and firms fine-tuned their operations (as illustrated in

[12] The layoff policies of the chaebol may have had something to do with the behavior of the unemployment rate and the maintenance of employment. Although Korea doesn't have a permanent employment system similar to Japan's, there is still *social and political pressure on larger firms to avert layoffs,* and the diversified business groups are able to transfer labor among affiliates. As the structure of industry shifted from light to heavy manufactures, and as the share in total employment accounted for by large firms and the chaebol rose (although less than their share in sales or shipments), employment possibly held steadier.

Figure 4.1 Relationship between Exports and Real Effective Exchange Rate (REER). The index of REER is the inverse of column 5, Table 3.1. An increase in the index indicates a depreciation in the won. Thus, the two variables presented in the figure are expected to move in the same direction. *Source:* Bank of Korea and International Monetary Fund.
Key: □   growth rate of exports
  +   REER

Chapters 11 and 12). In part it increased as the new political regime pursued the same agenda and tactics as the old one and forced chaebol in sectors characterized by overexpansion and "excessive competition" to amalgamate, to specialize, or to exit (Korea Exchange Bank, 1980). Industries subject to reorganization included automobiles, heavy electrical equipment, electronic switching systems, diesel engines, copper smelting, and power-generating equipment (see the discussion in Chapter 5).

Rising productivity diminished the costs of the economic contraction that workers had to bear. True enough, real wages fell in 1980 and 1981, and the growth rate of real wages only recovered in 1988 the height it had achieved in 1978. Nevertheless, even as inflation abated, workers continued to demand high nominal wage increases, and real wages in 1982 and 1983 increased at an average annual rate of over 7%. Because productivity was rising fairly fast, and workers were at least enjoying some real gains, wages began to increase more in line with unit labor costs. The nominal growth rate of unit labor costs declined steadily from 1979 and was negative in 1982–1984 (Table 4.10).

Added Austerity

At a time when the economy was already assured recovery and price increases were already well below historical levels (the CPI was 7.2% in 1982 compared with 11.6% in 1965–1973), the government departed from past practice and, in concert with the IMF, tightened the fiscal and monetary screws. The stated objective was to prepare the macroeconomic environment for the structural liberalizations that were supposed to be under way. An adjustment program was formulated that was supported by a standby arrangement with the Fund. The program envisioned a sharp deceleration in the growth of external debt and a substantial improvement in its maturity structure— long-term debt as a percentage of total debt had fallen from 74% in 1978 to 62% in 1982 (Table 4.7). To achieve these objectives, the government included in the program a steep reduction in both the public sector deficit and the rate of credit expansion, as well as a real depreciation of the currency. The public sector deficit fell by about 3 percentage points between 1981–1983 and 1983–1984; the rate of credit expansion was cut by more than half, to about 13%; and the real effective exchange rate was depreciated by about 7% in 1983 and remained stable thereafter.

The effects of such extreme austerity were wide ranging. In terms of distribution effects, austerity probably took its highest toll in agriculture because, in the budget crunch of 1983–1984, a prime target of revenue saving was agricultural price supports. Between 1982 and 1985 there was a mass exodus from agriculture (roughly 600,000 people), even larger than the migration associated with the 1980 harvest failure (about 85,000). The last wave of migrants, however, was believed to have consisted of relatively older people, unequipped to enter the urban labor force and unaccounted for in the unemployment statistics (Castaneda and Park, 1986). In 1984–1985 there were sit-down strikes by young farmers to protest the government's price and import policies. Between 1979 and 1983 imports of grains rose by 28%, whereas during the 1970s they had remained fairly stable (Economic Planning Board, 1984).[13]

Two other changes are less certain to have emerged from austerity. First is the question whether austerity reduced inflation. The GNP deflator fell from 7.1% in 1982 to almost nil in 1985–1986. Yet the decisive drop in prices came earlier, before austerity became trenchant, when the prices of oil and non-oil imports fell like stones (see Table 4.9). Second is the question whether price stability encouraged an increase in private savings. By 1987 Korea had passed a milestone. Domestic savings exceeded domestic investment.[14] Yet the extent to which a decline in inflation was responsible for such saving behavior is unclear. Private savings also reached what in the late 1970s was an historic high, at a time when inflation as well was at an historic high. Savings behavior, therefore, may be more responsive to factors other than the direction and rate of price change. Whatever the true causality between the Comprehensive Stabilization Plan, savings, and inflation, this much is clear: Austerity cannot claim chief responsibility for the restoration of rapid growth in Korea. It is also unrepresentative of twenty-five previous years of short-run macroeconomic policy.

THE GROWTH-PRODUCTIVITY DYNAMIC OF LATE INDUSTRIALIZATION

We come to the last facet of growth to be considered, the growth-productivity dynamic of late industrialization. It is easier to understand this dynamic now that we have a sense of how late industrialization starts, how it spreads to new industries, and how it is shielded from external shocks. The objective is to go further and to understand theoretically a dynamic between growth and productivity that

---

[13] For a discussion of farmers' protests, see J. S. Suh (1986). In 1985 the real income of the farmer, relative to that of the urban worker, was worse than in 1965, 1970, and 1975, although slightly better than in 1980 (Moon, 1987).

[14] See *Han'guk Kyŏng-je Sinmun* (1987).

appears to drive late industrialization forward. It is suggested below that, subject to institutional constraints, high growth rates of output generate high growth rates of productivity, and vice versa. There is circular and cumulative causality. Once started, a momentum builds between growth and productivity that drives industrialization forward. This is what we observe in countries like Japan, Korea, and Taiwan, whose economies have followed an upward spiral.

In countries whose industrializations date to earlier historical periods and whose leading firms are at the world technological frontier, we tend to see another growth dynamic at play, or at least we are conditioned by economic theory to see such a dynamic. It is a dynamic that runs from technological change at the world frontier to high productivity, and from high productivity to high growth. In such a growth relationship there is no reverse causality. Growth does not generate high productivity or technological change, although technological change generates high productivity and growth.

One-way causality characterizes the theoretical models of most economists, and so the general case. There exists a contrasting model associated with the work of Verdoorn and Kaldor that does express cumulative causality between increases in output and productivity.[15] Like the conventional growth model, it also presumes to describe a general case. Its explanatory power, however, may be greatest when applied specifically to late-industrializing countries and the learning process, and it is this application that is attempted below.

The conventional growth model takes the form,

$$\dot{g} = f(\dot{x}_1, \dot{x}_2, \ldots, \dot{x}_n)T \qquad (4.1)$$

where growth ($\dot{g}$) is a function of factor inputs ($\dot{x}_1, \ldots, \dot{x}_n$) and technological change (T), which is represented as a scalar and residual (dots indicate growth rates). The weakness of this formulation lies in its failure to explain its key component, technological change itself.[16] Technological change is taken as being exogenously determined, and not much in the way of theory is given to explain what underlies it. By implication, productivity is also left unexplained because it depends on technological change. Moreover, this formulation implicitly incorporates the view that productivity depends not just on technological change but on a particular type of technological change, the epochal breakthrough. While it is true that epochal breakthroughs probably occur erratically and are, therefore, best left

[15] For this literature, see Kaldor (1967; 1978), and Journal of Post Keynesian Economics, (1983).

[16] For a critical review article on growth models and growth accounting, see R. R. Nelson (1981).

undetermined within the economic system, there is more to productivity than epochal breakthroughs.

The conventional growth model is inappropriate for late-industrializing countries because it throws away valuable information. The information it discards is the source of productivity increases. Although productivity changes remain a mystery in advanced countries, where productivity increases come from in late-industrializing countries is quite obvious. They do not depend upon "creative genius"; they are plucked from the world technology shelf. First, increases in productivity come from imports of foreign technology. Second, they come from operating foreign technology on a scale sufficient to minimize unit costs. Third, they come from learning how to use foreign technology imports efficiently.

One may go one step further and suggest that all three of these determinants of productivity are collapsible into one variable, the growth rate of output. Ignoring for the moment the institutional setting, it can easily be appreciated that if foreign technology is embodied in plant and equipment, then to raise productivity by importing technology will depend on the rate of investment in new plant and equipment. The faster output is rising, the faster one may expect investment to rise, and hence technology imports to rise. If growth and investment are low, the import of foreign technology will also be low. Similarly, it will be easier to realize scale economies embodied in imported foreign technology when output is growing. When output is growing, income is also growing, and hence the size of the market is expanding, making it easier to reach minimum efficient scale. Finally, how efficiently foreign technology is used will depend on the experience of the user. The faster output is rising, the faster experience accumulates. In other words, learning-by-doing, which is one critical aspect of learning in general, depends on cumulative output.

If growth depends on productivity, then as just stated, productivity also depends on growth. The growth-productivity momentum is a closed loop. Once growth starts and invades newer and newer industries, it gathers momentum by triggering increases in productivity. The loop in which productivity depends on growth takes the form,

$$\dot{p} = \dot{g}(x_1, x_2, \ldots, x_n) \qquad (4.2)$$

where productivity ($\dot{p}$) is a function of growth ($\dot{g}$) and growth decomposes into three *growth effects*, $x_1, x_2, \ldots, x_n$. The three growth effects are investment-embodying technology new to the user, economies of scale, and learning-by-doing.

As just formulated, the growth-productivity dynamic is highly mechanical. While it is fairly easy to imagine how the government might intervene to great advantage to keep the growth momentum going, in reality higher productivity does not automatically follow from higher growth. In one scenario, higher growth may simply lead to higher prices. In another, it may generate gross inefficiency. The translation of high growth rates of output into high growth rates of productivity depends on what happens *inside the unit of production*. Closing the loop between growth and productivity, therefore, involves an analytical shift, a change in the center of gravity from the state to the other key institution of industrialization, the firm.[17]

CONCLUSION

This chapter examined three aspects of growth: diversification and entrepreneurship, short-run stabilization, and productivity. In the case of entrepreneurship, by historical standards the big businesses of late industrialization have curtailed the role of the private entrepreneur. On the one hand, as discussed in this chapter, the state has usurped the domain of the traditional private entrepreneur by making milestone decisions about what, when, and how much to produce. On the other hand, as discussed in later chapters, the salaried managers have carried the burden of implementing investment decisions because it is they who hold the technical expertise. The private entrepreneur of late industrialization is a pale reflection of the heroic figure of the past.

As for short-run stabilization, the way it has been managed by the state has been critical in late industrialization, which has been subject to sharp and recurrent external shocks. The management of stabilization by the state in Korea has been contrary to what has typically been the prescribed medicine of the Bretton Woods institutions. Rather than soften external shocks with austerity measures, the Korean government has been wont to adopt expansionary policies and borrow its way out of balance-of-payments difficulties. It has been able to do so because heavy foreign borrowing has been balanced by large productivity increases. Therefore, despite massive foreign borrowing to finance diversification, the debt/GNP ratio even fell slightly in Korea by the end of the Big Push into heavy industry in 1979.

---

[17] This suggests that Equation 4.2 should be estimated at the firm level. Chenery, Robinson, and Syrquin (1986) measured it instead at the most aggregate level, which may explain why their findings of a positive association between the growth of output and productivity were not stronger. There are severe statistical problems involved in measuring Equation 4.2. It is difficult to separate the three growth effects and to exclude the temporary impact of business cycles. For a discussion of measurement problems, see *Journal of Post Keynesian Economics*, Spring 1983.

Finally, the productivity increases of late industrialization ill-fit the standard growth model, whereby productivity growth induces output growth but output growth does not induce higher productivity, higher productivity being driven by breakthroughs at the world technological frontier independent of the growth rate of output. Productivity in late industrialization, by contrast, has nothing to do with breakthroughs at the world frontier. Instead it depends on how rapidly foreign technology is borrowed (which depends on the investment rate), whether foreign technology is utilized at the appropriate scale (which depends on how fast the market is growing), and how efficiently foreign technology is employed (which depends on experience related to cumulative production). In short, the growth rate of output may be hypothesized to depend on higher productivity and, in closed-loop fashion, higher productivity also depends on the growth rate of output.

On the one hand, this cumulative relationship between productivity and growth underscores the importance of government intervention to keep the growth momentum going. On the other hand, the fact that productivity has little to do with imminent events at the world technological frontier and much to do with production capability—investing in foreign designs, producing at the appropriate scale, and learning-by-doing—highlights the importance of firm-level management practices. The next chapter, therefore, opens an extended discussion of the firm and its human resources.

CHAPTER FIVE

The Spiraling of Market Power

MONOPOLY, COMPETITION, AND LIBERALIZATION: AN OVERVIEW

Big business as well as the state shouldered the burden of carrying Korea in to basic and high-tech industry. Beginning in the 1880s, big, oligopolistic firms became a general property of industrialization. Oligopoly, or a relatively small number of firms in control of the output of a single industry, is one meaning attached to the term *market power*. The term has, however, another meaning. This meaning relates to the tendency of big business to diversify into more than one industry, giving rise to high aggregate concentration. According to an account of industrialization in the United States, "The large modern corporation typically is not confined to a single industry but embraces many lines of business and its operations extend to all parts of the earth . . ." (Mueller, 1982, p. 427). Thus, a general property of the industrialization beginning in the late nineteenth century is high aggregate concentration along with industry concentration, the former referring to the accountability by a relatively small number of firms for a large share of national product.

The countries that industrialized still later through learning took high aggregate economic concentration even further, in the form of the diversified business group—zaibatsu in Japan, chaebol in Korea. A volume describing the proceedings of the International Conference on Business History testifies to the generalness of this form of business in late industrialization:

> In developing countries such as South Korea, Taiwan, the Philippines, Thailand, India, Brazil and Argentina . . . industrial groups which resemble Japan's former zaibatsu have sprung up since the Second World War. (Yasuoka, 1984, p. xi)[1]

[1] For information on Taiwan's business groups, see Chou (1988).

Table 5.1 Combined Sales of Top Ten Chaebol, as Percent of GNP,[a] 1974–1984

Groups	1974	1975	1976	1977	1978	1979	1980	1981	1982	1983	1984
1	4.9	4.3	4.7	7.9	6.9	8.3	8.3	10.5	10.4	11.8	12.0
2	7.2	7.5	8.1	12.5	12.9	12.8	16.3	19.1	19.0	21.2	24.0
3	9.0	9.8	11.3	16.0	16.9	17.6	23.9	27.6	27.4	30.5	35.8
4	10.3	11.4	12.9	18.2	20.7	22.1	30.1	35.2	35.6	38.7	44.3
5	11.6	12.8	14.5	19.8	22.9	24.6	35.0	41.3	42.2	46.7	52.4
6	12.7	14.1	16.1	21.3	24.7	26.6	38.2	44.9	46.0	51.0	56.2
7	13.5	15.3	17.5	22.8	26.4	28.5	41.0	48.0	49.2	54.2	59.4
8	14.3	16.2	18.4	24.0	27.7	30.3	43.6	50.9	52.2	57.1	62.1
9	14.7	16.7	19.3	25.2	28.9	31.6	46.0	53.3	55.1	59.8	64.8
10	15.1	17.1	19.8	26.0	30.1	32.8	48.1	55.7	57.6	62.4	67.4

[a](Aggregate net sales of the largest ten business groups/GNP) × 100 for each year.
Source: Seok Ki Kim (1987).

The extreme degree of diversification and concentration represented by the diversified business group is notable when one compares the chaebol with, say, General Motors and General Electric before World War II. These two American giants were highly diversified, but largely in related products (however remotely related). The leading Korean chaebol, by contrast, comprise major divisions that have no relation to one another whatsoever: consumer electronics and petrochemicals in the case of the Lucky-Goldstar group; finance and heavy machinery in the case of Hyundai; consumer electronics, heavy machinery, finance, and entertainment in the case of Samsung; and so on. What is more, while prewar General Motors and General Electric were larger in absolute size than Samsung or Hyundai, they never accounted for as high a share of total gross national product. As Table 5.1 shows, in 1984 the three largest chaebol alone accounted for a staggering 36% of national product in Korea.

Big business raises two sets of issues: its economic performance and its social effects. Concerning its social effects, they appear similar whatever the mode of industrialization. In Germany, the appearance of big business was associated with the trusts, gold and iron, an imperial style in politics and economics, and the rise of centralized state power.[2] In Japan, the modern industrial enterprise was associated with heavy industry, fascism, and war:

The whole period of military hegemony and fascism was very favorable to business. Industrial output rose from 6 billion yen

[2] See the account by Stern (1977). On the trusts see Maschke (1969).

in 1930 to 30 billion yen in 1941. The relative positions of light and heavy industry were reversed. The four great zaibatsu firms, Mitsui, Mitsubishi, Sumitomo, and Yasuda, came out of the Second World War with total assets of more than 3 billion yen, compared with only 875 million in 1930. (Moore, 1966, pp. 301–2)

In Korea, too, the rise of the diversified business group has been inseparable from the thunderous social change accompanying the decline of agrarian society, ushered in by the army and the state, with which it is associated.

Concerning economic performance, the supposed benefits of bigness have inspired a fair amount of skepticism. The major economic rationale for bigness is economies of scale.[3] Yet the case for economies of scale applies to *plant* size, not *firm* size. The major economic rationale for big diversified firms is economies of scope. That is, given fixed inputs, it can be demonstrated theoretically that producing a greater rather than a smaller variety of products may be cheaper under certain circumstances.[4] Yet the case for economies of scope has also come under attack. Writing about the world's beleaguered hegemonic power, the United States, Adams and Brock argued,

> The case for large *firm* size . . . rests upon alleged efficiencies of management rather than technology. Efficiency, it is said, is enhanced by spreading administrative expenses over multiplant operations; by eliminating duplication of officials, services, and record systems; by providing sophisticated statistical, research, and other staff services that would be ruinously expensive for smaller firms; by hiring more competent executives, more talented legal departments, and more effective lobbyists; by obtaining credit on more advantageous terms; and so forth. Some of these economies . . . reflect advantages of bargaining power; however profitable they may be to the particular firm they do not benefit the community at large. (1986, pp. 33–4)

Moreover, it is argued that the diseconomies of scope tend to overwhelm the economies. Adams and Brock quote a professor at Harvard Business School, Steven C. Wheelwright, as saying, "Companies always thought, 'Our people can manage their way out of the problems [that] size and complexity create.' But the evidence is that they can't" (1986, p. 153). The authors came to a related conclusion:

---

[3] While the principle of economies of scale is demonstrated repeatedly in the commonplaces of everyday life, its significance in the profit-making sphere is still open to debate among economists. For two interesting discussions, see Gold (1981) and Buzacott et al. (1982).

[4] On economies of scope, see Bailey and Friedlaender (1982) and Spence (1983).

By most objective standards, America's corporate giants have not performed very well over the last fifteen years. They have lost markets to the Japanese and the newly industrializing countries. They have lagged in innovation. The quality of their products has often been inferior and unreliable. And, taken together, America's five hundred largest industrial corporations have failed to generate a single new job since 1970. (1986, p. xi)

These arguments about bigness miss the point. America's corporate giants may not have performed well over the last fifteen years, and they have certainly lost markets to Japan and to late-industrializing countries like Korea. Yet the economies of Japan and late-industrializing countries are also dominated by corporate giants. Economies of scope, moreover, may benefit one firm at the cost of another, but society at large can still benefit if size improves the international competitiveness of the aggrandizer. The point, therefore, is that nothing can be said a priori about the effect of bigness on performance. Instead, how well big business performs depends on how well it is coordinated and on the context in which it functions.

In general, the chaebol's economic performance has been impressive even if its social effects have been sinister, the popular perception being that while the chaebol benefited from public subsidies, they have not shared their wealth (and their derived power) with the rest of society. In terms of economic performance, during the period from, say, 1962 through 1979, the chaebol may not have maximized every possible source of efficiency or minimized every possible scrap of waste. Yet they never intended to. As profit-maximizing firms, their objective was to grow, not to pare costs to the bone. Korea has one of the highest investment rates in the world. In 1983 the share of investment in GDP was 31 percent, a rate less than in Singapore, which reached a staggering 48%, but greater than in Japan (29%), India (21%), Mexico (17%), and so on (see Table 5.2). Moreover, as output in Korea has increased, so, too, has productivity, contributing to the eradication of national unemployment and acute poverty. As already noted, Korean industry was productive enough to allow Korea's debt/GNP ratio to remain unchanged at the beginning and end of the Big Push into heavy industry, in 1973–1979. And while international comparisons of productivity that include late industrializing countries are statistically problematic, the most careful attempts show Korea well in the lead. According to estimates of Chenery et al. (1986), *total factor productivity as well as output grew faster in Korea's highly concentrated economy than in that of almost any other country studied.*

We may take aggregate indicators of output, productivity, and investment as evidence for the time being of outstanding performance

Table 5.2 International Comparison of
Percent Share of Investment[a] in Gross
Domestic Product, 1973 and 1983

Country	1973	1983
Korea	24	31
Hong Kong	22	26
Japan	37	29
Singapore	34	48
Argentina	20	16[b]
India	15	21
Mexico	21	17
United Kingdom	20	17
United States	18	17

[a] Gross capital formation.

[b] 1982.

Source: U.N. Statistical Yearbook, various years.

on the part of the chaebol, insofar as it was the chaebol that dominated the economy described by the aggregate indicators. Like the
multidivisional enterprises of the United States, Germany, and Japan, those of Korea can be said to have acted as the agents of industrialization. They were responsible for developing the forces of production in economies that expanded at unprecedented rates.

This chapter is concerned with two issues related to big business.
The first concerns the magnitude and causes of concentration. As
yet, there is no systematic study of why big business groups have
evolved into critical factors in late industrializing countries. Some
proposed explanations take a market failure perspective (Leff, 1978,
1979, 1979a; S.K. Kim, 1987). According to one such study: "The
business group is an entrepreneurial response to the environment of
market imperfection" (HBS, 1986a, p. 9). This explanation, however, is not altogether satisfactory. It implies that if markets were
perfect, firms would pursue a strategy of specialization. In fact, there
is little evidence to support this. The United States—if any country—
industrialized under fairly competitive market conditions. Yet the
upshot was the multidivisional firm—and more recently, the conglomerate—not the specialized corporation. Another explanation for
the rise of diversified business groups could conceivably be developed from a transactions cost approach (see, for example Williamson, 1985), although this approach is almost impossible to test empirically.

Alfred Chandler's (1989) study of the multidivisional enterprise in
the United States, Britain, and Germany suggests that diversification

by business is an integral part of expansion whatever the country. We take this historical proposition as a starting point for understanding the rise of the big business group in Korea. From this stylized fact two further questions arise which are the subject of speculation in the first part of this chapter: Why did the chaebol exceed most multidivisional firms in diversifying so broadly; and why, despite a high degree of diversification, does coordination appear tighter in the chaebol than in, for instance, the American conglomerate?

The second major issue with which this chapter is concerned relates to discipline. As stated in Chapter 1, a defining characteristic of Korean industrialization has been not merely support but also discipline of big business by the government. Yet discipline has by no means been flawless. In this chapter we wish to air some of the limitations. In particular, we wish to focus on the government's waning ability to control a particular type of business activity, whatever its ability to control the overall performance of business to produce goods and services efficiently. The particular type of business activity with which we are concerned is the one that typically is anticipated to arise from a high degree of market power: namely, monopolistic abuses such as creating scarcities, price gouging, and ruining smaller competitors. The time period with which we are especially concerned is the 1980s, following the assassination of Korea's iron-fisted ruler, Park Chung Hee. It was in this time period that the new military dictatorship adopted a policy of "liberalization", one intent of which was to mitigate monopolistic abuses by strengthening freer markets as a particular form of discipline over big business.

MARKET CONCENTRATION

High levels of economic concentration exist in Korea at both the industry and the aggregate levels. Table 5.3 provides data on industry structure. The data for 1982 cover 2,260 commodities and suggest that only about 18% of all commodities that year, or 30% of all shipments, were produced under what are typically considered to be competitive conditions—that is, a three-firm concentration ratio of less than 60% (or a combined market share of the top three producers of less than 60%). The remainder of commodities was produced by either monopolies, duopolies, or oligopolies (see Table 5.3 for definitions).

Table 5.3 also suggests that over time, the share of shipments produced under a competitive structure declined, while the share of the remainder of shipments shifted among the three types of noncompetitive market configurations. Comparing 1982 with 1970, the percent share of shipments produced under monopolistic conditions in-

Table 5.3 Structure of Manufacturing Industry: 1970, 1977, and 1982

Year		Monopoly	Duopoly	Oligopoly	Competitive	Total
1970	No. of	442	279	495	276	1,492
	Commodities	(29.6)	(18.2)	(33.2)	(18.5)	(100)
	(% share)					
	Shipments[a]	110	204	439	498	1,252
	(% share)	(8.8)	(16.3)	(35.1)	(39.8)	(100)
1977	No. of	667	425	674	343	2,219
	Commodities	(31.6)	(20.1)	(32.0)	(16.3)	(100)
	(% share)					
	Shipments[a]	2,264.0	1,536	4,716	5,404	13,920
	(% share)	(16.3)	(11.0)	(33.9)	(38.8)	(100)
1982	No. of	533	251	1,071	405	2,260
	Commodities	(23.6)	(11.1)	(47.4)	(17.9)	(100)
	(% share)					
	Shipments[a]	5,649	3,275	24,967	15,481	49,372
	(% share)	(11.4)	(6.6)	(50.6)	(31.4)	(100)

[a] Billion won.

Concentration ratios (CR):
Monopoly (one-firm CR accounts for a market share of more than 80%).
Duopoly (two-firm CR accounts for a market share of more than 80%).
Oligopoly (three-firm CR accounts for a market share of more than 60%).
Competitive (three-firm CR accounts for a market share of less than 60%).

Source: Compiled from the Census of Manufacturing data base, Economic Planning Board, by K. U. Lee et al., (1986).

creased (having peaked in 1977). Duopoly proved to be a nonviable arrangement, and its percent share of shipments decreased. The share accounted for by oligopoly, however, rose by 15 percentage points, from 35% in 1970 to over 50% in 1982.

Korean industry is even more highly concentrated than that of Japan. This is suggested in Table 5.4, which compares the average three-firm concentration ratios of Korea, Japan, and Taiwan (or the average shares of the top three producers in all manufacturing industries).[5] Furthermore, in that high degrees of concentration at the level of individual industries are complemented by ultrahigh degrees of concentration at the level of the entire manufacturing sector, the whole may even be greater than the sum of the parts. In short, *Korea has acquired one of the world's most concentrated economies.*

[5] Nevertheless, Taiwan probably has a higher level of economic concentration than Korea in "upstream" industries like petrochemicals, shipbuilding, and steel, in which typically a government monopoly presides (Amsden, 1989).

122 THE STATE AND BUSINESS

Table 5.4 Comparison of Simple Average
Three-Firm Concentration Ratios for Korea,
Japan, and Taiwan

Country (year)	Average share (percent)[a]
Korea (1981)	62.0
Japan (1980)	56.3
Taiwan (1981)	49.2

[a] Average share of top three producers in all manufacturing
industries.

Source: K. W. Lee, et al. (1986).

Measured by sales, the ten largest diversified business groups accounted for a phenomenal 67% of total sales in 1984 (see Table 5.1).
Sales, of course, exaggerate the chaebol's share of manufacturing
activity because they include inputs purchased from other firms.
Nevertheless, concentration measures in terms of sales may give an
accurate picture of the chaebol's command over the economy insofar
as the development of a subcontracting system in Korea has rendered many of the chaebol's suppliers mere satellites (see Chapter
7). In terms of shipments, which are a close approximation of value-
added, the percentage accounted for by the chaebol is also impressive (see Table 5.5). In 1982 the top ten diversified business groups
accounted for as much as 30.2% of manufacturing activity (but only
12.2% of employment).

Table 5.6 compares aggregate economic concentration measured

Table 5.5 Percent Change in Concentration of Economic Power of
Business Groups,[a] 1974–1982

	Shipment			Employment		
	1974	1977	1982	1974	1977	1982
Top 5 business groups	NA	15.7	22.6	NA	9.1	8.4
Top 10 business groups	NA	21.2	30.2	NA	12.5	12.2
Top 15 business groups	NA	25.6	33.9	NA	14.4	14.5
Top 20 business groups	24.6	29.3	36.6	13.5	17.4	16.0
Top 25 business groups	NA	31.9	38.8	NA	18.9	17.1
Top 30 business groups	NA	34.1	40.7	NA	20.5	18.6

NA, not available.

[a] Manufacturing sector only.

Source: Compiled from the Census of Manufacturing data base, Economic Planning Board, as
cited in Lee et al. (1986).

Table 5.6 Percent Aggregate Concentration Rate by Shipment of the Largest Companies in Korea, Japan, and Taiwan,[a] 1970–1982

Year	Korea		Japan	Taiwan	
	Top 50	Top 100	Top 100	Top 50	Top 100
1970	33.8	44.6	NA	NA	NA
1975	NA	NA	28.4	15.8	21.7
1977	35.0	44.9	NA	15.2	22.4
1980	NA	NA	27.3	16.4	21.9
1982	37.5	46.8	NA	NA	NA

NA, not available.

[a] Manufacturing sector only. It is unclear how *company* as distinct from *business group* is defined.

Source: K. U. Lee et al. (1986).

in shipments for the largest companies (not business groups) in Korea, Japan, and Taiwan. Aggregate economic concentration is by far the highest in Korea, more than twice as high as in Taiwan and approximately 1.7 times as high as in Japan.

Countries that have industrialized since the 1880s share high aggregate economic concentration because huge firms tend to diversify. Chandler (1989) called such firms "modern industrial enterprises" and noted their synchronous emergence in the 1880s in the United States, the United Kingdom, and Germany. They emerged slightly later in Japan and considerably later in Korea because both countries industrialized later. We return again to Chandler's model of the modern industrial enterprise because it provides a benchmark to examine big business in late-industrializing countries. Here we are interested in one aspect of Chandler's model, the one that relates to diversification. For Chandler, diversification is a defining characteristic of the modern industrial enterprise, although there is considerable variation among the members of the family, which include the chaebol, zaibatsu, and American conglomerates. There is variation in the degree of diversification, measured roughly by the relatedness of products and the degree of *centralized management coordination*, in terms of financial and human transfers among firms within a single corporate group. In the standard case, diversification tends to be restricted to related products. The firms that produce these products also tend to be centrally managed, as evidenced by the rise of managerial hierarchies—another defining characteristic of the modern industrial enterprise—and by the multidivisional organizational structure—still another. Thus, in a graph with degree of diversification on the vertical axis and degree of coordination (of both financial and human resources) on the horizontal, the modern in-

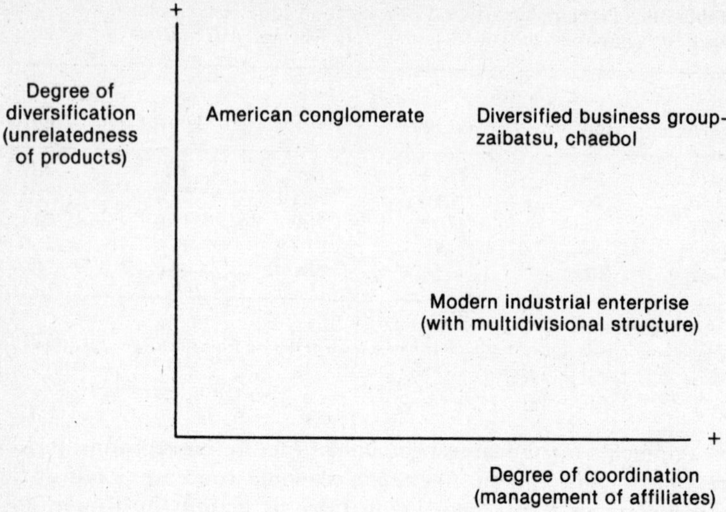

Figure 5.1 Degree of Diversification and Coordination of the Modern Industrial Enterprise.

dustrial enterprise falls in the lower right-hand corner (see Figure 5.1).

Although diversification in the United States has typically conformed to the pattern just noted—diversification into related products only, under fairly tight coordination—the United States has also been characterized by what has come to be called *conglomeration*. According to Chandler,

> The large, diversified [modern industrial] enterprise had grown primarily by internal expansion—that is, by direct investment of plant and personnel in industries related to its original line of products. It moved into markets where the managerial, technological, and marketing skills and resources of its organization gave it a competitive advantage. The conglomerate, on the other hand, expanded entirely by the acquisition of existing enterprises, and not by direct investment into its own plant and personnel, and it often did so in totally unrelated fields. (1977, p. 481)

Conglomerates are known to be coordinated to the degree that they have central budgeting. Nevertheless, there is little, if any, transfer of people across affiliates (Mueller, 1982). In terms of Figure 5.1, therefore, the conglomerate occupies the space in the upper left-hand corner.

We come now to the diversified business groups in Korea and Japan. We note first that they are far from homogeneous, showing significant variations among themselves. The new and old zaibatsu differ in degree of diversification, and the prewar zaibatsu and postwar keiretsu differ in degree of coordination.[6] Among the chaebol, too, there are variations in the extent of diversification, depending on the overall size of the business group. Moreover, the tendency of the chaebol before 1980 was to grow by internal investment; thereafter its tendency has been to grow by acquisition.[7] These variations notwithstanding, there is a single theme. The big business groups of both Korea and Japan are more diversified than the modern industrial enterprise described by Chandler, and they are more coordinated than the American conglomerate. Thus, in terms of Figure 5.1, the zaibatsu and the chaebol belong in the northeast quadrant, exhibiting high degrees of both diversification and coordination. This corporate structure—*more widely diversified than the modern industrial enterprise and more centrally coordinated than the conglomerate*—appears to be typical in late industrialization. Two questions follow: Why do business groups in late industrializing countries tend to diversify so widely, and how do they manage to stay closely coordinated?

CORPORATE STRATEGY TOWARD DIVERSIFICATION

As Chandler pointed out, whatever the national character of industrialization, whether driven by borrowing technology or by creating it, large corporations diversify into *related* business activities—where related refers to skills or markets—through vertical or horizontal integration. In Korea, the Hyundai group branched out vertically from construction to cement manufacture and shipbuilding, and from shipbuilding to shipping and steel structures. The Samsung group diversified horizontally in entertainment with a broadcasting company, a daily newspaper, and a hotel. The Hanjin group includes tourism industry business—an airline, a bus line, and a travel agency.

---

[6] See Hirschmeier and Yui (1981, pp. 132–42, 222–36, and 257–60).

[7] From 1981, when the Fair Trade Act was passed, until June 1986, there were 1,136 reported cases of chaebol beginning to own new businesses. Among these the number of horizontal integrations (intraindustry) was 324 (28.5% of the total), that of vertical integrations was 215 (19.9%), and that of diversifications into other industries (interindustry) was 597 (52.6%). The methods of expansion included acquiring stocks, establishing new companies, merging, acquiring management participation, and acquiring business rights. Acquiring stocks accounted for 45.7% of all cases; establishing new companies accounted for 19.8% (*Donga Ilbo*, 1986).

The KIA group makes vans and the machine tools that are used in their manufacture. The Doosan group makes bottling equipment and owns a bottling franchise. The impulse to diversify into related businesses is illustrated by a statement made by the chairman of the Lucky-Goldstar group, which reported 1984 sales of $9.2 billion. According to the chairman,

> My father and I started a cosmetic cream factory in the late 1940s. At the time, no company could supply us with plastic caps of adequate quality for cream jars, so we had to start a plastic business. Plastic caps alone were not sufficient to run the plastic-molding plant, so we added combs, toothbrushes, and soap boxes. This plastics business also led us to manufacture electrical and electronic products and telecommunication equipment. The plastics business also took us into oil refining which needed a tanker-shipping company. The oil-refining company alone was paying an insurance premium amounting to more than half the total revenue of the then largest insurance company in Korea. Thus, an insurance company was started. This natural step-by-step evolution through related businesses resulted in the Lucky-Goldstar group as we see it today. For the future, we will base our growth primarily on chemicals, energy, and electronics. Our chemical business will continue to expand toward fine chemicals and genetic engineering while the electronics business will grow in the direction of semiconductor manufacturing, fiber optic telecommunications, and eventually, satellite telecommunications. (Harvard Business School, 1985b)

The impulse to diversify into related businesses is illustrated by the lower right-hand corner of Figure 5.1, the area occupied by the modern industrial enterprise, or multidivisional firm.

Nevertheless, after the initial move into related businesses, the extent of diversification among firms differs. In the case of innovators, say those in the United States, *the tendency has been to build on expertise,* whether technological or marketing, and hence to diversify further only into related fields. On the other hand, in the case of firms with no expertise, for example those of late-industrializing countries, or of firms with expertise whose rate of return is narrowly bounded, the tendency has been to diversify into unrelated areas.[8] A large chaebol like Lucky-Goldstar has diversified in part because local in-

[8] In the United States, diversification into unrelated businesses occurred mainly when industry growth declined: "The creators of the first conglomerates embarked on strategies of unrelated acquisition when they realized that their own industries had little potential for continued growth" (Chandler, 1977: 481). Typical industries employing this strategy were textiles and ocean shipping.

puts were in short supply, and it needed to become its own supplier. In other cases market size was too small to specialize; or too risky to do so. The supposed relationship mentioned earlier between its plastic injection-molding operation and its oil refinery is farfetched. The so-named backbone of the group—chemicals (Lucky) and electronics (Goldstar)—is more like disconnected vertebrae.

Assuming an equal desire on the part of all firms to diffuse risk, the above suggests that quite possibly learners in late-industrializing countries tend to diversify widely because their level of experience in particular industries does not enable them to develop related products or processes, or to grow by moving into a higher quality niche in their existing markets. Instead, they are constrained to diversify widely and often to expand laterally. They compete on the basis of price and reliability at the bottom end and at the middle layers of many altogether unrelated markets. The choice between a competitive strategy of price versus one of high quality product differentiation is mused upon by the chairman of the Daewoo group, one of the most meteoric of chaebol and one that relied more than most on acquisitions in order to grow (because it started late):

> Up to the present, I have succeeded, to a certain degree, in building new businesses and increasing employment opportunities. I have done this through hard work and by turning around troubled companies. I believe that these accomplishments demonstrated to the Korean people *the possibility of succeeding with almost any business in Korea.* Looking back, however, I feel I could have concentrated on developing a Korean company which produced the best quality product in the world, rather than diversifying to various fields [wishful thinking?]. When we have spun off the present collection of companies [the chairman plans to free each of Daewoo's affiliated companies from equity control by the parent corporation by 1990], I shall resign as chairman of Daewoo and start a new venture. And the product I am going to develop will be the best quality product in the world from Korea, like those of Japan's Sony or Germany's Leica. (Harvard Business School, 1985a; my italics)

One leaves as speculation the zaibatsu's and chaebol's location in the northeast quadrant in Figure 5.1 as a function of their status as learners.

Diversifying widely is a big gamble, especially when diversifications occur in rapid succession as they did in most Korean business groups. How, then, did the chaebol manage to grow so fast and yet prosper?

First, as latecomers, they bought the industry-specific technical expertise they needed from foreigners. Second, they borrowed abroad with credit guarantees and subsidies from the government. This helped them to grow very large, with high debt equity ratios, *yet maintain their family ownership structure.* By contrast, in the business histories of advanced countries, the family form of ownership is diluted for want of finance to grow. Third, as they grew, the chaebol's finances and status rose, and they were able to hire the most experienced salaried managers. Family firms in advanced countries have had much trouble recruiting the best salaried managers, who prefer to work for firms that are not owned by families so that their chances of rising to the top are greater. In Korea, promotion opportunities were greatest in the chaebol, the remainder of firms being even more family oriented.

Fourth, in the mid-1980s most chaebol were still nurtured by first-generation owners who had personally witnessed their sales growth as it progressed from thousands to billions of dollars and who also held an intimate knowledge of the human resources of their entire group.[9] As will be demonstrated in later chapters, a new subsidiary would most likely be established by a task force typically formed at the group level and comprising qualified managers, engineers, and even supervisors from existing companies within the group. In the case of Hyundai, for example, managers from its construction arm were transferred to its shipbuilding arm to aid in project management. Later, engineers from its shipbuilding arm, who had a knowledge of anticorrosion, were loaned to its automobile affiliate where a new paint operation was coming on stream. Such transfers increased the capability to diversify and were facilitated by a central "brain" and a uniform group culture. Within a very short time, therefore, the business groups in Korea were multiproduct yet still under family management, with salaried managers in command at the industry level and with a capability to enter new industries quickly.

Under conditions of rapid growth and a succession of diversifications and capacity expansions, Korean management appears to have accumulated experience in the areas of feasibility studies, task force formation, purchase of foreign technical assistance, training, equipment purchase, new plant design and construction, and operation start-up. This experience became an invaluable competitive asset in the absence of proprietary technology because it allowed the chaebol to be Korea's first movers in many industries. Investment costs were also kept to a minimum, which enabled new affiliates to start operations with a relatively light financial burden. This control over costs complemented the group strategy of competing in a wide range of industries on the basis of price.

---

[9] See the study by Hattori (1984) on the family structure of the chaebol.

The group coordination pattern just described influenced the conduct of risk diffusion, which became more than simply a strategy of investing in unrelated industries. It meant shifting people and money around the group to increase the probability that risk-diffusing projects would earn profits. It meant converting ailing acquisitions into moneymakers. Group coordination implied a more proactive approach to averting risk and financial loss.[10] In general, one may venture to guess that *the group's ability to enter new industries rapidly and cost effectively became a major economy of scope.*

DISCIPLINE OF MONOPOLY POWER

Oligopolistic Competition

Korea's economy may be highly concentrated, but its leading firms appear to engage in intense competition with one another in overseas as well as in domestic markets. The Economic Planning Board controls most prices, so only firms supplying differentiated products have a chance to compete on price. However, big business competes primarily on the basis of nonprice factors, as do oligopolists in other countries.

The specific nonprice factors that the chaebol compete on are characteristic of a particular type of oligopolist—the learner. First, learners compete to get additional favors and industrial licenses from the government. They do so by wining and dining bureaucrats, by preparing investment packages that meet planners' specifications, and by distinguishing themselves on the basis of their achievements (like introducing products novel to Korea, winning Korea's equivalent of the Deming Award for quality, exporting Korean-made steel to Japan and Korean-made cars to the United States, etc.).[11] Second, they compete to get foreign technical licenses on the best terms from the

---

[10] As of April 1, 1987, 32 chaebol were reported to have 3,474 billion won in cross-investments among their subsidiaries. Such investments amounted to 43.9% of their net assets (*Maeil Kyŏngje Sinmun*, 1987a).

[11] For example, in the case of general trading companies (GTCs):

The government's primary objective in establishing Korean GTCs was to promote exports, and it has used all sorts of means to increase the exports of Korean GTCs. As a stick, the government annually increased the minimum requisite export amount that a Korean GTC must reach to retain its GTC title. As a carrot, the government created a variety of prizes, citations, and medals. More important, it provided low-cost financing for each dollar exported, which often more than compensated for losses incurred in export transactions. These government measures, together with the competitive spirit of the management, encouraged Korean GTCs to vie fiercely against each other to increase the export amount. (D. S. Cho, 1987, p. 57)

foremost international firms. Third, they compete in the labor market for the best college recruits and the most experienced skilled craftspersons, supervisors, managers, and engineers (see the discussion in Chapter 8). Fourth, they compete in the marketplace on the basis of quality and delivery. In the case of the automobile industry, domestic price is not a competitive factor because it is set by the government according to liter capacity. But the two major automobile companies compete—in the local market and abroad—on the basis of gas mileage, appearance, safety, service, and resale value (Amsden and Kim, 1985a). The spirit of competition between the two major automobile makers is such that one of them does not allow anyone driving the other's car to enter its parking lot.

The likelihood of intense competition also rises in the presence of uncertainty and multiproduct oligopolists. When it is unclear which markets will grow the fastest, and when demand is rising rapidly in a number of markets, multiproduct oligopolies will be inclined to compete vigorously in all of them to maintain parity in terms of, say, sales at the group level. Overall size could be considered critical for raising finance, attracting the best labor, winning the most favorable foreign licenses, and so on. Parity is particularly important when group affiliates are subject to central coordination. If resources can be shifted throughout the group, higher profits in one market may improve competitiveness in all. Finally, when the government dispenses largesse according to criteria that are corrupt but performance oriented, competition becomes almost a certainty.

Countervailing Power

Government policy was almost completely in harmony with the strategy of the chaebol to grow through diversification. Yet a consequence was a spiraling of market power. To curb the "appalling power of mammoth enterprise," policies were first conceived in the spirit of democratic pluralism (Park, 1962, p. 228).

The intention to curb monopoly power by protecting the interests of diverse social groups (one interest group being small- and medium-size firms) was articulated by Park when he still ruled by popular vote:

It is thought in many quarters, both capitalist and communist, that large-scale industries are unconditionally the best. But we cannot ignore the fact that there are many industrial fields where small and medium businesses may have independent domains. The present stagnation of these smaller businesses suggests they could be stimulated to increase their productivity through prompted coordination of management, and assistance rendered by the state and improvement of techniques, so that the income ratio of these businesses would not be less than that of the bigger enterprises. (1962, pp. 226–7)

With respect to consumers, Park wrote,

It is desirable that the state should give special attention to possible dangers to the public interest presented by some industries which face no competition to prevent their trespassing on the interests of the consumers. The state may grant some form of consumer groups a kind of admonitory voice over industrial operations. (1962, p. 236)[12]

Park even hinted at encouraging the growth of trade unions:

To protect against the mounting power of big enterprises, employes should be allowed, with the reasonable backing of the state, to have equality with management. Special measures should be worked out so that skilled laborers and others can utilize their creativity individually and collectively to contribute to the improvement of industry. By so doing, the state will be able to protect the interests of the employed and rally strongly the voluntary support of workers for the improvement and expansion of industry. (1962, p. 26)

However, none of these countervailing forces to big business ever gathered much strength under Park. Even when he pursued a strategy of socializing big business by pressuring leading companies to sell equity to the public, Korea's stock market remained moribund, and the chaebol remained closely held family concerns (see Chapter 4).[13]

The frenzy of activity surrounding the building of heavy industry in the late 1970s characterized a shift in power toward big business, because as subsidies sweetened, restricting entry became more difficult. Takeovers in the 1980s of smaller firms by the *chaebol* became endemic. The newspapers were filled with exposés of monopolistic abuses. The crisis surrounding the second oil shock and President Park's assassination led to an attempt by the government of Chun Doo Hwan, therefore, to restructure and liberalize the economy.

---

[12] Consumer advocacy groups are weak in Korea, as they are in other late-industrializing countries, but see Sobija Poho Danché Hyŏpŭihoe (1987) and Tachan Chubu Kŭllŏp Yŏnhaphoe (1987).

[13] As late as 1984, the Securities Supervisory Board was still attempting to upgrade the auditing and accounting practices of firms in order to strengthen the stock market (Chŭnggwon Kamdogwon, 1984). The stock market only began to boom in the late 1980s.

Restructuring

A period of restructuring appears to characterize most industrial expansions, each in its own form, for example, the merger movement at the turn of the century in the United States or the capacity reductions in Germany and Japan in the 1920s. By comparison, the reorganization of heavy industry in Korea in 1979–1982 seems relatively superficial because only a few industries were permanently affected. After much delay, the shipping industry was rationalized by a drastic reduction in the number of firms from about sixty to fifteen (World Bank, 1987).[14] The heavy electrical equipment industry witnessed a merger of major *chaebol* (Hyosung, Kolon, and Ssangyong), as did the fertilizer industry. But another move in heavy electrical equipment was temporary—a nationalization that was soon rescinded. An attempt to reduce capacity in the automobile industry through merger was also short-lived and abortive. As the Korean and world economies recovered and prosperity returned (eventually even to fertilizers and petrochemical producers), restructuring became as redundant as capacity had temporarily been. Restructuring was also limited in scope in the sense that the industries affected had accounted for only a small share of total investments in the 1970s. The machinery industry was the most vexed by excess capacity and by restructuring, yet the technology of adding capacity in the machinery sector is such that investments had accounted for only 10% of total investments during the Big Push (Y. C. Park, 1985, quoted in Amsden, 1987).[15]

The form that restructuring took under Chun Doo Hwan was in keeping with the spirit of state intervention practiced under Park Chung Hee (although the firms involved did not all acquiesce under Chun Doo Hwan). In exchange for the favors they had received, the big firms were rounded up and forced to merge. The World Bank observed, "It is clear from these cases that government has bypassed

[14] Reorganization of financially troubled firms had dragged on in the late 1980s, especially in the shipping and construction industries. H. Y. Song (1987) stressed the inequity of reorganization, since healthy firms are often forced to acquire ailing ones (and the taxpayer is forced to pay for all parties' mistakes). An article in *Han'guk Ilbo* (1986a) noted that reorganization resulted in higher levels of aggregate economic concentration. The government was reluctant to let ailing firms go bankrupt because commercial banks would have gone bankrupt simultaneously. In 1986 there were fifty-six firms under government reorganization (*Donga Ilbo*, 1986a).

[15] The machinery industry is typically given as an example of the failure of state intervention, presumably because the industry suffered from excess capacity beginning in late 1979. Nevertheless, the troubles of the industry after 1979 were as much a function of the world recession and the "teething" associated with developing a skill-intensive sector as they were a function of government blunders. By as early as 1986, the machinery industry in Korea was booming. See *Donga Ilbo*, 1986b, 1986c; *Maeil Kyŏngje Sinmun*, 1986b, 1986c.

competitive solutions in most of its restructuring operations" (World Bank, 1987, vol. 1, p. 50). On the other hand, American forms of regulation did not play a major role in restructuring. The enactment of a Monopoly Regulation and Fair Trade Act along the lines of American antitrust legislation appears to have been out of character and has not been vigorously enforced.

Although the number of corporations designated by the government as dominating their respective markets increased from 105 in 1981 to 216 in 1985, no more than 10 were accused of having abused their power. Out of 1,172 applications for "corporate integration," or horizontal merger, all but 2 were approved (K.-U. Lee et al., 1986). The act, moreover, did not include a restrictive clause on *conglomerate* integration because "there was a concern that such policies would harm enterprises that had fallen on hard times since the recession beginning in 1979." Further, as expressed by Lee et al., "the problem of the concentration of economic power is very complicated and difficult to solve by the Monopoly Regulation Act alone" (1986).[16]

Instead of regulation, liberalization was the means by which the new military rulers and economic advisors hoped to discipline big business and reverse the institutional legacy of two decades of state controls. In this reversal they were aided by the World Bank, which supplied Korea with a restructuring loan. Liberalization was supported in bits and pieces by the Federation of Korean Industries, the mouthpiece for big business. Basically, big business wanted trade barriers to remain, except on agricultural goods, but it also wanted privatization and freedom from government controls in financial markets.[17] At first, liberalization affected direct foreign investment, trade barriers, industrial licensing, state credit allocation, public enterprise, price supports, and price fixing. Ultimately, zeal was confined to two major areas—trade and finance. At U.S. prodding, the

[16] For earlier studies of monopoly regulation in Korea, see K. U. Lee and Kim (1981); K. U. Lee (1984); K. U. Lee and J. H. Lee (1985); and K. U. Lee and S. S. Lee (1985).

[17] In 1987 the Federation of Korean Industries lobbied for fewer government controls. Its representatives complained that it took 530 days and sixty-two steps to establish a new firm. Firms allegedly had to spend 0.77% of sales (33.4% of profit) on "tax-like" expenditures (official contributions such as defense tithes, donations to government-related organizations, charities, etc.). The government, according to the Federation, regulates prices, production volumes, inventories, and labor-management relations (*Han'guk Ilbo*, 1986b). The Federation of Korean Industries, along with four other federations representing business, wanted Korea's new constitution to minimize government interference in the economy [as well as to support infant and growth industries, to promote harmonious labor relations, and to deny labor the right to participate in management decision-making (*Maeil Kyŏngje Sinmun*, 1986d)]. There appears to be no study on industrial licensing in Korea, but for a review of government regulation of licensing, see *Donga Ilbo* (1987).

government liberalized imports; to compensate the chaebol, the government rewarded big business with freer financial markets.

Trade Liberalization

To assess the openness of Korean trade after liberalization is as hard as assessing godliness in a reformed heretic. As the World Bank pointed out,

> the automatic approval concept—whereby import items are transferred from a restricted to a nonrestricted list—is imperfect: [It] suggests more openness than it actually measures because items so designated may still be subject to some other possible administrative review procedures, such as the Special Law mechanism. Thus, the conventional "AA ratio" is biased upwards. (World Bank, 1987, vol. 1, p. 63)

Nevertheless, the World Bank believed that Korea had, in fact, liberalized trade: "Korea's liberalization program is very much on track, and government merits unequivocal high marks for its effective implementation." (1987, vol. 1, p. 74)

The United States disagreed. It took a lively interest in the matter in 1987 by virtue of a $7 billion U.S. trade deficit with Korea, which simultaneously ran a $7 billion trade deficit with Japan. The U.S. government pressured the Korean government to liberalize imports, which Korea did only by increasing imports from Japan (Korea Traders Association, 1987; Amsden and Min, 1989). According to a U.S. Embassy report, the extent to which Korea liberalized was fictitious:

> Use of the word "liberalization" in reference to Korea's shifting items off its restricted list is somewhat misleading in the first place. At the time of their "liberalization," duties on the 104 items "liberalized at U.S. request" averaged 33%, with none subject to duties of less than 20%, and many subject to duties of 30%, 40%, or 50%. Generally, other NTB's [nontariff barriers] (e.g., the rule that only Korean cosmetics manufacturers can import cosmetics) remained in place. (1986, p. 3)

Besides, of the 104 items that both sides agreed were "liberalized," the total value, according to the U.S. Embassy, was only 6% of the *growth* in Korean exports to the United States in a three-year period.

Financial Liberalization

In exchange for whatever trade liberalization actually occurred, the big business groups won critical concessions from the government in

the area of finance. (The United States also pressured Korea to liberalize its financial system.) First, the government reduced regulation of nonbank financial intermediaries (NBFIs), many of which had
long been controlled by the big business groups. [According to one
study, the chaebol had "controlling interest in some NBFIs such as
insurance companies and investment and finance companies" (Y. J.
Cho and Cole, 1986, p. 14).] As a consequence of deregulation, the
share of total deposit liabilities held by NBFIs increased from 27%
in 1980 to 42% at the end of 1984 (Ministry of Finance, quoted in
World Bank, 1987, vol. 1, p. 89). Second, the government began to
denationalize commercial banks in 1981 by divesting its shares. It
also restricted single shareholders of nationwide commercial banks
(except for joint venture banks) to 8% of total ownership, to prevent
the banking industry from being controlled by big business groups.

Shortly thereafter, it became clear that the government had by no
means altogether relinquished administrative control over the banking system.[18] It had also become clear that the big business groups
had not been prevented from taking equity control. Cho and Cole
remarked in a footnote in their study of financial liberalization:[19]

> While an effort was made to limit concentration of ownership
> by the private purchasers of these shares, it is widely believed
> that the large conglomerate groups . . . succeeded in gaining
> control of individual banks. (1986, p. 14f)

With increased deposits in the nonbank financial intermediaries
under chaebol ownership, and with their new major interests in national banks, the Korean big business groups became more like the
zaibatsu. They also became more liquid. They used their new financial resources for at least two purposes: to buy state enterprises that
were being privatized and to buy financially troubled firms, sometimes at the government's instigation.[20] One group, Sunkyong, was
catapulted into the league of the Big Ten chaebol as a result of the
privatization of a public oil refinery. In the 1980s, the chaebol grew
almost exclusively through acquisitions (S. K. Kim, 1987).

The result of such buyouts was a rise in economic concentration.

[18] According to the World Bank, "Government still has strong leverage over firms,
primarily because financial liberalization has not yet produced real banking auton-
omy" (World Bank, 1987, mimeo, vol. 2, p. 82).

[19] Son (1987) discussed how the chaebol circumvented legislation to limit their holdings of bank equity to not more than 8%. Son also gave figures on the extent of
private ownership of major commercial banks, local banks, life insurance companies,
and securities firms.

[20] For example, the government forced the Ssangyong group to acquire a bankrupt
textile-machinery manufacturing company employing about 400 workers in the interests of preserving the textile machinery industry in Korea.

As indicated in Table 5.3, the relative value of shipments produced under competitive market conditions declined between 1977 and 1982, whereas it had held fairly steady throughout the rise of heavy industry in the 1970s.[21] The increase in concentration was especially sharp at the aggregate level. As Table 5.1 indicates, the share of manufacturing output of the largest business groups rose from 32.8% in 1979, the year of the second energy crisis and the end of the Big Push, to 67.4% in 1984. This increase in aggregate concentration was about the same in percentage points as between 1974 and 1979, when one would have expected concentration to rise as a consequence of capital-intensive investments. *Liberalization, therefore, contributed to a rise, not to a decline, in economic concentration.* Nor should this have been unexpected. It is difficult to achieve equity through market forces in the presence of large agglomerations of economic power.

CONCLUSION

The big business groups in Korea were the product of a harmony of interests between the state and private enterprise. Private business groups, driven by what may have been a lack of technological capability to expand into higher quality niches, diversified widely into the bottom end and middle level of many markets; fairly close coordination of financial and labor flows among group members allowed this. The state supported such diversification because it promised to provide the clout necessary for Korea to penetrate deep into world markets and to compete against the big business groups of Japan (which provided a model that the Korean president consciously followed). Such harmony has stood at the heart of "Korea, Inc."

By the mid 1980s, the top ten chaebol accounted for almost 70% of GNP, yet out of the interstices of ultra high aggregate economic concentration has come rapid increases in GNP and productivity. As noted in earlier chapters, productivity rose against a backdrop of government discipline of big business, in the form of pressures to export, price controls, restrictions on capacity expansions and entry into certain markets, prohibitions on sending speculative capital overseas, and sweeping financial controls. An additional backdrop to rising productivity was provided by competition, which was stimulated by fast growth, rivalry among the big business groups, and oligopoly rather than monopoly at the industry level. Learners-cum-oligopolists competed for government favors, the most favorable foreign licenses, and the best managers, engineers, and workers.

In the 1980s, however, the government's forcefulness and credi-

[21] It is unlikely that the rise in concentration between 1977 and 1982 was confined to 1978, the year before stabilization and liberalization began.

bility declined and the private business groups augmented their power, prompting popular demands for reform. The response on the part of the government of Chun Doo Hwan was market "liberalization."

Nevertheless, big business grew even bigger and concentration increased further as a result of liberalization measures in Korea. As indicated in Table 5.1, aggregate economic concentration doubled in less than five years after liberalization was introduced in 1979. The ownership (if not the control) of commercial banks fell from government hands into those of the private sector. As the World Bank observed in a footnote in one of its reports: "There are, perhaps surprisingly, some similarities between Korea's and Chile's reforms. In both cases, big conglomerates bought major interests in the national banks" (1987, p. 82f).

In the presence of large concentrations of market power, reliance on the market mechanism for reform appears to produce some perverse results, not just in Latin America but also in the Far East.

CHAPTER SIX

Getting Relative Prices "Wrong": A Summary

FAILURE OF THE MARKET PARADIGM

Korea is an example of a country that grew very fast and yet violated the canons of conventional economic wisdom. There are many ways to analyze industrial expansion, but most can be grouped into one of two grand approaches—market oriented or institutional. It is well recognized among economists that the market-oriented approach represents a coherent body of economic "laws" or tendencies. Although these laws have largely been formulated to explain resource allocation or economic efficiency, rather than economic growth, they are considered sufficiently dynamic to analyze industrial expansion. So deep is the belief in the explanatory power of these laws, so firmly held the conviction that if, and only if, they are free to operate will industrial expansion succeed, that any departure from them, whether in theory or practice, tends to be discredited, dismissed, disregarded, or disbelieved. If industrial expansion succeeds, success is typically interpreted as being a validation of market principles and the institutions financially supporting them. If it fails, failure is seen as a result of the violation of market principles, perpetrated by perverse institutions.

In Korea, instead of the market mechanism allocating resources and guiding private entrepreneurship, the government made most of the pivotal investment decisions. Instead of firms operating in a competitive market structure, they each operated with an extraordinary degree of market control, protected from foreign competition. Nevertheless, most economists who recognize these realities greet them with an unfailing faith in market laws. They suppose that while state interference in Korea is pervasive, the economy operates with a set of relative prices that is not greatly distorted. In fact, little evidence supports this presumption. As was explained in Chapter 1 and illustrated in Chapter 3, not only has Korea not gotten relative prices right, it has deliberately gotten them "wrong."

Nor is Korea an isolated case. It is part of a general group of countries that I have termed *late industrializers*. These are countries that either just before or during the twentieth century began to grow from agricultural economies to industrial ones at what are now considered to be rapid rates. In Asia, the group includes Japan, Korea, and Taiwan (although not the city-states of Hong Kong and Singapore, which never transformed themselves from an agrarian base). Beyond Asia, other late industrializers are Brazil, Turkey, India, Mexico, and possibly Argentina. There is, of course, disparity in the economic record even among them, and what makes Korea especially interesting is its sterling performance. Just as their growth rates differ, so do the institutions of these emulating countries. Nevertheless, in broad respects the institutions of late industrializers have exhibited the same central tendencies, to the extent that an economic paradigm can be identified that is institutional in character and categorically distinct from the market model. It is suggested here, therefore, that the economies of these late-industrializing countries behave according to economic laws that constitute a new paradigm.

THE INSUFFICIENCY OF THE SCHUMPETERIAN ALTERNATIVE

There is nothing unique in offering an alternative to the venerable market model. The Schumpeterian view of industrial expansion is one such alternative, and it has commanded the respect of many economists to the degree that it is regarded by them as more than an appendage to traditional theory. Nevertheless, the Schumpeterian world view pertains to a set of socioeconomic conditions that originated in the Second Industrial Revolution. It was these historically specific conditions that inspired Schumpeter's ideas. These conditions were defined by the rise of the modern industrial enterprise—what Chandler calls the *multidivisional firm*—operating large-scale plants on the basis of managerial hierarchies. Simultaneously, the conditions included a transition from invention, which is defined here as the hallmark of the First Industrial Revolution, to innovation, defined here as the hallmark of the Second. At the time Schumpeter was writing, technical discoveries had ceased to be the property of individual inventors owning and managing small-scale firms and had begun to be commercialized on a massive scale by big business.

Late industrialization shares some of the conditions of industrialization in Schumpeter's period. It is also characterized by multidivisional firms operating large-scale plants on the basis of managerial hierarchies. Furthermore, big business, although organizationally distinct, is no less the dominant force that it was in the economic expansions that rocked Germany and the United States starting in the 1880s. However, what is conspicuously absent from late industrialization is innovation. Late industrialization, as defined in the foregoing chapters, is devoid of innovation and occurs on the basis of learning. Learning involves borrowing, adapting, and improving upon foreign designs. The Schumpeterian model provides insights into the process of late industrialization, but it cannot penetrate a process of industrial expansion in which the dynamic of new technical discoveries is missing. Thus, while there is nothing unique in offering an alternative to the venerable market model, the alternative that is offered here to explain late industrialization differs from any offered before.

THE HISTORICAL RECORD: DELIBERATELY GETTING RELATIVE PRICES "WRONG"

In honor of one crucial difference between the two paradigms—the market oriented and the institutional—one may use the terms *market conforming* and *market augmenting* to describe their respective overarching policies. In the context of late industrialization, market conformance refers to the minimum amount of government intervention necessary to get relative prices right. In "backward" countries some government intervention is believed to be necessary to correct existing market distortions, and proponents of the traditional view hold such distortions responsible for the delay in growth. The government is supposed to intervene only to liberalize markets from its own controls. Thus, Korea's economic success is attributed to a series of liberalizations introduced just prior to "takeoff." In or around 1965, the Korean won was devalued, interest rates were raised, tariffs were lowered, and taxes were increased (similar reforms were introduced in Taiwan).

As Fischer has noted, "A big event *must* have big results, we think. But this is the fallacy of identity" (1970, p. 223). The view that growth followed liberalization is based on such a fallacy. The events comprising liberalization occurred, but in conjunction with other policies, so that the logic driving Korean industrialization was not the freeing of markets. The historical record looks different depending on which paradigm one chooses. The historical interpretation set out in the foregoing chapters is the one that is summarized below.

The histories of late-industrializing countries differ. Those of Japan and Korea, for example, differ to the degree that one was the other's colony. But even among former colonies, there are differences. The involuntary "modernization" of Korea by Japan, although subject to exaggeration, has possibly given Korea an edge over other backward countries in terms of physical infrastructure in basic industry. Nevertheless, all late-industrializing countries that are former colonies tend to share the characteristic of a long history during which their economies were subject to free trade and to the pursuit of static comparative advantage, usually agricultural. From this perspective, the delay in growth in late-industrializing countries arose not from distorted prices but rather from the exemplary play of market forces. Growth began to accelerate when the central authority, once too weak to defend itself against foreign aggression, became strong enough to mediate market forces to advantage. In Korea, this transformation from weak state to strong state took almost a century. At the end of that period, and of foreign rule, South Korea had been separated from its northern half and was soon ruled by an oversized army, both the consequences of the Cold War.

Come the 1950s, Korea benefited from U.S. aid, even though most of it was designated for consumption and the aid designated for projects was subject to poor administration on both sides. The Korean economy was also routinely subject to interference from U.S. aid advisors, who put stability before growth when a century of Korean history suggested the precondition of growth for stability. The military government that seized power in a coup in May 1961, therefore, inherited a depressed economy, partly as a consequence of tough stabilization measures imposed in the late 1950s. The new government began by nationalizing all banks—aid advisors having persuaded Syngman Rhee to denationalize the banking system in the 1950s—and introducing emergency measures to stimulate the economy. These measures rekindled inflation (to around 30%) and were hostilely received by the aid administration. The liberalization reforms may be seen as an appeasement in reaction to threats by aid advisors to withhold food assistance until Korea deflated.

This period in Korea's history has been mined for information on the origins of Korea's economic miracle. Few studies, however, have descended to the industry level where more detailed information exists. In Chapter 3, we examined this period in Korea's history through the lens of its leading sector, cotton spinning and weaving.

In this industry one sees what for Korea at the time were integrated, large-scale firms employing management techniques that were modern by the standards of other industries. Firms were organized into a cartel that wielded substantial political power. However, in the early 1960s, the industry was suffering from excess capacity, not necessarily because import substitution had outgrown its "easy" stage but because most textiles firms had built excess capacity to take advantage of subsidized U.S. aid-related loans in the 1950s.

An analysis of the cotton textile industry sheds light on some long-standing debates in development economics. One debate relates to the role that aid advisors and the Bretton Woods institutions played in persuading Korea (and Taiwan) to orient their economies toward what were considered to be more market-conforming export activity. In this regard, it is noteworthy that cotton spinners and weavers were *prohibited* by U.S. law from exporting until the mid-1960s. Congress did not want countries receiving U.S.-subsidized raw cotton to export cotton products. Thus, the United States can hardly be credited with consistent support of export-oriented growth.

Another debate relates to the market-conforming paradigm, which says that countries need only get relative prices right and follow their comparative advantage in order to export. Pre–World War II history provides no example of an emulator that used relatively low wages as the exclusive entree into world markets. Neither Germany nor the United States overtook Britain on such a footing. They overtook it on the basis of superior technology and organization. As for Japan, it invaded Lancashire's markets for textiles in the 1920s on the basis of better trading companies to procure raw cotton, more modern equipment, and a more integrated process flow, as well as on the basis of lower wages. Beginning with Korea and Taiwan, late-industrializing countries were the first to attempt to penetrate world export markets with little more competitive advantage than low wages. As such, they represented a truly new international economic order.

However, analysis of Korean cotton-spinning and weaving firms suggests that they found low wages insufficient as a basis on which to compete against Japan. Even in a relatively labor-intensive industry like cotton textiles, which indisputably gave the comparative advantage to low-wage, "backward" countries, firms appear to have required subsidies to begin to compete in world markets. The Korean government offered generous subsidies to stimulate exports, including subsidized long-term loans to targeted industries and firms that are not included in calculations of the "effective exchange rate." This rate, therefore, understates the true degree of government support. The Korean government offered generous subsidies first as a response to the political demands of the spinners' and weavers' cartel, later as an article of faith in an industrialization strategy.

The subsidy serves as a symbol of late industrialization, not just in Korea and Taiwan but also in Japan, the Latin American countries, and so on. The First Industrial Revolution was built on laissez-faire, the Second on infant industry protection. In late industrialization, the foundation is the subsidy—which includes both protection and financial incentives. The allocation of subsidies has rendered the government not merely a banker, as Gerschenkron (1962) conceived it, but an entrepreneur, using the subsidy to decide what, when, and how much to produce. The subsidy has also changed the process whereby relative prices are determined.

Industrial expansion depends on savings and investment, but in "backward" countries especially, savings and investment are in conflict over the ideal interest rate, high in one case, low in the other. In Korea and other late-industrializing countries, this conflict has been mediated by the subsidy. Throughout most of the twenty-five years of Korean industrial expansion, long-term credit has been allocated by the government to selected firms at negative real interest rates in order to stimulate specific industries. The high real interest-rate policy that started in 1965—in the spirit of liberalization—ended in 1972 with a return to low real interest rates. However, even during those seven years, domestic savings were never sufficient to meet investment demand. The government, therefore, arranged long-term international credit for favored firms at rates far below those obtainable domestically. Thus, the government established multiple prices for loans, only one of which could possibly have been "right" according to the law of supply and demand. Moreover, the most critical price—that for long-term credit—was wildly "wrong" in a capital-scarce country, its real price, due to inflation, being negative.[1]

As for the foreign exchange rate, another key relative price in economic expansion, it has also been deliberately distorted by late industrializers, which need a high rate to export and a low rate to repay foreign debt and to import raw materials and producer goods that cannot yet be produced domestically. In Korea, exchange rates were not grossly distorted, but they did succeed in stimulating exports only when they operated in conjunction with other policies. Exports have been heavily subsidized and coerced, so inside the range of reasonableness, the relative price of foreign exchange has been altogether irrelevant. According to a survey of exporters in the mid-1970s that was conducted under the aegis of the World Bank, over half of the respondents claimed that export quotas had a negative overall effect on their firms. Exporters, however, were compensated for having to export by being allowed to sell in the domestic market

---

[1] Multiple exchange rates and multiple interest rates are possible, in principle, in the neoclassical general equilibrium model (see Arrow and Hahn, 1971). The strictures in the text, however, are directed against the IMF's and World Bank's policy prescriptions in which multiple interest rates and exchange rates are anathema, and which insist on a single, unique exchange rate or interest rate, presumably on the ground that this is the "equilibrium" rate.

at inflated prices. Such prices were distorted due to protection. Thus, tariff barriers and nontariff barriers have comprised a key ingredient in Korea's industrial policy. Even imports "liberalized" in the mid-1980s are subject to an average tariff rate that may approximate 30%.

WHEN "WRONG" IS RIGHT

Although Korea industrialized on the basis of relative prices that deviated sharply from free-market equilibria, such prices were less "distorted" and provided big business with fewer bonanzas than prices in India, Turkey, and the Latin American late-industrializing countries. Why?

If one believes that Korea began to grow rapidly in the 1960s as a result of "liberalization," then its adoption of relatively freer prices must be attributed to an embrace of market theory by Korean policymakers, coached by foreign experts. Yet an examination of cotton textiles suggested that the policy regime that Korea eventually adopted evolved out of a complex process in which the interests of opposing groups were reconciled, not out of theoretical conviction. One dimension of this conflict was a strong enough government to impose performance standards on the interest groups receiving public support. The insistence on performance standards by the government induced a level of productivity, and willingness to invest on the part of the private sector, that made greater price "distortions" unnecessary, and the ample price "distortions" that did exist more effective.

Therefore, it may be said that growth has been faster in Korea not because markets have been allowed to operate more freely but because the subsidization process has been qualitatively superior: reciprocal in Korea, unidirectional in most other cases.

THE DISCIPLINARY MECHANISM

Economic paradigms are largely defined by the internal mechanism that is built into them to exert discipline over firm behavior. In the case of the market paradigm, discipline is dispensed by the invisible hand. With the subsequent erosion of competitive market structures that were consistent with the market paradigm, Schumpeter analyzed a new basis for competition, a new mechanism to discipline firm behavior. He recognized such a disciplinarian in technological change. It was the creative gales of new technological discoveries that uprooted old monopolies and increased productivity, not steadily but in great spurts.

There is no mechanism in the market-augmenting paradigm that is equivalent to the invisible hand or to technological change. To the extent that oligopolists the world over compete, oligopolists in late-industrializing countries also compete, although the dimensions that they compete along relate to their status as learners. However, there is no neat mechanism in the market-augmenting paradigm that can be relied on to drive firms to be productive, because growth itself does not happen automatically. Growth in late-industrializing countries depends on government intervention to augment supply and demand.

Few aspiring emulators of the Korean expansion appreciate just how diverse subsidies have been, just how pervasive protection is, and just how encouraging government support continues to be in Korea, including bailouts and expansionary rather than contractionary policies in times of external shock (see the discussion in Chapter 4). With such discretionary power under the control of mere mortals, two questions arise: What mechanism will discipline subsidy recipients? And no less pertinent, What mechanism will discipline the donor of subsidies, the awesome state itself?

All paradigms have their hidden premises, a large number of firms confronting one another in the same industry in the case of the market-conforming paradigm, an undulating stream of new technological discoveries in the case of Schumpeter's. Although the market-augmenting paradigm does not have an automatic disciplinary device, it nonetheless has a premise on which industrial expansion depends. The premise of late industrialization is a reciprocal relation between the state and the firm. This does not simply mean close cooperation, which is sometimes the way business-government relations in Korea and Japan are simplistically depicted. Nor does it simply mean that sometimes the government wields the carrot and at other, unrelated times, the stick. It means that in direct exchange for subsidies, the state exacts certain performance standards from firms. The more reciprocity that characterizes state-firm relations in these countries, the higher the speed of economic growth.

Reciprocity in Korea was in no way free of corruption. No business in Korea could survive for the past forty years if it challenged the government politically. None could make it big if it did not support the government financially. Yet for all the venality, the evidence presented in later chapters suggests that beginning in the 1960s, the government's favorite pets—the big business groups that came to account for so large a share of GNP—were outstanding performers from the production and operations perspective. What with export targets—an objective, transparent criterion by which firm performance is easily judged—price controls, restrictions on capacity expansions, limits on market entry, prohibitions on capital flight, restraints on tax evasion, and government control over the banking system, the big business groups had to deliver.

The presence of discipline in Korea and its absence elsewhere does not reflect differential abilities among policymakers. It reflects differences in state power. The state in Korea was able to consolidate its strength with respect to both business and labor for what appear to be historical reasons. In the early 1960s there were no financiers to challenge the government's power because the state-owned banking system of the colonial period was renationalized; the business community was as weak as the financial community and beholden to the state for largesse; the working classes were small in number; and the countryside, through a land reform, was devoid of large landholders. In other late-industrializing countries such landholders challenge the state's authority or seduce it into rent-seeking. It is no coincidence that growth has been especially fast in Japan, Korea, and Taiwan, countries which all have reciprocal subsidy systems and which all have had land reforms.

Finally, it bears emphasizing that Korea has grown very rapidly and has done so on the basis of nationally owned firms. Even the first liberalization that the Korean economy underwent—in the mid-1960s—was notable for its omission of market-conforming measures that would have allowed an inflow of direct foreign investment. Korea, at the time, was too fearful of Japanese competition to open its doors to foreign equity ownership. There are fewer multinationals in Korea than in almost any other late-industrializing country, possibly even India. This has almost certainly made it easier for the state to discipline private sector firms, not least of all in the buildup of a domestic science and technology capability.

DEVELOPMENTALISM: A RESEARCH AGENDA

It is frustrating to model builders in "backward" countries to learn that Korea's success rests heavily on a strong state (one that is capable of implementing its own policies). It is frustrating because countries are "backward" mostly because their state is weak, an argument taken up in the first two chapters. The beauty of the market-conforming paradigm supposedly lies in its minimalist requirements of state activity. In principle, it promises industrial expansion if the state is strong enough merely to provide enough political stability for long-term investments, to point prices in the right direction, and then to exit.

Nevertheless, it would be altogether ahistorical to think that getting relative prices "right" requires any less strength on the state's part than getting them "wrong." "Backward" countries in search of a model to guide them do not present themselves as a tabula rasa. They have entrenched interest groups that would be hurt if relative prices were "freed" of distortions. Devaluations hurt firms by raising the cost of imported inputs. Upward adjustments in interest rates hurt investors. Equating of revenues and expenditures in the government budget threatens the livelihood of social welfare recipients, and so on. Whether one attributes the acceleration of growth in Taiwan and Korea to getting relative prices right or wrong, either outcome required strong state management, which is precisely what "backward" countries lack.

The policies that comprise the market-augmenting paradigm are heterogeneous, in keeping with the diverse tasks that states must perform to accelerate growth. In "backward" countries, the level of international competition, the technology gap, the investment barriers and savings deficiencies, are all so problematic that, without government intervention, little ever gets done to address these hurdles. The art is to get something done *with* intervention. A strong state is as dysfunctional as a weak one if it uses its power only to enrich itself. What, then, will discipline the state?

A disciplined (or developmental) state refers to one that advances capital rather than accumulating it, or at least does not allow its own enrichment to derail the development effort, as in Korea. The rise of developmentalism, as well as the relationship between it and democracy, eludes easy explanation (unenlightened much by the classical economists who focused on "rent-seeking" by private business, not the state). External threat, militarism, and few raw materials may have predisposed the Korean and Taiwan states to industrialize, but a state like Chiang Kai-Shek's refused to spend a dime on economic development until Taiwan demonstrated its economic potential (and retaking the Mainland proved fanciful) (Amsden, 1985). What remains to be analyzed in Korea's case is why, led by the student movement, the population has revolted at a low threshold of tolerance against states that overly abuse their power.

The relationship between developmentalism and democracy is complex, because reciprocity in the allocation of subsidies requires a strong state vis a vis business, not necessarily labor. What awaits systematic analysis is how much labor repression is critical for rapid growth. This question is intriguing in Korea's case because, as discussed in Chapter 8, average real wages have risen faster in Korea than in all other late-, and possibly earlier, industrializing countries.

COMPETITION IN LATE INDUSTRIALIZATION AND THE GROWTH DYNAMIC

Partly as a consequence of the theorocentric interpretations that many Western economists gave of Japanese economic growth, recognition of a unique economic paradigm in late industrialization was slow in coming. A major study undertaken by Kazushi Ohkawa and Henry Rosovsky was reasonable enough in its objective: "To fit Japan's experience into an historical growth model of the type familiar to economists" (1973, p. 1). A volume on "Asia's new giant," edited for the Brookings Institution, went further: "We gently suggest that Japanese growth was not miraculous: *it can be reasonably well understood and explained by ordinary economic causes*" (Patrick and Rosovsky, 1976, p. 6; my italics). A spin-off from the Brookings study went even further. After noting the oligopolistic practices that Japanese industrial policy had encouraged, it concluded: "We cannot detect any compensating gains" (Caves and Uekusa, 1976, p. 157). The message was that Japan might have grown even faster had it conformed to the market model. Yet this message is doctrinaire and misleading—the former because there is no evidence that Japan could have performed better had it allowed the free play of market forces; the latter because there is no evidence that free market forces could have achieved what Japan achieved.

Recognition that Japan's political economy was different from that inherited from either the First or Second Industrial Revolutions came from a political scientist, Chalmers Johnson, who wrote a history of MITI (1982). Johnson, however, explored Japan's uniqueness from the political angle and saw the economic side of political economy as merely conforming to the traditional market norms.[2] Understandably impervious to the issue of whether Japan had gotten relative prices right or wrong, Johnson associated market conformance with productivity and competition:

> The third element of the [Japanese] model is the perfection of market-conforming methods of state intervention in the economy. In implementing its industrial policy, the state must take care to preserve competition to as high a degree as is compatible with its priorities. . . . One clear lesson from the Japanese case is that the state needs the market, and private enterprise needs the state; once both sides recognized this, cooperation was possible, and high-speed growth occurred. (1982, p. 318)

[2] But see Johnson (1988) on the obtuseness of economists regarding the realities of Japan's political economy.

What Johnson took as evidence of market conformance was an industrial-licensing policy that favored oligopoly over monopoly. In Korea, too, most markets are oligopolistic rather than monopolistic (in terms of both shipments and number of commodities), few taking the extreme of either a single seller or of many. From this perspective, the relationship between the market-augmenting and market-conforming paradigms is complementary (see Table 5.3).

Nevertheless, one need not understand competition and productivity in late-industrializing countries in terms of industry structure. One may understand more about them in terms of lateness. In fact, markets in most advanced countries are oligopolistic. Competition in these countries, however, may be less intense than in Japan or Korea. One must, therefore, probe deeper than industry-level market structure to comprehend the competitive behavior of Japanese and Korean oligopolists. When one does, one recognizes the existence of a distinctive firm structure—the diversified business group—and a distinctive growth dynamic—that of cumulative causality between productivity and output.

The market-augmenting paradigm of late industrialization may now be extended as follows, by way of summarizing the discussion in Chapters 4 and 5. The government initiates growth by using the subsidy to distort relative prices. Then big business implements state policy. The role of small firms varies by industry, but basically the process of industrialization through learning involves the subordination of small firms to large ones in subcontractual relationships (until a turning point is reached when the state begins to support small-scale firms in the hopes of stimulating innovation). Oligopoly at the industry level and high aggregate economic concentration equip leading firms with the market power to survive the hardships of late entry. Two behavioral patterns are associated with high concentration in the learning context. First, once growth gets underway, there is little reason for the big business groups to collude and every reason for them to compete in a wide array of industries in order to maintain parity with one another in their overall size. *Competition tends to be a consequence of growth,* not a cause of it. Second, high concentration permits high rates of investment embodying foreign technology, the realization of scale economies, and the cumulation of output in a small subset of firms, thereby facilitating learning-by-doing. *Growth contains the seeds to increase productivity,* and increased productivity raises output further in an upward spiral.

To understand variations in growth rates among late-industrializing countries, therefore, one must explore two key institutions: the reciprocity between big business and the state (as discussed earlier);

and the internal and external behavior of the diversified business group, as summarized below.

THE DIVERSIFIED BUSINESS GROUP

The diversified business group is found in Japan, Korea, India, Taiwan, Brazil, Turkey, and other late-industrializing countries. Of course, not all diversified business groups in late-industrializing countries perform equally well, their degree of success being partly due to environment. Not all states are as solicitous of big business as are Japan or Korea. Nor are they as stern with it. The diversified business group is a variant of the modern industrial enterprise that is found in every industrialized country and that is multidivisional, comprised of large-scale production units, and managed hierarchically. Yet the diversified business group in late-industrializing countries is unique in that it is more diversified in unrelated products than the modern industrial enterprise on the one hand, and more centrally coordinated than the conglomerate on the other (in terms of intra-group flows of both human and financial capital). Its broad diversification and central coordination were explained in Chapter 5 as functions of lateness. Korea's business groups may have diversified widely because they had no technical expertise to build upon in related products or in higher quality product niches. Their widely diversified structures complemented their strategy to compete at the bottom end of many markets. In their diversification efforts, they had the full support of the government because the government's vision of industrialization fixated on bigness, and bigness and diversification overlap.

The chaebol were able to manage their diverse holdings by virtue of their ability to borrow abroad and buy industry-specific technical expertise from foreigners. This allowed them to grow very large, at first "organically," and at the same time remain under the control of their original family founders. The chaebol soon became the most progressive firms and attracted the best-salaried supervisors, managers, and engineers. A continuity in ownership and control contributed to a uniform group culture and a centralized knowledge of group resources. Both facilitated the intragroup transfer of money and personnel. *An economy of scope arose in the form of the capability to diversify.* Entering new industries at minimum cost and at lightning speed raised the firm's ability to compete in many markets. With state subsidies and a diversified structure, the chaebol became willing and able to undertake risk.

Government controls in commodity markets in Korea largely precluded the chaebol competing against one another on price. Like other oligopolists, they tend to compete on nonprice variables—quality, delivery, location. They also competed on those specific nonprice variables peculiar to learners: the best foreign technical licenses, the best labor, and most of all, the fattest state subsidies. By building a meritocratic element into its system of awarding subsidies, the state extracted from the chaebol—an institution of possibly unprecedented market power—a growth rate of output and productivity that may also have been unprecedented.

However one wishes to explain such results, one cannot do so by "ordinary economic causes." The forces of supply and demand, of course, do not cease whatever the paradigm, but the institutions that manage them are subject to change.

THE GROWTH-PRODUCTIVITY DYNAMIC IN LATE INDUSTRIALIZATION

The 1970s in Korea witnessed rapid increases in output as well as a transformation of Korea's industrial structure. GNP grew at an average annual rate of 9%, and exports grew by a phenomenal 28% (deflated by the U.S. wholesale price index). The heavy industries increased their share of manufacturing output from 40% in 1971 to 56% in 1980. Their share of manufactured exports over the same period tripled. To finance investments in the heavy industries, Korea borrowed abroad. Total debt rose from $4.3 billion to $20.5 billion during the Big Push. Nevertheless, total debt as a percent of GNP remained constant at the beginning and end of the Big Push, from 34% in 1972 to 32% in 1979. Korea's economy was sufficiently productive that a big increase in debt did not result in a heavier debt burden.

The productivity of the new industrial sectors may be understood partly as having been a function of their rapid growth. In response to the state's market-augmenting policies, firms invested more in new plant and equipment that embodied technology from abroad. This investment may be expected to have raised output per person employed. As firms expanded further in response to a growing market for their output, they also became more capable of importing the best foreign technology from the viewpoint of economies of scale. So productivity may be expected to have increased further. Finally, as the cumulative output of firms increased (at first under the tutelage of foreign technical assistance, later under local management), and as firms repeated the same task again and again and discovered process improvements, they may be expected to have raised productivity as a consequence of learning-by-doing. Initially, learning-by-doing may not have taken the form of fine-tuning. It may only have been of the type where, at the plant level, the production process was brought under control and, at the group level, the capability to diversify and to execute projects was advanced. Yet, with any luck, a firm was able to repeat a successful process and to continue to raise productivity interactively with growth, the one triggering the other.

In theory then, we have a dynamic that is quite distinct because industrializing on the basis of foreign technology rather than innovation is also quite distinct. In the case of the former, not only does higher productivity generate higher growth; higher growth also generates higher productivity by means of learning-by-doing, economies of scale, and investments embodying foreign designs. The growth-productivity dynamic in late industrialization is a closed loop involving the cumulative causality of productivity and output. As such, it differs from the dynamic that supposedly drives economic growth in the market model, a model that is focused on new technical discoveries, and one in which higher productivity generates higher growth, but higher growth does not generate higher productivity.

One may conclude by saying that the market-augmenting paradigm comprises a set of institutions and associated patterns of behavior, and that Korea has been a prime example of those patterns and institutions at work. Out of a highly politicized process of resource allocation, there has arisen a diversified economic base and a fast growth rate of output. Given rapid rates of industrial expansion, and out of a high degree of market power at the industry and aggregate levels, intense competition among leading producers and rapid increases in productivity have arisen. One may object to the implied perversities of such relationships, for fast growth is an unexpected consequence of government intervention, high productivity is an unexpected effect of fast growth, and competition is an unexpected outcome of monopoly. Nevertheless, perversity has a long tradition in economic theory. The Schumpeterian paradigm teases innovation out of monopoly power. The market-conforming paradigm turned moral philosophy on its head with the proposition that society benefits the most when each individual indulges in the most selfish behavior. What could be more Hegelian?

"WRONG" PRICES, RIGHT DIRECTION?

Although Korea distorted its relative prices, it could still be said to have conformed to the market mechanism in pursuing its comparative advantage through international trade. Can one argue, therefore, that distortion of relative prices is acceptable so long as economic activity is directed toward exports? Korea provides a near-perfect laboratory to study this question, because its growth has been exceptionally fast and its share of exports in national product has possibly been higher than that of any country in recorded history (see Table 3.6). Nor is the positive association between economic growth—meaning industrial expansion—and exports—meaning manufactured exports—limited to Korea. According to Feder,

> Empirical comparisons of countries tend to demonstrate that developing countries with favorable export growth records have generally enjoyed higher rates of growth of national income than other developing countries. (1986, p. 72)

The implied causality of the regression findings inclines one to examine the relationship between exports and economic growth in historical context, to explore causality further. Korea's export history falls into two phases, an early one from roughly 1965 to 1975 centered on labor-intensive manufactures (cotton textiles, apparel, plywood, wigs, and consumer electronics), and a later one from, say, 1976 onward centered on more skill- and capital-intensive manufactures (ships, steel, machinery, automobiles, and computer electronics). Assuming causality in the regression findings, the exporter of light manufactures ought to have prepared the ground for heavy manufacturing. One may expect two types of externalities from export activity, economic and technomanagerial. With respect to the latter, Feder wrote,

> An argument can be made for significant *inter*sectoral externalities. These follow from the beneficial effects of export activities on other sectors in the economy through the development of efficient and internationally competitive management, the introduction of improved production techniques, the training of skilled workers, and the spillover consequences of scale expansion. (1986, p. 273)

The first externality, economic in nature, appears to have been strongly positive in Korea. The foreign exchange earned by exporting light manufactures almost certainly improved Korea's credit ratings, which helped it to raise capital abroad to finance its heavy industry investments and to service its loans. The employment and income generated by light manufactured exports, higher than what would probably have existed in their absence, created a boom that secured the military government's power and emboldened it to proceed with its plans to develop industry beyond the light manufacturing stage.

Contrary to Feder's belief, though, technomanagerial externalities in Korea were far less apparent. In the case of cotton spinning and weaving, unambiguously Korea's leading sector at the time, there were almost no technomanagerial externalities. Since all this is the subject of a later chapter, here the point to note is that there was no natural progression in any tangible, organizational sense from cotton spinning and weaving in particular and light manufactures in general to more complex industrial activity. The initiative to progress came from the government in the form of subsidies to further import substitution. Import substitution then permitted a diversification of export activity—sometimes immediately, as in the case of steel and ships, sometimes with a ten-year lag, as in the case of chemicals and machinery, and sometimes with a twenty-year delay, as in the case of automobiles.[3]

The argument that relative prices in Korea were distorted but in the right direction, that is, toward exports, is therefore itself distorted. Prices were distorted in all directions in Korea—both for import substitutes and for exports—and often for one and the same product in the two categories.

CONCLUSION

The market-conforming paradigm rests on two pillars: marginal productivity theory and the law of comparative advantage. Marginal productivity theory is the formal expression of getting relative prices right, which as just suggested, is the antithesis of what actually happens in late-industrializing countries. The second pillar—the law of comparative advantage (or relative costs)—expresses the idea that specialization enhances economic growth. However, it is argued in the following chapters that this second pillar cannot bear the weight of the facts of late industrialization either. The principle of specialization is fundamentally at variance with the logic of late industrialization—to diversify into more industries in order to catch up. It is to the realities of catching up at the firm level that attention returns.

[3] In decomposing the Korean growth rate into its constituent parts—exports, import substitutes, and domestic demand—Westphal (1978) and K. S. Kim and Roemer (1979) trivialized the importance of import-substitution activity because of the way they defined import substitution and ignored quality. Instead of defining import substitution as a stream of activities, corrected for quality changes, they defined it as a one-time event. For example, import substitution of automobiles would have been counted as such in only one year, when automobiles began to be assembled from knockdown kits with a very small total value. Moreover, if an automobile engine had been manufactured since the Korean War in a backyard garage, even when its quality was later improved to supply the domestic automobile industry and motors ceased to be imported, the transaction would still have been recorded as an expansion in domestic demand, not as import substitution.

PART II

Professional Management and Human Resources

CHAPTER SEVEN

The Rise of Salaried Engineers: Automobile Manufacturing

THE SALARIED ENGINEER AND FIRM DIFFERENTIATION

This chapter will look at the salaried engineer in Korea's late industrialization with respect to two extreme typologies: the small- and medium-size firm and the huge diversified business group. Between the two lies the specialized big business—principally in publishing, pharmaceuticals, and cotton spinning and weaving. These firms will be discussed in a separate chapter within the context of the cotton textile industry.

Since the late nineteenth century, industrialization has been executed by the salaried manager, including and increasingly the salaried engineer. As Chandler wrote:

> Large industrial enterprises with their teams of managers . . .
> appeared suddenly and simultaneously in the United States and
> Europe in the last decades of the nineteenth century [and a little
> later in Japan, only because Japan was later to industrialize].
> They came in industries with much the same characteristics, and
> they continued to compete and to grow in much the same man-
> ner. The enterprises that became major players did so by mak-
> ing a threefold investment in facilities and personnel. They made
> an investment in facilities and personnel in the new technologies
> of production large enough to achieve the cost advantages of
> the economies of scale and scope. They created national and
> international marketing and distribution networks that took over
> the functions of existing commercial intermediaries—the whole-
> salers, suppliers and distributors. Most essential of all, they re-
> cruited the managers necessary to coordinate the new processes
> of production and distribution. (1989: pp. 2–3)

As a consequence of this threefold investment, the modern industrial enterprise evolved into an institution that comprises large-scale operating units, is multidivisional—producing many related products—and is hierarchical—key decisions are made by salaried managers who occupy various consecutive layers of authority and gradually supersede owner-managers as chief executives.

There are, however, notable differences in the way firms are managed. As Chandler reminded us:

> There were striking differences among different nations in the numbers and size of these large integrated enterprises, in the ways in which they were managed, and the industrial sectors in which they were located. (1989, p. 8)

A defining characteristic of late industrialization is the abundant supply of managers salaried from the start of accelerated growth. They do not have to pass through the ranks of production workers as they did in past industrializations, but originate in the universities. As for the distinctive features of Korean (and Japanese) salaried managers, they have been a key factor in economic expansion, but they have not driven overhead costs through the roof. Despite rapid industrialization, the ratio of managers to production workers in Korea has remained relatively constant, engineers have grown in number relative to administrators, and the number of levels in the managerial hierarchy has been kept in check. These features of Korean management suggest themselves as major factors underlying Korea's successful industrial growth.

This chapter looks at one of Korea's proudest industries—automobile making—to begin examining a general hypothesis about shopfloor management that is carried further in later chapters. The hypothesis is that leading firms in late industrializing countries, if they are to penetrate world markets, must adopt unusually pro-active production and operations management policies. By pro-active we mean policies that assign high-quality managers to the shopfloor and inspire initiative on the part of such managers to develop the skills of the work force and to improve process performance. Otherwise the gap in productivity levels with leading firms in advanced countries will not be bridged while the advantage in wage levels narrows.

The rise of the modern industrial enterprise in the 1880s witnessed a continuation in the existence of small-scale firms. What has happened with each sequential industrialization is that the diversity of the firm population has increased. Technological change has transformed all industries, but some have been made more capital intensive, others more complex in terms of the number of stages in the production process or the difficulty of process control. The re-

sult has been a far greater *range* among firms than in previous periods with respect to size, integration, capital intensity, and the employment of managers. This appears to have encouraged the
emergence of subcontracting systems.

Another theme of this chapter, therefore, is relations between big
and small business through subcontracting. The small-scale firm has
been a relatively unimportant element in Korea's growth. As a sub-
contractor, however, the small scale firm is becoming pivotal. It is
through subcontracting relations that Korea's management system is
being generalized.

THE SMALL- AND MEDIUM-SIZE FIRM

The definition of small- and medium-size firms is not fixed and relates variously to assets, sales, and employment. In terms of number
of employees, the threshold of small- and medium-size firms in late
industrializing countries varies from 50 to 500. In Korea, the threshold is typically 300, yet a firm producing a single product and employing 1,000 workers is commonly thought of as medium-size or
even small by comparison with a large chaebol. However defined,
the category is a catchall, comprising firms ranging from a handful
of high-tech start-ups to thousands of backyard shops employing only
family workers.

Its conceptual fuzziness notwithstanding, the small- and medium-
size-firm sector has given rise to conjectures that are central to the
topic of late industrialization. One theory concerns the extent to which
small-scale capitalism can serve as the basis for achieving rapid economic expansion. An affirmative answer has been given by vision-
aries ranging from Proudhon to Ghandhi in the past and by scholars
of methods of appropriate technology and flexible specialization at
present.[1] Another conjecture regards the extent to which small- and
medium-scale firms can provide the germ from which large-scale firms
can grow. David Anderson has attempted to measure such germi-
nation, and his answer is as follows:

> The shares in employment expansion in the large industry group,
> attributable to the growth of small firms through the size distri-
> bution . . . [are]: Korea 40%, Taiwan 53%, Turkey 45%, Col-
> ombia 70%, Philippines 42%, and India 67%. (1982, p. 925)

Korea stands out because it falls at the bottom of the list. Taiwan commands attention because it has been idealized as a model of

---

[1] Sabel (1982) and Sabel and Zeitlin (1985) examined the alternatives to mass production, past and present. A landmark in the literature on productive small-scale
enterprise is by Piore and Sabel (1984).

Table 7.1   Percent Distribution of Manufacturing Value-Added[a] by Firm Size, 1973

Country	Number of Workers			
	1–9	10–99	100–499	500 or more
Korea	5.8	13.8	27.7	52.7
Taiwan[b]	4.4	16.7	22.5	56.4
Hong Kong	7.4	30.2	32.1	30.2
Brazil	3.4	23.7	36.1	36.6
Turkey[c]	11.7	10.1	27.5	48.4
Peru	4.0	23.9	46.4	25.7
Japan[d]	8.7	28.4	24.9	37.9
Canada[d]	2.0	21.1	37.4	39.3
Czechoslovakia	0.2	5.4	18.2	76.1
Austria	0.8	21.5	36.2	41.5
United Kingdom		15.7[e]	24.4	60.0
United States[d]	2.4	18.3	30.5	48.7

[a] Generally, value-added in producers' values.

[b] Value-added in factor values, 1971.

[c] 1970.

[d] Net value-added in factor values.

[e] 1–99.

Source: All countries except Taiwan: United Nations (1979). Taiwan: Executive Yuan, *The Report of Industrial and Commercial Census of Taiwan and Fukien, District of the Republic of China, 1971,* quoted in S. Ho (1980).

fast-growth-cum-small-scale capitalism.[2] Big business is presumed to be negligible in Taiwan, while the facts that its state is as strong as Korea's and that its real-wage increases are lower are ignored. In reality, large state enterprises in the early phases of development in Taiwan accounted for over half of industrial output, and even though their share declined over time, they were first movers in cement, iron and steel, shipbuilding, fertilizers, heavy machinery, machine tools, banking and insurance, and so on (Amsden, 1985). One could say, therefore, that in terms of value-added, large firms in Taiwan provided the basis for the growth of small firms, not vice versa (Amsden, 1989).

Table 7.1 provides some supporting evidence. The data show how value-added is distributed among firms of different size in different countries. The data for Taiwan are from a 1971 industrial census; the data for the remaining countries were compiled by the United Nations for a special survey of world industry in 1973. About that time both Korea and Taiwan were enjoying rapid economic expan-

[2] See, for example, Lau (1986).

sion and were on the point of deepening their industrial structures. What is interesting is that of all the developing countries for which data are published, Taiwan has the highest share of manufacturing value-added in firms with 500 or more workers, 56.4%.[3] There can be no simple equation, therefore, of Taiwan's economic success and that of small-scale capitalism.

One practical problem confounding research on the small- and medium-size-firm sector is empirical. Because the sector is so heterogeneous and fraught with firms that are in a constant state of flux, it is a challenge even to gather data to describe it. There are at least five classes of measurement problems:

1. If small- and medium-size firms have exceptionally high rates of bankruptcy, and if data are collected only on existing firms, then the tendency is to overstate how well firms in this sector are performing.

2. It is hard to collect any data on existing firms because tax evasion tends to be high. Bhalla (1979) uncovered an informal sector in Korea that had escaped government statistical notice; he estimated that the sector contained half to two thirds as many workers as the formal sector.

3. Comparisons of the productivity *levels* in small- and medium-size firms on the one hand and large firms on the other are meaningless from the standpoint of relative performance, since the two firm sets rarely produce the same products.

4. Assessing relative performance from productivity *growth rates* is misleading because of a statistical artifact between large and small firms, although much seems to have been made of such findings in Korea. Table 7.2 presents data on productivity growth rates by firm size for 1967–1979. The data show large firms (with 500 or more workers) performing worse than small- and medium-size firms in almost every size range except that of 200 to 499 workers. The problem is that the 200 to 499 size range accounts for almost half the total value-added of all small- and medium-size firms in the period in question (see the last column in the table). Moreover, productivity growth rates are biased toward small firms because the base from which they grow is relatively small.

5. Growth rates of output and labor productivity in the small- and medium-size firm need to be corrected for poor-quality product. Poor quality hounded attempts to develop a subcontracting system in Korean industries like electronics, shipbuilding, and automobiles. According to a survey conducted by the Korean Auto-

[3] To the extent that the "informal sector" is excluded from the data, differences across countries may be misleading.

Table 7.2 Percent Growth Rates of Output and Total Factor Productivity by Size of Firm for Manufacturing Sector, 1967–1979

No. of Workers	Output	Labor Productivity	Capital Productivity	Total Factor Productivity	Percent of Value-Added[a]
5–9	11.1	12.8	4.9	7.8	1.5
10–19	13.9	11.5	5.2	7.6	2.0
20–49	20.1	11.5	6.0	8.0	4.4
50–99	22.7	11.7	4.5	6.8	6.4
100–199	25.8	12.5	4.1	7.6	9.3
200–499	22.1	8.6	0.7	2.4	18.2
500 or more	27.6	11.0	2.3	4.0	58.2
Total	24.0	12.3	2.6	5.0	100.0

[a] 1976.

Source: Size of firm: C. K. Kim (1981). All other data: Economic Planning Board (various years).

mobile Industry Association in 1976, only 10% of a sample of 1,200 parts and components supplied by small-scale firms approximated international standard. As much as 60% was far below it. (C. K. Kim and Lee, 1980)

Generally speaking, the small- and medium-size firm cannot be credited with developing the forces of production in late-industrializing countries, even in Taiwan. Nevertheless, the modern industrial enterprise in several key sectors in Korea would have been hard pressed to expand without it, as suggested below.

THE MODERN INDUSTRIAL ENTERPRISE

Korea provides yet another example of a country that supports Chandler's theses about the modern industrial enterprise. For instance, Chandler found that the world's largest industrial enterprises tend to be clustered in the same set of industries—food, chemicals, oil, primary metals, and machinery—and have been so arrayed ever since the late nineteenth century. The same industry pattern prevails in Korea, as Table 7.3 suggests, although in general, the incidence of large firms in textiles tends to be greater in Korea and in machinery smaller than in more advanced countries. Chandler also found that the activities of the world's largest industrial enterprises in capital-intensive industries are "monitored and coordinated by a small team (or perhaps an individual) of full-time executives who plan and allocate resources for the operating units and the enterprise as a

Table 7.3 Percent Distribution of 200 Largest Manufacturing Firms[a] in Korea, Japan, Germany, and United States, by Industry

Industry, Standard Industrial Classification	Percent Distribution			
	Korea[b] (1983)	Japan (1973)	Germany[c] (1973)	United States[d] (1973)
20. Food	14.5	9.0	6.0	12.1
21. Tobacco	4.1	0.0	3.0	1.7
22. Textiles	12.8	5.5	2.0	1.7
23. Apparel	1.7	0.0	0.0	0.0
24. Lumber	0.6	0.5	0.0	2.2
25. Furniture	0.0	0.0	0.0	0.0
26. Paper	1.7	5.0	1.0	5.0
27. Printing	0.6	1.0	3.0	0.5
28. Chemicals	16.3	17.0	15.1	14.9
29. Petroleum	2.9	6.5	4.0	12.1
30. Rubber	4.1	2.5	1.5	2.8
31. Leather	0.6	0.0	0.5	0.0
32. Stone, Clay, Glass	4.1	7.0	7.5	3.9
33. Primary Metal	11.6	13.5	9.5	10.5
34. Fabricated Metal	1.2	2.5	7.0	2.8
35. General Machinery	2.9	8.0	14.6	9.4
36. Electrical Machinery	10.5	9.0	10.5	7.2
37. Transport Equipment	9.8	10.0	7.1	10.5
38. Instruments	0.0	2.5	1.0	2.2
39. Miscellaneous	0.0	0.5	0.5	10.5
	100.0	100.0	100.0	100.0

[a] Ranked by sales.

[b] 172 firms. Some of the industrial categories were adjusted to conform with the SIC breakdown.

[c] 199 firms.

[d] 181 firms.

Sources: Korea: Economic Planning Board (1985); Japan, Germany, and the United States: Chandler (1987).

whole" (1989, p. 9). So, too, in Korea, managerial capitalism has arisen, as indicated in Table 7.4.

The first column in Table 7.4 provides data on the number of administrative employees per 100 operatives, or the ratio of indirect to direct labor. This number may be taken as a proxy for the density of management. By and large, managerial resources tend to be greatest in the same industries in which large firms are clustered—food, chemicals, oil, and machinery, especially transport equipment. The textiles industry, however, which according to Table 7.3 comprises a sizeable fraction of large firms, has a low ratio of administrators to operators. Thus managerialism does not necessarily characterize all

Table 7.4 Managerial Resources by Industry, 1983

Industry, Standard Industrial Classification	Administrative Employees/ 100 Operatives[a]	Family Workers/ 100 Administrative Employees[a]
Food	30.0	11.0[c]
Tobacco	17.0	0.0[d]
Textiles[b]	9.3	16.8[e]
Apparel[b]	8.7	20.4
Lumber	14.2	32.1
Furniture	12.2	37.5
Paper	20.8	12.0
Printing	34.0	14.5
Chemical	44.0	3.7
Petroleum	46.1	2.6
Rubber	7.3	6.2
Leather	12.1	18.8
Stone, Clay, Glass	18.5	13.6
Primary Metal	23.0	4.4
Fabricated Metal	19.3	14.3
Machinery	22.6	12.2
Electrical Machinery	17.7	4.5
Transport Equipment	31.1	2.9
Instruments	15.6	9.3
Miscellaneous	10.9	17.9

[a] Figures for administrative and family workers refer to males only to avoid inflating the administrative and family categories with female clerical workers. See discussion in text.

[b] Adjusted for the fact that many female administrative employees in these industries are front-line supervisors. Adjustment takes the form of inflating the number of male administrators in these industries by the ratio of males to total administrators in the all-manufacturing average.

[c] Average of food and beverages.

[d] A government monopoly exists in the tobacco industry.

[e] Excludes shoes.

Source: Economic Planning Board (1985).

large firms; rather, it characterizes those that operate in capital-intensive industries. In the labor-intensive sectors, or in sectors subject to capital widening,[4] expansion occurs with little change in the proportions of capital and labor used in the production process, and consequently little change in the production process itself. Therefore, the same equipment and labor (say, sewing machines and seamstresses) replicate themselves on an extended scale with little need for an abundance of managerial resources. By contrast, in the capital-intensive industries, or in industries that are subject to capital

---

[4] The distinction between capital widening and deepening originated with Hawtrey (1937). See further discussion in Chapter 10.

deepening, expansion occurs with an increasing proportion of capital to labor and therefore continuous changes in the production process itself. Chandler wrote,

> In the capital-intensive industries, the throughput [production time] needed to maintain minimum efficient scale requires not only careful coordination of flow through the processes of production but also of the flow of inputs from the suppliers and the flow of outputs to the retailers and final consumers.
>
> Such coordination did not and indeed could not happen automatically. It demanded the constant attention of a managerial team or hierarchy. The potential economies of scale and scope are characteristics of a technology. The actual economies of scale or of scope, as measured by throughput [or yields], are organizational. Such economies depend on knowledge, skill, experience and teamwork—on the organized human capabilities essential to exploit the potential of technological progress. (1989, pp. 14–15)

Finally, Korea has begun to conform to the international pattern of a decline in the importance of "family capitalism" and a rise in the importance of decision-making by salaried managers (although the family founder remains the highest decision maker). The second column of Table 7.4 presents data on the ratio of family workers to administrative employees. The ratio may be taken as a very rough approximation of the relative importance of family versus salaried managers. The lower the ratio, the less important family management. According to the chart, the ratio tends to be lowest in those industries that use capital-intensive production processes and that harbor large-scale firms. Family capitalism appears to be least prominent where modern technology and large capital investments are greatest.

Korea's modern industrial enterprise remains under tight family ownership and control, typically under the ownership and control of the original founder, who occupies the position of president.[5] As suggested in Chapter 4, however, the president does not exercise the fundamental function of the entrepreneur—that of deciding what, when, and how much to produce. In Korea's version of the modern industrial enterprise (i.e., chaebol), the government performs that function, particularly in the formative years of Korean industrialization, the 1960s and 1970s. The functions of chaebol presidents, therefore, have been limited to three areas. First, presidents have made strategic decisions for the group about which initiatives of the

---

[5] See the discussion of the family structure of the chaebol in Hattori (1984).

government to follow and by how much. Second, they have exercised power over the purse, to the extent of deciding how to shift funds among group members. Third, they have exhorted their work forces to work harder and have made key personnel decisions, including which top managers to hire.

Top Management

Top managers of modern industrial enterprises in Korea who are not related familially to the president are recruited from diverse sources. Tamio Hattori, in a 1984 study of Korean management during the period 1962 to 1978, examined 556 cases of recruits into the ranks of top managers and discovered the following breakdown: The most important sources of top managers were the government, financial institutions, and public enterprises. Relatively unimportant were the media, academia, politics, the military, and the Korean Central Intelligence Agency. Altogether unimportant was the law profession (see Table 7.5).[6]

Figure 7.1 presents Chandler's organizational chart for the typical

Table 7.5 Background of Top Managers,[a] 1962–1978

Background	Percent of Total
Government	23.0
Finance	12.4
Public Enterprise	9.9
Media	7.4
Academia	5.7
Military and Korea Central Intelligence Agency	5.2
Politics	4.1
Law	0.7
Religion	0.2
Cultural	0.2
Others	5.7
Unknown	25.4
Total	100.0

[a] Refers to a sample of 556 recruits among the largest diversified business groups.

Source: Hattori (1984).

[6] It is rumored that the chaebol employ a lot of retired military personnel either as a favor to the government or to obtain favors from it. The figure on the number of recruits with military backgrounds, therefore, may be understated, or the rumor may be false.

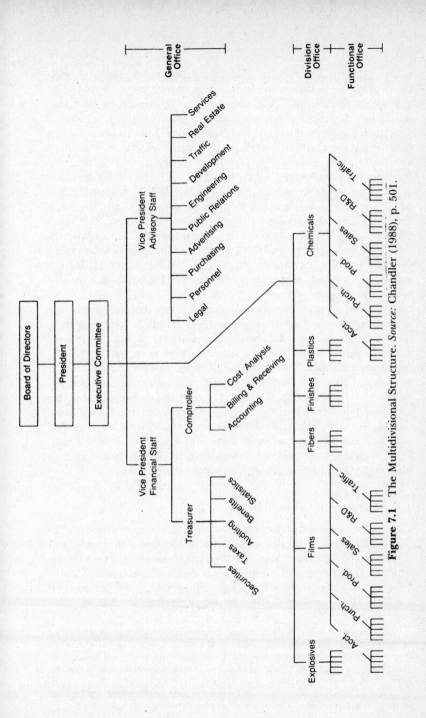

Figure 7.1 The Multidivisional Structure. *Source:* Chandler (1988), p. 501.

169

modern industrial enterprise. The structure for the chaebol is similar in principle to that of the world norm but different in kind. The chaebol's structure, like that presented in Figure 7.1, is multidivisional, but its general office tends to be relatively small (like those of American conglomerates). In fact, some large Korean firms do not have any general office, secretariat, or staff to serve the president and his retinue. Among 218 large firms surveyed by the College of Business Administration, Seoul National University (SNU), as many as 30% had none (Seoul National University, 1985).[7] Among the 200 or so firms (large and small) that did have general offices, the functions that they undertook on a regular basis were limited. Most functions were undertaken centrally only when the need arose, in which case managers operating at the group or company level were pulled together to form a temporary task force. Such task forces, for example, executed decisions about entering new industries (see the discussion in Chapter 5).

A small or nonexistent general office is a key characteristic of the Korean modern industrial enterprise and is indicative of how decision-making power is distributed between owners and salaried managers. Decisions at the top tend to be made by owners autocratically, rather than bureaucratically. Most decisions, however, are not made at the top. According to SNU's survey, salaried managers made decisions about production, R&D, and marketing, and these managers were assigned where their skills were needed most: to the shop floor, the plant, or the company level, respectively.[8] Firms concentrated over half their efforts on production and R&D (which in the mid-1980s typically concerned the absorption of foreign technology), with marketing taking up much of the remainder of their time.

The Distribution of Managers

This picture of the distribution of power—showing strategic and financial decisions in the hands of a single individual or family, and decentralized decision-making in other areas—is lent support by statistics on the growth and composition of Korean management. Table 7.6 provides data on manufacturing employment in the period 1960 through 1980, broken down into six categories: engineers, man-

---

[7] Furthermore, roughly 80% of a sample of 280 small firms had none. The survey of Seoul National University was conducted in 1984. It covered approximately 500 firms, depending on the survey question. The definition of small- and medium-size firm varies by question but usually refers to firms employing 500 workers or less. See Seoul National University (1985).

[8] It is assumed for simplicity that middle and top managers differentiate themselves by their assignment either to the company or to the group level, respectively.

Table 7.6 Managerial Resources in the Manufacturing Sector,[a] 1960–1980

Employment Category	1960	1970	1980	Increase 1980/1960
Engineers	4,425	16,252	44,999	10.2
Managers	31,350	47,166	69,585	2.2
Sales	5,025	27,778	68,716	13.7
Service	13,660	22,740	49,522	3.6
Clerical	17,330	143,849	356,362	20.6
Production	404,735	1,188,406	2,206,851	5.4
Total	479,975	1,447,520	2,797,030	5.8
Administrative[b]/production	0.13	0.10	0.10	—
Administrative, clerical/ production	0.18	0.22	0.27	—

[a] Includes transportation and communication workers in the manufacturing sector.

[b] Includes engineers, managers, sales, and service workers.

Source: Korea Institute for Educational Development (1983).

agers, sales, service, clerical and production workers. The data show that between 1960 and 1980 there was an increase in the absolute number of engineers, managers, sales, and service employees (call them white-collar workers, excluding for the moment the clerical category). Nevertheless, the ratio of white-collar to blue-collar, or production, workers *declined* from 0.13 in 1960 to 0.10 in 1980. This is a rather stunning fact. It suggests that *even as Korean firms learned, diversified, and evolved into modern industrial enterprises, complete with managerial hierarchies, they tended to keep their overhead expenses in check.* To use the terminology of the classical economists and Marx, they maintained a more or less stable or even declining ratio of "unproductive" to "productive" workers.

By contrast, Seymour Melman pointed out that "the businessmen [sic] charged with administering the manufacturing firms of the United States have devoted increasing resources to administration functions of their firms since the turn of the twentieth century" (1951, p. 89).[9] Melman's observation applies equally well to many European countries. In the period 1978–1985, there was an "alarming increase" in the number of white-collar workers in the United States, coupled with a decrease in the blue-collar category—+21% and −6%, respectively (Thurow, 1987).

If one includes clerical staff among white-collar workers in the

[9] See also the study of Delehanty (1986). In part, the ratio of managers to workers may be in check in late industrializing countries because of the availability of information technology, which may conserve on managers.

Korean data, then between 1960 and 1980 the ratio of white- to blue-collar workers also rose, from 0.18 to 0.27. Nevertheless, the fact that the increase in the white- to blue-collar ratio in Korea was accounted for by a rise in clerical workers has acted to contain manufacturing costs, not to inflate them. Most clerical workers in Korea are women with vocational or secondary high-school degrees. They handle a wide variety of bookkeeping functions that in higher-wage countries now tend to be computerized. Discrimination against women workers in Korea is so severe that not only are they paid far less than men (see Chapter 8), they are also induced to quit paid employment when they marry. Thus, clerical workers represent a variable cost that does not rise with seniority.

Furthermore, although both the number of managers and the number of engineers in Korea both rose absolutely between 1960 and 1980, the latter increase was far greater than the former. *The number of engineers increased tenfold, that of managers by a factor of only 2.2* (see Table 7.6). The ratio of managers to engineers fell from 7.0 in 1960 to 1.5 in 1980. This suggests an orientation toward production in Korean manufacturing firms rather than toward sales or finance, although in certain industries sales include technical people who are tied closely to production. Insofar as Korea competes in world markets on the basis of its manufacturing capabilities, it invests its money where its competitive advantage lies.

The number of levels in the managerial hierarchies of larger firms has also been kept in check. Table 7.7 indicates that larger firms have a greater number of departments and sections than do smaller firms. Their management is more extensive. They also tend to have

Table 7.7   Managerial Hierarchy, 1984

No. of Workers	No. of Departments[a]	No. of Sections[a]	B/A[b]	No. of Levels in Hierarchies	No. of Subordinates/ Section Chief
0–99	2.90 (116)	5.15 (120)	1.78	5.55 (120)	6.02 (121)
100–200	3.67 (87)	7.68 (79)	2.09	6.97 (87)	8.90 (83)
200–300	4.92 (65)	10.60 (65)	2.15	7.37 (68)	11.81 (67)
300–500	6.43 (41)	14.73 (41)	2.29	6.93 (41)	10.90 (42)
500–1,000	10.93 (60)	22.60 (60)	2.07	7.48 (60)	10.81 (58)
1,000–2,000	16.35 (60)	43.10 (58)	2.64	7.25 (61)	14.95 (58)
2,000–5,000	21.00 (42)	57.60 (40)	2.74	8.21 (43)	15.05 (41)
5,000 or more	54.62 (13)	156.15 (13)	2.86	7.23 (13)	9.69 (13)

[a]Parentheses refer to number of firms in sample.
[b]Column 3/column 2
Source: Seoul National University (1985).

a large number of subordinates per section chief. Nevertheless, they have only marginally more managerial layers. In fact, firms with 200 to 300 workers have more levels of hierarchy than firms with over 5,000. The compactness of the hierarchical structure suggests that engineers who have entered the manufacturing sector in increasing numbers in Korea since 1960 have kept in close touch with the ranks.

Korea's modern industrial enterprises tend to recruit their middle managers openly, through competitive examinations. Out of SNU's sample of 208 recruiting experiences by large firms, only 14% were closed (Seoul National University, 1985). (The comparable figure for small- and medium-size enterprises was 47%.) This is not to suggest that the recruiting process is altogether democratic. Most chaebol admit no women at all into the ranks of managers, and they conduct a first screening of male candidates against the criteria of quality of their university and personal recommendations. This tends to restrict chaebol manager recruitment to the elite. Among the elite, however, what could be called open recruitment exists and is based on candidates' "industrial insight and capacity." [10]

Elements of Technological Capability

The learning that falls on the shoulders of production managers is broken down into three different types of technological capability in Table 7.8. The first, production capability, refers to the skills involved in optimizing the operation of established plants. The second, investment capability, refers to the skills involved in executing new projects. The third, innovation capability, refers to the skills necessary to create new products or processes. This classification scheme is not perfect. For example, some skills in Table 7.8 are more important in certain industries than in others. Also, the distinction between innovation capability and production and investment capability is artificial. (Learning how to operate a plant optimally, for example, requires a large number of small innovations to achieve marginal improvements. Introducing a new innovation requires a process that is fully under control.) Nevertheless, Table 7.8 conveys the breadth of elements that the typical firm confronts in acquiring technological capability. The point is that the management patterns just described facilitated the acquisition of such technological capability. Those patterns included a minimum of hierarchy separating managers and workers, a high incidence of engineers at the plant level in total managerial resources, and more emphasis on managers' training and education than on their political pull.

[10] The term is Veblen's ([1915] 1965, p. 194), quoted in Chapter 1.

Table 7.8 Elements of a Technological Capability

Production Capability[a]

Production management—to oversee operation of established facilities

Production engineering[b]—to provide information required to optimize operation of established facilities, including the following:

1. Raw material control: to sort and grade inputs, seek improved inputs
2. Production scheduling: to coordinate production processes across products and facilities
3. Quality control: to monitor conformance with product standards and to upgrade them
4. Trouble-shooting to overcome problems encountered in course of operation
5. Adaptations of processes and products: to respond to changing circumstances and increase productivity

Repair and maintenance of physical capital—according to regular schedule and when needed

Investment Capability

Manpower training—to impart skills and abilities of all kinds

Preinvestment feasibility studies—to identify possible projects and ascertain prospects for viability under alternative design concepts

Project execution—to establish or expand facilities, including the following:

1. Project management: to organize and oversee activities involved in project execution
2. Project engineering: to provide information needed to make technology operational in particular setting, including the following:
   a. Detailed studies: to make tentative choices among design alternatives
   b. Basic engineering: to supply core technology in terms of process flows, material and energy balances, specifications of principal equipment, plant layout
   c. Detailed engineering: to supply peripheral technology in terms of complete specifications for all physical capital, architectural and engineering plans, construction and equipment installation specifications
3. Procurement: to choose, coordinate, and supervise hardware suppliers and construction contractors
4. Embodiment in physical capital: to accomplish site preparation, construction, plant erection, manufacture of machinery and equipment
5. Start-up of operations: to attain predetermined norms

Innovation Capability

Basic research—investigation to gain knowledge for its own sake

Applied research—investigation to obtain knowledge with specific commercial implications

Development—translation of technical and scientific knowledge into concrete new processes, products, and services through detail-oriented technical activities, including experimental testing

---

[a] Activities listed refer to the operation of manufacturing plants, but similar activities pertain to the operation of other types of productive facilities as well.

[b] This usage of the term departs from conventional usage in that the term is used far more broadly to include all of the engineering activities related to the operation of existing facilities. In this usage, the term encompasses *product design* and *manufacturing engineering* as these terms are generally used in reference to industrial production. See the entries under these headings in the *McGraw-Hill Encyclopedia of Science and Technology* (New York: McGraw-Hill Book Company, 1977).

Source: Westphal, Kim, and Dahlman (1985).

Analysis of the acquisition of technological capability will be presented now for the Korean automobile industry to suggest the significance of the management patterns just described. The time is the summer of 1985. The company is Hyundai Motors. It is operating under great strain because it has just expanded its capacity and is positioning itself to enter the U.S. market.

LEARNING AT THE HYUNDAI MOTOR COMPANY (HMC)

The Technology

HMC began operations, based on foreign licenses and technical agreements with Ford, as an assembler of the Cortina passenger car in 1967. Then the Long-Range Automobile Industry Promotion Plan promulgated by the Korean government in 1974 induced Hyundai to construct integrated automobile manufacturing facilities. Hyundai adopted a policy of obtaining technology from several sources rather than from a single one (sometimes it turned to two different sources for the same technology). From 1974 to 1976, HMC acquired technologies for engine block design, transmissions, and rear axles from Japan; for factory construction, layout, and internal combustion engines from England; and for car designs from Italy. Eighteen technology transfers took place before introduction of the first HMC model, the "Pony." The experience that allowed HMC to absorb these technologies was gained through its technical assistance from Ford. Production know-how, though, came from Japan (Amsden and Kim, 1985a).

The next phase of HMC's technological development began in 1979 when exports appeared on its agenda partly in response to the government's machinery-export-promotion policy. HMC established its own engineering center. To meet the quality standards of major car markets, HMC also licensed more than 30 different technologies from Japan, England, and the United States, although with mixed results. In 1982, HMC's cars met European Economic Community requirements on emission controls, noise levels, and safety, but they fell short of the more stringent U.S. standards. The Pony failed to meet 12 of 35 U.S. safety requirements, among them the ability to absorb adequately head-on and side collisions (*BK,* Dec. 1983).

When the Korean and world economies were severely depressed in the early 1980s, HMC pushed ahead with a project to design and produce a subcompact car embodying world frontier technology and aimed at export markets. Toward this end, HMC sold 10% of its equity to Mitsubishi (5% to the Japanese group's automobile subsidiary and 5% to its trading arm). Mitsubishi's role in Hyundai, however, is limited to technical assistance for engines and transmissions. Not only does Hyundai retain all managerial control, but it also reserves the right to import parts and technology from Mitsubishi's competitors and to compete directly in Mitsubishi's own markets, if it can.

The Plant Level

In the summer of 1985, managers of different departments at HMC described their problems in a way that is reproduced here as faithfully as possible. The manager of HMC's Machine Tool Department (MTD) reported that HMC began making its own machine tools in 1978:

> The department employs 317 people, including 175 workers, 58 clerks, and 84 engineers with college degrees. It has begun to make machining centers, about five a month. Controls are from Fujitsu Fanuc. The MTD gets technical assistance from SNK of Sweden. It has a foreign license with SNK that covers blueprints, specifications, and supervision. The MTD sends designers and inspectors to SNK for instruction. They send foremen and electricians to MTD. The MTD also has a short-term relationship with Cincinnati Milacron (CM). MTD relies on CM for some jigs and fixtures. The MTD has just started a CAD/CAM[11] team, but it is not yet at the software stage. The MTD mainly manufactures materials-handling equipment. The ideas come from the workers. The breakdown of capital equipment in HMC's new plant expansion is roughly as follows: 50% of capital equipment comes from Japan; 25% comes from Korean machinery builders; and 25% comes from the MTD. The MTD's equipment is for materials handling on the line as well as for the engine and transmission plant.

According to one of the managers of HMC's assembly operations, the assembly line at Okazaki, Japan, which is Mitsubishi Motor's headquarters, is about 1.5 times faster than the line at HMC. The rated capacity of HMC's new assembly line is about 60 cars per hour. Right now, however, HMC is operating only at about 85% of rated capacity. Following is the manager's explanation of the problem:

> There are three main problems. First, there are shortages of parts from subcontractors. Mando, Inc., for example, one of the Hyundai group's subsidiaries and major suppliers, is sometimes late with deliveries. Second, there are problems with Production Control. It keeps changing the sequence of lot production in order to accommodate changes in the schedule of the Sales De-

---

[11] Computer-aided design/computer-aided manufacture.

partment. Third, there is a lot of downtime of machinery, particularly in the body shop. The welding machines of the Machine Tool Division sometimes break down. There are also too many kinds of machines in the body shop, some from one supplier, some from another, some from the MTD. Maintenance is a problem.

In addition, the manager of the body shop said that there were some problems with local machinery and that the design of the line needed improvement:

There are too many stations, and the materials-handling system sometimes jams. Every station has to be finished before the line proceeds. The company is going to have to change the line in the body shop, and improve the jigs and fixtures. By comparison with Okazaki, there are more workers per job at HMC. There are approximately 2.5 more workers per job. There are also more subassemblies on the line. The number of tasks per station is also greater. HMC is forced to do a lot in-house because the quality of parts is so low. For example, it might take 10 seconds to tighten a screw at HMC compared with only 5 seconds at Okazaki. Several factors are involved. The screw is worse. The main parts do not match each other, hole for hole. The material is of poor quality. The design of the screw is poor, and the skills of the workers are inferior. There are no time-and-motion studies [done at] most parts suppliers.

A manager in the purchasing department confirmed that there were machinery problems in the press and body shops. Downtime was about 85%, due to new facilities and testing:

In the old facility, downtime is much less. Many small robots are made by the workers. There are small study groups of workers on each line. All have long experience at each station. If there are no absentees among the line people, then these workers [can] become floaters and develop new machinery. Absenteeism is very low at HMC.

The industrial engineers in the Methods Engineering Department have a high education level and high status in the plant. They are the people responsible for developing new production methods. They are then supposed to teach the foremen what to do. Members of the Methods Engineering Department are always traveling throughout the plant. If there is a problem a foreman cannot shoot, then the methods engineering people are asked to help. They are the people who get rid of the bottlenecks. The workers on the line are always working, they have no time to think about new methods. The boss•of the production line gives orders and controls. He has no time to think either.

The attitude at HMC is that everybody has to cooperate, to choose to work or to leave. According to a manager in the Production Engineering Department, when people work, they work hard—in spite of the fact that the government does not like to see HMC fire a worker:

If a worker is lazy, there is peer pressure. A few years ago, there were a lot of lazy workers. Now, everybody works hard. School and society teach them that they must work hard. The education level of workers is now higher. Workers obey fellow workers and supervisors. Workers and supervisors work together. About half of all supervisors are college graduates; about half are not. Young supervisors are all college graduates. A supervisor with a high-school degree has to have long experience.

Basically, inspection is done by workers themselves, of their own work. Workers at the next station also check the previous station's quality. There is also a big Quality Department. There is someone from the Quality Department at all major work stations, who [will] work together with the workers. Every five or six stations on every line has its own quality circle. Quality circles meet once a week, on average. HMC is trying to build a good quality circle movement. It cannot yet do as well as the Japanese. This is because workers do not yet have enough experience; they are not all experts in their jobs. They have to do more work than Japanese workers to improve quality. Quality circles set plans about how to achieve improvements in operations. Then they check actual progress against their goals. Sometimes they make the same mistake five times. They should do research to make and set their targets. Sometimes their problems prove too difficult to solve themselves. They have to call on the Methods Engineering Department. They have job rotation. The plant manager likes to do job rotation for learning purposes. Rejected cars become workers' teachers. HMC has introduced a new computerized system that allows a particular part to be traced right back to the worker responsible, or to the supplier.

The Engineering Center is responsible for design. HMC gets its platform designs from Italian designers and (now) designs the remainder of its cars. The Engineering Center was established at a fairly early stage in HMC's existence and has grown steadily. It is managed by a graduate from Seoul National University. (The plant manager graduated from the Korea Naval

Academy and has been a vice-president of HMC for a long time.)
It started with the Pony, and now its engineers are trying to
design everything, including all parts. The Engineering Center
is located in the same plant as the rest of HMC. People from
production departments and people from the Engineering Center meet every day. They always have discussions. Designers come
to the site because the Engineering Center has no experience,
they are not experts. Even if designers are right, they have to
meet the workers. When a new type of car [the Excel] got started,
the Engineering Center worked especially close with production. This is easily done since they are stationed in the same
plant.

Subcontracting

The foregoing suggests a relatively high educational level of shopfloor management, from the ranks of industrial engineers and supervisors down to the workforce. The pro-activeness of management
in attempting to raise productivity and quality is also evident, even
if the effects were not immediately positive. For example, the effort
on HMC's part to build some of its own on-line equipment had its
problems at the time of our visit. But this initiative promises to give
HMC tighter control over its process and costs in the long run. The
emphasis on quality is also evident, although quality control circles
were not yet functioning smoothly. Nowhere is pro-activity more apparent, however, than in HMC's efforts to forge a subcontracting
network, to which attention is now turned.

One of Chandler's main points about the modern industrial enterprise is that the ones that succeed do so by tailoring their organizational structures to their competitive strategies. In the case of General Motors (GM), Chandler wrote: "It . . . successfully creat[ed] a
general office [in the 1920s] to coordinate, appraise, and set broad
goals and policies for the numerous operating divisions" (1962, p.
130). Vertical integration—one competitive strategy that Chandler
mentioned—was closely connected with the expansion of GM's general office: "The corporation acquired a general office to administer
the many operating divisions that Durant [GM's founder] had collected in his strategy of vertical integration and constant expansion"
(1962, p. 162). Significantly, in the almost 50 pages that Chandler
devoted to a discussion of strategy and structure in GM, he made no
mention of a subcontracting strategy. GM subcontracted little possibly because it was an innovator, and few outside firms were familiar
with the parts that it required.

If one were to compare the strategy and structure of General Motors in the 1920s with that of Hyundai Motors (HMC) in the 1980s, one would notice some similarities, even though GM was by far the larger of the two companies. (In 1927 it was already building over 1.3 million cars per year, while in 1986 HMC was building only 168,000.) Like GM, HMC initially pursued a policy of vertical integration. Key parts and components were made in-house, by firms within the Hyundai group (for example, brakes and transmissions). Like GM, HMC also began to build a general office. The office was not positioned at the group level because the Hyundai group was diversified into a larger number of unrelated industries that was GM. Instead, it was located at the company level, but it played an analogous role to GM's general office on a much smaller scale. Nevertheless, it appears that HMC subcontracted to a far greater degree than did General Motors. As GM's volume rose, it increasingly integrated its operations, whereas HMC increasingly consolidated its subcontracting network as its volume rose.[12]

As will be discussed shortly, HMC expanded its managerial support staff at the company level to provide its subcontractors with technical assistance. Thus, the establishment of a subcontracting network did not altogether preempt the need for an in-house managerial support staff. Nevertheless, it probably reduced the size that such a support staff would have had to assume in the absence of subcontracting. One can say, therefore, that for all the similarities between GM and HMC in their youths, this was a significant difference in their development. GM emphasized an organizational structure whose epicenter was the general office and that had a complementary strategy of integration. HMC deemphasized the importance of a general office and of integration to the extent that it pursued a strategy of subcontracting.

HMC emphasized a strategy of subcontracting for two reasons. First, to subcontract was cheaper than to integrate. Subcontracting arose in recognition of the limited financial resources and technological capability of a learner. Second, the government pressured HMC to patronize the small-scale firm in the interest of wealth sharing. In its role as a learner and patron of the satellite firm, HMC was consciously following in the footsteps of the Japanese automobile industry of approximately thirty years earlier.

JAPAN'S INFLUENCE ON KOREA'S SMALL- AND MEDIUM-SIZE FIRM

The marked resemblance between the chaebol and the zaibatsu leads one to ask whether small- and medium-size firms in Korea and Ja-

---

[12] For information on GM, see Chandler (1964). Information on HMC was provided by HMC.

pan are also alike. It turns out that they exhibit both similarities and differences.

A striking difference concerns export behavior. In the early stages of Japanese industrialization, small-scale firms were the principal exporters. In the 1920s,

> Despite the strategic importance of the modern zaibatsu enterprises, medium and smaller factories employed the overwhelming majority of Japan's industrial workers. Even more important, the zaibatsu firms produced primarily for the domestic market, but the medium and smaller enterprises concentrated on production for export. With a few exceptions such as rayon, silk yarn, and cotton textiles, where large enterprises were also strong exporters, medium and smaller manufacturers of sundries such as bicycles, pottery, enamelware, canned goods, hats, silk textiles, and so forth were contributing from 50% to 65% of all of Japan's exports. And they were losing money doing it. (Johnson, 1982, p. 98)

In 1953, smaller factories in Japan employed 70.9% of all workers in manufacturing industries and accounted for 54% of value-added in output. They were estimated to be responsible for approximately 60% of all exports (Asia, 1957).

No comparable export figures are available for Korea, but it appears that, contrary to the historical pattern in Japan, small firms in Korea serve the domestic market, and large firms export. According to Samuel Ho, who in 1980 wrote about small-scale enterprises (SSEs) in both Korea and Taiwan, "because *most SSEs produced primarily for the domestic market,* the export promotion policies did not in general directly affect the small-enterprise sector" (emphasis added) (1980, p. 88). Youngil Lim's analysis of data from the Small and Medium Industries Bank in Korea suggests that its clients typically export between 10% and 20% of their output, whereas in the aggregate, Korea's exports amount to approximately 35% of output (1981). In a study of over 500 small- and medium-size firms in the machinery sector, Jae Won Kim found that approximately 60% did not export at all (1983). Small- and medium-size firms in Korea appear to be marginal exporters despite the fact that they account for a large share of employment, as do small firms in Japan. Table 7.9 indicates, however, that their employment share is decreasing. Korea's small- and medium-size firms (with fewer than 500 workers) employed as much as 88% of the work force in 1958, down to only 63% in 1983.

As for similarities, although small-scale firms in Japan have been better able than their Korean counterparts to take shelter behind monopoly legislation, small-scale firms in both countries have faced government discrimination during the heydays of heavy industry and

Table 7.9 Size Distribution of Manufacturing Firms by Number of Employees, 1958–1983

No. of Employees	No. of Firms (% of Year's Total)					
	1958	1963	1969	1973	1978	1983
5–9	44,064 (16.79)	60,564 (14.99)	103,620 (12.47)	74,729 (6.44)	69,731 (3.30)	90,261 (4.07)
10–99	129,720 (49.44)	167,607 (41.49)	235,804 (28.38)	259,291 (22.34)	479,259 (22.67)	660,366 (29.78)
100–499	55,557 (21.17)	84,418 (20.90)	215,862 (25.98)	318,982 (27.48)	635,816 (30.08)	639,119 (28.83)
500 or more	31,086 (11.85)	89,392 (22.13)	273,758 (32.94)	505,827 (43.58)	927,119 (43.86)	825,487 (37.23)
Total	262,385	403,944	831,013	1,160,802	2,113,903	2,217,216

Sources: Korean Reconstruction Bank and Economic Planning Board.

rapid growth.[13] The mastermind behind Japan's fast-growth strategy, Hayato Ikeda, had to resign as prime minister after his "slip of the tongue" in the Diet about not caring if a few small businessmen were driven to suicide (Johnson, 1982, p. 214). No politician in Korea ever resigned over abuse of the small-scale sector, but only because democracy, not discrimination, was less evident than in Japan.

The most striking similarity between the small- and medium-scale sector of Japan and that of Korea is subcontracting involvement in the automobile, shipbuilding, machinery, and electronic industries. Being older and operating in a larger domestic market, the Japanese subcontracting system in the automobile sector is more highly articulated than is Korea's, and it involves several layers of subcontractors. However, the two systems closely resemble one another. This is not surprising, since they are directly linked through technology transfer and both operate on the basis of a *just-in-time* (JIT) inventory system.[14]

The philosophy behind JIT is that production with minimum inventories forces firms to be efficient and quality conscious; if, in the absence of inventories, efficiency and quality are low, then delivery dates cannot be met. Furthermore, interviews with Korean automobile parts suppliers suggest that excess stocks do not disappear from the shelves of automakers only to reappear on those of their suppliers. The finished goods and work-in-process inventories of autoparts suppliers in Korea appear to be low. Profit margins are themselves too low to support more. Hence, inexperienced suppliers in Korea have had to learn in a very pressured and disciplined environment. Although the big automobile companies in Korea provide some technical assistance to suppliers, the big companies' expertise is itself

[13] In Japan, a law in 1925 allowed small- and medium-size firms to cartelize in order to remain in business without resorting to "dumping." Although this privilege was withdrawn in 1948 by the Supreme Commander of the Allied Powers, MITI introduced a law in the Diet as soon as the occupation ended in 1952 that enabled MITI to create cartels among small businessmen as exceptions to the Antimonopoly Law (Johnson, 1982). Very recent legislation in Korea is likewise intended to help small- and medium-size firms to cartelize. Some such firms also enjoy high market shares naturally. One-quarter of Jae Won Kim's sample of 500 machine shops had market shares of over 60% (J. W. Kim, 1983). Yet by Japanese standards, cartelization and monopoly among small- and medium-size firms in Korea is underdeveloped. For data on discrimination against small- and medium-size firms in credit allocation, see Y. J. Cho and Cole (1986). K. E. Lee (1984) looked at other forms of discrimination against them.

[14] Toyota's JIT system of "kanbans" does not operate in HMC, but HMC has adopted another system of just-in-time. For a discussion of the Japanese manufacturing system, including JIT, see Schonberger (1982). For a discussion of the JIT system at Toyota, see Ohno (1984) and Cusumano (1985).

limited. Hence, technology has had to be acquired by suppliers with minimum know-how, deliveries have had to be met with minimum inventories, and profit margins have had to be preserved in a business setting of intense competition.

What follows is an account of interviews with subcontractors in Korea's automobile industry that parallel the interviews, presented earlier, with Korea's largest automobile prime contractor, HMC.[15]

THE SUBCONTRACTING NETWORK OF THE HYUNDAI MOTOR COMPANY (HMC)

In 1985, a manager in HMC's Parts Supply Department, call him Mr. Shin, said that HMC subcontracts about 40% of value-added in a standard car. The following paraphrases Mr. Shin's comments:

Of this 40%, a "large" share is subcontracted to "independent" suppliers *within the Hyundai group* [e.g., Hyundai Precision Industries and Mando, Inc.]. The Korean government prohibits prime contractors from owning equity in subcontractors, but a company like Mando, Inc. is a legal entity within the Hyundai empire. (Mando, Inc. was divested by HMC to comply with the law.) The remainder of the 40% comprises small parts and components that are supplied by 185 small- and medium-size firms.

In 1980–1981, HMC established the Parts Development Department (PDP). This department was modeled on the vendor development department of HMC's competitor in Korea, the Daewoo Motor Corporation. *The Daewoo Motor Corporation organized its vendor development department in 1966 at the suggestion of its Japanese technology supplier, the Toyota Corporation, to raise the technical standards and quality of inexperienced vendors.* The parts suppliers of HMC were tiny and had no technology. It became HMC policy to bring them up to a higher standard. The Parts Development Department employs 150 engineers with college degrees. Typically, a group of three to ten engineers is formed and dispatched to a supplier. The group first studies the supplier's line, from receiving to inspection. It looks for bottlenecks to determine what parts of the line are responsible for delays. It examines jigs and fixtures to assess quality.

All parts suppliers that received assistance from the PDP made a giant step forward. They were taught how to clean house. They were taught the importance of visual control so that there were no hidden

---

[15] The names of subcontractors and the types of products are disguised. In all, twelve subcontractors were interviewed, six of HMC and six of its competitor, the Daewoo Motor Corporation (DMC). DMC is a joint venture between the Daewoo group and General Motors. (The DMC interviews are not reported.)

work stations. They were taught how to make their process a straight line. They were taught the basics.

The PDP got to know a lot about its suppliers. It would receive drawings from HMC's engineering center, study the drawings, and then choose a parts maker. Discussions would then begin with the supplier about how to improve the drawings and how to manufacture the parts at low cost and high quality.

Myongdo Industrial Co. (MIC)

According to Mr. Chung, former quality control manager at HMC, and currently plant manager at MIC:

The Myongdo Industrial Co. (MIC) has 170 employees in two plants. Most work is in the larger plant located in Ulsan, close to HMC. The president of MIC owns 90% of the equity of MIC, and the number-two man owns 10%. MIC makes pistons.

HMC has two piston suppliers, but MIC supplies 100% of its output to HMC. Almost all suppliers have the same relationship with HMC. MIC maintains about two days' inventory. It has problems with its vendors. Sometimes the steel they supply does not have the correct porosity. Each month, MIC receives an order from HMC for the following month and a forecast for the following two months (MIC also gets an annual sales forecast). For purposes of planning, it adds 10% variability to demand. Although HMC's monthly requirements are fixed, daily requirements fluctuate.

MIC negotiates with HMC on price. HMC knows everything about MIC's finances. Regular negotiations are held over the price of existing parts. In the case of new parts, the two companies calculate the cost of construction. Then HMC tests the part, and they renegotiate. Prices are fixed until there is a change in material prices.

MIC gets some financial assistance from HMC. In the case of a new investment at MIC, HMC gives it advance payment. HMC also gives it credit to buy new machinery from Hyundai Heavy Industries. Most of MIC's finance, however, comes from the Small and Medium Industrial Bank.

MIC gets technical assistance from HMC. When MIC starts to make a new part, HMC's people work together with MIC's. But HMC cannot give specialized technical assistance because it does not have the know-how. MIC had to ask a Japanese equipment maker to supervise it for a while.

MIC gets assistance for quality control from HMC. HMC taught it about inspection standards and how to develop quality. MIC and HMC meet to discuss quality. Usually HMC people don't come to MIC's factory unless there are problems with quality. In the case of a new part, HMC people stay at the factory, check the specifications with MIC people, and discuss how to troubleshoot. They test together and after the test report, HMC sends MIC feedback. HMC does random inspections of MIC's deliveries.

MIC has a big problem with fluctuations in demand and order quantity changes from HMC. HMC gives it too short lead times. This makes it necessary for MIC to carry excess capacity and to schedule overtime to meet delivery dates. Until now, HMC paid once a week. Now the government has said it must pay twice a week.

Relations between the two companies are "close." In most supplier companies, HMC has "friends." When people leave HMC, they usually go to work for a supplier. There are some exceptions in the Changwon Industrial Estate. Suppliers located there are not under HMC's control. They supply several companies. An example is a joint venture with a Japanese company that supplies HMC with carburetors. The more technically developed the company, the less control HMC has over it.

The Arirang Company

According to its president, a former HMC employee, the Arirang Company was established in 1976 when HMC started to assemble its first model, the Pony:

The plant manager also worked at HMC a long time before coming here. Arirang has 270 employees and makes mufflers.

Arirang has no "special" relations with HMC in financial terms, although when Arirang invests in new tooling, HMC gives it financial assistance in the form of advance payments.

Arirang carries about one day's inventory in assembled mufflers and two days' in work-in-process. Every month Arirang gets an order from HMC for the next month and a forecast for the next two months. It also gets weekly, daily, and hourly requirements. It communicates with HMC by telephone and by electronic facsimile. Although monthly orders rarely change, daily orders fluctuate about 10%. If demand fluctuates by more than 10%, Arirang can't meet HMC's order. Daily requirements depend on HMC's line situation, urgent schedule changes, and shipping releases. Arirang works under enormous pressure. Frequently it has to schedule overtime.

HMC has a much higher level of technology than Arirang. HMC, therefore, gives Arirang technical assistance and sends people to Arirang to ensure quality control. Arirang sells only to HMC, and HMC buys only from Arirang. HMC is kind to Arirang because there is no multiple sourcing by HMC for mufflers.

Sodaemun Company

According to the general manager, the Sodaemun Company has been making automobile parts and components for more than 10 years. It has five factories with a total of 240 employees. The factory in question is located in Ulsan, close to HMC. The company makes steering equipment parts and, on average, delivers to HMC once a day. It sells to HMC and to the Korean military. It also sells to Hyundai Heavy Industries. The company, however, is very dependent on HMC.

Sodaemun has no "special" ties with HMC. Nor does it receive financial assistance from HMC. It does, however, receive credit for new tooling. Often, the people from Sodaemun and from HMC get together to discuss technical problems associated with new designs. HMC's product development department, however, provides only the basic designs. Sodaemun does all the detail engineering. It also does cost breakdowns for new designs, which it gives to HMC for negotiation. HMC reimburses Sodaemun for tooling costs, sometimes by giving it a lump sum payment, sometimes by folding costs into unit price. Whatever the case, costs are never computed to include design work, prototypes, and samples. Moreover, there is a time lag between development and mass production, which HMC fails to consider. Sodaemun has lost money on some models.

SUBCONTRACTING: A SUMMARY

Subcontracting in late industrialization requires sufficient output volumes by prime contractors to enable suppliers to specialize.[16] In the automobile industry in Korea, this condition began to take hold in the 1980s, and a subcontracting system arose that was a microcosm of Korea's industrial economy. The system was hierarchical, but like Korea's factory system, without many layers, and like its economy at large, manipulated from the top by the government. The effects of subcontracting were also like those of other parts of Korea's economic system, more desirable from the viewpoint of economic growth and efficiency than from the viewpoint of equality.

The major piece of legislation from the government to stimulate subcontracting came in 1982, when global economic depression in-

---

[16] Subcontracting may be greater where prime contractors are locally owned firms. In the case of Daewoo Motors, for example, in which General Motors holds a 50% stake, subcontracting existed, but possibly on a smaller scale than in HMC. The scale was smaller because DMC imported more parts than did HMC. Moreover, instead of subcontracting to local firms, DMC formed joint ventures in Korea with GM's American suppliers, such as Delco Remy, that had established operations in Korea.

tensified competition from Japan. The Small- and Medium-Industry Systemization Law appealed to the better sense of big business by empowering the Minister of Commerce and Industry to reserve certain industrial spheres for small- and medium-size subcontractors (Article 5). The law also forbade prime contractors from swallowing up subcontractors through stock ownership. Additionally, the government undertook responsibility to provide more financial and tax incentives to enable subcontractors to modernize their factories and to acquire technical assistance. It introduced a scheme to reduce the risks they faced in commercializing new technologies. Finally, it provided guidelines on fair trade practices, for example, on the frequency of payments and the length of subcontracting contracts. These guidelines were enforced by a large bureaucracy in the Economic Planning Board. Subcontracting surged ahead after 1982.

In terms of equality between big and small business, Korea's subcontracting system, like Japan's, has left much to be desired. As a consequence of prime contractors' operating procedures, the day-to-day working environment of subcontractors is stressed. As a consequence of prime contractors' market power, the profit margins of subcontractors are squeezed. In terms of growth and efficiency, however, Korea's subcontracting system has been an ideal vehicle by which to spread the progressive practices of the modern industrial enterprise to the remainder of the productive economy.

Subcontracting has acted as a transfer mechanism in three respects. First, prime contractors have imposed on-time, on-spec[17] delivery conditions on subcontractors. Second, the production systems of subcontractors have become extensions of those of prime contractors, including the just-in-time inventory management system. Third, salaried managers themselves have been transferred to supplier firms, which has tended to raise the overall educational level of Korean business. In Korea managers of even small- and medium-size subcontractors are well educated. In the machinery sector, for example, of a sample of 441 subcontractors in 1983, as many as 73% employed college-educated managers (J. W. Kim, 1983). In part, such high educational attainments in the small- and medium-scale sector reflect Korea's high investments in education. In part, they reflect the interpenetration of prime contractors and subcontractors through the exchange of personnel. Subcontracting has tended to generalize the practices of salaried management, and the efficiency of salaried management has become one of Korea's competitive strengths.

[17] On-spec refers to deliveries that conform to predetermined quality standards.

CHAPTER EIGHT

The Paradox of "Unlimited" Labor and Rising Wages

LABOR IN LATE INDUSTRIALIZATION

By the standards of both contemporary and earlier industrializations, real average wage increases in Japan, and in Korea especially, are possibly unprecedented. Late industrialization is characterized by a labor supply that is almost unlimited, an absence of a cadre of skilled workers who could provide trade union leadership, and a lack of opportunity for mass international migration. All these factors have favored a low rate of wage increase. Yet real average wages appear to have risen, even if only desultorily, in most late-industrializing countries. They have risen sharply in Korea and Japan.

The rapid rate of wage increase in Korea and Japan during their periods of ultrafast growth has lent the industrializations in these countries a particular character. The low *level* of real wages has underscored the international competitiveness of both economies. The rapid *rise* of real wages has driven the more prudent firms to invest in greater technological capability for the future. The combination of low wage level and fast wage increase has contributed to the dynamism of Korean and Japanese growth.

The reasons for such wage behavior are in part unique and in part extreme variants of properties that are general to late industrialization. The unique factors include an ultralong workday and an especially high real income per farming family in Korea and Japan. The general property of the labor market of late industrialization that takes a particularly strong form in Korea and Japan is segmentation, by manufacturing industry and sex.

This chapter examines the forces behind the operation of the labor market and real wage increases in Korea. Because scarcity and supply and demand cannot alone explain the operation of Korea's labor market, the chapter ends with a discussion of the imperatives of technology and the skill set of late industrialization that have driven big business to pay more.

The argument is as follows. In industries in which the technology transfer problem was fairly complicated and in which Korea lacked experience, workers were paid relatively high wages not because of a shortage of particular skills but in order to induce them to exercise their intelligence and make imported technology work. The wage rate in Korea was driven up especially fast by the exigencies of learning because the learning experience in Korea was especially intense. The learning experience was especially intense because it was undertaken by local rather than foreign firms, happened in a great spurt, and occurred in large, bureaucratic enterprises. Business was also pressured by government to share its wealth with labor.

LABOR SUPPLY

Countries that have industrialized since World War II, by comparison with either England, the European emulators, or the United States, have done so on the basis of far larger labor reserves, or what Lewis (1954) called *an unlimited supply*. Greater labor reserves may be inferred from differences in population growth rates, international migratory flows, and obstacles to labor organization.[1] (They cannot be *inferred* from unemployment rates because these are statistically unreliable.)

Population

According to Kuznets' (1966) estimates for countries that are currently industrialized, the growth rate of population from the mid-1700s and onward was rarely more than 1.5%. One exception was the population of the United States, which grew very fast because of inward migration. The population of Japan, on the other hand, was

---

[1] There was not always overpopulation and excess labor in what is known today as the Third World. At first, the Americas were short of a voluntary work force and depended on European migration and slavery; the foreign plantations and mines in remote parts of Africa and Asia experienced severe labor shortages and relied on state coercion. Both slavery and coercion explain why a high-wage economy failed to develop in the face of labor scarcity:

Sometimes the pressure was applied directly, and the administrative power of the colonial government or indigenous rulers was used to direct labor to the mines and plantations. More frequently, the pressure was applied indirectly, by imposing a poll tax or a hut tax, which obliged the indigenous people in the subsistence economy to come out and work in the mines and plantations so that they could pay their taxes. (Myint, 1964, p. 61) .

abundant throughout the period of industrialization despite a very low population growth rate. From 1869 to 1940 the Japanese population is estimated to have grown at only about 1% per annum; after the war it grew by only about 1.1% (Patrick and Rosovsky, 1976). By contrast, in developing regions (excluding Latin America), the population growth rate steadily increased from about 1.5% in the 1940s to about 1.7% in the 1950s. In Latin America the average annual population growth rate was 1.9% in the 1930s, 2.3% in the 1940s, and 2.7% in the 1950s (Sanches-Albornoz, 1974), In the 1960s, population growth rates averaged 2.4% in "low income" countries, 2.5% in "middle income" countries (which include Korea and other late-industrializing countries), and 1.0% in industrialized ones (World Bank, 1979). All told, the typical colonial pattern produced abundant surplus labor. Minimal investments in health and sanitation by the colonial authorities enabled the population to grow; minimal investments in industry and agriculture dampened demand for labor's services; hence, the ultimate "distortion" of excess population brought about by colonial rule.

Given Korea's traditional high population density and inequitable income distribution, a scarcity of labor never existed, even in the mines and plantations of the Japanese colonialists. During the colonial period the labor market behaved as one would expect; between 1910 and 1940, real wages fell (Grajdanzev, 1944).[2] Further evidence of excess reserves came during World War II when 2 million Koreans were drafted to work in Japan's least remunerative industries, with no perceptible impact on Korean production. Although land reform in late-1940s Korea was labor absorbing, by 1960, one year before the military coup, it was estimated that perhaps one-fifth of the industrial and agricultural work force—2 million people—were unemployed (Reeve, 1963).

International Migration

By comparison with countries that industrialized relatively early in world history, Japan's industrialization marked a turning point after which countries experienced not only faster growth rates of population as they industrialized but far fewer opportunities to send their surplus populations abroad. Since the end of World War II, capital has become more mobile internationally, while labor has become far less so.

Permanent emigration from Korea is said to have begun in the eighteenth century when people in the northeastern part of the

[2] In Taiwan, by contrast, they appear to have risen. See Ho (1984).

country strayed into Manchuria. It reached a rate of 60,000 a year by the early nineteenth century and continued under economic and political duress during the period of Japanese rule (S. Kim, 1982a). When industrialization got under way, however, annual emigration was generally well under 10% of the natural increase in population. Fewer than half a million Koreans emigrated permanently in the two decades following 1962 (S. Kim, 1982a).[3]

The overall permanent migration from Korea and from the rest of the developing world has been relatively modest because of restrictive immigration policies in the developed countries. According to Kuznets,

> The significance of intercontinental, and presumably international, migration in the growth of countries of origin and of destination in the nineteenth and early twentieth centuries lends importance to the failure of Asia, Africa, and much of Latin America to participate—even before World War I—and to the sharp decline in these flows after World War I. Perhaps it merits specific notice that Japan, which entered the phase of modern economic growth well before the twentieth century, could not fully participate in the emigration toward the more developed areas. (1966, p. 56)

The contrast between present-day migration and that of the period from the second half of the nineteenth century to the end of World War I is striking. An estimate of European migration during the period 1851–1920, when the population of all of Europe was far smaller than that of the developing world today, puts the number at more than 40 million. About half of those who migrated did so in the last three decades of the nineteenth century—a number equivalent to over 40% of Europe's natural population increase during those years (Woodruff, 1973).

Obstacles to Labor Organization

By comparison with countries that achieved industrial transformation earlier in world history, countries that have industrialized since World War II have generally tended to do so in the absence of a

---

[3] Temporary emigration, or contract-labor migration, was initiated by the Korean government in 1963 when roughly 250 coal miners and later some 1,000 nurses were sent to the German Federal Republic. Then, in the late 1960s, approximately 25,000 construction workers migrated to Vietnam. Finally, beginning in 1974, the boom in the Middle East drew tens of thousands of Koreans to overseas construction sites. Annual migration to the Middle East skimmed the supply of able-bodied men and drove up wages at home. But the Middle Eastern migratory flow proved ephemeral (*Han'guk Ilbo*, 1986c; *Choson Ilbo*, 1986).

coherent trade union movement or of a parliamentary labor party. The weakness of trade union activity is partly tied to the demise of the skilled crafts, which says something additional about the skill base of late industrialization. Whereas skilled labor in earlier industrializing countries was at the vanguard of worker protest movements and trade union organization, a property of late industrialization is a relatively small role for the same type of manual skilled labor in any capacity—be it labor leader or scarce resource. Discussion here is restricted to the first, that of labor organizer.

In early-industrializing countries, the extreme difficulties of effective general unionization—due to rapidly increasing population, great labor mobility, very low real incomes, sharp economic fluctuations, and a hostile law—were chipped away by the class of skilled workers. In England, "Effective trade societies were first confined to the skilled handicraft workers—the 'aristocracy of labour' " (Mathias, 1969, p. 364). In Germany,

> At least some part of the developing working class in the second and third quarter of the nineteenth century would have been former artisans (using the term in a broad sense) who, although their earnings may have been higher in the factory, felt that their skill had been degraded and suffered a sense of deprivation. This kind of former artisan resentment contributed to the foundation of a labour movement, particularly of the Lassallian sort. (Kemp, 1985, p. 105)

In the United States,

> The experience of the post-Civil War decades clearly indicated the great difficulties trade unions confronted to sustain themselves in the face of periodic business depressions, bitter employer resistance, and hostile public authorities. To cope with these problems, Gompers and his associates . . . argued that unions had to "perfect" their organization and establish themselves on a "permanent" basis by providing their members with unemployment benefits, burial insurance, sick pay, and strike benefits. . . . This mode of organization was far easier to establish with unions that represented skilled rather than unskilled workers. (Shefter, 1986, pp. 259–0)

The part played by the artisan in late industrialization has depended on the country. In Japan, the role of artisans resembled more that of early industrializers than that of late ones. According to Sumiya,

> Manpower for Japanese industrialization came essentially from two groups. The first and major source was children of former

samurai, craftsmen, and peasants who migrated to the cities. They [children] were employed as apprentices and became modern factory workers after training.

Craftsmen themselves were the second source of factory labor. Since training of skilled workers was urgently needed for industrialization, the skills of traditional craftsmen were used whenever possible, while many were retrained to become skilled workers. (1974, p. 33)

As for unionization, Sumiya traced its origins to those Japanese who had gone to work in California in the 1890s and there formed a group patronized by Samuel Gompers. On returning to Japan, the group helped establish a union among iron workers and then railway engine drivers and printing workers. Sumiya wrote,

These unions not only were American-type craft unions in organization, . . . but also followed the AFL example; . . . [They] demonstrated not only the considerable increase in the number of industrial workers resulting from the growth of the factory production system but also the sense of unity that emerged among workers in the same craft or trade based on common interest shared and communicated as they moved from shop to shop. (1974, pp. 38–9)

In India, handicrafts had been highly developed at the time of foreign intrusion, but the artisan failed to play the role of union organizer because the sequence of industrialization differed from that in England, Germany, or the United States. Instead of modern machines displacing artisans directly and driving them to organize in defense, the displacement was indirect due to colonialism. In India, as in other late learners, industries that could use modern technology did so by way of import substitution, not by the destruction of artisanal production, which expired in the face of coercion and competitive imports from more advanced countries long before the arrival of factory production. The British Crown legislated the decrepitude of the handloom weaver in India in the interests of the East India Company, and then free trade furnished the final blow (Bagchi, 1982). The Governor-General of East India, and later Marx, wrote about the bones of the handloom weavers bleaching in the Indian countryside. When a modern textiles industry eventually emerged in India (in the last quarter of the nineteenth century), its victims were competitive imports, not skilled artisans, whose fortunes had long ago declined.

The sequence of events was somewhat different in Korea, because at the time of colonialism's arrival handicrafts were far less developed than they had been in India when the British arrived. When, after the Korean War, production with modern machinery finally commenced on a sizeable scale, surviving crafts that required traditional skills were accorded low status. Many skilled trades that hadn't been beaten down—furniture manufacture, tailoring, and tanning—began to be undertaken in the "informal sector." From special surveys, it seems that the informal sector was about 8 million people in 1979, or as much as one half to two thirds the size of nonagricultural employment (Bai, 1982; Lindauer, 1984). The application of surviving crafts in the informal sector has meant the following: (1) Such crafts were still frequently the pursuit of the self-employed rather than of the paid employee. (Of the estimated 8.3 million persons in the informal sector in 1979, roughly one third were either self-employed—2 million people—or family workers—half a million people.) (2) The remaining two thirds were regular, temporary, or daily workers, many of whom were low paid and had the lowest status. In either case, no material for labor leadership emerged from the informal sector.

In the formal sector, the technological changes that modern machinery had undergone by the time it began to be used, and the employment norms of paid labor that arose in tandem, created only moderate demand for traditional skills, as discussed shortly. A new "labor aristocracy" was established, but its skill base was nontraditional. This new labor aristocracy, moreover, was helped rather than hurt by modern machinery and, if for no other reason, played a negligible role in trade union growth in the 1950s through 1980s.

THE RATE OF PAY

Under conditions of repression, unlimited labor supply, absence of international migration, and weak grouping of skilled workers, one would expect at most stability—if not decline—in real wage rates. Yet average real wages in manufacturing have tended to rise somewhat in late-industrializing countries. In Korea, they have positively soared. Table 8.1 compares real wages in Korea, Brazil, Argentina, Mexico, India, Turkey, and Taiwan in the period 1970–1984. The 1970s were a period of rising real wages in all these countries, but in Korea wages rose spectacularly. The index of real wages in Korea increased from a base of 100 in 1970 to 238 in 1979.[4]

---

[4] Industrialization, of course, began before 1970 in all these countries, but wage increases were faster in Korea than in India, Brazil, or Taiwan also during the earlier period. Taking 100 as the base in 1957, the wage index in 1969 reached 77 in Brazil, 123 in India, and 156 in Korea. (Korea: see Richardson and Kim, 1986; Brazil: Souza, 1978; India: Lucas, 1986.)

Table 8.1 Comparison of Real Nonagricultural Wage Increases
in Seven Late-Industrializing Countries,[a] 1970–1984

Year	Korea[b]	Brazil[c]	Argentina	Mexico	Turkey	India[d]	Taiwan
1970	100	100	100	100	100	100	—
1971	102	110	105	103	100	100	—
1972	104	114	99	104	99	—	100
1973	119	119	107	104	98	106	107
1974	130	119	126	107	96	97	98
1975	131	127	124	114	116	110	110
1976	154	129	80	123	122	120	126
1977	187	134	76	125	146	116	138
1978	219	142	77	122	147	124	151
1979	238	134	87	121	155	130	163
1980	227	130	100	116	124		166
1981	225	118	91	119	130		171
1982	241	115	79	117	129		180
1983	261	97	97	86	130		188
1984	276	84	112	83	111		191

[a] Base = 100. Deflated by consumer price index.
[b] Real earnings manufacturing sector.
[c] Average wages for skilled workers in construction. Data are from the Central Bank.
[d] Rupees per hour for industrial workers.

Source: Korea: Richardson and Kim (1986). Brazil, Argentina, and Mexico: Paldam and Riveros (1987). India: Lucas (1986). Taiwan: Council for Economic Planning and Development (various years). Turkey: Institute of Statistics (various years).

Korea's wage behavior appears to be unrivaled in earlier industrial revolutions, although Japan's is almost as impressive. Of course, cross-sectional and intertemporal comparisons are by no means conclusive because of the universal fragility of wage data—the more distant the past and the less legitimate the political regime, the less reliable the data—and because of differences in the length of the time period considered—the shorter the time horizon (only two decades in Korea's case), the less the certainty that one is observing a secular trend. Overall, however, the average rate of real wage increases in Korea's post-World War II industrialization appears to be faster than that of earlier vintages.

In the case of England, Lindert and Williamson (1983) used new data and new methods of data manipulation to show that in the seventy-year period spanning 1781 to 1851, their "best guess" of the increase in the real full-time earnings of all British workers was 155%, 99% in the case of blue-collars workers. In their most pessimistic scenario, the gains were 100% and 62%, respectively. However rosy Lindert and Williamson's "best guess" estimate, it pales by compari-

Table 8.2 Average Earnings in Korean Manufacturing,
1955–1980 (in Thousand Won/Annum)

Year	Nominal Earnings	Real Earnings		
		Index Number (1975 = 100)	% Change from Previous Year	
1955	15	40.3	—	
1958	24	44.2	3.2[a]	
1963	40	47.0	1.3[a]	
1966	67	47.9	0.6[a]	
1967	82	52.7	10.0	
1969	129	66.4	13.0[a]	
1970	159	70.6	6.2	
1971	190	74.3	5.2	
1972	216	75.6	1.8	
1973	267	90.6	19.9	
1974	347	94.8	4.6	
1975	459	100.0	5.5	
1976	587	110.9	10.9	
1977	759	130.1	17.3	
1978	1,050	157.5	21.1	
1979	1,378	174.7	10.9	
1980	1,759	173.2	−0.9	

[a]The computed average annual percent change over relevant interval.

Source: All data are originally from the Mining and Manufacturing Survey or Census. Collection of these data has been the responsibility of various agencies, including, in chronological order: Bank of Korea, Korean Reconstruction Bank, and Economic Planning Board. For the years 1970–1979, the data are from the tabulations of the Small and Medium Industry Handbook (1980), as cited by Lindauer (1984).

son with Korea's. Table 8.2 presents a longer profile on real wages in Korean manufacturing, from 1955 through 1980 (and on average, manufacturing workers in Korea are among the *lowest* paid in the country [Richardson and Kim, 1986]). By comparison with English data, the following is striking: While it took English workers seventy years to raise their real earnings by rough 150%, Korean manufacturing workers achieved a comparable gain in about 20 years (from 1955 to 1976). In just one decade, 1969–1979, real wages in Korea rose by more than 250%.

The long-run trend in real earnings of workers in the United States, England, and the European emulators has been estimated by Brown (1986). The most authoritative source for comparative purposes, Brown's data are for the period 1860–1913 for five countries: France, Germany, Sweden, the United Kingdom, and the United States. Among the five countries, real average wages (expressed in composite units of consumables) grew fastest in the United States. Taking, therefore, the U.S. index at its trough and peak—approximately 45 in 1865, just after the Civil War, and about 130 in 1913, just before World War I—real wages increased in the United States by a factor of almost 3 in roughly fifty years. In Korea, however, real wages increased even faster: As indicated in Table 8.2, real earnings quadrupled from trough to peak in roughly half as much time, twenty-five years.

Japan's best wage data are divided into two subperiods, 1900–1935 and 1950–1968, and refer to workers in manufacturing establishments of thirty or more production workers (Minami, 1973). Ignoring gender differences, real wages for all production workers rose from about 120 yen in 1900 to about 430 yen in 1935, or by a multiple of 3.6 in thirty-five years. After World War II they rose even faster, following labor unrest in 1947–1949 and the onset of the prosperous postwar international division of labor. Real wages rose by a factor of 2.7 in eighteen years, from approximately 400 yen in 1950 to about 1200 yen in 1968. Again, however, real wages in Korea rose even faster—by a scalar of 4.3 between 1955 and 1980 and by one of 3.6 between 1966 and 1980. Wage rates in Korea, moreover, are understated in comparison with those of Japan. Whereas Korean data are restricted to firms with over ten workers, Japanese data are restricted to firms with over 30. Yet smaller firms in Japan are believed to have begun paying lower wages than larger firms after the 1920s (Minami, 1973, pp. 172–3).

THE REASONS BEHIND RISING REAL WAGES

When a price increases, one is inclined to think that scarcity is involved. Yet one cannot explain Korea's wage behavior simply by supply and demand analysis. Indirect labor, which includes managers, engineers, and technicians, is supposedly the scarcest type of labor in backward countries. Thus, one would expect late industrializers to experience abundance and scarcity of direct and indirect labor, respectively, the wages of the latter modestly pulling up the overall average, if at all. The pattern of wage increase in Korea, however, flies in the face of expectation. As Table 8.3 indicates, in four subperiods from 1965 to 1984, the rate of wage increase was higher for production workers than it was for professional, technical, or managerial employees in spite of the excess supply that is believed to have characterized both labor markets, especially the one for production workers.

In the late 1970s, Korea supposedly reached a "turning point" (Bai, 1982), its supply of surplus labor vanishing, with the outflow of

Table 8.3 Rate of Wage Increase in Korea for Production and
Professional, Technical, and Managerial Workers, 1965–1984

| | Wage Increase Rate | |
Period	Production Workers	Professional, Technical, and Managerial Workers
1965–1970	12.8	6.6
1971–1974	7.1	6.1
1975–1979	16.8	15.3
1980–1984	5.3	2.5

Source: 1965–1979, Bai (1982); 1980–1984, Ministry of Labor (1985).

workers—mainly to the Middle East—amounting to as much as 27%
of the male manufacturing work force (Ministry of Labor, various
years). Table 8.3 confirms that wages increased in the late 1970s especially fast. Nevertheless, such scarcity proved short-lived with the
collapse of the Middle Eastern construction market and a slowdown
in Korea's growth rate.[5] Thus, in the twenty years spanning 1965
through 1984, a tight labor market was the exception to the rule, yet
real wages rose persistently.

The wage question in Korea is further complicated by the fact
that, although all workers experienced some increase in real wages,
the increase was unevenly distributed across firms of different size,
industries of different capital intensity, and workers of different sex.
The lowest paid workers, say in light manufactures in the informal
sector and textiles in the formal one, have continued to receive what
even Korea's state-dominated labor federation has admitted are little
more than subsistence wages, whereas workers with comparable levels of experience and education in the heavy industries are among
the highest paid.[6] Thus, firm behavior toward labor has become increasingly differentiated, a reflection of a high degree of differentiation among firms in terms of size, capital intensity, organization, and
management (see Chapter 7).

The behavior of real wages in Korea therefore must be examined
not merely in terms of supply and demand, but also in terms of
institutions and history. To arrive at the explanation for why real
wages have risen more rapidly in Korea than in other late-industrializing countries, the following areas are explored: the fast rate of
capital accumulation; the low base from which wages in Korea have
risen; the structure of Korean agriculture— a consequence of land

[5] Unemployment of college graduates was especially sharp in the late 1960s and
1980s (*Donga Ilbo*, 1987).

[6] For a discussion of the subsistence nature of Korean wages, see J. C. Lim (1986).

reform in the late 1940s; the unrivaled length of the work week; and market segmentation—by gender, firm size, and industry. Before proceeding, one may note the striking extent to which the factors operative in Korea that help one to understand its rapid wage increases also tend to have been operative in Japan during its period of rapid wage gains. Nevertheless, the factors operating in both countries are not obviously "cultural" and confound any simple explanation for market behavior related to "the Orient."

The Demand Side

If Korea experienced faster real wage increases than did other late-industrializing countries, this is partly because its GNP grew faster. A rapid rate of capital accumulation provided the basis for rapid wage increases. Nam (1980) estimated an equation to explain the rate of change of nominal manufacturing wages in Korea during the period 1966–1977. He included variables to represent the demand for labor (the rate of GNP over the previous year), the supply of labor (the lagged change in manufacturing employment), and inflation (the lagged change in prices). The strongest explanatory variable is the demand for labor, or the previous year's change in GNP.

The period in question, 1966–1977, was the Golden Age of Korea's industrial expansion. Output, exports, and productivity were all growing rapidly. Not surprisingly, wages also rose. Even if the government did not intervene directly in wage determination, employers were under strong pressure from the government to share their gains with labor. However, as Table 8-4 suggests, beginning in 1965 the rate of real wage increase tended to stay below the rate of labor productivity growth (except in 1976–1979 and 1982). The wage strategy of big business amounted to gain sharing.

Nevertheless, ambiguity surrounds the determination of the impact of fast growth on real wage increases.[7] In Brazil, for example, it seems that the impact is weak. The average annual growth rate of the Brazilian economy during the period 1950–1975 was as much as 6.7%. Yet while real wages increased for the majority of the period, they did so very slowly (Paldam and Riveros, 1987; Souza, 1978). Growth in Taiwan has equalled that in Korea but wages have lagged.

[7] Nam's equation fails to explain why wages rose, notwithstanding the inclusion of a variable intended to measure labor supply. According to Nam, "the fit of the wage equation to the data is not excellent," although a similar model provided better correlation with the inclusion of a dummy variable for the period 1970–1977 (1980, p. 79). Norton and Rhee (1980) estimated a wage equation with a dummy variable, GNP, and a price deflator (but no supply effect) and got an R^2 of 0.88.

Table 8.4 Percent Change in Labor Productivity and Wages in Manufacturing, 1965–1984

	1965–1973	1974–1975	1976–1977	1978–1979	1980	1981	1982	1983	1984
				Percent Change					
Total wage									
Nominal[a]	21.6	31.2	34.3	35.6	19.1	20.0	14.7	11.3	8.2
Real[a]	9.8	5.1	19.5	19.2	−9.6	−1.3	7.5	7.9	5.9
Labor productivity	13.0	18.8	10.6	13.4	10.5	16.9	7.2	13.0	10.0

[a]Nominal minus consumer price index.

Sources: Office of Labor Affairs (until 1980) and Ministry of Labor; Bank of Korea.

The Supply Side

Korea's Low Wage Base

Korea's wages grew fast but they started from an exceptionally low base. In a symposium in the mid-1960s on wage trends in developing countries, it was asked why the Far East had experienced no structural inflation similar to Latin America's. Three answers were forthcoming, all of which hinted at the extreme poverty characteristic of Far Eastern economies at the time.

1. "The backwardness of these countries—even by the standards of developing regions—means that the industrial labor force tends to be unorganized and in no position to force wage rises when the cost of living increases . . ." (Smith, 1967, p. 27).
2. Because of the small size of the industrial sector, industrial expansion does not place excessive demands on agricultural output.
3. The marginal product of labor in agriculture tends to be low because of high population density, so rural-urban migration does not reduce agricultural output. Inhabitants per square kilometer in 1960 were 109 in South Central Asia, 86 in Europe 71 in East Asia, 48 in Southeast Asia, 14 in Southwest Asia, 11 in Central and South America, 10 in the Soviet Union, 9 in North America, and 8 in Africa (Smith, 1967, p. 27).[8]

Thus, from a low wage base in Korea, it was easier for employers to remain internationally competitive and yet raise wages, if only to improve the physical stamina and psychic motivation of their workers.

Land Reform and Small-Scale Agriculture

Rapid increases in productivity (and thus "implicit" wages) in Korean agriculture, acted to drive up wages in modern industry. The "implicit" wage of male workers in agriculture *exceeded* the average wage in manufacturing until the late 1960s (Ban et al., 1980). According to Bai's (1982) estimates, the male wage rate in agriculture exceeded that in modern industry until at least the mid-1970s. In the mid-1980s, the average income of a rural family exceeded that of an urban family (BOK, *Yearbook*).

It is misleading, however, to use the term, *agricultural wage rate,*

[8] One might add that neither of two tendencies operating toward a high wage level in Africa and Latin America operated in the Far East. In Africa, the relatively high pay scales of European civil servants in the British and French colonial services were adopted by locals during the period after independence (Amsden, 1971). In labor-scarce Latin America, early European settlers earned European pay scales. By contrast, Korea experienced almost no inward migration from advanced countries, and the pay scales of Japanese colonial administrators may have become only a dim memory after the chaos that terminated Japanese rule and the Korean War.

because Korean agriculture employed few proletarians. Instead, the agrarian reform of the late 1940s invested land in the tiller, so a tenure system of small-scale family farms evolved, which required few hired hands except at harvest. Given sharp increases in agricultural productivity as a consequence of government support, rural-urban migration and downward pressure on manufacturing wages can be assumed to have been less massive than it would otherwise have been. The labor retentiveness of Korean agriculture by comparison with less egalitarian land tenure systems is suggested by international comparisons of the share of agricultural employment in total employment. Despite the limited availability of arable land, Korean agriculture's share of the labor force in 1980 was as high as 34%, compared with, say, 30% in land-rich Brazil. The Korean share was even higher than that in Taiwan, although both countries had experienced land reforms (World Bank, 1982). Consequently, both a lower-than-otherwise flow of rural-urban migrants and a higher-than-otherwise rural household income buttressed manufacturing wage rates.

Women Workers

Nonetheless, one can still say that Korea has industrialized (and continues to do so) with unlimited labor reserves. To the question of how agriculture may preserve a society of family farms yet provide industry with enough labor to keep wages at a socioeconomic subsistence level, Lewis provided this answer: "There are the wives and daughters of the household. . . . The transfer of women's work from the household to commercial employment is one of the most notable features of economic development" (1954, p. 404).

Not only has Korea set world records with its growth rate in wages, it has also outcompeted other countries in its discrimination against women workers, although in some years (1984, for example), this dubious distinction fell to Japan. As Table 8.5 indicates, in 1980 the male-female wage gap was greater in Korea than in any other country for which data are available from the International Labor Organization.

Almost 60% of the male-female wage gap in Korea has been attributed to differences in human capital between the sexes. It is estimated that 27.6% of the gap is due to differences in education and 31.8% to differences in experience (traditionally, women have been forced to leave paid employment when they marry). Thus, ". . . part of the wage differential between the sexes in South Korea seems to be rooted in 'before labor market discrimination' in addition to . . . 'labor market discrimination,' . . . but both are closely interrelated" (J. W. Lee, 1983, p. 67). There are virtually no women in manage-

Table 8.5 Comparison of Manufacturing Wage Differential by Sex,[a]
1980

Country	%	Country	%
Sweden	89.3	Belgium	69.4
Burma	88.8	U.K.	68.8
Denmark	86.1	Syria	68.8
Norway	81.9	Ireland	68.7
Netherlands	80.1	Greece	67.8
El Salvador	78.9	Switzerland	67.7
Australia	78.6	Egypt	63.1
France	75.4	Luxembourg	61.2
Finland	75.4	Cyprus	50.2
West Germany	72.7	Japan	48.2
New Zealand	72.4	South Korea	44.5

[a] Female/male average wage × 100. Hourly wages except for Burma (monthly). Adults only for United Kingdom.

Source: International Labor Office, 1981, as quoted in J. W. Lee (1983).

rial or even entrepreneurial positions in the primary manufacturing sector (Grootaert, 1986).

The human capital explanation for the gender wage gap would lead one to expect discrimination to recede as women invested in more education and acquired more experience. Yet such is not the case:

> During the past few decades, gender inequality in educational opportunities at all levels of schooling has . . . continuously decreased. . . . The participation in the labor force of those with secondary and tertiary education increased at a much faster rate for women than for men with [a] decreasing proportion of primary school graduates. . . . Moreover, the proportion of women in [the] 25–29 age group, who have the burden of childbearing and childrearing, has increased, which suggests improved women's labor-force attachment. . . . In contrast, the male-female earnings gap remains large, without reduction. (Y. H. Kim, 1970, p. 4)

Korea's outstanding real wage increases and unrivaled gender wage disparities are related to one another insofar as an unlimited supply of women workers has allowed Korea's bifurcated wage structure to achieve dual ends. One end is the maintenance of international competitiveness in labor-intensive industries, which employ primarily females. The other is the entry into more skill-intensive pursuits on the basis of a relatively well-paid, highly motivated, male labor aristocracy.

Table 8.6 Hours of Work in Manufacturing, 1976–1985

Country	Average Workweek (hrs)
South Africa	47.0
Argentina	45.6
Mexico	46.0
Puerto Rico	38.0
United States	40.1
Hong Kong	47.1
Israel	38.7
Japan	46.0
Korea	53.3
Malaysia	48.4
Belgium	34.3
France	40.1
Germany	41.2
Norway	38.1
Sweden	37.8
United Kingdom	41.5

Source: International Labor Office (1986).

The Length of the Workweek

In the length of its workweek, Korea has set still another world record. For all persons employed in manufacturing in 1984, 73% of men and 62% of women worked at least fifty-four hours per week (Grootaert, 1986). By contrast, in other countries the average for persons employed in manufacturing was much lower (see Table 8.6).

The length of Korea's workweek can be understood historically against the backdrop of the length of the prevailing international workweek, particularly that of Japan. In turn, the length of Japan's workweek can be traced back to work hours in Europe at the time Japan was "opened" by the West.

It was, of course, in the 1870s that Japan began to industrialize, and Japan was undoubtedly influenced by the prevailing length of the workday in Western countries. By the turn of the century, moreover, "la semaine Anglaise" and the workweek in the United States were short by the standards of Continental emulators, which were most likely to have served as models for Japan. In 1908 the British Board of Trade found that a sixty-hour workweek was standard in all German trades except printing. In France, the Factory Act of 1900 had provided for the reduction of the maximum workday for all classes of workers to ten hours, but there was no legal requirement of any rest day. These long hours, moreover, prevailed until the end of World War I (Brown, 1968).

During the colonial period, Japan directly transferred a long workweek to Korea. The colonial factory system was harsh, and Korean workers grew accustomed to a workweek similar to what then prevailed in Japan and say, Germany at the turn of the century. According to one contemporary account,

> The men in large-scale enterprises in 1939 [in Korea] worked on an average of 10 hours a day, and women and children 10 hours and 15 minutes, and 10 hours and 20 minutes, respectively. . . . With respect to holidays, the usual arrangement is two rest-days a month, though in 1931, an investigation of enterprises with 10 workers and more revealed that 35% of these enterprises had no rest-days whatsoever. (Grajdanzev, 1944, p. 184)

These work hours exceed those that have won Korea its reputation for industriousness, and they were expended in a period of falling, not rising, real wages.

What is extraordinary about Korea is that long work hours have continued to persist. This may be understood in terms of both the weakness of organized labor to shorten hours for a given wage rate and labor's willingness to take advantage of rapid industrial expansion through higher wages for endless toil.

Segmentation

Upward pressure on wage rates came especially from large-scale firms in basic industry. Table 8.7 shows the origins of Korea's segmented labor market. The rate of wage increase during the labor-abundant period 1965 to 1971 varied according to industry, ranging from a low of 175% in rubber products to a high of 415% in petroleum and coal products. The upshot was a large dispersion in manufacturing wages.

Yet another world record that Korea holds is the degree of wage dispersion in the manufacturing sector. As Table 8.8 indicates, in both 1973 and 1982 the standard deviation of wages (in logs) was greater in Korea than in thirteen other countries examined, Japan taking second place. Nor has such manufacturing wage dispersion become more compressed in Korea over time (Richardson and Kim, 1986). The capital-intensive industries have continued to pay more than textiles, wood, and miscellaneous manufacturing. Wage dispersion also varies across firm size, especially when one disaggregates by gender.

The dispersion in interindustry wages is largely accounted for by

Table 8.7   Wage Increases in Selected Sectors of Manufacturing,[a] 1965–1971

Sector	Percent Increase 1971 over 1965
Food	336
Textile	227
Wood and cork	222
Paper	288
Leather	215
Rubber	175
Chemicals	354
Petroleum, coal products	415
Basic metals	222
Machinery	208
Electric machinery	363
Transportation equipment	313
Average	269

[a]Calculated from figures published in *Sanop Saingsan Yunbo* ("Annual Report on Current Industrial Production Survey") (Seoul: Economic Planning Board, 1972, pp. 68–81).

Source: Ewing (1973).

Table 8.8   Wage Dispersion among Manufacturing Industries in Selected Countries, 1973 and 1982

Country	Standard Deviation of Log Wages	
	1973	1982
Bolivia	.204	.168
Canada	.225	.239
France	.143	.126
Germany	.137	.141
Japan	.216	.263
Korea	.349	.314
Mexico	.147	.155
Norway	.075	.107
Poland	.126	.097
Sweden	.067	.081
USSR	.117	.101
United Kingdom	.087	.140
United States	.206	.241
Yugoslavia	.126	.120

Source: Krueger and Summers (1986).

blue-collar workers. According to J. W. Lee, "The interindustry differentials among white-collar workers are lower than among blue-collar with only a few exceptions" (1983, p. 172). In part, blue-collar workers earn different wage rates in different industries because they have different marginal products, those in the capital-intensive industries probably being higher. However, *it is unclear why capital-intensive firms pay a wage rate equal to their workers' marginal product rather than paying the all-manufacturing average.*

Wage dispersion by industry and by firm size is present in most countries that are now industrialized or that are in the process of becoming so. In the former, segmentation arose in response to a complex of factors, including trade union pressures (see Osterman [1984] for references). In the latter—Korea being the case in point—trade union pressures were weak, but political ones were strong. The Korean government routinely intervened in industrial relations (see the reference to the complaints of the Federation of Korean Industries in Chapter 5, footnote 17). In its populist posture, the government was undoubtedly responsible for narrowing the wage gap between managers and production workers (as indicated in Table 8.3). Populism took other forms besides higher rank-and-file wages, one example being a ban on color televisions to reduce social stratification. The fear was always one of a resurgence of political unrest and labor militance (in the 1960s labor affairs were placed under the jurisdiction of the Korea Central Intelligence Agency). In addition, big business began to pay high for reasons to do with efficiency, to which attention is now turned.

THE SKILLS OF THE NEW LABOR ARISTOCRACY OF LATE INDUSTRIALIZATION

To understand the rise of segmented labor markets in a late-industrializing country like Korea, one must understand the labor policies of the modern industrial enterprise—in Korea's case, the diversified business group. The reason that the diversified business groups may have paid their blue-collar workers above the all-manufacturing average was that the skills of such workers were in scarce supply because they tended to be firm specific. In the case of male workers, one year of "inside" experience (with the same employer) tended to raise wages on average by about 10%, whereas one year of "outside" experience (with a different employer) raised them on average by only about 3.8% (J. W. Lee, 1983). The interesting question then becomes what firm-specific "skills" were being rewarded.

One must start by understanding differentiation among firms. The firms to emerge in the basic industries—shipbuilding, steel, and so on—were different in almost every respect even from modern large-scale enterprises in cotton textiles, Korea's leading sector (see the discussion in Chapter 10). They were different if for no other reason than that their profitability depended on the exploitation of technologies for which they had virtually no operational first-hand experience.

Experience in textiles dated back to the Japanese colonial period, so expansions and modernizations in the 1950s exposed textiles entrepreneurs to few problems. By contrast, even the huge fixed-capital investments in the continuous-process industries that relied initially on turnkey technology transfers—cement, fertilizers, oil refining, and steel—created for managers the problem of trying to bring under control a process that the foreign experts themselves understood only imperfectly. Neophytes that they were, Korean managers could never hope to manage in a tight, "Taylorist," top-down fashion, at least not initially, *because no one at the top knew enough about the process to do so.* Under these conditions, it was imperative to rely on motivated workers, even if these workers possessed little more than formal schooling, to exercise the most fundamental skill of all—intelligence. In all of the new capital-intensive industries—continuous-process and especially fabrication-assembly operations and job shops of jumbo proportions—production workers were motivated with relatively high wage rates, first to get the product out the door, and later to improve quality. In short, they were motivated to adopt a reasonably scientific approach to problem solving in a milieu whose technology was tacit, implicit, and not yet procedurized.

For the purpose of gaining an appreciation of the skills of the new labor aristocracy, which were being rewarded with high wage increases during late industrialization, one may examine the personnel policies of one of Korea's premier producers, the state-owned Pohang Iron and Steel Company (POSCO).

The Personnel Policies of the Pohang Iron and Steel Company (POSCO)

POSCO maintains a three-tier wage structure. Managers are the highest paid and then come blue-collar workers, who are divided into two categories: "regular" and "contracted out." In 1984, contracted-out workers numbered 8,700 or 24% of a total work force of 25,700. Contracted-out workers are confined to menial tasks such as relining, cleaning, packing, preparing ingot molds, scarfing, and treating slabs. POSCO is estimated to save about 15% in wages by contracting this work rather than delegating it to regular employees (PaineWebber, 1985). Regular employees are well paid by Korean standards—about twice the manufacturing average, depending on the annual bonus—although POSCO claims that it never faced a labor shortage. In addition, POSCO provides its regular workers with paternalistic perks: a kindergarten-through-university school system from which new workers are recruited; a medical dispensary, including a room for surgery; five daily commuter trains "free" of charge to employees; about $50 per month lunch allowance, and more.

Thus, the internal wage structure of production workers at POSCO reflects the external one at the national level. Production workers are divided into high-paid and low-paid categories that are analogous to those of the permanent and transitory employees in Japan.

In exchange for relatively high pay and the job security that comes with employment in a company that is expanding rapidly, POSCO expects attentiveness from its workers throughout their long hours on the job. A century ago, steelmaking required strenuous physical effort on the part of production workers as well as proficiency in the art of steelmaking on the part of master steelmakers (earlier, iron-puddling would have been considered a skilled craft). The category of master steelmaker or "saint technician" still survives in POSCO, but largely as a vestige of the past. After a decade of operation, only one master technician and five submasters exist. Instead, steelmaking or ironmaking for production workers involves process monitoring and control as well as auxiliary operations such as overhead crane driving. *POSCO has approximately 425 job categories, and the largest number of workers can be found at data-collection stations positioned at well defined set points in the process.* Workers check sensors for temperatures in different process zones, note the chemical composition of gases, and register flow rates. For this, however, they must have a fairly good understanding of the physical and chemical reactions involved in ironmaking and steelmaking—in order to ensure high quality—since steel production is not all in closed-loop control and the acceptable limits of materials change.

To increase productivity POSCO provides its workers with extensive training. In a single year, 1984, 9,924 workers out of 23,700 received training in one form or another (see Table 8.9). Of interest even beyond the quantity of training, though, is the curriculum. The aim is to instill in all workers a general knowledge of POSCO's operations and operating principles. Only to a lesser extent is training oriented toward building in-depth specialized skills.

Table 8.9 Status of Training and Education at the Pohang Iron and Steel Corporation (POSCO), 1968–1984

Training and Education	Number of Employees		Total (1968–1984) (percent)
	1968–1979	1980–1984	
General training			
Job Instruction[b]	17,246	6,343	19.4
Manager	863	2,045	2.4
Site Supervisor	2,041	1,736	3.1
Subtotal	20,149	10,125	24.9
Specific training			
Steelmaking	2,517	3,205	4.7
Computer	—	2,259	1.8
Sales	—	160	0.1
Subtotal	2,517	5,624	6.6
Language	4,738	2,435	5.9
Quality control	1,368	19,962	17.5
Trainer and PWI	1,343	1,538	2.4
Irregular education	10,244	16,922	22.3
Consigned education	4,239	3,325	6.2
Job training (out of company)	5,081	7,324	10.2
Others	11,769	3,886	12.8
Total trained	61,448	60,331	100[a]

[a] Sums to more than 100 due to rounding.
[b] Company orientation.
Source: POSCO.

The "general training" referred to in Table 8.9 involves two to three weeks' introductory education for new recruits, designed to familiarize them with the company's organizational structure, management system, and production system and to build occupational "morale, mentality, and attitude." "Specific training" in steelmaking refers to specialized education programs that encourage operation and maintenance technicians to promote or to diversify their on-the-job training by learning more theoretical and practical knowledge in the field of their specific job. "Irregular education" refers to occasional education programs for employees who need particular training for special occasions; for example, for new facilities or systems, new quality controls and production scheduling, and so on. Overall, a good deal of training involves general instruction, including training in quality control, computer literacy, foreign languages, and the training of trainers.

A normal workweek at POSCO consists of fifty-six hours (eight times seven): forty-five regular hours and eleven overtime hours for which no premium is paid. Every worker is entitled to *only one day of leave per month*, plus one day for each year with the company. In 1977 labor turnover at POSCO was 4.4%, below the national average of approximately 5.1% in manufacturing. In 1984 labor turnover had fallen to only 1.2%, well below the national average of approximately 5.4% (Ministry of Labor, 1985). Absenteeism in POSCO is not a problem. In 1984 absenteeism was only 0.07% of labor days. Low absenteeism and turnover are believed to be essential for high productivity. Although the overwhelming majority of POSCO's 23,700 workers cannot be described as possessing highly developed craft skills, steelmaking remains something of an art and learning its technology makes in-house experience invaluable.

POSCO operates with the motto, "Resources are limited, but human creativity is unlimited." Limited resources, or scarcity, therefore, does appear to have influenced POSCO's wage policy by driving it to pay more than average to attract the "best" workers. "Best" should be understood in a general sense, however, rather than with reference to specific skills.

CONCLUSION

We have repeatedly suggested that a firm's history conditions its behavior. In particular, firms that industrialize late, on the basis of learning, tend to behave differently from those that date from the nineteenth century and that expanded over the years on the basis of commercializing new processes-cum-products. Yet there is a convergence of behavior in at least one critical respect—the advent of labor market segmentation. Taking the example of the steel industry, it appears that integrated steelmakers in a late-industrializing country like Korea, no less than in a country like the United States, tend to pay relatively high wages by their respective all-industry average.

Segmentation, however, does not imply that in both types of firms the management of workers converges *in other respects*. There appear to be significant differences in the way labor is managed in the two sets of firms. Moreover, at least some such differences seem to derive from structural distinctions in the learning and innovating mode.

In the case of the learner, as exemplified in this chapter by POSCO, the absence of experience (or skills) in steelmaking on the part of its work force—both manual and managerial—forced the adoption of management practices that minimized the costs of such a shortfall. Such practices may be simply stated as follows (and are presented in detail in later chapters): First, there was a tendency for management to be very clear and specific about job descriptions and workers' responsibilities (see the discussion in Chapter 12). Even before POSCO poured any steel, it practiced steelmaking in an open field, workers shouting orders to one another so that there was no uncertainty about tasks. This procedurization and intense attempt to overcome the variabilities of a foreign technology paid off in tight process control, which ultimately facilitated process improvements and higher quality. Second, lack of experience on management's part forced a greater reliance on worker inputs and participative labor relations. Even before quality control circles were officially formed, work groups were established in POSCO to facilitate vertical and horizontal networks of communication. Finally, inexperience coupled with unfamiliarity with an imported technology directed management's attention to the shop floor. POSCO put its best managers on the line and formed decentralized "technostations" to provide line managers with ongoing technical assistance. Overall, this approach opened the door to sustained productivity improvements, making relatively high wage increases also sustainable.

Turing to the mode of industrialization based on innovation in the United States, one cannot, of course, generalize across firms in all industries. There does, however, appear to be a pattern in the behavior of leading firms in the traditionally high-paying sectors—steel, autos, machinery, petrochemicals, and others—that suggests a different approach to managing labor from the one just described. For one, the residue of skills (and bargaining power) on the part of the work force often contributed to work rules that lent a rigidity to the production process and intensified labor-management hostility. A legacy of skills on the part of the work force may have hurt productivity more than a base case of no skills at all. For another, the tendency of innovators in advanced countries to compete globally on the basis of new products and labor-saving machinery often meant, in practice, a second order of importance accorded to incremental productivity improvements on the shop floor. Implicitly, firms were managed as though higher wages alone would generate the worker response necessary to realize higher productivity. Such a strategy, however, has increasingly proved unsustainable, particularly under competition from learners.

CHAPTER NINE

The Boom in Education

LATE INDUSTRIALIZATION AND THE LEVEL OF EDUCATION

One reason Japan, Taiwan, and Korea appear to have industrialized rapidly is that they have invested relatively heavily in education.[1] A well-educated work force, both white- and blue-collar, is a general property of late industrialization, distinguishing it from earlier industrial change. Late industrialization is premised on the learning of production processes and procedures that are characteristic of more advanced economies. Thus, formal education of the work force and the apprenticeship of firms to foreign technical assistants (rather than the apprenticeship of workers in particular crafts) lie at the heart of late industrial expansion.

One cannot quantify historical differences across countries in foreign technical assistance. Yet, with greater codification of knowledge, improvements in transportation and communication, and widening in the information gap between backward and advanced countries over time, it is very likely that more recent industrializations have experienced more thoroughgoing technology transfer. Korea may have grown especially fast among late-industrializing countries because it received the preponderance of its technical assistance from Japan, whose mindset was that of a learner and whose industrial competitiveness was waxing, whereas India and the Latin American countries received most of their technical assistance from Britain and the United States, respectively, inventors and innovators whose industrial systems were in need of reform.

This chapter, therefore, is devoted to both formal education and foreign technical assistance, and ends with a firm-level illustration of

---

[1] Y. C. Kim and Kong (1983) studied the contribution of education to economic development in Korea, as did Y. B. A. Kim (1975). J. I. Yoon and Park (1977) examined the issues surrounding the education budget in the critical years of the late 1970s.

interaction between the two. Learning is explored in the second manufacturing affiliate of the Samsung Group, Cheil Wool Company, founded in 1954.

Despite the obvious importance of education, however, it is hard to see how the relationship between education and industrialization in Korea can be said to have obeyed a kind of Say's law, the supply of educated personnel creating its own demand. The quality of education in Korea was sometimes strained and education itself appears as a passive rather than an active agent in the industrialization process. Educated unemployment was massive until the government introduced its subsidies in the 1960s, and the industrialization process in general has been short on college graduates spontaneously forming their own companies. It has been long on the bureaucracies in business and government driving up the returns to education by placing heavy demands (sometimes erratic) on the supply of salaried managers, which, in turn, has generated heavy demands for more educational services on the part of the population, which has enabled the bureaucracies to expand further, and so on. Bureaucracy and mass education appear to go hand-in-hand.

The evidence that sequentially later industrializations have been characterized by higher levels of mass education is particularly striking at the university level. In 1903 there were 5 students in British universities or university colleges per 10,000 population and 7.87 in Germany per 10,000 (Musgrave, 1967, p. 83). In 1985 the comparable figure for Korea was 217.5 students (Ministry of Education, 1984). In 1899 the number of boys in public secondary schools per 1,000 population was only 4.3 in Birmingham (England) and 10.0 in Berlin (Germany) (Musgrave, 1967, p. 81). In 1984 the comparable figure for Korea, including both sexes, was 20.0 (Ministry of Education, 1984). Table 9.1 provides evidence that sequentially later industrializations have been characterized by greater access to higher levels of education. Table 9.1 is based on data collected by Easterlin (1965) and relates to the estimated percentage of the total population enrolled in schools below the college level. The estimates are subject to conceptual and measurement bias, most notably to variations in the proportion of school-age population to the total. Nonetheless, the rough orders of magnitude are revealing. First, they suggest that the Second Industrial Revolution, in the United States and Germany, involved a more educated population than did the First Industrial Revolution, in England. Second, they show that, in 1954, Japan and Korea were about to begin massive industrialization with more educated populations than that of either Germany or the United States eighty years earlier. The latest data available for purposes of comparison are for 1954. Already in that year, Japan was educating

Table 9.1 Estimated Percent of Total Population Enrolled in School, Selected Countries, 1830–1954

| Country | Percent of Population in School | | | | | |
	1830	1850	1878	1887	1928	1954
England and Wales	9	12	15	16	16	15
Germany	17	16	17	18	17	13
United States	15	18	19	22	24	22
Argentina				7	14	16
Mexico				5	9	12
Brazil				3	—	9
Japan				7	13	23
South Korea				—	4[a]	17
India				2	4	7

[a] Includes North Korea and date is 1938.

Source: Easterlin (1981a).

a larger fraction of its population than was either the United States or Germany at the close of the nineteenth century. In 1954, one year after the end of the Korean War, Korea was in the process of vastly expanding its educational system, with as much as 17% of its population already enrolled in school

THE AMBIGUITIES OF KOREA'S OUTSTANDING INVESTMENTS IN EDUCATION

Clearly, late-industrializing countries tend to promote greater accessibility to education than was customary in earlier periods of industrial expansion. What is noteworthy here is the relative preeminence of Korea, by contemporary standards, in this area of social progress. Table 9.2 provides data on human resources in seven late-industrializing countries. *Even among late-industrializing countries, Korea tends to excel in most indices of education, standardized for population size:* secondary students as a percent of eligible secondary-age students, scientists and engineers per capita, and so on. Korea scores higher in most educational indicators than even Singapore, which adopted a high-skill growth strategy before Korea.

In the 1960s, Korea compared favorably with other developing countries in terms of *overall* level of educational attainment (although not necessarily in terms of the proportion of population enrolled in either primary, secondary, or higher education). In both 1960 and 1965, Korea's overall educational attainments exceeded what one would have expected from its per capita GNP (Harbison, Ma-

Table 9.2 Indicators of Human Capital in Seven Late-Industrializing Countries

Indicator	Year or Period	Country						
		Korea	Singapore	Argentina	Brazil	Mexico	Turkey	India
Secondary students as percent of secondary age population	1965	29.0	45.0	NA	NA	17.0	16	29.0
	1978	68.0	57.0	46.0	17.0	37.0	34	30.0
Postsecondary students as percent of eligible postsecondary age population	1965	5.0	9.9	NA	NA	3.0	4.4	4.0
	1978	9.0	8.8	18.0	10.0	9.0	7.7	9.0
Postsecondary students abroad as percent of all postsecondary students	1970	2.0	NA	1.0	1.0	1.0	NA	1.0
	1975–1977	1.7	12.5	0.3	0.7	1.0	3.2	0.3
Engineering students as percent of postsecondary age population	1978	26.0	40.8	14.0	12.0	14.0	17.6	—
Scientists and engineers in thousands per million population	Late 1960s	6.9	NA	12.8	5.6	6.6	NA	1.9
	Late 1970s	22.0	5.2	16.5	5.9	6.9	15.9	3.0
Scientists and engineers in R&D per million population	1974	NA	NA	323	75	101	NA	58
	1976	325	263	311	NA	NA	222	46
	1978	398	317	313	208	NA	NA	NA

NA, not available.

[a]1975.

Source: Adapted from Westphal, Kim, and Dahlman (1985) for Argentina, Brazil, India, Korea, and Mexico. United Nations, *Statistical Yearbook* (various years) for Singapore and Turkey.

ruhnic, and Resnick, 1970), and the nation's educational resources were perceived to be both plentiful and well balanced.

A barometer of the importance that a society attaches to education is the relative status and salary it accords to the teaching profession. *The status of teaching in Korea's militaristic society is relatively high, as suggested by a comparison of teachers' pay and that of military officers.* In 1983 the starting base salary of elementary school teachers was about equal to that of captain in the armed forces. College and university teachers' starting base salary in 1983 exceeded that of the rank of army major (W. S. Yoon, 1986). In 1984 the average monthly salary of teachers (539,000 won/month) was below the average of managers (631,700 won/month) but above the average of all professional, technical, and technically related workers (432,000 won/month) (Ministry of Labor, 1985).

Korea, therefore, is both a general case of a well-educated late industrializing country and a special case of an exceptionally well-educated one. One might infer from these facts that education in Korea has acted as a determinant of economic development, driving the economy to the heights of per capita income achievable by a high level of formally educated human resources. This inference, however, is overly deterministic, particularly when one recognizes the flaws in Korea's educational system. All that glitters is not gold.

The counterpart of large enrollments is large classes, so the quality of Korean education has been called into question. Moreover, a look at the content of what is taught in the classroom suggests that formal schooling has largely served the purpose of political socialization, not technical preparation for industrialization. According to one account,

> What distinguishes the curriculum of Korean schools from that of countries whose attempts at development have failed is not its emphasis on science and technology. The major difference seems to be that Korean education places a heavy stress on moral education and discipline. (McGinn et al., 1980, p. 228)

Furthermore, the elitism of Korea's educational system is emphasized in a cultural interpretation of Korean development:

> The desire of the government to indoctrinate, and of parents to obtain the validating credentials which would enable their offspring to exploit opportunities denied most Koreans under the Japanese, generated strong pressures to expand the educational system. Though not to be faulted, such enthusiasm has been a mixed blessing. . . . Education may be free, but books and services are not, eliminating most of the poor in rural areas. Enter-

ing numbers are high, but attrition is high also. Hence, although education is legally open to all, increasingly as one goes up the educational ladder, the system serves the select few. Yet, simultaneously, even at the highest level, the numbers of students are many in relation to the available faculty. The consequence is didactic lecturing rather than discussion, and authoritarian methods to control great numbers of potentially disruptive students. All this smacks of the Japanese colonial past. (Jacobs, 1985, p. 269)

As suggested in Chapter 2, the view that the Japanese colonial education system left a stock of human resources that served as the foundation for later industrialization is overdrawn. Literacy in Korea may have been higher than the colonial norm, but there was little in the nation's school curriculum that matched that of the universally admired developmental education of Meiji Japan.[2] In Japan itself, the goal had been to

produce not only a diverse labor force with the necessary knowledge and skills to handle various levels of technical work but a core of scientists and engineers who could actually perfect and advance the current state of technology. Korea's colonial government, on the other hand, was interested mainly in ensuring the existence of a labor force in Korea that possessed the rudimentary education required to carry out orders from factory managers who were for the most part Japanese. . . . The Japanese had shown little interest in developing even industrial education for Koreans beyond the most elementary level. (Eckert, 1986, pp. 296–7)

Nor did the United States aid administration do much to correct the deficiency in industrial education. Between 1952 and 1961, aid to technical education totaled a mere $5 million. A history of U.S. educational assistance to 1966 reads as follows:

The major part of the [vocational high schools] were vocational in name only as they lacked both equipment and the instructors qualified to demonstrate practical work skills. As a result, these schools became a refuge for students unable to pass examinations for the academic schools, or who lacked funds. (Dodge, 1971, p. 103, quoted in McGinn et al., 1980)

---

[2] Han'guk Kyoyuksa Yŏnguhoe (the Association for the Study of the History of Education) has published a book that forcefully makes this point (1972). A study by G. E. Han (1973) examined the influence of Confucianism and nationalism on Korean education during the Japanese colonial period.

As for the educational "portfolio of investments," balanced across different levels, it too has been imperfect. At times Korea has tended to produce a surplus of trained personnel at the middle and higher educational levels. This is not unexpected in emulators that have caught up rapidly, an historical case in point being Germany. The German state in the late nineteenth century poured resources into education to spur economic development, and one consequence was an oversupply of educated labor power:

> By the 1890s, there were signs that these Hochschulen were producing too many engineers. . . . There was also a large number of unemployed lawyers. . . . By 1890 the Kaiser was afraid that the expansion of secondary facilities would create an academic proletariat. (Musgrave, 1967, p. 84).

In Korea, as well, heavy investments in education created temporary excess supply and fears by the military of social unrest.

Educated unemployment in Korea began "perhaps as early as 1953," and a decade of aid did little to alleviate the problem (McGinn et al., 1980, p. 95). In 1960 it was reported that 9,000 of 15,000 college graduates were unable to find jobs (J. E. Kim, 1973). Further, when the military government initiated serious economic planning in 1963, it discovered an excess of high-level personnel. Park's government attempted to curtail enrollments in higher education in 1961 and again in 1968. Through the 1960s, Korea was an exporter of educated persons. As late as 1972, only 60% of graduates in engineering and related sciences were estimated to have found employment, and long-range forecasts indicated continued oversupply (McGinn et al., 1980). When the government launched its drive into heavy industry, educated unemployment was relieved, but only temporarily. The government imposed a tight college quota system in the 1970s to dampen enrollments. The quota was later modified to increase enrollments and, along with slower growth, contributed in the 1980s to a rise in educated unemployment (Castaneda and Park, 1986).

Rather than Korea's economic development responding spontaneously to educational attainments, the 1950s and 1960s seem to have produced a corps of managers and engineers who were part of a nationally directed industrialization.

THE EDUCATIONAL LEVEL OF PRODUCTION WORKERS

The educational attainments of Korea's work force are indicated in Table 9.3. The gains over time are most striking at the lower levels of schooling. Illiteracy, defined as absence of any schooling whatsoever, declined from about 40% of the work force in 1946 to virtually

Table 9.3	Education Level of Work Force, 1946–1983
(Percent of All Workers)

Year	All Sectors[a]	Manufacturing
1946		
No schooling	39.6	NA
Primary	53.0	
Secondary	7.4	
College	—	
Total[b]	99.0	
1963		
No schooling	5.5	NA
Primary	53.0	
Secondary	33.9	
College	7.6	
Total	100.0	
1970		
Primary and No schooling	67.4	50.1
Secondary	26.4	42.0
College[c]	6.1	7.7
Total	100.0	100.0
1980		
Primary and No schooling	49.1	30.7
Secondary	43.0	61.4
College[c]	7.8	7.8
Total	100.0	100.0
1983		
Primary and No schooling	41.2	23.8
Secondary	48.6	65.7
College[c]	10.2	10.5
Total	100.0	100.0

NA, not available.

[a] In 1946 and 1963, sectors include mining, manufacturing, commerce, service, and agriculture. Thereafter, sectors also include electricity, construction, transportation, and finance.

[b] All totals include a small amount of unknown.

[c] Includes graduate work.

Source: 1946 and 1963: Ewing (1973). 1970, 1980, and 1983: Castaneda and Park (1986).

nil by 1963, although some of the poorest workers are still barely educated. Among these are factory girls, some of whom attend night school to learn to read and write (Commission of the Churches on International Affairs, 1979). The share of the work force with secondary schooling rose from 7.4% in 1946 to almost 50% in 1983, and in the manufacturing sector educational attainments were even higher. As Table 9.3 indicates, only one quarter of manufacturing workers had *less* than a secondary education in the early 1980s.

In the field of technical education, progress has been slower, and *Korea probably performs no better in this area than do other late-industrializing countries.* The problem is characterized by one expert who uses the term *confusion* to describe Korea's system of vocational training (K. W. Lee, 1983, p. 12). Confusion reigns in two areas: At which level should technical education be provided, high school or junior college? Who is to assume responsibility for funding, the public or private sector?

In terms of training level, the first area of confusion was generally understood at the time of the fourth five-year plan (1977–1981). Technical vocational high schools would foster broadly educated technicians to support scientists, engineers, and other professionals. Technicians would be supported by skilled and semiskilled workers who would be trained at vocational training centers, both inside and outside factories. This structure, however, became otiose as values changed and technical workers aspired to become college graduates. Vocational high schools transformed themselves into junior colleges; junior colleges, in turn, tried to emulate full-fledged colleges in their instructional programs (K. W. Lee, 1983). The identities of high school and college technical training, therefore, became blurred.

The second area of training strategy confusion concerned finance. An amendment to the Vocational Training Law at the time of the fourth five-year plan imposed a penalty on firms that employed over 300 workers and failed to provide in-plant training (firms were to provide in-plant training as a matter of principle or pay a levy in exceptional cases). Yet the amendment has three weaknesses: The quality of in-plant training is uncertain because trainees are not subject to compulsory skill tests, most programs go no further than providing workers with elementary skills, and the levy that is assessed is not high enough, so that firms find it less costly to be fined than to train.[3]

The crux of the problem of training lies in the partial demise of skilled craftspersons. They still perform critical tasks in Korea, such as the following (the skills listed here are some of the skills subject to trade tests):

Piping	Electrical repair
Welding	External wiring
High-pressure gas handling	Electrical welding
Mechanical drawing	Chemical analysis
Auto maintenance	Rock drilling
Architectural carpentering	Radio operating
Surveying	Precision finishing

[3] See the discussion by S. Kim (1982b, pp. 18–24).

Watch repair	Forest seeding
Printing	Textile fabric finishing
Type casting	Embroidering

Yet the quasi-derogation of even these skills is reflected in the relatively short duration of most training courses for craftspersons. Furthermore, craft skills have never really constituted a bottleneck to industrialization, although experienced craftspersons have been in scarce supply in certain areas and time periods.

At the start of the First Industrial Revolution, a typical apprenticeship lasted from five to seven years. A traditional apprenticeship system, covering anywhere from forty to seventy trades, endured in Germany well into the second half of the nineteenth century (Samuel and Thomas, 1949). Thereafter,

> The German secondary schools, especially the six-year Realschule, . . . served the labor force at this level excellently by giving a broad "modern" education of a liberal nature, fitted to the needs of future salesmen or technicians. The latter, after practical experience, attended centralized technical schools of a very specialized nature full-time, and one would have expected this second part of their education and training to have built soundly on the theoretical foundations of the first part. (Musgrave, 1967, p. 87)

Technical training in Korea is nowhere near as comprehensive. According to K.W. Lee's analysis of skill formation in a representative big business group in the automobile industry, of 911 newly recruited production workers below the university level, 27% were given minimum in-plant training, 38% were poached from other firms, about 10% had acquired their skills in a vocational training center (typically a one-year program), and only 21% had attended vocational high school. Skills being taught in the vocational training centers springing up in the 1970s were sufficiently simple that the centers had no trouble graduating thousands of craftspersons each year (graduation depended on passing a trade test). Approximately 125,000 and 130,000 craftspersons passed trade tests in 1976 and 1979, respectively, two peak years (Ministry of Labor, 1980). Vocational high schools have been relatively inconsequential. Of approximately 2 million high school students in Korea in 1984, only 9.6% were enrolled in technical courses (Ministry of Education, 1984).

On the other hand, the deskilling process in industry has not advanced to the point where the demand for skills is wholly satisfied. "Experienced and skilled" workers have become especially scarce over time. Table 9.4 reports the 1984 findings of a survey on labor scar-

Table 9.4 Labor Shortage by Occupation, 1984

	Percent Shortage	
Occupation	Small and Medium Firms	Large Firms
Engineers	14.1	17.7
Managers	1.8	1.4
Skilled[a]	39.4	40.5
Clerical	1.1	1.4
Sales	2.2	4.7
Unskilled	17.3	17.7
Temporary	3.2	0.5
None	20.9	14.4
Other	—	1.9
	100.0	100.0

[a] The direct Korean translation is skilled and experienced workers.

Source: Seoul National University. 1985.

city in the manufacturing sector conducted by the School of Business Administration at Seoul National University. According to the findings, neither engineers nor managers were found to be the scarcest resources (Table 9.4 suggests that by 1984 managers were one of the *least* scarce resources). Rather, "experienced and skilled" workers appeared to be in shortest supply, *particularly in the textile and apparel industries,* although neither harbors large numbers of "skilled" workers as traditionally defined. *Experience is the key in these lower paid industries.*

Reluctance on the part of the private sector to train is assumed by the Korean government to run contrary to the public interest. In response to its concern with how to increase training, therefore, the government's expert on technical education has advised a course that is characteristically Korean. He recommended that the government devise "a strong incentive system to help motivate business enterprises to voluntarily provide in-plant training for their workers" (K. W. Lee, 1983, p. 28).

THE EDUCATION LEVEL OF MANAGERS AND ENGINEERS

On the whole, Korea's cadre of managers and engineers is very well educated. Even owner-managers—across the spectrum of company size—have generally been found to hold advanced degrees (see the discussion in Chapter 7).

The employment of salaried managers with university degrees, however, is a fairly recent phenomenon in the history of world industrialization. In the early stage of the Second Industrial Revolution in Germany, for example, the old pattern still prevailed whereby managers at the top (inclusive of owner-managers) knew their business inside out and had a keen sense of technical factors gained solely through long first-hand experience. By the end of the nineteenth century, a new pattern had emerged:

> For instance, Alfred Krupp was rarely in Essen; he traveled the world on sales trips, tried to influence governments, or engaged in the politics of industry. Men like August Thyssen, Hugo Stinnes, and Krupp von Bohlen, son-in-law of Alfred Krupp, were financiers-businessmen, who left highly qualified technicians to run their works. In the 1980s, Lowthian Bell spoke of the German class of "scientific men . . . who seem to devote themselves almost entirely to industrial science." At the Union Works, Dortmund, the managers at this time were reported to have "the usual German technical training," be familiar with English, and to be regular readers of English engineering and metallurgical journals; the two leading chemists and the head draughtsman had attended Polytechnics, though to an English manager of a Bavarian engineering works, such men lacked practical experience. (Musgrave, 1967; pp. 80–1)

It was the latter pattern that characterized the earliest stages of Korean industrialization. Managers and engineers work themselves up through the company, but the lowest rank from which they start is first-line supervisor, a management position. They do not work themselves up from the ranks of production worker.

The Second Industrial Revolution in the United States underwent a transition similar to Germany's, and with considerable social conflict:

> One source of ideological and actual conflict within the industrial system was between technical graduates and intermediate managers, foremen, and top executives who had made their way to the top by personal skill rather than by formally attained qualifications or credentials. The uneducated did hire the educated, but often, like Thomas A. Edison, bragged about how they were hiring (at low salaries) men with high pretensions and only marginally useful abilities. (Calvert, 1967, p. 147)

The tension between school and shop coincided with other major changes. First, the college curriculum was transformed to admit the discipline of engineering as a legitimate science.[4] Second, the transition from employing experience to employing education planted the seeds for a new way of innovating, through research and development (R&D). Despite Edison's convictions, the salaried engineers soon proved their worth. Not only did they raise shop-floor productivity, but they innovated as well. A person like Alexander Holley, chief engineer at Carnegie Steel who proselytized the virtues of technical education, was the epitome of the educated as well as innovative manager (McHugh, 1980).

In Japan, the university-trained engineer-manager appears to have arrived earlier in the trajectory of industrialization than in either Germany or the United States. The trajectory in Japan was itself different because, as in still later industrializing countries, it was consummately defined by catching up, not by a backlog of experience and inventiveness. After the Meiji Restoration, the new state found itself in urgent need of all kinds of modern skills and knowledge, and, according to Eisuke Daito, turned to three sources: First, the Meiji entrepreneurs tried to depend on the small number of people who had somehow acquired Western business practices and technologies for themselves, but these were in short supply. Second, many promising young men were sent abroad or went on their own to learn how commercial and manufacturing businesses were conducted in advanced countries. Third, foreign experts and advisors were brought into Japan. "To gain independence from foreign experts, ministries and newly formed government enterprises often set up training programs of their own," but these were costly and could be carried out only by a profitable government-owned enterprise. Private firms "had to recruit well-trained people in one way or another from outside or attract personnel of such high caliber and determination that little internal instruction seemed necessary." Yet the prevailing social climate put "official above private life," and so private-sector "employers could not attract university graduates." It was only after the turn of the century that the graduate recruitment situation began to change rapidly (Daito, pp. 155–8).

INEXPERIENCE

One-hundred years after the Meiji Restoration, Korea relied on the same sources as Japan had relied on to relieve it of ignorance—a small number of experienced personnel, overseas training, and foreign experts. However, private firms in later industrializing coun-

---

[4] See the discussion of the relationship between education and private industry in Noble (1977).

tries differed from those in Meiji Japan in being able to rely on university graduates—who could ultimately replace the foreign experts—at an earlier stage of industrialization. Private firms in Korea appear to have had access to a relatively plentiful supply of such graduates early on.

Nevertheless, the inexperience of university-trained managers presented acute problems. The naiveté of these managers was compounded by the inexperience inherent in the process of late industrialization—the import of foreign technology. In innovating firms, experience is developed pari passu with new technical development. In firms that must catch up, this development process is absent. Alexander Holley, in his capacity as a founder of the American Institute of Mining Engineers, not only proselytized the virtues of technical education but also those of practical knowledge: "In the chasm between science and art," he stated in one speech, "how much effort and treasure, and even life, are swallowed up year by year" (McHugh, 1980, p 268).

Although modern industrial enterprises in Japan and Korea followed similar paths to overcome the inexperience of their managers, these paths were not necessarily identical ones. According to Daito,

> Since universities [in Japan] offered minimal vocational training, new recruits were assigned to positions at the bottom of managerial hierarchies and were trained mainly on the job. Vacancies above the bottom level were filled not by the hiring of qualified men on the open market but by internal recruitment, promotion from within, and transfer. Decision making on promotions depended heavily on seniority as well as competence. (1986, p. 167)

Similar procedures of hiring, on-the-job training, and promotion have been followed in Korea insofar as new university recruits have tended to be assigned to the lowest managerial positions and promotion has depended heavily on seniority.[5] Newly recruited managers in diversified business groups tend to be trained first at the group level, in short courses that are oriented toward exposing them to company culture.[6] They are then assigned to operating affiliates where they are trained both on the job and in outside courses. Managers in Korea are sent to courses offered by the Korea Bureau of Standards (on quality control), by the Korea Advanced Institute of Science and Technology (on technology management), and others. Managers are sent to overseas courses as well, sometimes for formal education,

---

[5] For a discussion of seniority practices in Korea, see S. Kim, (1982b.)

[6] See the discussion by J. H. Park (1987) on groupwide training of managers.

sometimes to acquire in-plant experience. The key difference with Japan is that top positions in Korea are sometimes filled not by internal promotion but by recruitment of experienced personnel from outside the firm (as discussed in Chapter 5).[7]

Employers in Japan expected young engineers to plunge into the shop to deal with technical difficulties and problems of factory management. The engineers, Daito reported, took over several functions from the foremen and tried to control such factors as "manufacturing costs, product quality, inventory levels, intensity of work, and so on in greater detail than ever before." Their offices were near the shop floor because "their main duty was to maintain a high operating ratio of expensive equipment, some of which had been imported from advanced countries, and their technical knowledge had to be supplemented by practical experience on the shop floor" (Daito, 1986, p. 173). As we shall see in later chapters, the acquisition of experience by Korean managers was also a two-pronged process, involving the application of formal techniques to shop floor control (although not necessarily at the foreman's expense, whose power in Korea probably never equaled what it once was in Japan), supplemented by informal shop floor experience. In the shipbuilding industry, which is examined in Chapter 11, even the first crop of managers in the most modern yard strove to standardize operating procedures while simultaneously learning more about how ships were built through close contact with the ranks. The imperative to work closely with the ranks was echoed, in general, in an organizational structure that tended to comprise relatively few layers of managerial hierarchy and indeed relatively few managers (see the discussion in Chapter 7).

REWARDS FOR THE ELITE

A jaundiced view of the educated engineer-manager, held by practical people of antiintellectual persuasion like Thomas Edison, has never become thematically dominant in Korean industrial culture. By and large, managers and especially engineers are well respected. They have performed a critical function, of putting imported technologies and machinery into operation. The respect they have commanded is reflected in their remuneration. *The wage differential in Korea between managers on the one hand (including engineers) and production workers on the other has been large,* as suggested in Table 9.5. On average, in the period 1971 through 1984 managers earned about four times more than production workers.

[7] This, however, was also true of Japanese firms circa the 1920s, the period Daito described, before the entrenchment of permanent employment practices.

Table 9.5 Relative Monthly Earnings[a] by Occupation,
1971–1984

			Earnings (won/month)			
Year	Technicians	Managers	Clerical Workers	Salesmen	Service Men	Production Workers
1971	280	428	243	140	107	100
1973	253	406	206	151	99	100
1975	266	458	215	123	104	100
1977	271	439	206	131	100	100
1979	256	436	176	107	97	100
1981	230	367	163	96	100	100
1983	241	343	155	129	101	100

[a] Figures include regular pay, overtime, and special earnings (bonus payments).

Source: Ministry of Labor, *Yearbook of Labor Statistics,* 1972–1985, as cited in Castaneda and Park (1986).

The gap in earnings between managers and production workers reflects a large gap in earnings related to educational level. Higher education in Korea tends to be well rewarded and so is in great demand. This is suggested by data in Table 9.6. Between 1975 and 1984, college and university graduates earned about three times the salaries of primary school graduates and about one and one-half times those of high school graduates.

International wage comparisons of managers and production workers are difficult to draw because of intercountry variation in the indirect component of managerial salaries (bonuses, stock options,

Table 9.6 Relative Monthly Earnings[a] by Education, 1975–1984
(Men Only) (Primary School = 100)

	Earnings (won/month)				
Year	Colleges, University	Junior College	High School	Middle School	Primary School
1975	306	200	154	109	100
1976	330	219	156	110	100
1978	301	205	147	106	100
1980	256	170	127	100	100
1982	252	161	126	100	100
1984	240	145	121	100	100

[a] Figures include regular pay, overtime, and special earnings (bonus).

Source: Ministry of Labor, *Yearbook of Labor Statistics,* 1976–1985, as cited in Castaneda and Park (1986).

Table 9.7 Comparison of Relative Occupational Wage Structure in Korea with that in the United States (Production Workers = 100)[a]

Country (Year)	Technicians	Managers	Clerical	Sales	Service	Production
United States (1977)	160	179	109	117	51	100
South Korea (1980)	246	395	162	89	100	100

[a]Index = 100.
Source: J. W. Lee (1983).

cars) and the wide dispersion in salaries among managers. By comparison with Brazil, the wage gap between managers and production workers in Korea is narrow (according to Souza, by 1975 the pay of a general manager in the manufacturing industry in Brazil had come to be *162 times as large* as that of an unskilled laborer [1978]). On the other hand, by comparison with middle managers in the United States and undoubtedly Japan, Korea's wage gap is wide (see Table 9.7 for a comparison between Korea and the United States). In the case of returns to education, the well-educated in Korea probably earn a premium by the standards of most developing countries. The rate of return to primary education tends to be greatest in most developing countries, whereas the rate of return to higher education tends to be greatest in Korea (Psacharopoulos, 1985).

Korea's supply of managers and engineers is abundant by the standards of most developing countries. One is surprised, therefore, that its managerial-production worker wage differential is sizeable. It appears to be sizeable partly because of segmentation in the market for managers and engineers. On the demand side, the big chaebol tend to hire only the top graduates from the best universities, thereby driving up their price. On the supply side, most university graduates prefer to be employed in big companies, which seems to induce smaller firms to bid up wages to attract managerial recruits.

FOREIGN TECHNICAL ASSISTANCE

Korea may have the dubious distinction among late learners of having been occupied militarily not just by one but by two world powers—Japan and the United States. Yet in terms of technology transfer, Korea possibly got the best of both worlds. In 1945 through 1965, technology transfers through tied aid came mainly from the United States, which was then at the height of its technological supremacy. In the case of military-related projects from the United States, technology transfers also had the virtue of not being subject to profit-maximizing goals on the part of the teacher. After 1965, Korea relied primarily on technology transfers from Japan, which was itself in the process of becoming the world's premier producer.

American process technology in individual manufacturing projects may have been unrivaled, but the process of technology transfer itself was flawed. Technology transfer as it related to the disbursement of foreign aid was discussed in Chapter 2. It was characterized by delays and technical bungling, as a consequence of confusing administrative arrangements and the use of inexperienced military personnel on civilian projects. The military-related technology, however, appears to have been better communicated, so not only the Korean army but also civilian subcontractors to the American forces, like the Hyundai Construction Company, acquired high operating standards. According to Hyundai Construction, which now ranks among the world's top five international contractors, the contribution of the U.S. military to its technological development was fourfold:

1. Hyundai and other construction firms learned how to prepare a bid in the international format, as required by American military procurement.
2. Hyundai and other construction firms learned Western specifications and were forced to upgrade the quality of their construction work, as required by U.S. federal regulations concerning subcontractors.
3. Hyundai and other construction firms acquired construction management and quality control techniques.
4. Hyundai in particular, because of its experience in automotive repair, obtained war surplus construction equipment that allowed it to mechanize operations.

However, with the termination of U.S. aid and its tied provisions, Japan soon became Korea's major technical assistant, supplying it through diverse channels. Technical assistance arrived in Korea from Japan in the form of foreign licenses. Typically a foreign license transferred proprietary technology from firm to firm. The foreign technical assistance accompanying a foreign license varied in comprehensiveness and could cover anything from a blueprint to details on standard operating procedure to a turnkey plant. Table 9.8 provides data on cases of foreign licenses and reveals that their number increased dramatically in 1977–1981, during Korea's foray into heavy industry. The source of licenses was overwhelmingly Japan, accounting for 56% of the total, about the same share that the United States held as Japan's source of technology imports between 1950 and 1970 (Ozawa, 1974, p. 26).

Table 9.8 Cases of Approved Technology-Licensing Agreement by Country, 1962–1983

Country	1962–1971	1972–1976	1977–1981	1982–1983	Total
United States	74	90	301	144	609 (23.1[a])
Japan	214	280	629	363	1,476 (56.1)
West Germany	10	13	70	34	127 (4.8)
England	5	16	49	27	97 (3.7)
France	1	6	40	26	73 (2.8)
Other	14	29	132	74	249 (9.5)
Total	318	434	1,221	668	2,631 (100.0)

[a] Figures in parentheses denote composition ratios.

Source: Ministry of Finance.

Emulation in Japan and Korea does not parallel that of nineteenth-century European emulation. Although Europe abounds with stories of the British expatriate entrepreneur-engineer migrating to the Continent to teach, there are few if any stories of Europeans traveling to England to learn. By contrast, Japan, and Korea thereafter, sent thousands of managers and engineers to foreign countries to learn. Korea sometimes even sent skilled workers abroad to study on the shop floor. The total human outflow is undocumented, typically occurring as a subpart of a technical license, but company histories, some to be presented in later chapters, suggest that the numbers were large and the experience was critical. Overseas apprenticeship telescoped years in the classroom into months on the factory floor.

The data in Table 9.8 are typically taken as representative of Korea's technology imports, but they understate the extent of foreign technical assistance. They understate it because they exclude *informal* transfers from machinery suppliers and independent consultants. Instruction from machinery suppliers is an ideal form of technology transfer from the viewpoint of learners, because it is provided as part of a purchase of a capital good and is therefore less restrictive than if provided by a competitor. Capital goods are a major means through which both production processes and procedures are transmitted across countries. In the case of assembly line equipment in the electronics industry, for example, Japanese exports to Korea influenced Korea's adoption of a certain type of assembly line, the free flow or worker-paced line, believed by Japanese suppliers to enhance productivity by comparison with a direct drive or moving assembly line, on the model of Henry Ford's (Harvard Business School, 1986d). Table 9.9 provides data on Korea's capital goods imports from two

Table 9.9   Capital Goods Imports from the United States and Japan, 1973–1984

	Imports (% of total)											
	1973	1974	1975	1976	1977	1978	1979	1980	1981	1982	1983	1984
All machinery												
United States	26.4	20.8	24.9	20.4	22.7	17.5	21.0	23.8	25.6	29.4	—	—
Japan	52.5	55.3	49.6	45.9	54.1	61.0	49.6	49.2	44.3	37.7	—	—
General machinery[a]												
United States	12.6	16.4	18.9	18.4	17.0	14.1	15.5	17.5	23.9	24.7	28.4	25.7
Japan	65.8	65.4	52.8	43.5	55.1	59.7	49.5	53.4	45.1	40.2	49.7	52.1

[a] Excludes specialized industrial machinery.

Source: Korean Machinery Builders' Association.

major sources, Japan and the United States. Throughout the 1970s, Japan's share of Korea's capital goods imports far exceeded that of the United States. By the mid-1980s, Japan's share averaged approximately one half of the total, that of the United States only about one quarter. In importing the preponderance of its capital equipment from Japan, therefore, Korea was indirectly importing Japanese production practices.

Informal technology transfers were also facilitated by independent consultants. However, while the British entrepreneur-engineer who starred in the nineteenth-century tale of technology transfer to Continental Europe settled abroad as a resident teacher (Henderson, 1954), the equivalent figure is largely absent in Korea. Few expatriates live and work in Korea as employees of even the largest firms. They are considered too expensive to hire. Instead, *the star of technology transfer to Korea is the short-term independent consultant.* Typically such a figure is Japanese, either retired or still in the permanent employment of a Japanese enterprise, consulting in Korea on an ad hoc basis. The figure appears in almost every leading Korean firm, in diverse industries: a retired engineer from Mitsubishi Motors in Hyundai Motor's Ulsan automobile assembly plant; a university professor in its shipyard; a computer specialist in Samsung Electronics; a textile engineer in a large cotton spinning and weaving mill, and so on. The independent consultant from Japan has constituted a gold mine for Korean industry. As an independent, the consultant is free from many of the constraints on teaching that characterize firm-to-firm transfers. As a Japanese, the memories of backwardness and catching up are still fresh, the possibilities of success are communicable, and the knowledge conveyed has in recent years become state-of-the-art expertise. Access to such technical assistance placed Korea in an enviable position. Other late-industrializing countries further afield from Japan culturally and geographically have lacked such a resource to draw on.

THE CHAEBOL AS YOUNG MANUFACTURERS

The process whereby the chaebol reoriented their activities away from rent seeking and toward profit maximizing contains the seeds to understanding an important part of the process of economic development in general. Rent seeking refers to what the classical economists meant by buying cheap and selling dear, or earning profits on alienation. By creating scarcities and speculating, rent seekers realize windfall gains. The realization of windfall gains, however, is neither easy nor effortless. A few are rewarded but many are ruined. Economic activity, therefore, may be inclined to move toward profit maximizing, depending on whether capital accumulation can be shown to be profitable.

Two factors in Korea worked toward the creation of profitable investment opportunities. The first was discussed in Chapter 3, namely the state, which subsidized diversification into new industries. The second was suggested above, namely education and apprenticeship, or the creation of a cadre of foreign technical assistants and university-trained managers and engineers. Once the entrepreneurs saw that the managers were capable of managing, that the engineers were capable of producing products that worked, capital investment became a viable option. A long-run approach to learning evolved gradually and laid the groundwork for the replacement of the foreign expert. One illustration of this process is presented below.

Cheil Wool Affiliate of the Samsung Group

Today the Samsung group is regarded as one of the most tightly managed chaebol, with a compulsive emphasis on efficiency and quality. Little in the background of the company's founder, however, presaged such a management approach.

The chairman of Samsung, P. C. Lee, was, like most other Korean entrepreneurs, the scion of a rich landowning family. (According to Jones and Sakong, "It was primarily the larger holders who produced entrepreneurs . . . very few entrepreneurs have risen from the poor masses" [1980, p. 228]). Yet unlike most entrepreneurs, Lee was not well educated. ("Korean business leaders are extraordinarily well educated, in both an absolute and a relative sense" [Jones and Sakong, 1980, p 231].) Lee dropped out of high school and then enrolled in college in Japan, but dropped out of that, too. Nevertheless, he made a lot of money during World War II and later during the Korean War by buying cheap and selling dear. Then he turned his attention to amassing a fortune at the cost of contributions to Syngman Rhee's political campaigns. His activities in the post-Korean-war period were divided between "trade" and the manufacturing of daily necessities. Samsung's first manufacturing affiliate was Cheil (meaning first) Sugar Company (1953), followed by Cheil Wool (1954). The 1950s also witnessed Samsung's acquisition of companies in the insurance business—life, fire, and marine.

After the roundup of businessmen in the aftermath of the military coup of 1961, Lee's illicit wealth was estimated at about 19% of the national total (C. L. Kim, 1980, quoted in Jones and Sakong). Lee, however, was exonerated in 1963 after payment of a fine. Then in 1964 he founded the Han'guk Fertilizer Company, one of the largest projects of the period. Whereas it took over seven years for the U.S. aid administration to complete a fertilizer plant in the 1950s (see Chapter 2), Samsung's plant was completed in record time, commencing production in early 1967 after only thirty months. Even before production began, however, Lee appears to have succumbed once again to the attractions of speculation. It was discovered that saccharin, a commodity then in heavy demand in Korea, was being smuggled into the country by Han'guk disguised as a raw material for fertilizer production. After a presidential investigation, Lee "donated" 51% of Han'guk shares to the government. Undaunted, Lee followed the government's lead in establishing a string of new companies in the 1960s (a daily newspaper, a broadcasting company, a papermaking company to supply the newspaper, a department store, a real estate development and construction company, a university, a hospital, and Samsung Electronics—which began assembling black-and-white color TVs in response to the government's promotion of the electronics sector). Cheil Wool Company, however, "became very profitable as it gradually replaced foreign-made woolen textiles and became the backbone of today's Samsung group."[8]

The choice of the Samsung group to enter the worsted subbranch of the textiles industry was clever insofar as it placed Cheil Wool in a relatively protected market niche (none of the major chaebol ventured into the highly competitive area of cotton spinning and weaving). Cheil's production of worsted in 1957 amounted to 1,750,000 pounds, or 43% of total national output. Nevertheless, worsteds were riskier than either cottons or woolens because they required more sophisticated production processes and quality control. To meet both requirements, Cheil bought top-quality machinery, hired the best-

[8] Jones and Sakong, 1980, pp. 352–3. These authors gave further details about the life of P. C. Lee.

salaried managers, and relied on extensive foreign technical assistance. Lee's background became less and less important as a determinant of Cheil Wool's operating procedures.

Cheil purchased modern equipment in 1956 from a West German textiles machinery manufacturer and paid extra to have West German engineers come to Cheil to assemble the machinery and to supervise start-up. Cheil also dispatched five engineers to West Germany, England, and Australia to be trained and to observe a modern plant in operation. Cheil was successful to the extent that a decision was taken to expand capacity in the early 1960s despite excess capacity at the industry level. (In 1961 the worsted industry was estimated to be operating at only 45.9% of capacity [Bank of Korea, 1962].) Cheil increased spinning capacity by 50% without having to resort to foreign technical assistance. It also began to produce "top-making" wool, for which it did require foreign expertise (again inviting West German equipment manufacturers to assemble and start up the new machinery and again dispatching local engineers overseas for training). Cheil attributes the fact that it could expand its capacity when other worsted manufacturers were experiencing overproduction to the superior quality of its product.

In 1963, about the time the military regime began to push exports, Cheil entered a second stage of technology development in order to penetrate foreign markets. It tightened its quality control system and, interrelatedly, improved its process. It did so gradually, making errors along the way. For example, Cheil engineers (who numbered only 2% of the work force when Cheil was founded, later 6%) recognized after a visit to textile plants overseas that advanced countries were using double-apron drafting whereas Cheil was using only a single system. Double drafting was more efficient and produced higher quality fabrics. In 1967, therefore, Cheil engineers attempted to develop a double-apron system on the basis of available literature, catalogs obtained from foreign manufacturers, and imitation of foreign models. They failed, and then sought technical assistance from their West German machinery supplier. In 1965, Cheil became the first company in Korea to have high enough quality standards to obtain the right to use the "all wool" trademark. In 1969 it became the first company in Korea's textile industry to win an "Invention Award" from the government. In the late 1960s, it patented seven minor process improvements.

Investments to improve quality coincided with an improved management system in the Samsung group. All new managers were recruited and trained at the group level. They were then dispatched, at the company's discretion, to affiliates. Interaffiliate communication was facilitated by the closeness of graduates of the same training class, and all affiliates were ensured of professional management.

The Samsung group began to attract the best high school and college graduates and to become one of the most prestigious companies for which to work.

Some strategic decisions from top management concerned with long-run growth came relatively late in Cheil's history, however. Only in the 1980s did Cheil begin to integrate vertically, by establishing joint ventures in Australia to rear sheep and to manufacture woolen tops for smoother operations, and by acquiring an apparel-making plant in Korea. As late as 1979, twenty-five years after its founding and in response to government pressure, Cheil established a central R&D laboratory (the R&D budget for 1983 was $1.7 million). It was only in 1970 that Cheil established an in-house training institute, although ahead of government legislation making it compulsory to do so. The 1970s were devoted largely to producing enough output to meet escalating domestic and overseas demand.

Nevertheless, even at the very onset of operations, Cheil showed a belief in its ability to survive, and planned for the long term. This is illustrated by its policy toward technology transfer. In 1955, just after the end of the Korean War and one year after Cheil's founding, Cheil unpackaged its foreign technical assistance. In addition to buying technical assistance from its machinery supplier, Samsung independently hired an experienced Japanese textiles engineer as advisor. The advisor developed a master engineering plan with a long-range time horizon. The master engineering plan envisioned Cheil's first plant to have a 30,000 worsted spindle capacity, which was believed at the time to be the optimal size, although only 5,000 spindles were initially installed. Consequently, as Cheil expanded and reached 30,000 capacity twenty years after establishment, no subsequent engineering was necessary until a strategic decision was taken to open a second plant.

Here, then, is a brief example of one of the earliest subsidiaries of a leading chaebol practicing pro-active production and operations management in order to absorb foreign knowhow. The quality of management is rather high despite rent-seeking and technical ignorance at the top. Such quality may be attributed in large measure to the education of salaried managers in the broadest sense—acquired from Korea's own school system and from technology transfers from abroad.

CONCLUSION

The view that a high-level of education is a key determinant of industrialization is borne out in Korea to the extent that a well-educated population in general, and a plentiful supply of trained engineers in particular, appear to have been critical inputs into the industrialization process (but note that Brazil grew by over 6% per annum for more than twenty years without much emphasis on education). However, the role played by education in economic development ought not to be deified. Although education was highly supportive in Korea's development, its quality was modest and its role was largely passive.

Of equal importance with formal education was foreign technical assistance. Formal education builds the human capital of the individual. Foreign technical assistance builds the technological capability of the firm. Moreover, as the next chapter suggests, late industrialization, in Korea especially, has been largely a process of big business groups diversifying into new industries on the basis of their technological capability rather than individual entrepreneurs acting as independent agents of further industrial change on the basis of their personal experience and education. It is to this intragroup dynamic of creating comparative advantage that attention is now turned.

PART III

The Dynamics of Dynamic Comparative Advantage

CHAPTER TEN

The Switch in Industrial Leadership

NONLINEAR DIVERSIFICATION

Korea has diversified from less to more complex industries in a nonlinear fashion. Diversification may be thought of synonymously with realization of comparative advantage, or better yet, creation of dynamic comparative advantage, although the term *dynamic comparative advantage* is conceptually fuzzy. Korea can be said to have diversified in a nonlinear fashion because it experienced no simple transition from less to more skill- and capital-intensive industries. Part III contains a discussion of what the dynamics of dynamic comparative advantage actually are in late industrialization.

This chapter suggests that cotton spinning and weaving, Korea's leading sector in terms of production volume, did not serve as the springboard for further industrialization in any organizational sense. Insofar as the diversified business group acted as the agent of expansion, it had its origins in the government's more management-intensive, early import substitution projects, not a labor-intensive industry like cotton textiles. Chapter 11, within the context of the shipbuilding industry in the acutely competitive decade of the 1970s, examines the hypothesis that the diversified business group provides a multitude of capabilities and a protective cover to latecomers wishing to enter world trade. Chapter 12 examines the hypothesis that climbing the ladder of comparative advantage is a matter of creating competitiveness, usually with government assistance, rather than stepping into it. The evidence comes from Korea's integrated iron- and steel-maker, the centerpiece of basic industry and a public enterprise.

According to a "law" of economic development, there are stages of comparative advantage in the export activity (and underlying production trends) of developing countries; the stages running from less to more skill- and capital-intensive.[1] The law holds that economic activity typically begins with, say, cotton textiles or even more labor-intensive goods and progresses in stages to more complex capital- and skill-intensive products, in step with the fledgling country's accumulation of greater stocks of capital and human resources.

Korea has obeyed this law to the extent that the progression of its structural diversification shows no significant deviations from the expected pattern. Korean industry graduated from less to more complex, there being no great leaps to sophistication. One notices the expected pattern even in the growth trajectories of leading firms. Almost all started with small plants and only later moved to the very large. Almost all started with simple production processes (manual versus automated process controls; general purpose versus special purpose tools) and only then moved to the more challenging. Korean industrialization is very much a progression to technologically more complex industries, although the "less complex" industries are not all labor-intensive.

Nevertheless, no matter how solid the empirical support for the "law" of stages of comparative advantage, the concept of dynamic comparative advantage remains as fuzzy as ever. This is because the law of stages of comparative advantage suffers from the same shortcoming that afflicts all stages theories: *It fails to specify the mechanism by which progress from one stage to another is realized.* It is, moreover, the mechanism of graduating from one industry to another that constitutes the dynamics of comparative advantage.

There are, in fact, two presumed paths of expansion that are implicit in the law of stages of comparative advantage. One path involves a succession of entrepreneurs responding to market signals, flanked by salaried managers if need be, all supported by the formal education system, as the driving force behind diversification into new industries. Nothing, however, could be further from the truth in Korea. As Jones and SaKong have pointed out;

> A high percent of the expansion of industrial output has come from existing rather than new firms. . . . What has to be explained is not how new entrepreneurs were found, but how old firms grew, and why new firms were so much larger than the old. (1980, xxxii, p. 170)

The relative unimportance of the new entrepreneur is possibly extreme in Korea, as the reference to Anderson's (1982) study in Chapter 7 indicates. Nevertheless, the ubiquity of the diversified business group

---

[1] Stages of comparative advantage have been measured empirically by Balassa (1981, 1984). Chenery et al. (1986) attributed a lawlike quality to Balassa's empirical findings.

in all late industrializations leads one to think that the budding entrepreneur is the exceptional rather than general pattern. That growth has largely taken the form of *intraenterprise expansion* suggests a wholly different dynamic of comparative advantage from what is typically presumed.

The second path of expansion that is implicit in the law of stages of comparative advantage involves the *spin-off* firm. In this growth path new industries are formed supposedly by entrepreneurs or managers from existing industries, who break away to form more specialized enterprises. Stigler (1951) referred to this as a process of vertical *dis*integration. Rosenberg (1976) documented this process of disintegration in the case of the United States, when for example, specialized textile machinery manufacturers broke away from the textile manufacturing branch. From a late-industrializing country like Taiwan is the example of its machine tool industry, which spawned several specialized parts producers (Amsden, 1977).

Nevertheless, this second growth path does not fully characterize late industrialization in Korea either. For one, the spin-off firm has not been terribly important. According to Jones and SaKong, "Growth in value added is due first to expansion of existing firms, *second to entry of offspring firms,* and only to a minor extent to net entrance of new entrepreneurs (emphasis added)" (1980, p. 176). Moreover, however secondary the importance of the spin-off firm, *what is noteworthy is the complete unimportance of Korea's leading sector in early growth, cotton spinning and weaving, as an industry that spun off sequentially more complex industrial activity.*

The cotton textiles industry (defined in this chapter to include the spinning of fibers and the weaving and finishing of fabrics) accounted for as much as 20% of GNP in the 1950s (the manufacture of apparel accounted for another 7%). It was considered the most modern industry at the time.[2] After the 1960s, even as light manufacturing declined in importance—from approximately 60% to 40% of GNP—cotton textiles maintained a share of about 12% of total output. In the 1980s cotton textiles remained Korea's largest export. Nevertheless, despite the undisputed leadership of the cotton spin-

---

[2]   "In the pre-liberation period, when most of the modern industries were transplanted from Japan, this industry (textiles) utilized the most contemporary production and management methods, and its output value and employment contribution led other industries. During the period of the reorganization of Korean industries after the liberation of 1945 and during the reconstruction of the war-damaged industries in the 1950s, the textile industry was instrumental in the recovery and modernization of production facilities.

   With the beginning of formal economic development efforts in the 1960s, the industry was transformed into Korea's leading export industry." (Y. B. Kim, 1980, p. 190)

ning and weaving industry in Korea, it never acted as an agent of further industrialization: It transferred little know-how to new industries, it transferred few people to new industries, and it extended no organizational linkages to them. With possible unanimity, no chaebol can claim cotton spinning and weaving as the focus of its group's activities, historically or otherwise. The closest exception to the rule is the Samsung group, which had a major subsidiary in the worsted industry; but worsted textiles are more up-market than cotton textiles and are produced under a less competitive market structure.

There being no significant linkages between cotton textiles and newer industries, the dynamics of comparative advantage are less straightforward—or less linear—than the stages theory would suggest. Instead of emerging from the leading sector of cotton spinning and weaving, the diversified business group in the Korean model (and one suspects in the model of most other late industrializing countries) emerged directly or indirectly from the government's early import-substitution projects in basic industry. (See the discussion in Chapter 2 on the birth of the chaebol.) Such basic industries, or heavy industries as they are often called, included sugar refining, large construction projects, cement making, fertilizer manufacture, and oil refining.

The point to note about these heavy industries is that they differ from cotton spinning and weaving and other "light" industries. They are both more capital- and skill-intensive. They rely heavily on salaried managers to control a production process that is more science-based and less of an art. Hawtrey referred to the differences between the two types of industries as *capital widening* and *capital deepening:*

> The process by which the capital equipment of a community is increased may take two forms, a "widening" and a "deepening." The widening of the capital equipment means the extension of productive capacity by the flotation of new enterprises, or the expansion of existing enterprises, without any change in the amount of capital employed for each unit of labour. The deepening means an increase in the amount of capital employed for each unit of labour.
>
> The latter involves an increase in the period of production and a change in the structure of production. The former involves no change in either. (1937, p. 31)

Insofar as expansion in the heavy industries involves a change in the structure of production, the learning process underlying such expansion is more taxing than the process of expansion in the light manufactures. Expansion under conditions of capital-deepening requires greater technological capability and a different skill mix on the part of management and labor. Productivity gains are realized differently and the whole process of competition is distinct. *Such technological capability, skill mix, and mode of productivity growth and competition provide the basis for diversifying into new industries.*

To understand the differences between the light and heavy industries, this chapter compares the learning process in cotton spinning and weaving (by examining two representative integrated spinners and weavers[3]) with the learning process in one of the first heavy industries to emerge in Korea, cement-making. Whereas the textile industry failed to act as an agent of further industrialization, at least two of the biggest chaebol used the cement industry as a stepping stone to more complex economic pursuits. We conclude this chapter with a discussion of how managerial capability in the Hyundai Cement Company was diffused within the Hyundai group. Through a comparison of the learning process in cotton textiles and cement we can appreciate the importance of the early import substitution activities that the government encouraged, the life cycle of a leading sector, and something of the dynamics of comparative advantage.

THE TEXTILES INDUSTRY

D and L were founded during Korea's colonial period by Japanese textiles firms that are still prominent in Japan today—Kanebo and Toyo, respectively. The present owner of D was one of the few Koreans to receive training in textiles engineering during the Japanese occupation. He learned his craft working in a textiles plant established by a Korean entrepreneur in Manchuria. When the Japanese fled Korea, the government entrusted the man in question to manage the plant, and in 1955 he bought the plant from the government. Thus, D's history under the same management spans roughly forty years. Similarly, L, founded in 1935, was confiscated by the Korean government after World War II and sold to the Korean man who had managed it under the Japanese. L's history under the same management, therefore, spans roughly half a century.

[3] The tale of Korea's leading sector is told in this chapter through the histories of two firms, disguised by request, here referred to as "D" and "L." They were chosen for their ordinariness. Although more technologically advanced than many of Korea's small weavers, D and L are roughly comparable, in level of advancement, to any of the twenty or so large-scale integrated manufacturers that comprise the membership of Korea's cotton spinning and weaving cartel. In the early 1980s, D employed 3,500 workers and was among the largest of the integrated spinners and weavers. During the same period, L employed 2,500 workers and was in the medium-size range of the larger firm set.

The accumulation of experience, however, was disrupted by both the Second World War and the Korean War. As a result of the latter, the cotton textiles industry lost about 70% of its production facilities (Y. B. Kim, 1980). However, it rapidly recovered with foreign aid and with government patronage. In 1953 one of L's current plants was rebuilt on a turnkey basis with U.N. funding by two leading textiles machinery manufacturers, British Platt and Japanese Howa. D's facilities were also modernized after 1955 with the help of both foreign loans and machinery suppliers.

Beginning in the 1960s, export demand favored synthetic fabrics, and the growth of the textiles industry was spurred by government support for a domestic chemical fiber industry. Both D and L responded to export incentives by developing fabrics of polyester and cotton blends. In 1963, L received the President's Industrial Award for its contribution to the development of polyester/cotton (P/C) blended fabrics; it was the first Korean firm to do so. With government subsidies and with minimal foreign technical assistance from Japanese synthetic fiber manufacturers, L had no trouble developing such blends in-house. Thereafter, however, its investments in new product development diminished rapidly. Throughout the 1960s and 1970s, L's product line was highly stable and standardized. It included only P/C blends of carded and combed yarn, and poplin, shirting, duck, and gray fabrics—although these basics were manufactured in large varieties.

D developed P/C blends in 1968 by the same devices as those used by L: subsidized in-house efforts and minimal foreign technical assistance. Thereafter, though, D's investments in product development were somewhat greater than L's. It added a few new product lines in the 1970s and 1980s, sometimes with, sometimes without, foreign technical assistance. In the case of sanitized yarn, the most specialized of D's products, foreign technical assistance was forthcoming from both independent consultants and machinery suppliers. But D's in-house efforts at product development, although greater than L's, were still small. Table 10.1 provides a breakdown by technology-related functions of the time spent on each function in 1984 by D's professional and technical staff. The two functions that relate to product development—product engineering and R&D—absorbed only 1.1% of D's total technology-related efforts.

Furthermore, a shift in output from the home to the international market left both company modes of technology acquisition unchanged. Machinery suppliers and independent consultants, mainly from Japan, continued to be the primary source of know-how. These suppliers were selected after visits by firm presidents and by only one or two technical staff people to foreign textiles plants and ma-

Table 10.1 Technology-Related Functions, "D" Company, 1984

Function	Year Function Undertaken	Equivalent "Person Year," Professional and Technical Staff Involved, 1984	Percent
Plant maintenance	1955	720	50.0
Repair	1955	370	26.0
Quality control	1955	8	0.5
Testing	1955	7	0.5
Process engineering	1962	5	0.5
Product engineering	1962	5	0.3
Plant expansion	1967	313	22.0
Technical information services	1972	6	0.4
Research & development	1976	12	0.8
Total		1,436	100[a]

[a] Sum of listed items exceeds 100 because of rounding.

Source: D Company.

chinery builders. Until as recently as the late 1970s, the ring-spinning frame and the shuttle loom were the basic technologies procured. Suppliers of this equipment provided technical assistance on layout, start-up, and maintenance for capacity expansions that involved a new plant or a new vintage of the same basic technology. When a new variant of the same basic product line was involved, machinery suppliers also provided advice on production methods. D's and L's own engineers managed the task independently only when capacity expansions involved the same vintage of technology they had used before.

Learning-by-Doing

In the late 1960s, Japanese textiles firms began to lose world market share to competitors from Korea, Taiwan, Singapore, and Hong Kong. The textiles exports of these four economies combined were already 82% as great as those of Japan in 1970. By 1976 they had exceeded Japan's export share by a factor of 1.4 (Yamazawa, 1982). Further, Korean and Japanese nominal wages in the cotton-spinning industry had risen at approximately the same rate between 1945 and 1975 (Woo, 1978, p. 194). Therefore, Korea's further incursions into Japan's textiles market were not underwritten by a slower rate of wage increase, but rather by more rapidly rising labor productivity (Woo, 1978, p. 194). Labor productivity in the Korean cotton textiles in-

Table 10.2   Learning Curve Estimates for Firm "D," 1955–1981—
Regression: $\ln(L/V) = \ln(A) - B \times \ln(\Sigma V)$

Industry	Period	$-B$	t	R	2^{-B} (Learning Rates)
Spinning	1955–1968	−.384	.0000	.78	.766
	1968–1981	−.507	.0000	.82	.703
	1955–1981	−.451	.0000	.91	.716
Weaving	1955–1968	−.500	.0002	.69	.707
	1968–1981	−.511	.0003	.68	.702

L, employment; V, value-added.
Source: D Company.

dustry rose as a consequence of investments in foreign-made equipment, in Japanese technical assistance, and in learning-by-doing.

Estimates of a learning curve for company D are presented in Table 10.2. D's learning history is divided into two periods: 1955–1968, the years when a new plant came on-stream; and 1968–1981, the years when a new spinning technology—the open-end rotor—was imported. Ignoring momentarily any differences in the rate of learning between the two subperiods, what is striking about the estimates is how low they are by conventional standards (the lower the percentage, the faster the rate of learning or the rate at which labor inputs decline per doubling of output). Learning curves were first estimated during World War II in the American airframe industry (Yelle, 1979). The typical learning rate was found to be about 85%, compared with learning rates in the 70% range for D's spinning and weaving operations.

These results are consistent with the fact that cotton spinning and weaving are relatively labor-intensive operations—rates of learning tend to be especially sensitive to labor's skill and motivation and to management's artfulness in smoothing and improving the production process. Each of these factors is examined here in turn.

The Role of Young Female Labor

Notwithstanding the fact that the technology for making textiles is highly embodied in machinery, and that the machinery itself is relatively standardized, textiles manufacture remains an art. The young women who worked in Korea's textiles mills could not have been replaced by those who worked on the assembly lines in its electronics plants without causing an immediate fall in productivity. Through-

Table 10.3 Wage Differences in Manufacturing Industries: 1970, 1974, 1978, and 1981

| Industry | Wage Differences | | | |
	1970	1974	1978	1981
Average wage	100	100	100	100
Food	111.0	106.1	115.3	121.7
Textiles	78.6	85.3	74.6	79.3
Wood products	102.9	96.3	101.5	96.2
Paper	129.7	120.2	134.5	124.6
Chemicals	123.5	115.7	113.6	115.1
Nonmetallic minerals	104.5	116.3	127.1	114.6
Steel	143.9	160.1	150.7	138.4
Machinery	109.9	101.9	109.2	107.7
Other	73.7	73.8	76.2	78.3

Source: F. Park (1983).

put time and quality in textiles manufacture depend on the skills of operators in mending yarn breaks and repairing fabric imperfections. Yet, although the Korean trade union movement has been especially active in the cotton textiles branch, the wages in the textiles industry have been consistently 15% to 25% below the all-industry average (see Table 10.3). According to J. J. Choi,

> Factory production of textile goods represents the largest and oldest manufacturing industry in Korea; cotton textile manufacture especially constitutes its core. It was in this branch, therefore, that large textile mills were represented by one of the most well organized employers' associations, . . . and that the unionized workers staged some of the largest strikes . . . in the midst of the Korean War and . . . in the Syngman Rhee era. (1983, p. 441)

The labor unrest that swept over Korea beginning in the late 1970s was particularly acute in textiles (Commission of the Churches on International Affairs, 1979; Pallais, 1986), not least of all in company D.

The long and short of the labor strategies of both D and L was their intent to avoid any acceleration in wage increases and to raise productivity by means of both quality control circles (QCCs) and paternalism.

QCCs were viewed as an important vehicle for raising worker commitment and output because neither D nor L offered its workers any formal training. Introduced to D and L by Japanese consultants in the early 1970s, QCCs were studied further, in the case of D, by its president, who traveled to Japan under the auspices of the Korea Management Association. Then still more was learned about QCCs from the Korean Standards Association. The rate of wage increase in all Korean industries began to accelerate at this time, and the government made vocational training in large-size firms compulsory. Like many other textiles firms, however, D and L exempted themselves from this legislation. They provided their workers instead with primary school—and sometimes even secondary school—education, a compromise that the government found acceptable.

According to D, the establishment of primary schools on company premises had the effect of sharply reducing labor turnover. Although full-time workers were required by law to be 16 years or older, many of D's workers were younger, with barely any formal schooling. With the provision of formal schooling, D's factory girls became better workers; thus paternalism came to operate round the clock. Factory girls slept and ate in company-owned dormitories, spent nine and one-half hours on the job, and devoted evenings to study in company-owned night schools.

The Role of "Hands On" Management

Year-to-year productivity changes in the L Company are presented in Table 10.4. Ignoring for the moment the data that relate to the new technology of open-end spinning, Table 10.4 presents company figures on labor productivity and machine productivity for ring

Table 10.4 Labor Productivity in "L" Company, 1977–1986

	Labor Productivity			Machine Productivity		
Year	Ring Spinning (kg/man·8hr)	Open-end Spinning (kg/man·8hr)	Weaving (m/man·8hr)	Ring Spinning (kg/sp·8hr)	Open-end Spinning (kg·sp·8hr)	Weaving (m/mach·8hr)
1977	52.39	—	216.22	0.199	—	36.11
1978	55.87	—	218.17	0.199	—	36.28
1979	56.97	137.06	203.14	0.203	0.913	36.54
1980	56.37	157.39	183.02	0.204	1.073	36.04
1981	59.52	178.82	187.68	0.206	1.076	36.01
1982	61.60	177.54	199.43	0.210	1.089	35.11
1983	66.68	199.75	199.11	0.214	1.107	34.78
1984	70.12	178.13	186.15	0.222	1.186	34.34
1985	71.05	214.38	196.49	0.221	1.250	34.73
1986	78.49	210.30	224.05	0.225	1.259	35.38

kg, kilogram; m, meter; sp, spindle; mach, machine; 8 hr, 8 hours.
Source: L Company.

spinning and weaving for the years 1977 through 1986. Although capital investments in L were not altogether constant during this period, they could not have had much of an impact on productivity behavior. As indicated in Table 10.5, between 1977 and 1984 L added only 3,024 ring-frame spindles and 162 looms to its capacity, whereas its existing stock of ring-frame spindles and looms equaled up to 120,000 and 1,200, respectively. Table 10.4 indicates that productivity in weaving stayed practically constant, but that labor productivity rose more than machine productivity and labor productivity in ring spinning rose by a factor of 1.5 in a decade—even though ring spinning was an old process.

These productivity improvements stand as a monument to L's technical staff. In 1983 as much as 59.7% of L's staff of engineers had held their current jobs for more than five years, and 36.1% had more than ten years' experience. To raise productivity, the accumulated skills of these managers were deployed throughout the production process.

First, they were deployed in maintaining and repairing machinery, tasks that required a lot of know-how, given the age of L's capital stock. Second, they were deployed in devising optimal machinery-operating conditions for the manufacture of different types of yarns or fabrics, a task that required a lot of know-how, given a large number of "changeovers" (i.e., resetting of machinery conditions for production lots of different types of yarn or fabric). Changeovers were frequent because L produced a large variety of the same product in order to minimize risk. Third, they were deployed in mixing different types of cotton and synthetic fibers to achieve an optimal blend. Better maintenance, smoother runs, and better mixing all contributed to reduce breaks; reduction in breaks, in turn, reduced labor requirements. Break reduction depended, too, on the selection of machinery settings. Slower running machines, which might lower machine productivity, often meant higher output per worker and lower energy requirements. Better maintenance and synchronization of machines also allowed loading and unloading of larger size bobbins, which further reduced labor requirements.

Structural Stagnation

The 1970s were a Golden Age for the Korean cotton textiles industry, with profits, output, and learning-by-doing all rising rapidly and an average annual real output growth rate of 20% (World Bank, 1987). Nevertheless, although the cotton textiles industry was enjoying incremental productivity improvements and earning lots of money, it was engaging in short-sighted profit-maximizing behavior. Year

Table 10.5 Capacity Additions in "L" Company, 1963–1984

Date	Investment	Technology	Machinery Supplier	Technical Assistance (Engineers)	Major New Product
Sep., 1963	Spindles, 10,000	Ring frame	Platt (U.K.)	5, British	—
Sep., 1966	Looms, 100	Shuttle	Howa (Japan)	2, Japanese	—
Jul., 1967	Spindles, 10,000	Ring frame	Howa (Japan)	2, Japanese	—
Nov., 1967	Spindles, 11,200	Ring frame	Howa, Platt	2, Japanese	—
Oct., 1970	Spindles, 2,000	Ring frame	Platt	None	—
Jan., 1971	Spindles, 10,176	Ring frame	Platt	2, British	—
	Looms, 305	Shuttle	Enshu (Japan)	2, Japanese	—
Mar., 1973	Spindles, 7,344	Ring frame	Howa	None	—
Aug., 1973	Looms, 206	Shuttle	Enshu	None	—
May, 1974	Spindles, 30,072	Ring frame	Platt	None	—
	Looms, 94	Shuttle	Enshu, Picarol (Belgium)	1, Belgian	—
Apr., 1975	Spindles, 10,365	Ring frame	Platt	None	—
	Looms, 100	Shuttle	Enshu	None	—
Aug., 1977	Looms, 112	Shuttle	Picarol, Enshu	1, Belgian	—
Oct., 1979	Spindles, 840	Open end	Ingolstadt (Germany)	1, German	Open-end spun yarn for weaving
Apr., 1983	Looms, 50	Shuttleless	Ishikawa (Japan)	3, Japanese	—
Sep., 1983	Ring frames, 3,024	Ring frame	Howa, Samwhan Platt[a]	None	—
Dec., 1984	Spindles, 1,152	Open end	Schlafhorst (Germany)	2, German	Open-end spun yarn for knitting

[a]This firm is a joint venture between a Korean firm and Platt (U.K.).

Source: L Company.

after year it produced the same mix of standardized products at the low end of the quality range. As a result, its competition increasingly came from lower-wage countries that were trying to enter this market segment, rather than from higher-wage countries that were trying to exit from it. Such a short-run strategy was unsustainable since Korean wage rates were rising fast. Because product-mix constancy enabled textiles firms to operate with an unchanged process, little qualitative improvement in skills was needed. Therefore, even though the textiles industry experienced some intermarginal improvement in skills as a consequence of learning-by-doing, no inframarginal improvements occurred in the form of shifts in its skill set. An unchanging process also created little need for foreign technical assistance, which meant firms were denied the opportunity to ratchet-up their know-how. However, such stability in learning was made tolerable by the relatively labor-intensive technology of textiles manufacture.

The nature of the production process technology of spinning and weaving enabled textiles firms to grow rapidly by adding capacity in small increments. Thus workers were not induced to learn new skills, because as the firms enlarged their operating capacity, their process technology did not change. As Table 10.5 shows, L added to its capacity eighteen times in twenty-one years. Yet each increment to capacity embodied roughly the same ratio of capital to labor (or what is sometimes called capital widening). After ten years of intense investment activity from 1972 to 1983, the share of labor costs in L's total manufacturing costs was slightly higher, not lower. In D, labor's share in the same period remained almost constant. The aggregate industry capital labor ratio ranged from only 1.72 million won per worker in 1966 to 3.55 million won per worker in 1977–1979 (see Table 10.6).[4] Such a low capital labor ratio suggested minimal change in the production process.

In part, each increment in capacity embodied roughly the same ratio of capital to labor because the technology employed by textiles firms in Korea remained fairly stable for a long stretch of time. As indicated in Table 10.5, from 1963 to 1977 L used the same basic technology to spin—the ring frame—and from 1963 to 1983 it used the same basic technology to weave—the shuttle loom. Even though the global diffusion of a substitute for the ring frame, the open-end rotor, began in the 1970s, neither L nor D introduced the rotor until 1979 or slightly thereafter, and then only on a trial basis. The open-end rotor was a radical innovation because it simplified certain aux-

---

[4] Whereas fixed assets per worker had increased by 8.1% during 1971–1982 in all manufacturing, fixed assets per worker had increased by only 5.67% in the textiles industry (Hong and Park, 1986).

Table 10.6 Average Capital[a]/Labor Ratios
in Korean Textiles and Cement Industries,
1966–1979 (in Million Won per Worker)

Period	Textiles	Cement
1966	1.72	27.72
1967–1971	2.29	32.06
1972–1976	3.20	48.12
1977–1979	3.55	49.18
1966–1979	2.84	41.16

[a]Gross capital stock in millions in real prices. Level of
aggregation: textiles: Korea Standard Industrial Classification (KSIC) 321; cement: KSIC 36921.

Source: Computed from Korea Development Institute,
Korean Industry Capital Stock Calculations, 1982.

iliary steps in the process flow that formerly required high labor and
capital inputs. Yet the adoption of the open-end rotor was slower in
Korea than in any major competing country. Antonelli (1986) calculated the penetration level of the open-end rotor in twenty-eight
countries during the period 1975–1983, and some of his data are
presented in Table 10.7. They show that whereas the rotor's penetration levels in 1983 were 9.88% in Hong Kong, 6.76% in Singapore, and 2.83% in Taiwan, penetration in Korea was only 0.72%.

Table 10.7 Penetration Level[a] of the
Open-End Rotor, 1975–1983

Country	1975	1983
Korea	0.08	0.72
Hong Kong	5.33	9.88
Singapore	4.21	6.76
Taiwan	0.39	2.83
India	0.00	0.02
Mexico	0.51	1.20
Argentina	0.11	2.15
Brazil	0.50	1.14
Japan	1.83	2.72
United States	0.88	2.15
United Kingdom	1.19	4.29
Germany	1.36	4.58

[a]Measured as ratio of open-end rotors to ring spindles.
One rotor is equivalent to two spindles.

Source: Data from International Textiles Manufacturers'
Federation, as prepared by Antonelli (1986).

This constancy in Korea's textiles industry technology implied a constancy in its set of textiles skills.

The textiles industry in general was slow to introduce new technology because to do so would have represented a radical departure from past investment practice. In the 1960s and 1970s, the investment practice in the textiles industry was to minimize capital expenditures per unit of labor, with two corollaries. First, such capital-minimizing meant substituting existing for new equipment, where possible, even at the expense of quality. Whereas, over time, both D and L introduced more advanced generations of shuttle looms and ring spinners, they stopped short of introducing the latest generations that featured greater automation and computerized process-monitoring control. By 1986 both D and L lagged behind less-experienced firms in newer industries in their rate of introduction of computerized process-monitoring controls. In 1985, L had invested in applying electronic sensors to some of its weaving machinery, because that investment promised quick returns, but it had not made the same investment in its spinning machinery, because the payback period was too long. It also had decided against investing in special machinery—automatic levelers and high-caliber yarn clearers—to control quality.

Second, capital minimizing meant running existing machinery for as long as possible. Both D and L stressed that a lot of its technically outmoded equipment was highly profitable to use. In 1986 the average age of L's looms was 12.9 years, and the age of its ring frame spindles averaged 18.2 years. Figures produced by the Ministry of Commerce and Industry (MCI) in 1982 caused alarm because they revealed a high degree of machinery obsolescence in the textiles sector. The MCI defined obsolescence as over ten years old for looms and spinning and knitting machines, and over seven years old for dyeing and sewing machines. Using these definitions, MCI estimated that more than 40% of Korea's spinning machinery and more than 50% of its looms and dyeing machines were obsolete (see Table 10.8).

The Difficulties of Diversification

The unchanging skill base of the textiles industry made it difficult to "upscale" and all but impossible to act as agent of further industrialization through diversification into new industries.

According to the 1967 census of manufacturing, 150 establishments in all of manufacturing employed more than 500 employees. Of those large establishments, 29% were in the textiles sector (which accounted for roughly 14% of GNP at the time) (Economic Planning Board, 1967). Thus, at one time cotton spinners and weavers were

Table 10.8   Share of Obsolete[a] Machines in the Textile Industry, 1982

Type of Machine	Total Number (A)	Number Obsolete (B)	% Obsolete (B/A)
Spinning	4,246,246	1,740,921	41.0
Loom	187,827	94,578	50.4
Dyeing	7,576	3,853	50.9
Knitting	75,418	33,767	44.8
Sewing	169,759	53,570	31.6

[a]Obsolete spinning machines, looms, and knitting machines are over ten years old; obsolete dyeing machines and sewing machines are over seven years old based on their depreciation period.

Source: Ministry of Commerce and Industry.

the cream of the country's manufacturing establishments in terms of size and modern management. Yet none of the veterans in the cotton textiles industry in the 1950s and 1960s became the leading chaebol of the 1970s and 1980s. Most of the chaebol did profit in one way or another from the textiles boom—by trading in textiles or by entering the related fields of synthetic fibers, apparel, and in one case (that of Cheil Wool) worsteds. But among the top sixty-five chaebol in 1984 (ranked by sales), only five at any time had a major focus in cotton textiles. The largest among these five, Chungnam Spinning, ranked only fortieth among the total top business groups (S. K. Kim, 1987).

Furthermore, companies like D and L on the one hand, and the Samsung group's Cheil Wool subsidiary on the other, differed sharply in their ability to use textiles as a springboard to other manufacturing activities (see the discussion on learning by Cheil Wool in Chapter 9). The Samsung group looked outward for its industrial competence, to fresh university graduates and the experienced engineers of competitors, whereas D and L looked inward. The Samsung group was a generalist in manufacturing skills, whereas D and L were specialists in textiles.

The capability of the chaebol to diversify into newer and more complex industries is taken for granted, but diversification depends on skills—in preinvestment feasibility studies, in project execution, in training, and in production—that the managerial resources of companies like D and L did not possess. Instead, D's and L's managerial know-how derived from their long-term accumulation of experience on-the-job, the thread of expertise extending back to the time of Japanese management. Company presidents at D and L did complain about the lack of "internationalism" on the part of their technical people. Even on D's Board of Directors, only one of nine members had had any formal education outside Korea. Few salaried managers at either company could speak or read a foreign language. This impeded diversification.

When L's future in the cotton textiles industry became clouded with competitors from lower-wage countries, L attempted—unsuccessfully—to diversify into yachts, construction, and computer software. The company's diversification into yachts was misguided because Korea had few internal waterways and because Taiwan posed as a formidable competitor in international markets. Its diversification into the construction sector failed because its engineering and project coordination know-how were minimal and competition was fierce. Its diversification into computer software failed because it had little firsthand experience with either business or process computers and was unable to mobilize sufficient technical talent at a time when venture capital was pouring into the computer software field. Because L's annual sales in the early 1980s were as much as $85 million, and it had had a long time to accumulate capital and to develop credit channels, it cannot be said that L's failures at diversification were caused by capital shortages.[5]

In the case of D, it attempted instead to diversify into related fields, forming a joint venture with a Japanese apparel manufacturer and a Japanese synthetic fiber manufacturer. In addition, it established a wholly owned subsidiary to produce knitted fabrics as a way to diversify its yarn output and to supply its joint venture with knitted as well as woven fabrics. It also formed a trading company with the intention of distributing its own exports. Nevertheless, a decade after its joint venture was founded, less than 5% of D's total sales was accounted for by garments. Instead, yarns rose in importance to almost 80% of sales, with woven fabrics accounting for the remainder. The problem associated with integrating into quality apparel were of two types: (1) Wholly owned apparel subsidiaries found it difficult to

[5] Many economists in Korea and in the World Bank attribute part of the decline in the textile industry to government intervention (see, for example, World Bank, 1987). They argue that the government allegedly discriminated against the textile industry in its allocation of subsidized credit to build up the heavy industries. In fact, there is no evidence that the textiles industry was starved of capital—to the contrary. According to the findings of Hong and Park (1986), the textiles industry received above-average subsidized bank loans in 1974–1979 and 1980–1982 and average subsidized bank loans in 1971–1973. Hong and Park calculated loan to value-added percentages in twenty-three industries and in all of manufacturing for the period 1971–1982. They then calculated the ratio of the percentage in each industry to the all-manufacturing average. In 1971–1973, the ratio for the textiles industry was 1.0, implying a loan to value-added percentage equal to the all-manufacturing average. In 1974–1979 and 1980–1992, however, the ratio was above the all-manufacturing mean: 1.2 and 1.1, respectively (see Table 4.2).

compete against high-fashion houses, especially those in Hong Kong. (2) Prestigious foreign joint-venture partners were hard to find because Korean spinners and weavers had little to offer, being neither especially low cost nor particularly innovative in product development.

The Uncertainties of Upscaling

Those weaknesses in managerial resources that prevented D and L from acting as agents of further industrialization also undermined their ability to meet low-wage competition by "upscaling," that is, by moving into a higher-quality market niche in the textiles sector. Therefore, one of the first steps L took, when threatened by competition in the mid-1980s, was to recruit an engineer with a master's degree in textiles engineering from Seoul National University, Mr. Kim. Textiles engineering is one of the oldest engineering disciplines taught in Korean universities, and between 1963 and 1980, 5.8% of a total of roughly 100,000 university graduates with engineering degrees had majored in textiles engineering (Ministry of Education, various years). Most graduates, however, were believed to be unable to find jobs in the textiles sector, and Kim considered himself lucky to be working for L.

According to Kim, there were some weaknesses in L's capability, productivity being lower than in Japan, but he believed that there were also some strengths and that progress was being made. In a 1977 study by the Korea Productivity Center, which measured productivity by the number of hours of labor needed to produce one unit of output, labor hours were found to be 2.2 times higher in the Korean than the Japanese textiles industry (Han'guk Saengsansŏng Cent'a, 1979). Kim said that there were many causes for this.

The first cause of L's lower relative productivity was its reluctance to invest in new machinery. L was hesitant despite the dramatic productivity increases it had realized from the small amount of new technology it had introduced. As indicated in Table 10.4, the introduction of the open-end rotor in 1979 had led to an immediate jump in productivity above the level of the previous technology on the order of 2.4 in labor and 4.5 in capital. Although learning-by-doing continued to increase productivity on ring-spinning technology, it could not substitute for buying the new. According to Kim, L was slow to invest in new technology because the company was conservative. It adopted a wait-and-see attitude and followed the lead of other members of the industry's cartel. Nevertheless, L had begun to invest more in spite of obstacles to its "learning." It was building a new plant because an old one had burned down and it was equipping it with the latest technology—open-end rotors and shuttleless looms. L's transition to shuttleless looms in 1983–1984 had been very difficult. The company sent its best engineers to Japan to learn new operating methods, and Japanese machinery suppliers stayed at L for about a month.

Productivity was higher in Japan, according to Kim, because of better repair and maintenance. L's experienced engineers could operate the new machinery, but they could not repair it because it contained printed circuit boards and electrical parts that were unfamiliar to them. They didn't know enough Japanese or English to read the user manuals provided by machinery suppliers. In addition, most of the old-timers were resistant to the new machinery so that, in 1984, L had begun selecting young boys for training in electronics and repair. New machinery was worth maintaining, but Kim concluded that maintenance went against the grain at L. It was regarded as a waste of time and expensive because wages had to be paid for the duration of the time machinery was down. Furthermore, the Japanese maintained their machinery better because it was newer, and therefore the variable wage component in total costs was lower.

Kim said that L was just beginning to learn theoretical know-how. The company began to document every process, and it had introduced a computer in 1985 for the purpose of furthering statistical quality control. The capability of every machine had to be determined in order to decide whether to accept new orders for higher quality yarns and fabrics. While the old-timers were good at mixing, they had used a fixed combination of cottons, changing the mix only slightly from one material to another. Because fine fabrics required more complex mixing, Kim wrote a computer simulation program for mixing raw cotton. However, even though he had consulted a University of Texas program, which he then modified to suit L's conditions, his program failed. Kim concluded that mixing remained an art and that the old-timers were indispensable.

Royalties paid by the textiles sector for foreign technical assistance rose dramatically in 1978-1979, indicating an attempt on the part of the industry to upgrade. Of total royalties for the period 1962–1983, almost 90% were incurred after 1976. By the late 1970s–early 1980s, almost all of the textiles industry's proprietary imports for foreign technical assistance were related to product rather than to process: 40.6% of technical assistance was designated for new products and 37.5% was designated for product improvements (Federation of Korean Industries, 1984). However, Kim suggested that in spite of this industry trend, a company like L was reluctant to invest in product development because it was still more profitable to operate at the bottom end of the market.

TEXTILES MANUFACTURE VERSUS CEMENT-MAKING

Like the textiles industry in Korea, the cement industry originated during the Japanese colonial period. During the post-Korean-War era, it underwent first import substitution and later export promotion (a decade behind textiles). The cement industry also resembled the textiles industry in that it produced relatively standardized products and learned in an intensely competitive milieu. Nevertheless, the ways each industry created value and competed were quite distinct because of sharp differences in capital and skill intensity.

As indicated in Table 10.6, the average capital labor ratio in 1966–1979 was 41.16 million won per worker in the cement industry compared with 2.84 million won per worker in textiles. In 1980 the percentage of college graduates in total employment was lower in textiles than in most manufacturing industries: 0.8% compared with the all-manufacturing average of 8.1% (Economic Planning Board, 1983). Differences in skill intensity are also suggested by international data that compare across industries the number of engineers per 1,000 persons engaged. According to a 1970 study, data for the United States show that the manufacture of textiles involved seven engineers per 1,000 persons engaged, whereas the manufacture of glass, stone, and clay products involved as many as nineteen (Zymelman, 1980). Data for other countries also show that cement-making generally demands three times more engineers per 1,000 persons engaged than does textiles. The difference in technical and managerial resources of the two industries and the difference in management approaches that these resources entail—more scientific in the case of cement, more artistic in the case of textiles—underscore the difference in the ability of the two industries to diversify. Whereas no integrated cotton spinners and weavers transformed themselves into major diversified business groups, two cement firms (of a total of nine) later became chaebol affiliates: the first was the manufacturing facility of Korea's largest chaebol, the Hyundai group (see the discussion below), and the other, which accounts for almost 50% of cement output, became the major component of the seventh largest chaebol, the Ssangyong group (whose first manufacturing affiliate was in the soap industry).

Differences in skill and capital intensity in the textiles and cement industries reflected different modes of learning, competing, and realizing value in three respects:

1. Foreign technical assistance was far lower in the textiles industry than in that of cement. This is indicated in Table 10.9, which presents data on proprietary transfers of technology by industry for the period 1962–1981. Both royalty payments and value-added

Table 10.9 Proprietary Transfers of Technology in Korea, by Sector and Plan Period, 1962–1981

Distribution by:	Foreign Investment		Percent Distribution of Cumulative Values Licensed Technology		Production
	Approvals Granted	Amount Invested	Approvals Granted	Royalty Payments	Value-added
Sector, 1962–1981					
Food, beverages, tobacco	2.6	3.6	2.5	1.1	24.0
Textiles, apparel, leather	9.7	7.2	1.6	1.1	19.0
Pulp, paper products	0.4	0.1	0.8	1.5	2.5
Pharmaceuticals	2.0	1.6	2.9	0.4	a
Synthetic fibers, resins	14.4	30.9	2.7	4.5	2.8
Petroleum refining, other chemicals	1.1	8.2	18.7	36.8	20.2
Cement, ceramic products	3.2	1.6	3.0	2.4	5.1
Basic metals	9.1	6.7	9.7	11.4	7.1
Nonelectrical machinery	17.2	8.9	31.6	21.3	2.3
Electrical machinery	24.8	22.4	19.5	12.3	9.3
Transport equipment	1.0	5.0	3.0	3.3	5.3
Other manufacturing	14.4	3.9	4.0	3.7	2.3
Total manufacturing	100.0	100.0	100.0	100.0	100.0
Plan Period					
1962–1966	2.0	2.5	1.6	0.1	4.4
1967–1971	20.1	6.7	14.2	2.7	11.5
1972–1976	56.4	47.3	22.5	18.4	28.3
1977–1981	21.5	43.5	61.8	78.8	55.8
Total 1962–1981	100.0	100.0	100.0	100.0	100.0
Aggregate cumulative total cases	693	1,249	1,840	565	156,351

aValue is included in other chemicals.

bValues used to compute percentages are in millions of U.S. dollars: at current prices for amounts invested and paid and at constant 1975 prices for value-added. Total may not reconcile due to rounding.

Source: Westphal, Kim and Dahlman (1985).

for each industry are cumulative. The data suggest that the textiles industry (defined to include apparel and leather) accounted for 19.0% of manufacturing value-added in 1962–1981, but for only 1.1% of total royalty payments. By contrast, the cement industry (defined to include ceramics) accounted for 5.1% of value-added and 2.4% of royalties. The intensity of foreign technical assistance may be represented by the ratio of royalty payments of value added: the higher the ratio—call it the transfer ratio—the greater the intensity. In neither the textiles nor cement industry was the transfer ratio as high as in, say, petrochemicals or machinery. But it was far lower in textiles than in cement, 0.059 and 0.471, respectively.

The textiles industry's relatively low transfer ratio meant that foreign technical assistance left the breadth of know-how of individual managers almost unchanged. A defining characteristic of foreign technical assistance for capacity expansions in the heavy industries, cement included, has been the training of large numbers of administrative and technical personnel overseas, both on-the-job and in formal courses. The results of such overseas training have tended to include a sharp rise in the familiarity of engineers, front-line supervisors, and sometimes even skilled workers with state-of-the-art production processes. By contrast, foreign technical assistance in the textiles industry involved very little overseas training. On two occasions in the 1960s, L sent five or six engineers to Japan in preparation for new plant or major capacity expansion. But such training all but ceased in the 1970s. Overall, the effects of this lack of internationalism were that the professionalism of managers remained at a low level and that the lack of either an international outlook or a means for communication persisted. These effects contributed to a failure on the part of textiles firms to branch out into other manufacturing industries.

2. Divergent learning paths in textiles and cement firms were reinforced by differences in the content of the foreign technical assistance that was provided not just abroad but also on-site in Korea. The cement industry's transfer ratio was high partly because cement firms spent a lot on "software," that is, the detailed instructions that cement process specialists provided on how to operate a cement mill. This constituted the starting point for the industry's systematic in-house approach to experimentation in order to find the optimum operating conditions. By contrast, textiles firms spent far less on software because their standardized equipment did not warrant it. Instead, to achieve optimum production conditions, textiles firms relied almost entirely on the accumulated

experience and intuitive know-how of their technical staff. Thus, the relatively uncodified technology of cement-making gave rise to a more procedurized mode of learning, whereas the explicit technology of textiles manufacture gave rise to a mode of learning premised more on art than on science. Such a learning mode was difficult to transfer to other manufacturing industries.

3. Although both textiles and cement firms competed largely on the basis of price, they competed differently: Capital costs were the more important determinant of price in the cement industry, whereas in textiles labor costs were the more important determinant of price.

Capital costs per unit of output in the cement industry depended on three dimensions of the production process—technology, scale, and process automation. The industry's cost-minimizing strategy, therefore, became one whereby firms adopted "state-of-the-art" technology, larger scale, and greater process automation. The cement industry leader of the 1960s, which failed to introduce a new generation of technology and instead followed a strategy of fine tuning an existing one, was taken over by the Ssangyong Cement Company during a period of severe price competition in the mid-1970s. In 1986 Ssangyong Cement operated a total of sixteen kilns in three plants, one of the kilns the world's largest. During the course of its twenty-year history, it introduced three new generations of technology: a wet process in the early 1960s, a dry process in the late 1960s–early 1970s, and a new dry process in the late 1970s. During the same time period, the scale of its kilns increased by a factor of 7. Its earliest kilns had a yearly capacity of roughly 400 TMT (thousand metric tons) its next generation of kilns had an annual capacity of roughly 1,300 TMT, and the kilns installed in the late 1970s–early 1980s had an annual capacity of 2,800 TMT. As scale increased, more automated process controls were appended. Ssangyong installed a semicomputerized process-monitoring system in its largest plant. By 1986 a newer plant of a competitor had become fully computerized.

As technology, process automation, and scale changed, capital-intensity changed pari passu. As indicated in Table 10.6, the capital labor ratio in the cement industry rose from 27.72 million won in 1966 to 32.06 million won in 1967–1971 to almost 50 million won in 1977–1979. A change in the capital labor ratio signaled a change in the production structure, or what Hawtrey called capital deepening, *and with such change came pressure on cement firms to learn different skills.* The introduction of new vintages of technology demanded adaptations in investment and in production capability. As the scale of operations increased, production and quality know-how had to adjust, because technical parameters did not change linearly and the introduction of computerized process controls induced more vigorous efforts to monitor quality.

We turn now to a discussion of how managerial capability in the Hyundai Cement Company was diffused within the Hyundai group.

THE HYUNDAI CEMENT COMPANY

The Hyundai group accumulated its first fortune in the construction industry, having been founded by C. Y. Chung, a man of modest means and little formal schooling. [Most Korean entrepreneurs are well educated, from rich backgrounds (Jones and Sakong, 1980).]

Chung impressed the U.S. military authorities in Korea after World War II largely with a brother who spoke fluent English. Hyundai Construction began repairing bridges, paving roads, and building army barracks, simple dams, and reservoirs, using "appropriate technology" specified by the Corps of Army Engineers. Although Hyundai began working for the military in 1947, its first bulldozer was deployed as late as 1951. With the start of the Korean War and in its aftermath, however, construction projects became more technologically complex and also more lucrative. Between 1963 and 1966, for example, military projects accounted for 26% of Hyundai's total construction revenue but for almost 77% of its total profits.

Even when U.S. aid began to wind down in the mid-1960s, Hyundai proved sufficiently confident about the future to petition the government for a license to establish its own cement-making affiliate. Cement-making never became one of Hyundai's major enterprises. The mill that it established was uncharacteristically small, in fact one of the smallest in Korea. The mill, however, was critical for Hyundai's internal development and was a first for Hyundai in two respects: It was its first manufacturing affiliate and it was its first attempt to construct an industrial plant. For both reasons and with an eye toward the future, Hyundai attempted to involve itself as much as possible in all aspects of project execution.

To maximize involvement, Hyundai unpackaged technology transfer, much as D and L had done. Technology transfer in the case of a cement mill, however, is a much more complex procedure than in the case of a textiles plant. The latter mainly concerns the import of standardized pieces of stand-alone equipment, whereas in a cement mill, all parts are integrated and are less standardized individually. Hyundai, therefore, signed a technical consulting service agreement with George A. Fuller Company of the United States, a

Table 10.10 Hyundai's Involvement in Plant Erections

	Initial Plant 1964	First Expansion 1968	Second Expansion 1974
Basic engineering	Allis Chalmers	Fuller	Fuller
Detailed engineering	Allis Chalmers	Fuller	Fuller, Hyundai
Procurement	Allis Chalmers	Hyundai	Hyundai
Supervision	Allis Chalmers	Hyundai	Hyundai
Construction	Hyundai	Hyundai	Hyundai
Start-Up	Allis Chalmers	Fuller, Hyundai	Fuller, Hyundai

Source: Amsden and Kim, 1985b.

cement-plant process manufacturer, which provided general engineering advice on the overall project (it was incumbent on Hyundai to deal only with American suppliers because finance had been arranged through U.S. aid). On the Fuller Company's advice, Hyundai signed a contract with another American cement-plant process manufacturer, Allis Chalmers, for all project-related services except construction, but including a performance guarantee.

Hyundai's success at technology assimilation is suggested in Table 10.10. In the initial plant erection, the only function Hyundai undertook was construction, under Allis Chalmer's supervision. Then in an expansion four years later in 1968, Hyundai undertook the functions of procurement and supervision as well as construction, and even collaborated on start-up with Fuller. By 1974 the only function Hyundai did *not* engage in was basic engineering, which is typically left to cement-plant process specialists by all cement-makers, no matter how experienced.

The assimilation of cement-making technology was the basis for Hyundai's successful bid, ten years later, on a turnkey cement plant export to Saudi Arabia worth as much as $208 million. As for manufacturing capability, Hyundai used its cement plant as a laboratory to train its managers with backgrounds in construction, before assigning them to other manufacturing affiliates. Trainees gained experience in inventory management, quality and process control, capacity planning, and so on, thus spreading basic production skills throughout the Hyundai organization. After Hyundai Cement, the next manufacturing affiliate in the group was founded in 1967 and named Hyundai Motors. Twenty years later it became the first independent automaker from a late-industrializing country to export globally. The first president of Hyundai Motors was a former president of Hyundai Cement.

CONCLUSION

The dynamic of dynamic comparative advantage in Korea is one wherein growth emanates primarily from the diversified business group, secondarily from the spin-off firm, and only insignificantly from the specialized, independent entrepreneur. Moreover, the biggest Korean business groups of the 1970s and 1980s cannot trace their lineage to a specialization in the leading sector of the 1950s and 1960s, cotton spinning and weaving. In this respect the progression from labor-intensive to capital- and skill-intensive industry in Korea was nonlinear. The chaebol have their antecedents not in cotton spinning and weaving but in the simpler import-substitution heavy industries that the government encouraged on the periphery of the light manufactures.

This dynamic attests to the importance of early import-substitution activity. The importance of such activity stems from the fact that even the simple heavy industries like cement have qualitatively different technologies—and hence, modes of competition—from those of the labor-intensive pursuits like cotton spinning and weaving. The heavy industries expand by *capital deepening,* or a rise in the capital/labor ratio, rather than *capital widening,* or a multiplication of production units with the same ratio of capital to labor and hence production processes and skills. Capital deepening requires a relatively large cadre of salaried managers, who approach production more like a science than an art. It is on the basis of this science that the big business groups diversified into an ever-widening range of new industries.

Diversification into shipbuilding and steel will be considered in the next two chapters.

CHAPTER ELEVEN

The World's Largest Shipbuilder

THE COMPETITIVE CHALLENGE

Hyundai Heavy Industries (HHI), a subsidiary of the Hyundai Group, began building its first ship, a very large crude carrier, in March 1973.[1] Less then a decade later, HHI had become the world's largest shipbuilder, with cumulative deliveries exceeding 10 million deadweight tons (DWT) by 1984. South Korea's share of world orders for new ships vied with Japan's, having reached 17.4% by the mid-1980s—a 15 percentage point increase over ten years (see Table 11.1). Japan had led the way in building mammoth shipyards since World War II. Outfitted with up-to-date capital equipment, it was able to undermine the supremacy of European and American shipbuilders. Japanese shipbuilding companies, moreover, were of relatively long standing, predating World War II (Shiba, 1986; Vogel, 1985). What was unique about HHI, in comparison with its Japanese counterparts, was its rise to power on the basis of a complex, "greenfield" yard without any prior experience in shipbuilding. This chapter will explain the learning that underlay HHI's ascent.

By comparison with the Pohang Iron and Steel Company (POSCO) discussed in the next chapter, HHI's investment in a shipyard at Mipo Bay was relatively small—$900 million versus $3.6 billion for POSCO. Nevertheless, in several technical respects and in almost all economic ones, HHI's investment was the most difficult of the two to manage. Whereas POSCO was oriented to the domestic market and enjoyed excess home demand for its steel for over a decade after its founding, HHI was premised on exporting but awoke to an acute and protracted worldwide shipbuilding depression. As indicated in Table 11.2, between 1974 and 1976 the annual volume of

[1] Shipbuilding was first organized as a department within the Hyundai Construction Company. In 1973 the Hyundai Shipbuilding and Heavy Industries Company was founded. In 1978 this company changed its name to Hyundai Heavy Industries. HHI produces both ships and heavy machinery and equipment.

Table 11.1 Percentage of New Ship Orders Placed, 1974–1984

Year	Japan	South Korea	European Economic Community	Comecon	Rest of World
1974	38.4	2.8	27.0	2.9	28.9
1976	56.0	2.5	10.6	10.0	21.0
1978	43.2	3.7	14.9	11.5	26.7
1980	52.7	9.0	12.1	4.2	22.0
1982	49.7	9.6	13.5	9.4	17.8
1984	55.9	17.4	10.0	2.5	14.2
1986	37.1	18.9	8.9	8.2	26.9

Source: Lloyd's Register of Shipping (various years).

ship orders placed worldwide fell by over 50% and had not recovered by the mid-1980s. Hyundai's production volume over the
same period grew fitfully rather than steadily (see Table 11.3).

It was thus against a gloomy international background of excess
capacity and cutthroat price competition that HHI learned how to
build ships. Demand shortfalls drove HHI to alter its product mix
away from very large crude carriers (VLCCs) to smaller higher-value
ships, as well as to branch out into offshore structures, to diversify
into steel structures and industrial plants, and to integrate forward
in order to stabilize demand—all the while struggling to learn the
ABCs of shipbuilding proper. Diversification helped to offset the losses
HHI sustained in shipbuilding. HHI's hedging activities were supported by membership in the Hyundai group, possibly Korea's larg-

Table 11.2 Annual Shipbuilding Orders and
Completions Worldwide, 1974–1984
(in 1,000 Gross Tons)

Year	Annual Volume of Orders Placed	Annual Completions
1974	28,370	33,541
1976	12,937	33,922
1978	8,026	18,194
1980	18,969	13,101
1982	11,232	16,820
1984	16,000[a]	18,000[a]

[a] Estimates.

Source: Lloyd's Register of Shipping (various years).

est chaebol. This chapter is therefore concerned with the creation of competitive advantage in a particular context, that of the diversified business group.

Japan was HHI's main competitor. As the world slump in shipbuilding sharpened, Japan's share of new orders rose from roughly 40% in 1974 to roughly 56% ten years later, largely at the expense of the United States, Europe, and to a lesser extent Brazil. Then its share fell back to 37% in 1986 (see Table 11.1).[2] Although Japanese yards, like Korean yards, were menaced by excess capacity, they were able to retain their share of a smaller global volume amidst greater world competition by dint of their low costs and efficiency. With respect to demand conditions, Japan had a clear edge over Korea. The world leader in shipbuilding had a far larger domestic merchant marine than did Korea, and Japanese shipping companies tended to buy Japanese-made ships. By contrast, Korean shipping companies tended to import their fleets in the form of used vessels with favorable finance terms and fast delivery. In the early 1980s, about 80% of Korea's demand for ships was satisfied by imports (Korea Exchange Bank, 1983). Although the Korean government did operate a public procurement system, the Japanese system was far more comprehensive, enabling Japan to stabilize demand for locally built ships (Chung, 1982). With respect to costs, just as the total costs of POSCO and of the Japanese integrated steel mills ran neck and neck in the late 1970s and early 1980s (see the discussion in Chapter 12), the total costs of HHI and of Japan's "Big Seven" shipbuilders appear to have been fairly evenly matched.

International cost data on shipbuilding in the early 1980s for all Korean shipyards, not just HHI, suggest a 2.8% rate of profit in Korean yards (Harvard Business School, 1986b). (See Table 11.4 on the shipbuilding industry's cost breakdown.) The data, however, are too crude to indicate anything definitive about profitability. Rather, they are useful only to the extent that they provide some support for the overall picture: on the one hand, similarity in total costs between Korea and Japan, and on the other, dissimilarity in the relative shares of cost elements—labor and materials and components—in the total. The share of labor costs in total costs in 1983 was about 2.5 times higher in Japan than in Korea, a difference of the same order of magnitude as in the steel industry. Assuming wage rates in the shipyards and steel mills of Japan and Korea also differed by

---

[2] The decline in Japan's share appears to be due to the appreciation of the yen. In the first quarter of 1987, Korea for the first time surpassed Japan in orders for new ships (*New York Times*, 1987).

Table 11.3 Principal Shipbuilder's Production, 1973–1986 (in Gross Tons)

Company	1973	1974	1975	1976	1977	1978
Hyundai	126,000	451,700	512,000	573,500	505,568	614,790
Korea Shipbuilding & Engineering Corporation	2,980	2,980	75,400	52,450	76,322	116,694
Daewoo	—	—	—	—	—	—
Samsung	—	—	—	—	—	—

Source: Ministry of Commerce and Industry.

roughly the same order of magnitude, labor productivity in Japanese shipyards was about 1.6 times as great as in Korean yards.[3]

Labor productivity in shipbuilding is largely a function of the degree of equipment automation, the skill level of operators, the quality of ship designs, and throughput time (time taken for raw materials to be converted into final product). From the outset of operations, *learning at HHI was driven by the imperative to reduce throughput time in order to meet delivery schedules.* Meeting delivery schedules was no easy matter, however, because the process flow involved a large number of discrete operations and varied with the type of ship under construction. A large shipyard is tantamount to a giant job shop: The number of job descriptions and the number of components and sub-

Table 11.4 Value Chains of the Shipbuilding Industry,[a] 1983

	Western Europe	Japan	Korea
Materials and components	70.0%	63.0%	70.0%
Labor	36.0	30.0	12.0
General and administration	5.0	5.0	3.0
Design cost	0.1	0.1	0.2
Commission	1.0	1.0	1.0
Corporate overhead	NA	NA	11.0
Total	112.1	99.1	97.2

NA, not available.

[a]Percentages of 1983 ship prices for medium-sized bulk carriers.

Source: Harvard Business School (1986b).

[3] It is difficult to make interfirm wage comparisons because of differences in seniority and skills. Starting salaries in POSCO and HHI in 1985, however, were approximately the same for what appear to be roughly comparable skills.

Table 11.3 (continued)

1979	1980	1981	1982	1983	1984	1985	1986
383,763	518,565	907,040	861,206	864,782	1,320,904	1,423,378	1,262,478
103,060	60,448	137,655	186,988	129,573	152,781	124,484	186,535
—	—	21,500	148,329	128,270	571,800	929,600	722,101
—	13,858	52,000	126,000	73,400	123,974	273,074	378,100

assembly operations are far greater than in a continuous-process industry like steel. To gain firmer control over its process, to ensure more timely delivery of both inputs and outputs, to reduce costs, and to achieve parity with Japanese shipyards on all fronts, HHI decided to develop basic design capability in-house and to produce its own engines and core electrical equipment.

The guiding slogan became "our own ships, our own engines, our own designs." Forward vertical integration to offset demand fluctuations, backward vertical integration to produce key inputs, and the acquisition of basic design capability to meet delivery schedules, all combined to propel HHI's learning. Like the Hyundai Group itself, *the strength of Hyundai Heavy Industries came to rest on its total capabilities.*

The government's role in helping HHI create comparative advantage exemplified government industrial policy in general. The total capabilities on which HHI depended for its competitiveness enabled industrial policy to horse-trade discipline on the one hand and support on the other in the context of the diversified business group. Initially discipline over HHI was largely imposed by the sheer size of operations: HHI had to export to survive and the government licensed other Korean firms to enter shipbuilding as competitors. Support was provided in exchange for risk taking: Shipbuilding may have been relatively unprofitable, but the industrial plant unit of HHI was given a temporary monopoly over steel structures, which required massive yard space to construct and were highly profitable. Support was also provided as the need arose. The government, for example, ordered Korea's crude oil deliveries to be carried by the Hyundai group's newly created merchant marine as a way to strengthen stagnating demand for HHI's ships, once HHI had demonstrated its capability in shipbuilding. Support was also forthcoming in anticipation of comparative advantage: Government patronage of shipbuilding has a long history in Korea that intensified at

HHI's birth, and which continued into the R&D phase of HHI's activities.

It is to the government's extensive support that attention is first turned before examining the emergence of HHI's total capabilities.

GOVERNMENT ASSISTANCE TO SHIPBUILDING

The history of the Korean shipbuilding industry until the time of HHI's founding is one of slow progress characterized by scattered government attempts to accelerate growth. Evidence of the government's early interest in developing a shipbuilding industry is its establishment of a department of naval architecture at Seoul National University (SNU) in 1946, at Pusan National University in 1950, and at Inhas University in 1954. The number of naval architecture graduates from these universities, however, was only a fraction of those from the University of Tokyo. Table 11.5 provides evidence of this and also of the fact that the number of naval architecture graduates who still continued to work in the shipbuilding industry was far higher in the case of the University of Tokyo than of SNU—57% in the former versus 23% in the latter for the period 1950–1977 (although the number at SNU rose to 36% in 1970–1977).

The reasons why so few Korean graduates in naval architecture continued to work in the field before 1970 are the same reasons why government efforts to develop the shipbuilding industry were sporadic. The absence of a local steel industry made shipbuilding a questionable growth pole (although in theory cheap steel was avail-

Table 11.5 Comparison of Number of Graduates from the Department of Naval Architecture (NA), Seoul National University and University of Tokyo, 1940–1977

Graduation Period	Number of Graduates, Seoul National University[a]		Number of Graduates, University of Tokyo[b]	
	Total	Still Working in Shipbuilding	Total	Still Working in Shipbuilding
1940–1949	0	0	556	220
1950–1959	180	11	381	227
1960–1969	153	27	341	234
1970–1977	174	63	316	221
Total	435	101	1,594	902

[a] Private communication.

[b] Directory of Alumni of the Department of Naval Architecture of the University of Tokyo.

Source: Hyundai Heavy Industries.

able from Japan), and the absence of sufficient domestic technological capability hampered attempts to build any other than small-size vessels. Together, these shortcomings rendered shipbuilding a slow-growth industry, which caused both the government and naval architects to look elsewhere for more promising ventures, which reinforced slow growth, and so on.

From 1945 to 1968, the government demonstrated its commitment to shipbuilding (and to the Korean navy) by owning and operating Korea's then largest shipyard, the Korea Shipbuilding and Engineering Corporation (KSEC). KSEC was originally founded by the Mitsubishi group in 1937 as an instrument of the Japanese government's war policy. From the 1950s (when it employed about 500 people) until the time HHI began building ships, KSEC was Korea's largest and technologically most advanced shipbuilder. The government's patronage of KSEC indirectly benefited HHI because HHI recruited a large number of experienced engineers from KSEC. The government patronized shipbuilding in the 1960s by helping yards to convert from building wooden to building steel vessels. (The share of steel vessels in total tonnage increased from 8.2% in 1962 to 92.1% in 1971.)[4] As a way to upgrade shipbuilding quality, the government funded a Korea Shipbuilding Society project to develop a series of standard model ship designs. KSEC, Seoul National University, and Pusan National University collaborated in the project and developed sixty standard designs that were made available to all builders in the country.

When HHI arrived on the scene, the level of technological capability that KSEC had accumulated was still rather low. Two years before HHI's founding, KSEC had built a ship three times larger than the largest ship it had ever built before. Although the ship it built was quite small (a tanker one fourteenth the size of HHI's first tanker) and the duration of KSEC's accumulated experience was quite long (over thirty years), KSEC still had to resort to a foreign license for technical assistance.

The reasons behind HHI's relative success are complicated. The government's supportive role in the establishment of HHI is not altogether known, but its influence is generally recognized as having been decisive. First, analogous to the government's battle with the Bretton Woods institutions to create a large-scale steel mill, the government waged the fight against the international aid agencies to create a large-scale shipyard. Neither project relied on aid, but both depended on international finance, hence the blessing of the IMF and the World Bank, both of which influenced private overseas

---

[4] These data were provided by the Ministry of Commerce and Industry.

lending. Second, the government raised overseas credit for HHI directly and indirectly, the latter by guaranteeing HHI's own foreign loans. Third, the government provided extensive subsidies for infrastructure, much as it had done in the case of POSCO. Fourth, the government provided extensive financial guarantees to help HHI win its first order. Fifth, as will be discussed shortly, the government provided HHI (and other shipbuilders) with continuous support extending beyond start-up, although the visibility of the government's hand diminished (as had been true of POSCO) with the arrival of foreign technical assistance and with the initiation of production.

FOREIGN TECHNICAL ASSISTANCE

While KSEC existed for some thirty years with virtually no foreign technical assistance, HHI was nursed on it. HHI's foreign technical assistance came in four forms: dockyard designs from a Scottish naval architecture firm, A&P Appledore; ship designs and operating instructions from a Scottish shipbuilding firm, Scotlithgow; experienced European shipbuilders who worked as employees of HHI for the first three years of operations; and production know-how from the Kawasaki Shipbuilding Company of Japan.

The A&P Appledore technology transfer began in 1972 and involved the dispatch of over seventy engineers from HHI to Scotland for instruction in how to lay out a yard. What was to become HHI, the Department of Shipbuilding in the Hyundai Construction Company, coordinated the technology transfer. Dispatchees to Scotland were mostly new recruits, naval architects recruited from the construction and machinery building sectors. A&P Appledore designed the layout of the yard and provided drawings, and the Hyundai Construction Company supervised civil engineering and the actual physical labor involved.

HHI won its first order for two 260,000 DWT VLCCs from a Greek shipowner, George Livanos, on the condition that it build an *exact replica* of a ship that had been built in Scotlithgow's shipyard. Scotlithgow provided HHI with detailed drawings because HHI was required by Livanos to procure the identical equipment from the same sources as had the Scottish firm and to mimic every detail of design. For example, HHI bought over thirty cranes from the same suppliers in Europe that Scotlithgow had patronized. Angle bars were bought in England, steel was sourced from Japan, and Scotlithgow reviewed each size and thickness of plate to be used.

Fabrication and welding began when steel plate arrived at HHI in April 1973, with only one of seven drydocks completed. At this point, HHI employed five experienced European shipbuilders, for periods ranging from two to three years—one for personnel training, one for production planning, one for hull construction and production, one for machinery and electrical installation, and an experienced Danish shipbuilder was even appointed HHI president.

HHI learned general work procedures from the Kawasaki Shipbuilding Company of Japan. In fact, as a consequence of its full order backlog in 1974, Kawasaki subcontracted HHI to build two tankers and provided the company with the ships' proven designs. The Japanese shipbuilders trained HHI engineers and technicians both on-site and in Japan: A total of 200 people were sent to Japan for training, 40 a month, and Japanese foremen were stationed at HHI to help. As a consequence of working on-site with Japanese shipbuilders, HHI learned how to read blueprints, coordinate drawings to the job, and install machinery.

The Kawasaki ships were both to be 232,000 DWT tankers, very similar in design to the VLCC HHI had constructed for Livanos. HHI's first twelve ships, therefore, were also VLCCs, of two or three different types that were among the easiest to build. Next, HHI was fortunate, in a depressed market, to receive orders for a series of twenty-four multipurpose cargo vessels from different sources, all of the same basic design. Once again, the design had originated in a Scottish shipyard, Govan, which was going out of business during the time that HHI was collecting famous designs for different types of ships. When the Hyundai group's representative in London read in a British newspaper that Govan was going bankrupt, he contacted the company and bought its designs at a bargain price. Soon afterward, HHI received an order for four container vessels, and then for nine more containers. The virtue of receiving multiple orders for the same type of standardized ships was twofold: (1) It enabled HHI to take advantage of scale and to build in series, which promoted significant cost economies (Harvard Business School, 1986b). (2) It greatly facilitated learning-by-doing.

In time, foreign technical assistance and learning-by-doing advanced HHI's shipbuilding know-how. Nevertheless, when the Kawasaki order was complete and the experienced European shipbuilders employed by HHI departed, HHI could not be said to have been in control of its process. This was evidenced by repeated delays in deliveries. Early learning was slower at HHI than at a company like the Pohang Iron and Steel Company because of the differences between steel-making and shipbuilding technology. In steel-making, the process is highly embodied in capital equipment. In shipbuilding, the process is highly embodied in people. Consequently, no matter how great foreign technical assistance, when assistance reached its limit, the nontrivial matter remained of mastering an uncodified technology in-house.

THE ACQUISITION OF DESIGN CAPABILITY

Despite the fact that HHI built its first ship with the tested designs and proven capital equipment of an experienced European ship-builder, replication was not 100% successful. Scotlithgow only had enough capacity to build half a ship at a time. Consequently, it built VLCCs in two parts, and HHI had to do likewise. But when HHI put the two halves together, *they didn't fit.* This prompted the establishment of a design office employing 300 people, in order to modify the mistakes that delayed deliveries. Nevertheless, problems in hull construction delayed the launching of HHI's first ship from October 1973 to February 1974. Then problems in machinery installation (outfitting) delayed delivery until October. This was in spite of the fact that everyone was working overtime, the length of the working day running in some instances from 6 a.m. one day to 3 a.m. the following day. Learning-by-doing notwithstanding, Livanos' second ship was also delayed. The contract deadline was passed at the time of the project launch, and by the time of completion, the market for ships having collapsed, Livanos refused delivery. Up to the contracted time of delivery, the total exposure of ship buyers is only about 15% of the ship's price. In bad markets, therefore, it is not unheard of for ship buyers to refuse delivery—either by holding builders to contract in the event of delayed deliveries or by delaying delivery by finding minor defects. Delivery was refused again when HHI was late in delivering two VLCCs to the Japan line, and refused a third time when it was late in delivering two others to Hong Kong Inc.

It was at this juncture that the Hyundai group vertically integrated forward and founded the Hyundai Merchant Marine Company. HMMC had two purposes: first and foremost, to provide shipping services to Hyundai's newly founded general trading company; second, to absorb HHI's undelivered vessels. On August 31, 1976, all of HHI's undelivered vessels were sold to HMMC. HHI's strategy of forward integration had been largely underwritten by the government. As owner of Korea's oil refinery, the government dictated that all crude oil deliveries to Korea be carried in Korean-owned vessels, namely those of HMMC.

There were no additional instances of undelivered vessels after the five just mentioned, but there were still repeated delays. As the market worsened, HHI's marketing people traveled the world over looking for orders. By chance, they won the two contracts mentioned earlier for a total of twenty-four multipurpose cargo vessels of the same design. However, these ships posed two design problems. First, they were small (23,000 DWT), whereas HHI's yard and experience were geared for larger vessels. Second, although the basic design of the two vessels was the same, the two ship buyers involved wanted distinctive modifications. The first problem led to the purchase of basic designs for smaller vessels from Govan. The second problem led to more in-house design activity both to achieve desired modifications and to control costs. Design modification became necessary for cost control because a change in the machinery (including engine) for the purpose of sourcing less expensive parts meant a change in the design encasing that machinery.

Little by little, HHI acquired capability in design modifications, but it still lacked capability in basic design—making lines, estimating volume and weight, calculating DWT displacement and speed of engine, and so on. Consequently, it started out buying basic designs from European consulting firms. HHI managers discovered, though, that consulting firms took no responsibility for reaching rated capacity, and if rated capacity were not reached, delivery was delayed, each day in arrears incurring a heavy penalty. To avoid such delays, HHI decided to invest in a basic design capability, even though most shipyards do not possess such a set of skills. In 1978 HHI increased the size of its design department from 300 to 500 people, a fairly heavy overhead. By 1983 the number of designers totaled 900, and HHI had dispensed with buying designs from outside except for special-purpose vessels. Three years later, HHI calculated that it would cost $200,000 to buy basic designs outside whereas it cost $300,000 to make them in-house, but in the long run, in-house capability was expected to be cheaper.

HYUNDAI ENGINE AND HEAVY MACHINERY MANUFACTURING COMPANY, LTD.

HHI took the strategic decision to invest in an engine shop at the same time that it invested in a basic design capability. The company had been sourcing its engines from Japan, which built marine engines under license from a handful of longstanding European firms. But, according to D. S. Cho and Porter (1986), Japanese engine manufacturers charged higher prices to foreign shipbuilders than to Japanese ones. Consequently, to provide HHI with an alternative to high-priced Japanese engines, the Hyundai Engine and Heavy Machinery Manufacturing Company (HEMCO) was founded in 1978. HHI had decided to take a big risk and invest in an engine shop in order to compete, in the long run, against integrated shipbuilders. In the short run, such an investment was deemed necessary to ensure more reliable delivery of engines and to save costs. At the time, however, depressed demand made it certain that no ship buyer would purchase a ship with an untried engine. HHI, therefore, decided to make a ship of its own design, with its own engine, for its own sister firm, Hyundai Merchant Marine.

Building a marine engine is a microcosm of building a ship, and the broad outlines of HEMCO's learning process were similar to those observed at HHI: infusions of foreign technical assistance, the dispatch of large numbers of trainees overseas, sequential import-substitution of parts and components (vertical integration), attempts to develop a local subcontracting network (a marine engine has approximately 20,000 parts), and diversification. Emerging on the scene in 1978, just in time for the second energy crisis, and supplying a derived demand, HEMCO learned in an environment even more ravaged by depression than that faced by HHI five years earlier. In 1986 HEMCO had capacity to build 120 to 150 sets of diesel engines a year. It had, however, only 50 sets on order, so even though engines had originally been intended to comprise 80% of total capacity, it diversified and used half of its capacity to build other machines.

HEMCO's development was different from that of HHI, however. Whereas eight years after its founding HHI was easily as price competitive as Japanese shipyards, eight years after its founding HEMCO's engines were still overpriced relative to those of Japan. This stemmed largely from the fact that HEMCO continued to import key components from Japan: its fuel injection pump, turbo chargers, and electronic control equipment, all of which amounted to about 25% to 30% of the value of an engine. In addition, HEMCO surpassed HHI, from the outset of operations, in paying close attention to production and quality standards. This was an imperative imposed on it by its mode of technology transfer. HEMCO built brand name engines under rigorous supervision from its licensers, B&W of Denmark and MAN, Sulzer, and SEMT Pielstick of West Germany (the same licensers used by Japanese engine manufacturers). HEMCO followed detailed instructions in drawings and built strictly in accordance with standards. By contrast, HHI's relations with its foreign licensers were more distant, and it had to tailor its own standards and quality controls. We turn now to a discussion of this process and of its development at HHI.

INTERMARGINAL CHANGES

Quality

According to J. B. Park, the first person to hold the position of manager of HHI's Department of Quality Control (QC), HHI's priority at the outset of operations was to keep to schedule and to build ships that could float:

Quality was of secondary importance. I didn't recognize at first what quality was. I thought it was only delivering a ship that satisfied a client, not building a ship that conformed to predetermined specifications. But, I tried to keep an open mind. I failed at first, and quality defects were pointed out by the coast guard, by classification societies, and by QC representatives of the ship owner. So my policy became one of not repeating the same mistake.

In accordance with my policy, I tried to develop feedback between production departments and QC. At first workers didn't work very hard. But soon people became very busy. Every morning production people would speak on the microphone to workers about the Saemaul movement,[5] urging them to work harder. The general manager of the yard thought that quality was a waste of time, so I worked with section chiefs (assistant managers). I noticed variations in quality across different production sections, so I called a joint meeting in order to compare performance. Then I called two more meetings in which I presented a monthly evaluation of quality differences. At the fourth meeting, I made section chiefs undertake their own monthly evaluations and then compete against each other.

When I visited Seoul in 1975, I heard about quality control circles (QCCs) and was surprised to learn that the kind of activity that I had started at HHI was also going on outside. Although QCCs operated in Hyundai Motors, located in the same town as HHI, I didn't investigate quality control at this sister firm. Because ships were custom-built while cars were a market product, I believed that quality meant something different in the two cases. I learned about QCCs from the Korean Standards Association. Then I incorporated outside theory into HHI practice.

In 1973 the QC Department began to establish quality standards and procedures. Park consulted the standards and procedures of ship classification societies and of Japanese and European shipyards, but workers and managers at HHI found it difficult to meet strange regulations. One problem was that workers were inexperienced and afraid. When cutting plate, they wanted to leave extra material. Another problem was that experienced foremen who were recruited from smaller shipyards had their own standards and procedures. To achieve uniformity, a small training center was established early in HHI's history and foremen were sent there for one to three months.

---

[5] The *Saemaul* movement was begun by President Park Chung Hee to build commitment to economic development among the Korean people. It consists of an ideology and community-level investment projects.

The training center received feedback from inspection stations, and inspection stations fed information to the line.

In 1978–1979 HHI launched an intensive campaign to improve quality. The QC Department revised all its standards and issued a new worker quality manual. Every production department had to conform to the same standards and was linked to procurement. Statistical quality control (SQC) was introduced in the hull production department for the purpose of learning where and by whom errors were committed. The big campaign included reeducation and retraining. HHI's Training Center was expanded, and qualifications were set for welders, fitters, pipers, and painters. Certificates of qualification were canceled if poor workmanship was discovered. Technical assistance was extended to 100 of HHI's subcontractors, and incoming inspection standards were raised.

HHI began to tabulate data for a yardwide quality measure: the ratio of total acceptances by foreign inspectors to total work applications (requests for work approval) to foreign inspectors. The higher the ratio, the higher the quality conformance (see Figure 11.1). Quality measures show considerable improvement after 1978. The slowdown in the rate of improvement in 1982–1983 is attributed to what the QC Department called "quality dumping." Analogous to competition in the steel industry after the second energy crisis, quality dumping referred to competition from Japanese shipyards, which raised quality standards while holding prices constant. By 1983, HHI had succeeded in winning three quality assurance certificates: from Lloyds, Det Norske Veritas, and the American Bureau of Ships. These certificates testified that HHI's quality standards met international specifications.

Time and Motion Studies and Cost Control

The 1978–1979 campaign to ratchet up quality was part of a larger initiative at HHI to raise productivity and reduce unit costs. The initiative was taken in response to heightened competition, both foreign and local. Further deterioration in world demand for ships had sparked foreign competition (see Table 11.2), and HHI was threatened domestically by the specter of new Korean entrants into the shipbuilding sector. HHI's opportunity to reduce unit costs through better control of flows of information and materials was provided by the internalization of both the basic design function and the manufacture of engines. With its own designs and engines, HHI could tighten its production system.

Greater control over costs was approached from two directions: the systematization of material flows and time studies of individual

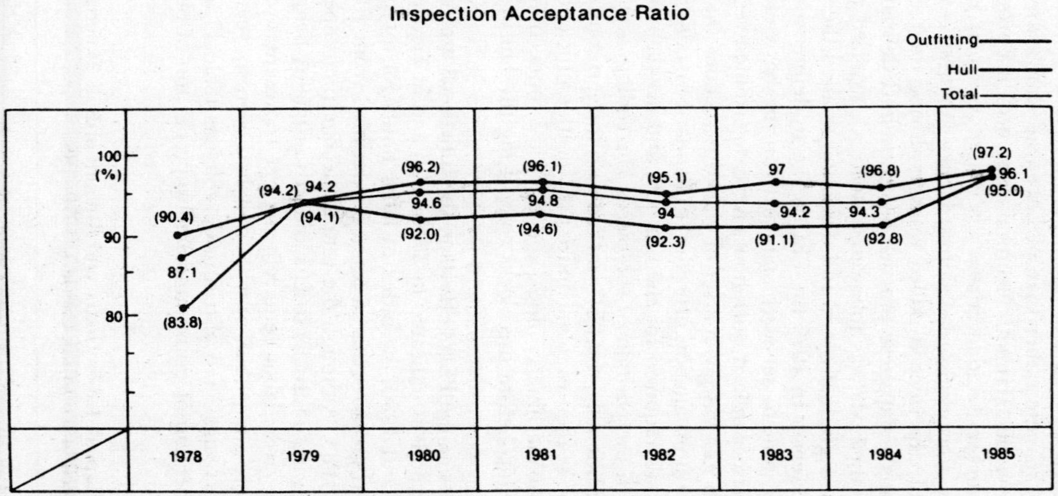

Inspection Acceptance Ratio

Figure 11.1 Inspection Acceptance Ratio (Quality Measure Used by Hyundai Heavy Industries). Outfitting is upper line. Hull is lower line. *Source:* Hyundai Heavy Industries.

jobs along with job sequencing. Both functional areas were sub-sumed under the Production Engineering Department (PED), which from the outset of operations had modeled work organization along the lines of Japanese rather than of European shipyards. Although both had provided HHI with technical assistance, in European prac-tice skilled workers wielded greater discretion over their job content and methods. Because Korean shipyards, like Japanese before them, were short of experienced skilled workers during their early years of operation, the Japanese practice of centralized definition of job content and methods was followed instead. Centralized job defini-tion happened gradually, and full definition awaited the accumula-tion of experience. In 1979 the PED began to define work content and methods and to set work standards on the basis of time and motion studies. Standard work hours were determined vessel by ves-sel, and each job was given a set of work instructions that included information on installation procedures (standard or nonstandard), a list of materials required for the unit job, and installation drawings complete with the position of the pieces, the coding, and the speci-fications. Additionally, the PED worked with foreign consultants and redefined job sequences to maximize preoutfitting efficiency (i.e., the installation of machinery, pipes, and electrical connections into the hull of the ship before the blocks comprising the hull were assem-bled).

The success of the PED's efforts in the functional area of job con-tent and methods is indicated in Table 11.6 and in Figure 11.2. Be-tween 1980 and 1986, the index of labor hours for a typical vessel (compensated gross registered tonnage) declined from 100 to as lit-tle as 66 in 1983. Although the rate of decline then tapered off in 1983–1985, with unusually strict standards of quality being imposed by Japanese yards, labor requirements per representative vessel by mid-1986 were almost half of what they had been six years earlier.

Materials savings were also considerable. As table 11.6 suggests, steel input per ton of output and steel pipe per ton of output each

Table 11.6 Capital, Labor Hours, and Amount of Bulk Material for 60,000 Deadweight Ton Bulk Carriers, 1979–1986

Year	Labor Hours	Capital (Machinery)	Bulk Material	
			Steel	Pipes
1979	1,000,000	(increase)	12,000/ton	330/ton
1986	550,000		9,100/ton	250/ton

Source: Hyundai Heavy Industries.

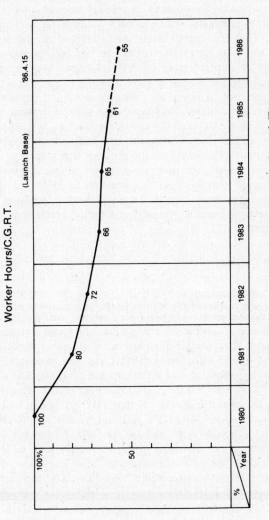

Figure 11.2 Labor Hours per Compensated Gross Registered Tonnage, 1980–1986. *Source:* Hyundai Heavy Industries.

decreased by a quarter of their original levels. When HHI first started building ships, it had no cost-accounting system. It had a very primitive numbering system to code materials and very poor interdepartmental information flow. Delays in delivery were blamed on the hull production department, which in turn blamed the steel-cutting department. The steel-cutting department blamed delays on steel deliveries at the same time that steel inventories were overflowing. With the decline in ship prices in 1978, HHI began work on a "system development system"—a set of rules to budget and control materials. The company relied solely on common sense at first; later it consulted other shipbuilders and computer systems specialists. It also increased its own computer services department to 300 people. Those people vetoed the idea of introducing a fully computerized on-line system for materials control on the grounds that control of materials touches on all production and cost-control systems. The systems specialists believed that because the situation at HHI was constantly changing—organization was shifting and work procedures were altering—material control required constantly evolving rules to remain flexible.

ORGANIZATION

Chaebol Membership

HHI's formative years were filled with intense activity aimed at both mastery of the art and science of shipbuilding and a strategy of integrating and diversifying to offset heavy financial losses from the nose dive in world ship demand. HHI was able to advance on both fronts simultaneously through the support it received as a member of one of Korea's largest diversified business groups. Organizational structure, in several respects, abetted HHI's strategy of becoming internationally competitive as a fully integrated shipbuilding company. First, although HHI had no specialized experience in shipbuilding proper, the Hyundai group had experience in technically related fields—especially construction—and engineers were dispatched to HHI to transfer their know-how. The top-ranking Korean manager of HHI was formerly a high-level manager of the Hyundai Construction Company (HC), and when HHI ran into problems keeping to schedule, engineers from HC were mobilized. In addition, Hyundai Construction provided HHI with many of its front-line supervisors, managed the construction of the Mipo dockyard, and helped supervise feasibility studies. Hyundai Motors dispatched engineers to help in the struggle to reduce throughput time and also provided technical assistance in assembly line and training techniques. Hyundai Cement sent people to work in production control. All in all, as HHI managers pointed out, "a lot of people joined." *The possibility of mobilizing such personnel enabled HHI to act quickly and to avoid the delays of recruiting fresh talent in the market.*

Second, group affiliation enabled HHI to recruit the best people outside the Hyundai enclave. The Korea Shipbuilding and Engineering Company claims to have lost one third of its most experienced people when HHI came on stream. HHI could afford to pay higher salaries and to offer better opportunities for promotion than could KSEC or most other shipyards. Turnover was even greater in Korea's seven medium-size shipyards than it was at KSEC. In 1979 only 4% of employees in these yards had been with the same company for longer than four years, and 55% had a tenure of under one year (Korean Shipbuilding Association, 1980).

Third, HHI's group affiliation made possible the simultaneous accomplishment of intermarginal and inframarginal tasks—of fine-tuning operations and improving quality while constantly expanding in large chunks through integration and diversification. The inframarginal tasks were undertaken at the group level by people from group subsidiaries with experience in executing new investment projects. The intermarginal tasks of learning to produce, and then learning to produce better, were undertaken at the level of the operating unit by people with industry-specific know-how.

Fourth, group membership allowed HHI to take a long-run approach to profit maximization. The fall in demand for HHI's ships was offset by the rise in demand for the Hyundai groups' automobiles and electronics. The financial backing of a large diversified business group allowed HHI to adopt a long-run approach to learning, in the form of acquiring a capability to design and to undertake R&D. In the case of R&D, HHI's welding research activities began in 1978 and then were integrated and substantially expanded during the following five years until a Welding Research Institute was opened in November 1983. According to an international shipbuilding trade journal,

The main purpose of the Institute is to research, develop and manage new welding technologies, monitor quality control, provide information to welders in the shipbuilding and offshore sections of the complex and find solutions to welding problems. Welding research activities are oriented toward high productivity levels, which reduce manhours and costs while maintaining quality standards. The Institute's researchers are endeavoring to increase the proportion of automatic welding with special emphasis on the future possibility of using robotic systems. (*Shipping World and Shipbuilder,* 1985, p. 561)

In October 1984, HHI inaugurated the Maritime Research Institute, "one of the most well-equipped institutes of its kind in the Far East. . . . The research staff of approximately 100 are gaining experience in naval architectural matters as the yard continues to be involved in virtually every ship design" (*Shipping World and Shipbuilder,* 1985, pp. 561, 565).[6]

Production Organization

Like the management of Korea's modern industrial enterprises in general, the management of HHI was "lean." As Table 11.7 points out, in the fifth year after HHI's founding, the share of engineers and technicians in total employment was only 10.8%, compared with 19.8% in Japanese shipyards. Administration in HHI accounted for 7.6% of total employees compared with 14.2% in shipyards in Japan. As in the case of the Pohang Iron and Steel Company, HHI's project management system decentralized control to compensate for a sparseness of experienced staff. *Primary responsibility for ship completions was taken by line managers.*

An effective project management system was key to HHI's success because the dockyard grew to vast proportions, necessitating inventive controls over information flows. Employing 25,000 workers (roughly 14,000 in shipbuilding), HHI's dockyard was 1,400,000 me-

Table 11.7 Comparison of Distribution of Employment in Shipbuilding, Korea and Japan, 1978

	Engineers, Technicians (%)	Administrators (%)	Direct Labor (%)	Total No.
Hyundai Heavy Industries (Korea)	10.8	7.6	81.6	21,586
Total Korea[a]	11.2	9.4	79.4	34,702
Total Japan	19.8	14.2	66.0	164,006

[a]Excludes all small shipyards. In 1978, neither Daewoo's nor Samsung's shipbuilding facilities had come on-stream.

Source: Korea Shipbuilding Association (1980).

[6] The progenitor of HHI's Maritime Research Institute was established earlier, in the mid-1970s, with an initial staff of only 10 engineers.

ters in area and comprised seven drydocks, four graving docks for ship repair, three quays, four goliath cranes, and facilities to build not merely merchant ships but also naval vessels, industrial machinery and equipment, industrial plants, onshore and offshore steel structures, and steel towers. Shipbuilding itself required complex coordination because of the large number of materials and tasks that had to be timed and sequenced. Complicating such coordination was the fact that HHI built ships in series.

Given its membership in a business group that originated as a construction firm, HHI adopted a project management system typical of construction sites, whereby construction managers move from project to project, taking full responsibility for overseeing the project on which they are working at the moment.[7] This new project management system took effect at HHI during a period when many of the problems this system is designed to address began to surface. Although late deliveries had ceased to be a problem by 1983, the economic downturn elevated the importance of good client relations. Good client relations were "by far the most important objective" HHI wanted to achieve, and its managers believed that its new management system would help them achieve it by improving the flow of information from builder to buyer. In addition, as HHI developed basic design capability and began to build more sophisticated and specialized vessels, the buyers to whom it catered became more discriminating, and quality control became more demanding. The merit of the new system was that it allowed quality standards to be tailored to the requirements of specific ships.

Apart from liaisoning with owners and customizing quality standards, the project manager was responsible for troubleshooting, for expediting and reviewing the production planning department's master schedule, for reviewing problem production procedures and getting assistance from the most qualified designers/engineers, for proposing minor budget revisions, and for following up a project with documentation.

[7] K. S. Choi, vice president, Shipbuilding Division, was responsible for devising HHI's new project management system (PMS). According to Choi, it is difficult to specify precisely the degree to which Japanese practice influenced HHI, with respect to either HHI's old system or its new one. In some Japanese shipyards, a project coordinator may be responsible for all seven phases of shipbuilding. But unlike the practice in most Japanese yards, whose project coordinators are highly experienced, HHI's project coordinators have the backing of their own technical group, whose size varies depending on the complexity of the ship being built. Once HHI decided on its new PMS, Choi was influenced by a manual on project control prepared in 1983 by a Norwegian, Sven R. Hed.

SUMMARY: SURVIVAL OF THE FITTEST

In the discussion just completed, HHI's success and survival in the shipbuilding industry was attributed to its diversified structure. Therefore, if something like the law of survival of the fittest operates, other successful shipbuilders in Korea ought to have a strategy and structure similar to (or, in the same terms, better than) HHI's. In fact, they do: Two other major shipbuilders are members of Korea's two largest chaebol, the Samsung and Daewoo groups. However, the fourth and oldest shipbuilder, the Korea Shipbuilding and Engineering Company, deserves further mention because although it is a chaebol member, it declared bankruptcy in the spring of 1987.[8]

Three points about KSEC's behavior are pertinent. First, the government sold KSEC in 1968 to a shipping magnate who owned one of the largest commercial shipping fleets in Korea. Thus, from the start of its expansion under private ownership, KSEC, like HHI, protected itself from demand vagaries by being vertically integrated forward. Second, KSEC had an extensive backward vertically integrated network, supplying it with certain key components and parts. Third, KSEC diversified: It not only built ships but also repaired them and built machinery and rolling stock as well. In 1983 the ratio of nonshipbuilding exports to total exports was 33% for HHI, 26% for Daewoo's shipbuilding affiliate, and over 45% for KSEC (*Han-'guk Kyŏngje Sinmun*, June 1984). By 1984 KSEC had become Korea's thirty-eighth largest diversified business group, with thirteen subsidiaries (including one of Korea's seven medium-size shipyards) (S. K. Kim, 1987).

Nevertheless, one may infer from KSEC's financial failure that the group of which it was a part was not large enough or diversified enough into unrelated products, or aggressive enough in marketing ships. It represents a case in the annals of the creation of competitive advantage in which long industry-specific experience and know-how did not compensate for the staying power that derives from membership in a financially and managerially cohesive huge group.

Such membership, however, may be an insufficient condition for survival. In 1989 Daewoo Shipbuilding was suffering from depressed demand and labor strife, with no relief in sight from the Daewoo group, whose automobile, consumer electronics, and computer divisions were also ailing. Whether politics or economics will guide the government's response to Daewoo remains to be seen.

---

[8] The government will not allow KSEC to go bankrupt, but may revive it under new management (*Han'guk Kyŏngje Sinmun*, Apr. 1987).

CHAPTER TWELVE

The Triumph of Steel

AN UNPROPITIOUS START

The technical skills and economic resources necessary to produce steel efficiently were absent in Korea when the government decided to promote an integrated iron- and steel-making facility. With the experience of India and Turkey in mind, a World Bank study team in the 1960s "expressed the view that an integrated steel mill in Korea was a premature proposition without economic feasibility" (Pohang Iron and Steel Co. Ltd., 1984, p. 23). A study of the trade regime in effect in Korea in 1968 concluded that most of the steel being made was "prominent among the inefficiently produced import-competing products . . ." (Westphal and Kim, 1982). Thus, Korea faced several challenges in entering the steel business (in addition to those associated with World Bank hostility): Integrated iron- and steel-making is highly capital intensive, but Korea lacked capital. Costs are sensitive to scale, but Korea's domestic market was small and the largest nearby market, Japan, lodged the world's most efficient steel producer. Korea lacked iron ore resources and was located far from the main sources of supply. Finally, Korea lacked steel-making skills. As is typical of many mature industries, the steel-making process is embodied in the equipment. The process technology is well diffused (except for very high quality specialty steels) and can easily be imported at arm's length from machinery suppliers and from technical consultants. Nonetheless, the nature of the process necessitates complex engineering. For example, of a sample of nineteen industries in the United States in 1970, iron and steel ranked tenth in engineering intensity (measured by number of engineers in total employment) (Zymelman, 1980).

In spite of all these obstacles, the Pohang Iron and Steel Company, Ltd., familiarly referred to as POSCO, became one of the lowest-cost steel-makers in the world. An ironic indicator of the speed of its progress was a joint venture it entered into with United States Steel (USX) in 1986 for the purpose of modernizing USX's Pittsburg, California, plant. At that time POSCO was supplying half of the capital requirements, or $180 million, for the modernization—providing the PittCal cold-rolled sheet facility with hot-bend coil, undertaking basic design of the facility's modernization jointly with USX, and training American managers and workers in operations and maintenance. Thus, less than twenty years after its founding, POSCO was exporting technology.

The dynamics of comparative advantage suggested by Korean steel-making, therefore, are those of overcoming obstacles to create advantage, of rejecting the current endowment of resources as arbiter of how income is to be earned in the future. Creating competitiveness in late industrialization amounts to taking the risk of deciding what skills, on the part of individuals, and what technological capabilities, on the part of firms, are both possible and profitable to learn. Then competitiveness depends on investing heavily in learning.

The risk of pressing ahead with an integrated iron and steel mill—at $3.6 billion, Korea's largest single investment to date—was assumed entirely by the state. POSCO has been a state-owned enterprise, although privatization is probably on the agenda. Not only the first integrated iron and steel complex in Korea, but also the second, is under POSCO's management, challenging the now fashionable view that state enterprise is invariably inefficient. POSCO represents a microcosm of Korean public policy in two respects: It is both supporter and disciplinarian of the private companies that patronize it. It is a supporter insofar as it provides high-quality steel at low prices. It is a disciplinarian insofar as it serves as a standard of an excellently managed enterprise. That POSCO itself is excellently managed may reflect the industrial environment in which it operates: most of the bigger businesses in Korea are also well managed, at least in the production and operations management sense. There may be a general tendency for public enterprises to mirror the management standards of the private sector at large.

Generally, creating competitive advantage through learning rather than innovation is less risky because the learner has both a model and a teacher to guide it. In POSCO's case, its model and its teacher was the Nippon Steel Company of Japan (which also commenced life as a state-owned enterprise). Yet creating advantage through learning is tenuous in one respect: The learner faces more competition than the innovator. The innovator protects its competitive position with a new product or low-cost process. The learner has nothing to protect it but lower wages, and these become increasingly insignificant as a competitive weapon the more skill and capital intensive the sector. The creation of competitiveness in steel was a watershed in Korean industrial history because it represented a major sector in which competitiveness depended on higher productivity (not lower wages) in a struggle against experienced producers from more (not less) advanced countries. In POSCO's case, its model and teacher was also its major competitor, the formidable Japanese steel-producing giants.

The fight to raise productivity in the Korean steel industry is the subject of this chapter.

POSCO'S FOUNDING

The government created the Pohang Iron and Steel Company, Ltd., in 1968; five years later POSCO began production in the southwest city of Pohang with an annual capacity of 1.03 million metric tons. After several expansions (in a total of four phases, with the last phase divided into two stages), the mill reached an annual capacity of 9.1 million metric tons of crude steel in 1983 (see Table 12.1). Because steel is liberally consumed by industries such as shipbuilding, automobiles, and construction, the founding of POSCO signaled Korea's turn to heavy industry.

The history of the Korean steel industry dates back to 1941 when Japan established two steel mills in southern Korea as a way to support its war efforts in China and Manchuria. These mills were severely damaged during the Korean War (1950–1953), so that until the late 1960s the industry comprised roughly 109 facilities—predominantly rolling mills, several steel-making minimills, and a few iron-making installations. Most of these firms suffered from obsolete plants and equipment. According to a 1967 study prepared for the prime minister by the Office of Planning and Coordination, of a total of thirty-seven steel-making furnaces (mostly electric), thirty-one were outmoded (dating to the 1940s), six were modern (dating to the 1950s), and none was contemporary (dating to the 1960s) (Korea Advanced Institute of Science, 1976). Furthermore, even though there were three small blast furnaces in existence (60 cubic meters in size compared with 1,660 cubic meters in POSCO's first phase), due to accidents and mismanagement none was operating. Quality was poor, and there was a market imbalance between the steel shapes that were being supplied and those that were being demanded.

Therefore, when the government set about founding an integrated iron and steel works, it chose not to build on any existing structure (although many experienced steel workers were later recruited by POSCO). Instead, the government founded POSCO as a wholly new entity. The government's failure to assign steel-making to one of the emerging chaebol remains a mystery. Some say it was because no chaebol was willing at the time to undertake the risk involved (although later the top business groups lobbied hard for the rights to POSCO's second integrated facility at Kwangyang in 1986).

Table 12.1 Capacity Additions and Plant Specifications of POSCO, 1970–1988

Items		Phases at Pohang					Phases at Kwangyang	
		I	II	III	IV-1	IV-2	I	II
Periods of construction		Apr. 1970–Jul. 1973	Dec. 1973–May 1976	Aug. 1976–Dec. 1978	Feb. 1979–Feb. 1981	Sep. 1981–May 1983	Mar. 1985–Jun. 1987	Nov. 1986–Dec. 1988
Capacity (1,000 ton/year)		1,030	2,600	5,500	8,500	9,100	2,700	5,400
Sinter plant	Spec.	DL type 130m	DL type 204m	DL type 400m	DL type 400m	—	DL type 400m	DL type 400m
	Cap.	1,322,000 T/Y	2,197,000 T/Y	4,292,000 T/Y	4,292,000 T/Y	—	4,426,000 T/Y	4,426,000 T/Y
Coke oven	Spec.	68 ovens	106 ovens	146 ovens	150 ovens	75 ovens	132 ovens	132 ovens
	Cap.	584,000 T/Y	912,000 T/Y	1,552,000 T/Y	1,552,000 T/Y	733,000 T/Y	1,430,000 T/Y	1,430,000 T/Y
Blast furnace	Spec.	1,660m	2,550m	3,795m	3,795m	II Relining)	3,800m	3,800m
	Cap.	1,011,000 T/Y	1,697,000 T/Y	2,752,000 T/Y	2,752,000 T/Y		2,840,000 T/Y	2,840,000 T/Y
Steel-making	Spec.	100 tons/heat x 2	100 tons/heat x 1	300 tons/heat x 2	300 tons/heat x 1	—	250 tons/heat x 2	250 tons/heat x 1
	Cap.	1,032,000 T/Y	(2,000,000 T/Y[a])	3,300,000 T/Y	(6,500,000 T/Y)	—	2,784,000 T/Y	(5,568,000 T/Y)
Continuous casting	Spec.	—	4 strand x 1 machine	—	2 strand x 2 machine	—	2 strand x 2 machine	2 strand x 1 machine
	Cap.	—	1,026,000 T/Y	—	(3,844,000 T/Y)	—	2,700,000 T/Y	(5,400,000 T/Y)
Hot-strip mill	Spec.	RF 150 ton/hour x 1	RF 150 ton/hour x 1	RF 150 ton/hour x 1	RF 250 ton/hour x 3	RF 300 ton/hour	RF 300 ton/hour x 2	RF 300 ton/hour x 1
	Cap.	606,500 T/Y	(775,500 T/Y)	(1,410,000 T/Y)	3,311,000 T/Y	—	2,660,000 T/Y	(4,433,000 T/Y)
Cold-strip mill	Spec.	—	TCM, CGL	—	TCM, CAL	—	—	—
	Cap.	—	711,00 T/Y	—	1,000,000 T/Y	—	—	—
Plate mill	Spec.	RF 100 ton/hour x 1	—	RF 235 ton/hour x 1	—	—	—	—
	Cap.	336,000 T/Y	—	1,243,000 T/Y	—	—	—	—
Wire rod mill	Spec.	—	—	2 strand	—	1 strand	—	—
	Cap.	—	—	446,000 T/Y	—	350,000 T/Y	—	—

Spec., specification; Cap., capacity.

[a] ( ) = capacity after expansion.

Source: POSCO.

Others say it was because the government did not want to give a monopoly to any one chaebol over an input that impinged on both the country's security and the competitiveness of major downstream industries. Nor did the government recruit the leadership of POSCO from the major import-substitution projects in chemicals that were begun in the 1960s, projects that took the form of joint ventures between the government and foreign partners. Instead, the government appointed as POSCO's president a competent retired army general and friend of President Park Chung Hee, Tae Joon Park, a man with a track record of having turned around the government-owned Korea Tungsten Corporation.[1]

The government first tried to finance entry into steel-making in 1961, then again in 1962 (with a group of German steel-makers), and still again in 1967 (with an international consortium that included the World Bank). All efforts collapsed in disagreement over scale—the Korean government driving for a multiple of the capacity that its foreign collaborators were willing to entertain. All efforts had the virtue, however, of providing the Korean participants with an understanding of the economics and geopolitics of steel-making (Korea Advanced Institute of Science, 1976). Finally, finance was forthcoming in the form of reparations from the Japanese government for "36 years of hardship under Japanese rule" (Pohang Iron and Steel Co. Ltd., 1984, p. 18). The engineering consultant to POSCO was designated the "Japan Group" and consisted mainly of Nippon Steel and, to a minor extent, Nippon Kokkan Steel.

Two points about the technical assistance that the Japan Group provided are noteworthy. First, according to POSCO, the Japan Group, in the name of friendship and economic development, was very enthusiastic about providing assistance at the time. Second, while steel mills in other developing countries had suffered from second-rate technology at the hands of the only source of finance available to them,[2] POSCO was fortunate to raise capital in a country that boasted the most efficient steel-making process. Concerning scale, POSCO's President Park "persuaded the Japanese that a larger four-stage plant was necessary with a capacity of 9.1 million tonnes—not

---

[1] Much has been made of POSCO's militarylike qualities—its strong leadership, the discipline and regimentation of its workers, and so on. Nonetheless, although Korea's military may be assumed to keep a sharp eye on the country's only integrated iron-and steel-making capacity, POSCO has no stronger leadership or greater worker regimentation than some of the chaebol. Moreover, the internal organization of POSCO is not drawn along administrative lines that are generally associated with the military (see Mintzburg, 1979). Rather, POSCO's organization is said to reflect that of its mentor, the Nippon Steel Company of Japan.

[2] See, for example, Lall (1987) on Indian steel.

the 2.6 million tonne figure that was the basis of the first plan received from Nippon Steel's technical cooperation department" (PaineWebber, 1985, p. 2-1).

Construction of Pohang began on April 1, 1970, and the plant was dedicated on July 3, 1973, two months before the first worldwide energy crisis.

PROFITABILITY AND SUBSIDIZATION

According to a report by PaineWebber directed to the American financial community, POSCO was a profitable venture from the beginning of its operations:

> Quite remarkable is the fact that POSCO has been profitable every year since it began production in 1973. In fact, in recent years, the company has had to resort to the use of accelerated depreciation and other accounting conventions to hold down reported profits. . . . This profit record is all the more remarkable when considering,
> —Major start-up and training costs have been incurred over this period.
> —POSCO has provided steel at bargain price levels to both its domestic and foreign customers (1985, pp. 1–2).

Three factors appear to have underscored POSCO's apparent profitability:

1. Korea's labor costs per ton shipped were lower than those of any major competitor. In 1973, labor costs per ton shipped of hot-rolled product were $7.06 at POSCO, $23.83 in Japan, $27.06 in the United Kingdom, $32.86 in Germany, and $37.83 in the United States (PaineWebber, 1985). Obviously POSCO's advantage largely reflected its far lower wage rates. Furthermore, over time, increases in POSCO's labor productivity (which will be discussed shortly) offset increases in its wage rates, enabling the fledgling firm to keep labor costs per ton shipped more or less constant.
2. POSCO incurred relatively low construction costs. For a capital-intensive investment like steel, construction delay is extremely expensive. POSCO managed to complete construction of the first phase of its mill to a mere twenty-seven months with major construction work subcontracted to Korea's leading construction firms. Of a total of twenty-seven facilities, twenty-three were completed *ahead of schedule* (Korea Advanced Institute of Science, 1976). In fact, delays in the construction of a hot-strip mill led to a crash project in which, with round-the-clock construction, workers

completed five months of work in two months, laying down 700 cubic meters of concrete daily (Pohang Iron and Steel Co. Ltd., 1984). When construction on the first phase of the Pohang mill was completed in June 1973, work on the second phase began almost at once, in December. A comparison study by the Korea Steel Association indicated that construction costs per metric ton of integrated mills after the oil crisis were the following: $1,750 for Brazil, $820 for the United States, $700 for the European Economic Community, $590 for Japan, and roughly $400 for POSCO.[3]

3. POSCO's profitability was shored up by government subsidization of costs of capital and investments in infrastructure—roads, harbors, and electricity generation. According to the Korea Advanced Institute of Science (KAIS), the Korean government supported the establishment of POSCO through various measures, as enacted in the Iron and Steel Industry Promotion Law of January 1, 1970. It provided POSCO with access to long-term low-interest foreign capital for the purchase of equipment and for the erection of a port building, water supply facilities, an electricity-generation station, roads, and a railroad line. Korea's electricity charges are among the highest in the world, but POSCO is self-sufficient in 80% of its electricity requirements. The government also provided POSCO with discounted user rates for many government services, such as a discounted railroad rate of 40%, port rate of 50%, water-supply rate of 30%, and gas rate of 20%. KAIS has estimated that the government spent a minimum of 13.3 billion won ($42 million at the nominal 1970 exchange rate) just for the "massive supporting facilities" of POSCO (Korea Advanced Institute of Science, 1976, p. 87).

Under conditions of heavy subsidization to a degree that is often underestimated by outside analysts, corporate profitability figures have little meaning. What becomes clear, however, is that *even after adding in subsidies to POSCO's costs, POSCO was operating with a cost structure that was neither less nor more favorable than that of Japan, the world's premier producer.* To remain competitive, POSCO had to compete on the basis of higher productivity and match Japan's incremental productivity improvements.

---

[3] Specifically, $400 per ton for phases I and II, $460 per ton for phase III, and $427 per ton for phase IV. The Mitsubishi Research Institute (1981) provided similar estimates in a study based on data in Fukunishi et al. (1980). Construction costs were not defined in either of these studies, but presumably included interest charges as well as direct costs (labor and materials).

THE COMPETITION

International cost comparisons of efficient integrated steel mills for both hot- and cold-rolled steel (POSCO's major products are hot rolled) show POSCO's total costs running neck and neck with those of Japan and of West Germany (see Figure 12.1 and Table 12.2). Figure 12.1 indicates that throughout the period 1973–1984, the margin of cost differences between POSCO, West Germany, and Japan was negligible. Table 12.2 gives a detailed breakdown of costs as well as input prices for cold-rolled coil in the integrated steel mills of five countries in 1984. In this case, Korea's costs are slightly above those of Japan (due, in part, to the short-run movement of exchange rates).

The explanations for cost differences between Japan and Korea in cold-rolled coil may be grouped into two sets: those related to finance (depreciation, interest, and taxes) and those related to prices,

Table 12.2 Cost of Producing Cold-Rolled Coil in an Efficient Integrated Steel Firm, Five Countries, 1985

Item	United States	West Germany	Japan	South Korea	Brazil
	Dollars per ton of finished product				
Operating costs	403.00	324.00	286.00	270.00	274.00
Labor	129.00	70.00	63.00	25.00	26.00
Iron ore	67.00	47.00	44.00	48.00	24.00
Scrap	18.00	11.00	—	—	—
Coal or coke	50.00	48.00	52.00	55.00	68.00
Other energy	24.00	22.00	15.00	24.00	27.00
Miscellaneous	115.00	126.00	112.00	118.00	129.00
Depreciation	24.00	24.00	29.00	77.00	27.00
Interest	12.00	15.00	27.00	14.00	80.00
Taxes	7.00	1.00	5.00	1.00	3.00
Total costs	446.00	364.00	347.00	362.00	384.00
Addendum					
Input prices					
Labor (dollars per man-hour)	22.50	11.90	11.70	2.85	2.90
Iron ore (dollars per ton)	40.00	26.00	24.25	25.00	12.50
Coal (dollars per ton)	55.00	58.00	59.50	59.00	60.00
Exchange rate (national unit per dollar)	—	2.90	240	800	8,500

Note: Costs are based on 90% utilization/capacity.

Source: Barnett and Crandall (1986).

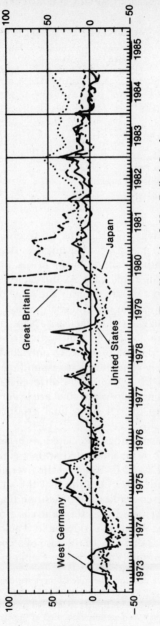

Figure 12.1 Comparison of Cost per Ton Shipped of Hot-Rolled Steel (percent difference from Pohang Iron and Steel Co. Ltd., Korea), 1973–1985. *Source:* PaineWebber.

Table 12.3   Efficiency Measures of Steel-Making, 1985[a]

Efficiency Measures	United States	West Germany	Japan	Korea	Brazil
Man hours per ton	5.75	5.85	5.35	8.20	9.00
Yield to finished product (percent)[b]	78	80	89	82	80
Iron ore per ton of finished product	1.67	1.81	1.81	1.92	1.92

[a]Derived from data in Table 12.2.

[b]Yield defined as output per unit of input.

Source: Barnett and Crandall (1986).

yields, and productivity.[4] Turning to the second set of explanations, the degree to which Japan's competitiveness depends on productivity and on yields, rather than on factor prices, may be inferred from the data presented in Table 12.2. As this table suggests, the *prices* of two inputs, iron and coal, are roughly the same per ton in Japan and Korea. Yet the *costs* of iron ore and coal per ton of steel are lower in Japan, suggesting higher yields. Similarly, labor productivity is higher in Japan: Wages are about four times greater in Japan than in Korea, but labor costs per ton of steel are only 2.5 times greater. Table 12.3 presents efficiency measures corresponding to the data in Table 12.2. As suggested by asymmetrical differences in wage rates and wage costs, labor hours per ton of steel are lower in Japan. The most common measure of overall yield, final product per unit of crude steel, is also higher.

The monetary magnitudes associated with variations in yields in the steel industry can be illustrated with a simple example, using data from Table 12.2 and focusing on the overall yield of final product per unit of crude steel. Assume that the value of a lost unit of final product represents a lost sale.[5] Assume that the value of a lost sale is equal (conservatively) to the unit costs of the least efficient producer. The least efficient producer in Table 12.2 is the United States, with unit costs of $442. In the case of a company like POSCO, therefore, with an annual capacity of 9.1 million tons, a 1% increase

---

[4] In terms of yields, or what may be called process or organizational productivity, output (or by-product) per unit of input depends on the performance of all factors combined. For example, yield with respect to finished product per unit of crude steel depends on the quality of raw materials embodied in the crude steel that is about to be converted, as well as on the performance of the labor and capital involved in the process steps whereby crude steel is actually converted into final product. To express productivity in terms of output per unit of input at this processing stage, input must be defined to include all factors. Such a productivity measure we refer to as a *yield*.

[5] This further assumes that a unit of steel produced is equal to a unit of steel shipped.

in yield raises output by 91,000 tons. At a "price" of $442 per ton, a 1% improvement in yield offsets a loss in revenue by $40.1 million— not an inconsequential saving.

Ignoring finance-related costs, the fact that Japan has defended its market share in the steel industry on the basis of superior productivity and yields has forced POSCO to invest in human and material capital to keep pace with Japan's technological progress. As will be discussed shortly, yields depend on labor skills, on process engineering, and on both the age of capital equipment and the vintage of technology embodied in it. Accordingly, POSCO has religiously reinvested its profits to upgrade its capital stock—prompting the acquisition of investment capability—and it has emphasized labor training and process improvements. In so doing it has embarked on a learning trajectory different from those of the labor-intensive industries (e.g., textiles) that preceded it.

POSCO has competed in both the international and domestic markets against steel from the integrated mills of the advanced countries as well as from Brazil and Taiwan. In the case of steel sold to local consumers who will market their final product domestically, imports are subject to a 25% duty. However, Korean steel consumers receive duty drawbacks if they reexport the imported steel in a more processed form (such consumers include numerous minimills, which account for roughly 35% of Korea's steel output and a sizeable share of POSCO's shipments). In the case of its minimill market, POSCO faces direct competition from abroad because it enjoys no tariff protection. A 1983 study of hot-rolled steel and its end users indicated that 26.5% of hot-rolled product was exported, 39.5% was sold to local consumers that were eligible for duty drawbacks, and only 34% was sold to consumers that would have had to pay a 25% duty had they imported steel (PaineWebber, 1985).

Despite excess home demand for steel throughout most of its history, POSCO has exported in order to accomplish the following: Ensure long runs and full-capacity utilization for all types of steel, earn hard currency to repay its foreign debt, take advantage of the government's export subsidies, and drive a stake in the international market in anticipation of future capacity expansions. POSCO has set itself an export target of 30%. In 1974 and 1975, however, when production was first getting under way, and then again in 1982, its ratio of exports to total shipments exceeded 40%; its major export markets are Japan and the United States.[6]

[6] In 1984 the Korean government and the U.S. Trade Representative reached an agreement that limits Korean steel exports to 1.9% of the U.S. market. The agreement imposes no product mix restrictions with the exception of slabs, which are limited to 50,000 net tons per year. POSCO's ratio of exports to total shipments averaged 28% between 1973 and 1984.

FOREIGN TECHNICAL ASSISTANCE AND THE NATURE OF STEEL-MAKING TECHNOLOGY

For the initial installation of Pohang, POSCO imported technology related not only to investment capability (preinvestment feasibility studies, manpower training, project execution), but also to production capability (process engineering, production control). The Japan Group provided both preliminary and master engineering reports, although POSCO had enough experience from earlier failures in project proposals to write the project plan. Lacking deeper capabilities in the area of engineering investment analysis, POSCO signed a contract with the Broken Hills Proprietary Corporation (BHP) of Australia to review and evaluate the engineering reports prepared by the Japan Group and also to advise it on signing procurement contracts for individual plants (almost all with Japanese plant exporters). Then POSCO hedged by engaging the services of a Korean steel specialist living in Japan to review the work of both BHP and the Japan Group (Korea Advanced Institute of Science, 1976).

POSCO ordered sixteen plants with facilities to cover the full spectrum of integrated steel mill activity. A railway system within the plant was even included. All contracts but one were given to Japanese companies (the exception was a hot-rolling plate mill awarded to Voest-Alpine, an Austrian firm.) Plant exporters supplied credit and were responsible for basic design and start-up in accordance with the Japan Group's master engineering plan. Plant exporters were also responsible for civil engineering and building construction designs. The Japan Group, however, instructed POSCO in process engineering for each plant and in overall inventory management, production scheduling, and maintenance. It also supervised all construction, POSCO being responsible only for the actual physical labor involved. In short, the initial installation was accomplished almost entirely on a turnkey basis.

The distinguishing characteristic of this turnkey transfer was the degree to which POSCO actively participated in it. POSCO engineers worked closely with their counterparts in the Japan Group—learning what was being taught to them, assimilating what was not being taught to them directly. The single most distinct feature of this participation was the dispatch of a large number of engineers and front-line supervisors for overseas training. Even before operations had commenced, 597 POSCO personnel had received training on or off the job in Japan and Austria in a total of eleven fields, among them iron-making and steel-making. This afforded a tremendous accumulation of experience and know-how and set a precedent for overseas training that continues today (see Table 8.9). Simulta-

Learning Curves for Blast Furnaces

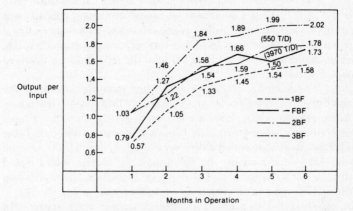

Figure 12.2 Learning Curves for Blast Furnaces. 1BF, 2BF, and 3BF refer to first, second, and third blast furnaces, respectively. FBF refers to foundry cast furnace. Output is in metric tons per day. *Source:* POSCO.

neously, the training of personnel on site at Pohang was taken with great seriousness. Before operations commenced, steel workers rehearsed their jobs in an open field, shouting orders to one another.

By all accounts, the first technology transfer was successful, a tribute to both the students and teachers involved. When operations finally started—the first molten iron poured forth on June 9, 1973—they did so smoothly, and within a short amount of time showed considerable improvement. The operating rate (production divided by rated capacity) for the last half of 1973 was 44.5%, or roughly 90% if prorated over the entire year. In 1974 it reached 114%, indicating that rated capacity had been exceeded. The operating rate of the first basic oxygen furnace (BOF) was 44% in 1973 and 112% in 1974. The first blast furnace produced 0.67 ton/day/cubic meter within one month of operation; within six months its output had more than doubled to 1.58 T/D/m^3 (see Figure 12.2).

Capital Deepening

Technology transfer, however, and its accompanying in-house investments in learning was not a one-shot transaction. Whereas capacity expansion in the textiles industry tended to involve *capital widening*—that is, small, divisible additions embodying the same technology and capital/labor ratio—capacity expansion in the steel industry tended to involve *capital deepening*, or large, indivisible additions embodying new technology and a higher capital/labor ratio (Hawtrey, 1937). Under conditions of capital deepening, POSCO was continuously confronted with process changes. Simultaneously, it broadened its product line, inducing further changes in process. Unlike the textiles industry, creating value in the steel industry involved dynamic learning.

Phase I presented a challenge even after start-up because of the large number of stages in the process flow. POSCO had to learn how to operate a sintering plant, a coke oven, a blast furnace, a basic oxygen furnace, an ingot-casting facility, and a plate mill (see Table 12.1). Each stage demanded a different set of technical skills. Overall productivity depended on the following: the correct mixture and quality of raw materials, the balancing of capacities, the scheduling of material flows, and the relieving of bottlenecks.

In phase II POSCO added a larger sintering plant, more coke ovens, a bigger blast furnace, a basic oxygen furnace, and for the first time, continuous casting and a cold-strip mill. Most facilities were enlarged still further in phase III—and the larger the facility, the more difficult the process control. Continuous casting capacity was not expanded, but a wire rod mill, a silicon steel mill, and a billet mill were added for the first time. Again, in phase IV continuous casting and cold-strip capacity were increased, and in the second stage of phase IV all major facilities were stripped and relined (with Japanese technical assistance).

Along with its process changes, POSCO's product mix grew more sophisticated. In addition to hot-rolled strip products, POSCO added wire rod, plate, billet, electrical, and cold-rolled and galvanized steel sheets. In 1985, about 4% of the value of the products that POSCO sold could be described as high grade (wire rope, high-carbon steels, railroad rails, and silicon steel). In addition, 7% could be called special steels. These require a higher level of process engineering and quality control than do basic steels. However, local demand for such steels is limited; according to POSCO this is the reason that higher grade steels do not comprise a larger percentage of total output.

PRIORITIZATION

From the time of the founding of POSCO to the time of the second energy crisis (1978–1979), POSCO's priority was to increase volume, given excess demand for steel in the home market. It did this by increasing productivity and yields and by expanding capacity. After the second oil crisis, while capacity continued to expand priority emphasis shifted to improving product quality and introducing new products. In the discussion that follows, POSCO's learning is described in two sections because it falls into two periods.

Productivity and Yields

To raise productivity (both labor and capital), POSCO attempted to minimize downtime, stabilize operations, and improve the performance of each piece of equipment. To minimize downtime POSCO adopted preventive maintenance of equipment. Stable operations depended on joint effort, and thus it worked at improving a broad set of skills. The degree to which operations were stabilized may be inferred from data on operating rates. Because a high operating rate suggests control over a process (at least enough control to prevent output from slipping below a specified level), the higher the operating rate the more stable the operation. Operating rates suggest a repetitive cycle of improvement, addition of new capacity, improvement, and so on. After POSCO added new capacity, operating rates tended to exceed rated capacity, indicating an above-average degree of process control (PaineWebber, 1985).

These early attempts at process control were not aided by computerized process-monitoring control systems. Despite the fairly widespread use of such systems in modern integrated steel mills in other countries, POSCO decided against their introduction in its first two phases of expansion. *It believed computerization would confound the accumulation of operating experience.* Therefore, it developed process engineering know-how through manual process-monitoring control. All data were collected and analyzed by hand. POSCO did not introduce a process computer until 1975, and then only in a select number of plants. Only in phase III were process computers introduced generally. As for business computers, they didn't appear until 1974. They were introduced in production control functions beginning in 1975, but a decade later POSCO was still involved in "totalizing" its computer system.

To improve the performance of each piece of equipment, POSCO provided training to its workers. As suggested in Table 8.9, the amount of training that POSCO has provided to all grades of employees is extraordinary. Between 1968 and 1979, training courses of one form or another involved roughly 61,400 workers. Approximately 4,200 people were trained outside the company, 1,513 overseas. In 1984 alone, 9,900 workers had received training, some 1,000 of them in computer applications. POSCO also runs technical training schools in the town of Pohang, and in 1986 it established an engineering college that it hopes will evolve along the lines of MIT.

The significant improvement of labor productivity over time is depicted in Figure 12.3. Employee hours per ton shipped dropped from 32.65 in 1975 to 9.62 in 1984. By comparison, the average Japanese integrated steel mill is estimated to have used 10.8 employee hours per ton in 1975 and 6.5 per ton in 1984.[7] Therefore, despite Japanese gains, the gap in labor productivity between Korea and Japan has narrowed (PaineWebber, 1985). Total factor productivity growth is difficult to estimate for POSCO because of measurement problems with capital (as mentioned earlier, POSCO artificially increased the value of its capital stock in 1982 to take advantage of accelerated depreciation). To illustrate the extent to which capital productivity has increased in conjunction with labor productivity, adjusted estimates of capital per unit of output are plotted against labor per unit of output over time (Figure 12.4). The closer the plots lie to the origin, the better both productivities. Figure 12.4 shows that the capital/output ratio was relatively low in 1973–1976, rose in 1977–1980 (with new investments in capital equipment), and then returned to its lower level in 1981. Over the whole period, the labor/output ratio generally declined.

To raise yields, POSCO concentrated on reducing rejects (as will be discussed shortly) and increasing the quantity and quality of continuous casting. In the belief that continuous casting was technically too difficult to operate at the start, it was not introduced until phase II. Then it was omitted in phase III and expanded only in phase IV, after the phase II operation had proved successful (Kwangyang will use 100% continuous casting). By 1985, POSCO was right on target: It had attained the expected yield of final steel product to crude steel (88.5%) given its continuous casting ratio (51.3%).

To meet rising demand at home (and to continue to serve the export market at a 30% target), POSCO expanded capacity, first at Pohang and then, beginning in 1985, at Kwangyang (another small village chosen as a steel mill site because of its good harbor). Foreign technical assistance continued through all four phases at Pohang. But POSCO progressively import substituted all the elements of investment capability initially supplied by the Japan Group. As percents of incremental output, foreign engineering fees and labor hours declined steeply over the four phases (see Table 12.4), despite the fact that each increment in capacity was larger than the previous one.

---

[7] Estimated at 90% operating rate for comparability with Japan.

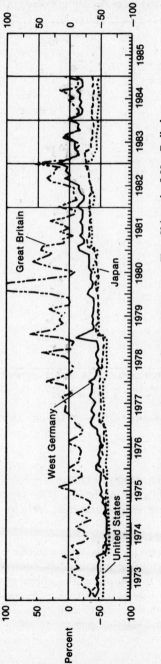

Figure 12.3 Comparison of Man Hours per Ton Shipped of Hot-Rolled Product (percent difference from Pohang Iron and Steel Co. Ltd., Korea), 1973–1985. *Source:* PaineWebber.

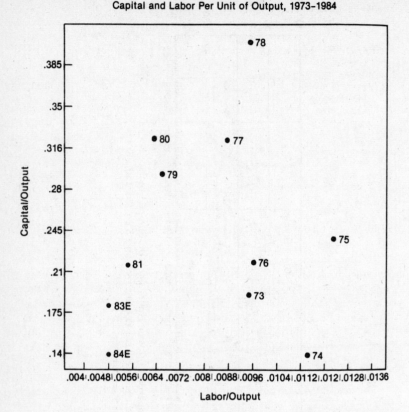

Figure 12.4 Capital and Labor per Unit of Output, POSCO, 1973–1984.
Source: POSCO

On the basis of participating in plant erections and in operating the integrated mill established in phase I, POSCO acquired capabilities to undertake the following engineering tasks in phase II:

Preliminary engineering planning
Preparation of procurement specifications for auxiliary facilities (power transmission and distribution systems)
Preparation of common specifications for general technology
Review and evaluation of manufacturers' specifications
Preparation of civil engineering and building construction design
Preparation of testing and start-up plans

Table 12.4 Dependence on Foreign Engineering at POSCO

	Phase I	Phase II	Phase III	Phase IV
A: Payments to foreign firms for engineering services ($ millions)	6.31	5.98	7.01	0.38
B: Foreign engineering hours involved	119,070	64,200	491	NA
C: Incremental capacity (million tons)	1.03	1.57	2.9	3.6
A/C: $/ton	$6.13	$3.81	$2.42	$0.11
B/C: Hours/ton	0.116	0.041	0.0002	—

Source: Derived from data from POSCO.

The Japan Group, however, reviewed all of POSCO's engineering work both during this phase and through phase III.

In phase III, the extent of local participation in project execution became even larger, although the master engineering plan continued to be the responsibility of the Japan Group. The Japan Group also assisted POSCO in establishing its computerized process-monitoring control system. New contracts with foreign consultants were entered into for specialty steels and for more advanced training. However, POSCO undertook all remaining engineering tasks itself. By the time of phase IV, the Japan Group's only function was to evaluate POSCO's own master engineering plan.

The technical assistance that POSCO has received for its Kwangyang mill has also been massive, but with two new twists. Most technology has come from Europe, Japanese steel makers being increasingly reluctant to transfer know-how to their erstwhile student. Most assistance has also been provided by plant exporters, and with the exception of evaluation, POSCO has executed all the tasks previously undertaken by the Japan Group (in addition to financing two thirds of the new mill with retained earnings). Within little over a decade, therefore, it can be said that POSCO learned enough and earned enough to reproduce itself.

Quality

In its second stage of learning (1978–1986), competing against a high-wage country like Japan took on a new dimension for POSCO. On the one hand, both an excess supply of steel in the world market and tighter measures to conserve the use of energy made customers' quality requirements far stricter than international standards hitherto existing. On the other hand, Japanese steel mills began to engage in what POSCO called *quality dumping,* or raising quality while keeping the price of steel constant. To compete, POSCO had to increase the quality of its products.

According to Sang Bok Hong, manager of POSCO's Quality Control Department, there was "not one word in the contract with the Japan Group about quality, although quality is the heart of steel-making know-how." This did not mean that the Japan Group provided POSCO with no quality control know-how whatsoever—it taught POSCO about quality indirectly, by teaching it how to make steel that met international standards. What Hong meant was that there were no quality guarantees in the contract and no explicit stipulation about instruction in how to improve quality.

Training apart, POSCO placed quality on its own agenda as early as 1973 when quality control circles were formed at the outset of operations. POSCO also established a quality control (QC) department, which functioned in practice, and launched a Zero Defect campaign, which existed in theory. The job of the QC department was sevenfold: systems analysis, laboratory work, mechanical testing, product design, investigation of the chemical and mechanical properties of different steels, monitoring of quality results across departments (steel-making, iron-making, etc.), and evaluation of quality. POSCO had not systematically collected data on reject rates until 1976, but in 1979 quality began to receive far more attention. Statistical quality control was furthered by the introduction of process computers, and investments in more sophisticated equipment enabled better testing and inspection. The Zero Defect campaign began to be taken seriously, and selected people were sent to Japan to learn more about the movement. POSCO workers began to be paid for suggestions that reduced defects.

By 1977 POSCO had as yet undertaken no R&D. Technical problems were solved either by the QC department, by technosections within production departments (to be discussed shortly), or by the Japan Group. Spurred by the second energy crisis and the need to introduce process and product improvements to reduce energy requirements, an R&D center was established in 1977. R&D expenditures between 1977 and 1986 averaged 0.70% of sales (or roughly 16.2 million dollars in 1985 when sales equaled $2.3 billion). In 1985 R&D employed 260 people: 148 researchers (12 with PhD's) and 112 technicians. The POSCO R&D department generally sets its own research agenda but also works on projects proposed to it by production departments. Major projects have included making the blast furnace an oil-free operation, reducing the consumption of refractories for steel-making, and improving the tundish for continuous casting. The R&D center's own agenda aims to consolidate technological know-how by 1990, to systematize know-how between 1991 and 1996, and to create new technology between 1996 and the year 2000.

New product introduction thus has involved the QC department, R&D, and technosections within production departments. Of the total of 432 steel grades that POSCO is aiming to establish as its fully conceivable product spectrum, 399, or 92.4%, were already being produced in 1986. An examination of quality measures of selected POSCO products makes possible the placement of an upper bound on the firm's technological attainments because its latest technological effort concerned quality. Both external and internal sources of information on quality were utilized: interviews with users of POSCO steel conducted by Mitsubishi Research Institute (MRI) and reject rates from POSCO itself. The two sources correspond fairly closely and show a mixed picture: quality equal to Japan's for some products but not others, and variations in quality along different dimensions for products whose quality is not yet under control.

The MRI survey results are presented in Table 12.5. According to users interviewed by MRI, Korean wire rod was equal in quality to Japanese wire rod. Figure 12.5, which presents POSCO's data on reject rates for wire rod, confirms the achievement over time of a defect rate that approximates zero. By contrast, user interviews suggest quality problems for plate, hot coil, and cold coil. Consistent with this finding, Figures 12.6 through 12.8 show reject rates for these products and indicate the persistence of quality problems. In the case of plate POSCO claims that the reject rate rose as customers

Table 12.5 Quality Competitiveness of Korean Steel Products Relative to Japanese Products, 1986

	Delivery	Dimension	Finish	Manufactur-ability	Weldability	Durability
Wire rod	OK[a]	OK	OK	OK	OK	OK
Concrete bar	OK	OK	OK	OK	OK	OK
Angle	OK	OK	OK	OK	OK	OK
Construction plate	OK	OK	OK	OK	OK	OK
Shipbuilding plate	NG	OK	OK	OK	NG	OK
Hot coil for pipe	NG	NG	OK	NG	OK	NG
Cold coil for car	NG	OK	NG	NG	OK	OK

[a]OK, as good as Japanese; NG, less satisfactory than Japanese.

Source: User Interviews, 1986, Mitsubishi Research Institute.

The Quality of Wire Rod

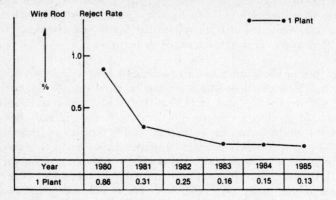

Year	1980	1981	1982	1983	1984	1985
1 Plant	0.86	0.31	0.25	0.16	0.15	0.13

Figure 12.5 Quality of Wire Rod at POSCO as Measured by the Reject Rate. *Source:* POSCO.

The Quality of Plate

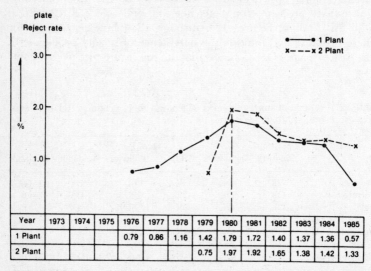

Year	1973	1974	1975	1976	1977	1978	1979	1980	1981	1982	1983	1984	1985
1 Plant				0.79	0.86	1.16	1.42	1.79	1.72	1.40	1.37	1.36	0.57
2 Plant							0.75	1.97	1.92	1.65	1.38	1.42	1.33

Figure 12.6 Quality of Plate at POSCO as Measured by the Reject Rate. *Source:* POSCO.

The Quality of Hot Coil

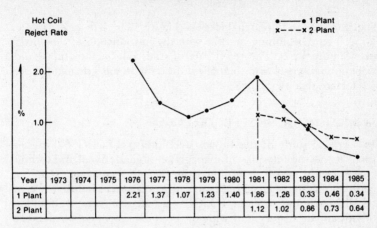

Year	1973	1974	1975	1976	1977	1978	1979	1980	1981	1982	1983	1984	1985
1 Plant				2.21	1.37	1.07	1.23	1.40	1.86	1.26	0.33	0.46	0.34
2 Plant									1.12	1.02	0.86	0.73	0.64

Figure 12.7 Quality of Hot Coil at POSCO as Measured by the Reject Rate. *Source:* POSCO.

The Quality of Cold Rolled Coil

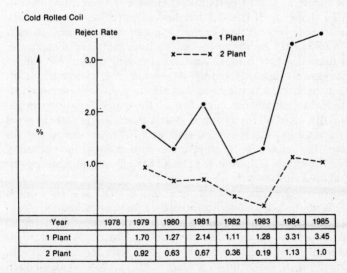

Year	1978	1979	1980	1981	1982	1983	1984	1985
1 Plant		1.70	1.27	2.14	1.11	1.28	3.31	3.45
2 Plant		0.92	0.63	0.67	0.36	0.19	1.13	1.0

Figure 12.8 Quality of Cold-Rolled Coil at POSCO as Measured by the Reject Rate. *Source:* POSCO.

began to demand greater thickness (Figure 12.6). The reject rate of hot coil rose beginning in 1978 with the introduction of new products (Figure 12.7). The reject rate of cold coil, on the other hand, went out of control as automobile industry customers demanded better surface quality (Figure 12.8).

SUMMARY: THE SHOPFLOOR FOCUS

In a critical study of the Indian steel industry, Lall (1987) argued that, "it was the interplay of managerial, organizational and technological factors which determined the [negative] outcome." The organizational and managerial issues in Korea's steel industry are especially intriguing, because POSCO is a state enterprise without any organizational history and without any of the benefits of membership in a diversified business group.

The nature of steel-making technology helped POSCO organize production without the group-level administrative support that the operating units of the chaebol enjoyed. While technological complexity characterizes the internal process flow of steel-making, the external linkages between steel-makers and feeder firms are relatively few. By comparison with, say, shipbuilding or automobile manufacture, steel-making depends on few supplier relationships. Steel production is dependent on tight internal coordination but not on the timely arrival of parts and components from multiple vendors. To make steel, POSCO has had to purchase raw materials, market its final product, and execute approximately 425 jobs. In each case, POSCO has taken steps to simplify its organizational exposure. It has formed a joint venture with a coal-mining firm in the United States to ensure a steady supply of raw material, although this investment probably has not been cost effective. It has distributed its own steel domestically but has relied on the general trading companies of the chaebol for overseas distribution. To reduce internal transactions it has subcontracted roughly 8,700 lower skilled jobs (as discussed in Chapter 8). By comparison with many of the operating units of the chaebol, therefore, POSCO has enjoyed relative organizational insularity.

Even more than the chaebol, however, POSCO was confronted initially with the task of building an organization of committed workers and managers. The argument that it has succeeded in doing so is lent support by its low turnover rates. As Chapter 8 noted, turnover for all POSCO employees due to quit rates fell from 4.4% in 1977 to 1.7% in 1980 and to a mere 1.2% in 1984 (PaineWebber, 1985, pp. 7–13). These quit rates are well below the all-manufacturing average for Korean industry. POSCO, however, has not created commitment by playing up the fact of its public ownership. To the contrary—most POSCO managers denied that the company was even a state enterprise. In fact, POSCO's status is both quasi-governmental and private in orientation. The company is a closed corporation and its stock is not traded on any exchange. Currently POSCO's ownership is held 30% by the government, 40% by the Korea Development Bank (government owned), and 30% by private commercial banks (which, however, are government controlled). Government approval is required on all management appointments and top policy management. As stated in Chapter 8, when POSCO was first founded the creation of a team of committed managers was aided by the educated unemployment that existed at the time, and POSCO workers are highly paid by Korean standards.

Nevertheless, although POSCO exploited its technology in a way that allowed it to operate outside the protective umbrella of a big business group, it organized production in the same way as the leading chaebol, which used a strategy that allowed them to compensate for their status as inexperienced learners: They gave power to managers directly involved in production. The twenty-seven different facilities that POSCO had to manage in phase I and the multiple stages in the process flow that had to be stabilized put a tremendous strain on an evolving management team that included newly returned trainees from overseas. To overcome these organizational weaknesses, POSCO gave a lot of power to the line. Each plant manager of a new facility was appointed as a counterpart to the corresponding consultant from the Japan Group, and worked closely with the responsible machinery supplier as well. The plant manager did overall planning and also participated in procurement, specification, construction management, test operation, and start-up. He (all managers are males), therefore had a total familiarity with the process of his plant at the outset of production. In the initial phases of growth, moreover, the best people were assigned to the line. Even shift foremen were experienced engineers with college degrees. Additionally, POSCO emphasized on-the-job operations training for all its technical managers. Newly recruited engineers with university backgrounds were required to work on all three shifts in order to become familiar with every operation. On-the-job training in steel-making lasted for six months; in iron-making it lasted for one year. The staff of the quality control department had to work in the plant for three months.

Only gradually were engineers gathered into centralized departments: a master engineering planning department, a construction department, an R&D center, and others. But greater centralization notwithstanding, each production department retained its own fifteen- to twenty-engineer "technosections." These technosections were important because they embodied a cross section of production and investment capability. Production capability was derived from providing technical assistance to operations managers; investment capability was derived from working with foreign technical assistants on successive capital expansions. Housed under the same roof, both skills fed one another.

CROSS-SUBSIDIZATION

When Y. S. Chough, the first plant manager of POSCO's number one blast furnace, was asked how POSCO managers learned to make steel, he responded:

> Total devotion. There were a lot of educated unemployed, and everyone wanted to learn. To learn, I had to make everything clear in every detail. We had to be in a position of preparedness to encounter the unknown. It was no use if information was known only to me. We had to concentrate everyone to one point. I always gave them tasks, homework. We would meet with the Japan Group. Then we would have a meeting of Koreans until late at night.

Determination alone, however, did not overcome the lack of capital, raw materials, markets, skills, and technology necessary to make steel. The planning that created Korea's comparative advantage in steel took two forms, both of which transcended market forces: political intervention by the government and a long-run approach to profit maximization by POSCO.

Political intervention by the government occurred in two market contexts: (1) The government intervened to raise capital. After failing to raise capital of the desired sum in the international market, the government arranged capital in political horse-trading with Japan. (2) The government intervened in POSCO's product market by a growth strategy that ensured a high level of home demand for steel. Although exports were encouraged, steel was primarily an import-substitution industry. Therefore, to ensure sufficient home demand to realize the ambitious scale at which the government wished POSCO to operate, a Big Push was necessary into the steel-consuming industries. This Big Push was a major source of government assistance to POSCO.[8]

---

[8] POSCO's principal domestic customers are minimills, which themselves serve the heavy industries—major shipbuilders and heavy equipment manufacturers—and two automobile makers. All three industries—shipbuilding, heavy machinery, and automobiles—can trace their origins to government support in one form or another.

In turn, fast growth created a stimulating environment in which to learn. It made possible two types of learning-by-doing: one associated with the acquisition of investment capability and the other associated with the acquisition of production capability. High demand allowed POSCO to run "full and steady," and steady made the acquisition of production-related skills more straightforward. Rising demand also enabled POSCO to undertake capacity expansions in rapid succession, thereby accelerating the acquisition of project execution skills and technological knowledge of the steel-making process. Finally, rising demand and the prospect of establishing a second integrated steel complex provided the government with a measure of discipline over POSCO managers. Every manager queried stated the pressure he felt to perform well in order to secure the contract for the second steel mill and the possibility of a promotion.

As POSCO expanded, it in turn increased the demand for the products of upstream industries. Its demand was of two types: it needed consumables for day-to-day operation (for example, refractories, spare parts, and abrasives), it needed capital goods. Thus, POSCO could meet government requirements for higher local content in consumption for capacity expansions. In 1977 POSCO bought about 44% of its consumables from local suppliers. By 1984 this figure had risen to 75%. The percentage of capital goods purchased locally for capacity expansions (ratio of localization) has also increased steadily over time. During the course of Pohang's four growth phases, the localization ratio rose from 12.5% to 15.5% to 22.6% to 35.1%. For the two phases of Kwangyang, the ratios are currently expected to be 50% and 56%, respectively. Furthermore, with each capacity expansion, local firms supplied more complex capital goods. In phase I of Pohang, local firms supplied simple materials; in phase II, steel structures; in phase III, single elements of equipment; in phase IV, unit facilities (power-receiving and distribution facilities and unloaders). In phase I of Kwangyang, local capital goods suppliers are building auxiliary plants (a power-generating plant and an automated warehouse). In phase II they are reaching the point of supplying major plants (a raw materials handling plant, a sintering plant).

Government subsidization of electricity afforded POSCO a cost advantage relative to minimills, and POSCO, in turn, subsidized minimills by providing them with steel at prices below those prevailing internationally (with the exception of the European "spot" market). According to PaineWebber (1985), the August 1985 price of hot-rolled coil in South Korea for domestic usage was $264 per metric ton. In comparison, the August 1985 "spot" price of hot-rolled coil was $342 per ton in the United States (list price was $524 per ton), $285 per ton in Europe at the French/German border, $346 in East Canada, and $358 for "big buyers" in Japan.

POSCO's technique for mediating market forces and creating competitive advantage in the labor market took the form of paying wage rates well above the going norm, thus accelerating the advent of a skill base also well above average. In the market for technology, foreign know-how at POSCO was rapidly supplanted by in-house investments in skill. Conceived in violation of static comparative advantage, the company might have followed an alternative path—acquiring production, investment, and innovation capability separately, in linear progression, the easiest first and the most difficult last, in a chain of static comparative advantage defined for different skill elements of a single product, analogous to one that is typically defined for many products. Instead, POSCO invested in acquiring different elements of steel-making skill more or less simultaneously. Linearity was present to the extent that POSCO first began to learn how to make steel, then how to expand steel-making capacity, and lastly how to innovate new steel products and processes. But the acquisition of investment and production capability occurred almost simultaneously. Indeed, certain elements of investment capability were acquired before POSCO turned attention to fine tuning its production skills. Sizable investments in R&D, moreover, occurred not long thereafter. *The time interval between POSCO's founding and its initial investment in R&D was barely half a decade. By contrast, twenty-seven years elapsed between the time the United States Steel Corporation was founded in 1901 and its establishment of a central R&D laboratory in 1928*[9] (Chandler, 1989). By historical standards, POSCO's learning has been less of a linear progression than a broad, frontal sweep.

---

[9] The United States Steel Corporation was formed from a merger of several existing steel companies, many of which began making steel in the 1870s. Therefore, the lag between the commencement of steel production and the establishment of a central R&D laboratory was far longer than twenty-seven years.

CHAPTER THIRTEEN

From Learner to Teacher

BACK-DOOR COMPETITION

Late-industrializing countries such as Japan and Korea appear to challenge existing economic powers such as the United States precisely in those areas in which the challengers excel by virtue of their *recent histories as learners.* Consequently, this book concludes with the major lessons that the learning paradigm of late industrializing offers to countries wishing to *re*industrialize. In addition to illuminating the path of late industrializers, the paradigm's reflection also suggests where innovators might change their rules of behavior to compete in a world that now includes a generation of latecomers reared on the learning tradition.

The competition in the late twentieth century between Japan, the quintessential learner, and the United States, the greatest economic power, unmistakably parallels a competitive relationship of the past. The United States has been challenged by Japan just as Great Britain was challenged a century earlier by the United States—on a new competitive front, using a new institutional framework. Neither Great Britain nor the United States could be said to have been attacked on its own turf, in its own area of preeminence—inventiveness in the case of Great Britain, innovation in the case of the United States.

Great Britain's inventiveness went unchallenged long after its economy had succumbed to competition from abroad. In the late nineteenth century, although England was responsible for pathbreaking inventions such as chemical dyes, it was Germany that gained dominance in the international dye-making industry. At the same time, and assuming Nobel Prize laureates in chemistry, physics, and physiology/medicine may reasonably be considered an indicator of inventiveness, Great Britain prevailed in that arena until at least 1960 (United States Department of Commerce, various years).

Today, U.S. innovativeness probably remains preeminent even as Japan continues to take market share from it in high-technology industries.[1] In terms of Britain's former province and one component of innovation—inventiveness—the United States is now indisputably master at the world technological frontier (forty of sixty-two Nobel Prizes in chemistry, physics, and physiology/medicine in 1976–1985 were awarded to Americans; only one was awarded to a Japanese) (United States Department of Commerce, various years). Moreover, in terms of the other component of innovation—the commercialization of inventions—the United States probably remains supreme. Nevertheless, although the United States was first in bringing to market such high-technology products as semiconductors, audio equipment like videocassette recorders and stereos, robots, flexible manufacturing systems, computer numerically controlled machine tools, and continuous casting in steel-making, Japan took leadership in the areas of production and growth. At the micro level, American industry appears less capable than does its Japanese equivalent of producing high-quality products efficiently and bringing new generations of the same product to market quickly. These are precisely the areas in which learners, lacking novel technology, have built their competitive advantage and excel. The macroeconomic consequence is a weaker than otherwise association between innovation and growth.

Thus, where challenge comes from a new paradigm, the new paradigm, to be contained, must be understood by its own logic rather than by the logic of the paradigm that it is upstaging. It is therefore to a summary of the lessons of late industrialization that attention is now turned.

FROM LEARNER TO TEACHER

The most elementary lesson from late industrialization is that Japanese competition is not a unique, culturally specific phenomenon. There exists a much larger set of countries that include Japan, Korea, India and Brazil, each having similar institutions that have evolved in response to the exigencies of industrializing late through learning. These institutions include an interventionist state that deliberately distorts relative prices to stimulate economic growth, business groups that diversify widely to compete initially at the lower end of many markets, a strategic focus on shopfloor management, where respected engineers strive to achieve incremental productivity and quality improvements, and a politically and economically weak labor movement (motivated in Korea by high real wage increases).

Culture and history enter into this paradigm by determining how well it operates in particular countries. As already suggested in sev-

---

[1] See, for example, Brooks (1985, p. 334).

eral chapters, the paradigm operates especially well in Japan and Korea because the state in both countries is willing and able to exact performance standards from big business in exchange for trade protection and subsidies. Moreover, although the modern industrial enterprise and managerial hierarchies are dominant in the industrial sectors of all late-industrializing countries, Korea and Japan have been unusually successful in keeping overhead in check by allocating responsibility to engineers rather than to administrators, and in stressing the importance of shop floor management. The essential features of the learning paradigm, however, are shared by enough late-industrializing countries that the world economy can expect the arrival of more like Japan. Moreover, most European countries have spent much of their industrial lives as learners, trying to catch up with either England or the United States. They, too, share many of the institutions of late industrialization, because these institutions are first and foremost a function of catching up. Therefore, if the United Kingdom and the United States have found it difficult to adopt some of these characteristics of their erstwhile followers, it is not because the institutions of these followers are especially exotic, as they believe them to be. Rather, it is because their own institutions are the exception to the general rule.

There appears to exist, therefore, a discontinuity along the continuum connecting innovating and learning, and it is unidirectional. It stops innovators from becoming learners rather than the reverse. Successful learners appear to slide easily into the role of innovator, propelled forward by large investments in R&D and habituated to scanning the world for new technology and mastering it in-house. Innovators, however, appear to find it difficult to cultivate the role of learners, because of neglect of the shopfloor and of other innovators as sources of new ideas, as well as hostility toward the state.

In the following, references to "late-industrializing countries" are restricted to Korea and the other high performers, Japan and Taiwan. References to innovators are restricted to the leading firms against which the high-performing learners have had to compete. The contest has occurred so far in mature industries or in the mature segments of high-tech industries that the innovators established. The innovators' country tends to be the United States because the mass-production industries that American firms created to compete against Britain at the turn of the century have been more susceptible to competition from late-industrializing learners than the engineering-intensive industries that German firms pioneered.

The deep ideological commitment of the United States to the market mechanism is widely recognized. In a 1965 book that comes close to predicting the U.S. economy's subsequent decline, Shonfield observed "The hostility to public initiative has deep roots in American traditional mythology" (pp. 298–9). What is less recognized is just how deep the ideological commitment of late-industrializing countries like Japan and Korea also is to the free market. The Korean president who masterminded industrialization under state initiative in the 1960s and 1970s apologizes in his autobiography for introducing planning and for intervening to control the necessarily "mammoth" big businesses of industrial growth (C. H. Park, 1963). Moreover, a commitment to market ideology in Korea was reinforced by the continuous monitoring of the Korean economy by the Bretton Woods institutions. It was stiffened further with neoclassicism by Korean graduate students returning from economics departments in American universities.

What distinguishes the United States from Korea is not economic ideology. Rather, the difference lies in how the two states define *free market* in practice. Because the productive forces in Korea have never been developed according to free market principles, Korea's workable definition of the free market is loose, satisfied by the existence of private property and intense rivalry among the big business groups. The divergence between theory and practice has been disguised by two rites of liberalization (in the early 1960s and then in the early 1980s), which left, in practice if not in theory, the fundamental relations between business and government and the institutions of economic growth unchanged. The United States, on the other hand, adheres to a much more orthodox definition of the market, despite its having been one of the most protectionist countries in the past. Ignoring its own history, the United States credits the free market with having developed the productive forces. The limits to the influence of this ideology in the United States are few. Nevertheless, late industrialization suggests that four aspects of the market mechanism have become dysfunctional and are in need of rethinking.

The first relates to allowing private rates of return rather than social rates of return to determine investment behavior. Proponents of the market view place unconditional faith in the capital market profit rate in making decisions about how much should be invested in which projects. They believe that because this rate is determined by market forces it is inviolate. Yet there is nothing sacred about it. It reflects the sociopsychic view of financiers about what rate of return they require in order to accept risk. Late-industrializing countries tend to operate with social rates of return that are much lower than the capital market profit rates that are in effect in innovating countries. Consequently, late-industrializing countries are prone to invest more, run a trade surplus, and thereby outcompete innovating countries in an ever-widening range of industries, many of which are interrelated and benefit (suffer) from each other's growth (decline). In a global economy where learners abide by social discount rates, innovative economies would be ousted from one industry after another if they left their investment decisions wholly to capital markets.

The second area in need of rethinking relates to two intersecting ideals of classical liberalism—that the state acts in the best interests of the entire nation and not those of any one group, and that the pursuit by firms other than monopolies of their private interests redounds to the benefit of society at large. *These ideals have been turned inside out in late industrialization.* Even in a democracy like Japan (and certainly in what was once a dictatorship like Korea), the state has acted unabashedly in favor of business. At the same time, the state has acted on the premise that the interests of business, even nonmonopolistic business, do not necessarily overlap with those of society at large. Hence, the support of business by the state on the one hand, and the discipline of business by the state on the other. Nevertheless, the United States persists with the two liberal market ideals that together are self-defeating: Business cannot be singled out for support, yet the economy must coast on the accomplishments of business.

The third aspect of the market mechanism that is in need of rethinking relates to productivity. The growth models of the market paradigm equate higher productivity with technological change, and then take technological change as exogenously determined. As suggested in earlier chapters, these models are irrelevant for learners because they make productivity improvements exclusively dependent on innovation, whereas learners by definition do not innovate. In practice, and in the theory of the economics of late industrialization developed in earlier chapters, the growth rate of output increases as the growth rate of productivity increases, and in closed-loop fashion, depending on institutional constraints, the growth rate of productivity increases as the growth rate of output increases—through investments that embody foreign designs, economies of scale, and learning-by-doing. While the closed-loop growth-productivity dynamic describes economic behavior in late-industrializing countries especially well, its applicability also extends to innovators. The dynamic has the virtue of drawing attention to the dependence of productivity improvements on institutions, firm size, managerial hierarchies, learning-by-doing, and so on, not just myopically on R&D, or on high wage levels that are insufficient in themselves to motivate high productivity among the workforce.

The fourth aspect of the market paradigm that is especially in need of rethinking relates to the law of comparative advantage, or the idea that countries should specialize in a limited number of industries, the choice depending on resource endowment. The law rationalizes the tendency of many American firms to withdraw from competition in "mature" industries (say, consumer electronics or steel, each of which requires significant amounts of production labor), once these markets are challenged by countries industrializing late.

Withdrawal, however, may be defeatist rather than discrete. The experience of late-industrializing countries suggests a wide latitude for improvement in such industries, in terms of productivity, quality, and service. Cumulative incremental improvements may prove decisive in winning over competitors in the areas of delivery, price, and product performance.

The potential of the mature industries is also suggested by the investments of learners in R&D. In 1983–1984, for example, the standard deviation across industries from the national mean of industrial R&D as a percent of sales was almost identical in the United States, Japan, and Korea (standardized for absolute mean differences). But the inter-industry pattern of deviation from the national mean differed. In Japan and Korea, R&D in most mature industries (food, textiles, chemicals, and nonferrous metals) fell below the all-industry average but by less than it did in the United States, and R&D in most machinery branches exceeded the all-industry average but by more than it did in the United States (World Bank, 1987). This gives some indication that in comparative terms, R&D in mature industries in the United States is lackluster.

The rate of innovation worldwide appears to be accelerating, making growing segments of high-tech service and manufacturing industries "mature" overnight. Countries unwilling or unable to compete in mature industries may discover specialization in high-tech too limiting, particularly since the social returns to investments in high-tech are higher when the new technology is applied in mature sectors.

LABOR RELATIONS

Of all the characteristics of late industrialization, labor relations show the least consistency across countries. Repression of labor dissidents and hostility toward trade unions are quite general among late-industrializing countries, but contentiousness and adversarialism between management and labor differ in degree and kind.

The Korean government has a policy with respect to every conceivable aspect of economic development except labor relations. Responsibility for labor relations within the government bureaucracy has largely been left to the Korea Central Intelligence Agency or to the police. Economists who have worked for the government, particularly for the dictatorship that came to power in 1980, have limited their labor policy to calls for wage restraint.

Korea's big diversified business groups have also treated the function of labor relations differently from other functions such as production, marketing, finance, and so on. These other functions have largely been arrogated to salaried managers, whereas that of labor relations has been retained under the personal control of the owner/chief executive. The personnel function in general, and the labor relations function in particular, are almost nonexistent as a staff responsibility, whether at the group or subsidiary level. Whatever professionalism creeps into the exercise of this function in Korea comes indirectly through the production function, in the form of quality control circles. Otherwise, labor relations are left to the charisma and paternalism of group chairmen to energize or smooth.

Paternalism in Korea since the military coup in 1961 has witnessed almost three decades of relatively peaceful labor relations. The causality between paternalism and peace is unclear because both operated in conjunction with state repression of labor, on the one hand, and rapid increases in real wages, on the other. Moreover, labor peace in the 1970s and 1980s in Korea was in keeping with international practice. The 1970s and 1980s were decades of relatively quiescent labor relations worldwide. In the United States, labor relations were quiescent despite the failure of real earnings to rise beginning in 1973 and despite the local upheavals associated with plant closings.

Nevertheless, the labor peace that has characterized both Korea and the United States may be misleading from the viewpoint of each country's capability to compete, assuming that labor peace is vital to sustaining competitiveness. In Korea, labor peace has been interrupted by explosions of unrest, as workers have demanded not merely better working conditions but also greater democracy at the workplace (as well as at the national level). In the United States, labor peace has been accomplished in conjunction with a decline in the growth rate of productivity. Although the causes of this productivity decline extend beyond labor relations, there is undoubtedly some connection between the two.

The entry of the late-industrializing countries into the world economy has resulted in an intensification of competition across markets. Competition has increased as the flow of technology across international borders has increased and the once gargantuan gulf in technological capabilities among nations has narrowed. With the notable exception of Japan, late-industrializing countries, including Korea—and many of the early-industrializing countries as well—have a long way to go before their labor relations can be described as conducive to sustained economic development. Yet, as the technological gap narrows further, one may venture to guess that competitiveness will increasingly depend on the achievement of such labor relations and of industrial peace.

Epilogue

Unlike earlier Olympic games, those held in Seoul in 1988 signified more for their host than a hollow gesture. In Korea's case the Olympics created a glare of international publicity that illuminated the intensity of domestic struggle for political change, and helped extract concessions from a government on its best behavior. The monetary rewards which the Koreans calculated as a by-product of hosting the Olympics were multiplied immeasurably by the political benefits: the emergence of relatively free elections for political officeholders.

The advent of a modicum of political democracy in Korea casts Korean industrialization in a new light. In the past it was easy to admire Korean industrialization from an economic angle. And while many Koreans also wished to have their industrialization praised from the standpoint of income equality, the case for a high degree of income equality in Korea has become uneasy. Until very recently, Koreans were not subject to financial disclosure and could hold bank accounts under assumed names. If for no other reason, this distorted the most careful attempts to calculate the distribution of wealth, a distribution that became all the more suspect with the entrenchment of Korea's mammoth diversified business groups, many of whose private owners paid no income taxes.

Now, however, one must respect Korean industrialization not only for its economic success but also for its political transformation. Economic success on the basis of strong government intervention, heavy industry, and big business is evidently compatible with political democracy. Indeed, one can make the case that the concentration of large groups of workers under one roof, and the priming of large numbers of students-cum-salaried managers, furthered political mobilization. The implications are twofold for what in the economics profession has come to be called the "new political economy" or the "new institutional economics": economic success in Korea challenges their assumption, based on psychological "laws," that government intervention degenerates into "rent seeking." Now free elections in Korea also challenge their related assumption that more government intervention results in less democracy. Korea supports the proposition that the reverse may be true, or that the degree of government intervention and the degree of democracy may be unrelated.

In Korea's practical world of policy making, democratization holds other implications. The near future in Korea is almost sure to be marked by intensified pressure from the United States for liberalization, particularly if Korea remains a trade surplus nation. In exchange for access to its home market, the United States wants access for its exports in the Korean market, and the freedom to enter Korea's financial markets to buy into Korean prosperity.

Greater liberalization is inevitable, but is being pushed independently by many Korean economists on grounds of efficiency. Past industrialization on the basis of learning, however, suggests that there is no simple equation between freer markets and greater efficiency. Moreover, liberalizing financial institutions in the presence of large conglomerations of economic power, as represented by the chaebol, has created greater inequality, not greater efficiency. Aggregate economic concentration in Korea more than doubled since financial liberalization began in 1979. Under conditions of high degrees of monopoly power, it may be preferable to keep major financial decisions in the government's hands. This is especially true now that the government is popularly elected.

The Olympics also witnessed Korea in the process of another transition: from learner, or borrower of foreign technology, to creator of new products and processes. Of course, this transition is in its infancy, and may be no easier to achieve than political democracy. But one can only be impressed by the large amounts of money that the Korean economy is currently investing in R&D and technical education. Between 1976 and 1986 the number of engineering graduates with higher degrees increased sevenfold. R&D as a percentage of GNP was .39 percent in 1970. By 1986 it had reached 2.0 percent, even as GNP soared. It is planned to reach 2.8 percent in 1990 and around 5 percent in the year 2000.

R&D in Korea has received two stimuli, one from the government and one from the institutions created by leading firms to import foreign technology. In the case of the government, rapidly rising wage rates in the 1970s alerted officials to the importance of thinking long term. The Technology Development Promotion Act of 1972 had little immediate effect on private R&D expenditures, but in 1978–1979, almost like clockwork, the biggest chaebol opened an R&D laboratory in their major industries, and then the smaller enterprises followed suit. As the government reformed tax credits and sweetened its incentives, the number of centralized corporate R&D laboratories rose from 3 in 1967, to 14 in 1976, to 52 in 1980, to 138 in 1984.

The foundations for such laboratories were often the technical offices created to facilitate the transfer of designs and production processes from overseas. In the case of the Ssangyong Cement Company, for example, its R&D laboratory began by testing the qualities of the cement Ssangyong was producing. Then the firm built a prototype of a mill to learn the optimum cement process to import from abroad. Now it has begun to experiment not merely with how to optimize cement making but also with how to develop ceramics.

The establishment of technical offices themselves were evidence that technology import is not a passive process. To be successful, technology transfer requires imagination and investments in the capability to improve and adapt. In the future, therefore, we may expect leading firms in Korea to continue practicing the high art of learning, as they scan the world frontier for new technologies and plan long-term expansion. Japanese and now Korean economic history, however, also teaches that we may expect not merely imitation and copying from learners—the longstanding stereotype. We may also expect creativity, because learning itself turns out to be a highly creative process.

Bibliography

English Language Works Cited

Adams, W. and J. W. Brock. 1986. *The Bigness Complex: Industry, Labor, and Government in the American Economy.* New York: Pantheon.

Agarwala, P. N. 1986. "The Development of Managerial Enterprises in India." In *Development of Managerial Enterprises,* K. Kobayashi and H. Morikawa (Eds.). Tokyo: University of Tokyo Press.

Aghevli, B. B., and J. Marquez-Ruarte. 1985. "A Case of Successful Adjustment: Korea's Experience during 1980–84." Washington, D.C.: International Monetary Fund.

Amsden, A. H. 1971. *International Firms and the Labour Market in Kenya.* London: Frank Cass.

_____. 1977. "The Division of Labor Is Limited by the Type of Market: The Taiwanese Machine Tool Industry." *World Development* 5 (3):217–33.

_____. 1985. "The State and Taiwan's Economic Development." In *Bringing the State Back In,* P. B. Evans, D. Rueschemeyer, and T. Skocpol (Eds.). Cambridge, England: Cambridge University Press.

_____ 1986. "The Direction of Trade—Past and Present—and the 'Learning Effects' of Exports to Different Directions." *Journal of Development Economics* 23:249–74.

_____ 1987a. "Imperialism." In *New Palgrave Dictionary of Political Economy.* New York: Macmillan.

_____ 1987b. "Republic of Korea." Stabilization and Adjustment Policies and Programmes, *Country Study No. 14.* Finland: World Institute for Development Economics Research of the United Nations University.

_____ 1989. "Big Business and Urbanization in Taiwan: The Origins of Small and Medium Size Enterprise and Regionally Decentralized Industry." Mimeo, Massachusetts Institute of Technology, Cambridge.

_____, and L. Kim. 1985a. "The Role of Transnational Corporations in the Production and Exports of the Korean Automobile Industry." Working paper 9-785-063, Division of Research, Harvard Business School, Boston.

_____. 1985b. "The Acquisition of Technological Capability in South Korea." Mimeo, Development Research Department, Productivity Division, World Bank, Washington, D.C.

_____, and S. Min. 1989. "The Limited Ability of the United States to Export Manufactures to South Korea." Mimeo, Harvard Business School, Boston.

Anderson, D. 1982. "Small Industry in Developing Countries: A Discussion of Issues." *World Development* 10 (11):913–48.

Antonelli, C. 1986. "Technological Expectations and the International Diffusion of Process Innovations: The Case of Open End Spinning Rotors." Mimeo, Politecnico di Milano, Milan.

Arrow, J. K., and F. H. Hahn. 1971. *General Competitive Analysis.* San Francisco: Holden-Day.

Ashworth, W. 1952. *A Short History of the International Economy, 1850–1950.* London: Longmans, Green.

Asia Kyokai. 1957. *The Smaller Industry in Japan.* Tokyo: Asia Kyokai.

Bagchi, A. K. 1982. *The Political Economy of Underdevelopment.* Cambridge, U.K.: Cambridge University Press.

Bai, M.-K. 1982. "The Turning Point in the Korean Economy." *The Developing Economies* 20:117–40.

Bailey, E. A., and A. F. Friedlaender. 1982. "Market Structure and Multiproduct Industries." *Journal of Economic Literature* 20:1024–48.

Balassa, B. 1981. "A Stages Approach to Comparative Advantage." In *The Newly Industrializing Countries in the World Economy,* B. Balassa (Ed.). New York: Pergamon.

———. 1984. "Comparative Advantage in Manufacturing Goods: A Reappraisal." Discussion paper, Report No. DRD90, Economics and Research Staff, Development Research Department, World Bank, Washington, D.C.

Baldwin, F. 1969. "The March First Movement: Korean Challenge and Japanese Response." Dissertation, Columbia University, New York.

Ban, S. H. 1971. "The Long-Run Productivity Growth in Korean Agricultural Development, 1910–1968." Dissertation, University of Minnesota, Minneapolis.

———, P. Y. Moon, and D. H. Perkins. 1980. *Rural Development.* Cambridge, Mass.: Harvard University Press (for Council on East Asian Studies, Harvard University).

Bank of Korea. 1963. *Review of Korean Economy in 1962.* Seoul: Bank of Korea.

———. Various years (a). *Economic Statistics Yearbook.* Seoul: Bank of Korea.

———. Various years (b). *Quarterly Economic Review.* Seoul: Bank of Korea.

Baran, P., and E. J. Hobsbawm. 1961. "The Stages of Economic Growth." *Kyklos* 14:234–42.

Barnett, D. F., and R. W. Crandall. 1986. *Up from the Ashes: The Growth of the U.S. Minimill Steel Sector.* Washington, D.C.: Brookings Institute.

Bernal, J. D. 1965. *The Scientific and Industrial Revolutions.* Vol. 2 of *Science in History.* Cambridge, Mass.: MIT Press.

Bhalla, S. S. 1979. "Aspects of Income Distribution (and Employment) in South Korea." Employment and Rural Development Division, World Bank, Washington, D.C.

Bloomfield, A. I., and J. P. Jensen. 1951. *Banking Reform in Korea.* New York: Federal Reserve Bank.

Bohn, R. E., and R. Jaikumar. 1986. "The Dynamic Approach: An Alternative Paradigm for Operations Management." Mimeo, Harvard Business School, Boston.

Brandt, V. 1986. "Korea." In *Ideology and Competitiveness: An Analysis of Nine*

Countries, G. C. Lodge and E. F. Vogel (Eds.). Boston: Harvard Business. School Press.

Braverman, H. 1974. *Labor and Monopoly Capital.* New York: Monthly Review Press.

Bresnahan, T. F. 1987. "Competition and Collusion in the American Automobile Industry. The 1955 Price War." *Journal of Industrial Economics* 35 (4):457–82.

Brooks, H. 1985. "Technology as a Factor in U.S. Competitiveness." In *U.S. Competitiveness in the World Economy,* B. R. Scott and G. C. Lodge (Eds.). Boston: Harvard Business School Press.

Brown, E. H. P. 1986. *A Century of Pay.* London: Macmillan.

de Brunner, S. E. 1928. *Rural Korea.* New York: International Missionary Council.

Bum-Shik, S. 1970 (comp.). *Major Speeches by Korea's Park Chung Hee.* Seoul: Hollym.

Business Korea. 1983. "Revving Up for a Rough Ride." December.

_____. 1984. "Business Concentration in Korea: A Critical View." July.

_____. 1985. "Where is the Edge?" August.

_____. 1986. "Technology Transfer: Targets and Tactics." February.

_____. 1987a. "Chairman's Death Makes Waves." May.

_____. 1987b. "Exports Continue to Fuel Growth." June.

_____. 1987c. "Samsung's Transition." June.

_____. 1987d. "In Search of the Linkage Effect." January.

Buzacott, J. A., et al. (Eds.). 1982. *Scale in Production Systems.* New York: Pergamon.

Calvert, M. A. 1967. *The Mechanical Engineer in America, 1830–1910.* Baltimore, Md.: Johns Hopkins University Press.

Castaneda T., and F.-K. Park. 1986. "Structural Adjustment and the Role of the Labor Market." Mimeo, Korea Development Institute and World Bank, Washington, D.C.

Caves, R. E., and M. Uekusa. 1976. *Industrial Organization in Japan.* Washington, D.C.: Brookings Institute.

Chandler, A. D. Jr. 1962. *Strategy and Structure: Chapters in the History of the American Industrial Enterprise.* Cambridge, Mass.: MIT Press.

_____. 1964. *Giant Enterprise: Ford, General Motors, and the Automobile Industry.* New York: Harcourt, Brace and World.

_____. 1977. *The Visible Hand: The Managerial Revolution in American Business.* Cambridge, Mass.: Belknap.

_____. 1988. *The Essential Alfred Chandler: Essays Toward a Historical Theory of Big Business.* T. K. McCraw (Ed.). Boston: Harvard University Press.

_____. 1989. *Scale, Scope, and Organizational Capability.* Mimeo, Harvard Business School, Boston.

Chang, Y. 1971. "Colonization as Planned Change: The Korea Case." *Modern Asian Studies* 5:161–86.

Chen, I.-te. 1968. "Japanese Colonialism in Korea and Formosa: A Comparison of Its Effects upon the Development of Nationalism." Dissertation, University of Pennsylvania, Philadelphia.

Chenery, H., and M. S. Ahluwalia. 1974. *Redistribution with Growth.* Oxford, England: Oxford University Press.

———, S. Robinson, and M. Syrquin. 1986. *Industrialization and Growth: A Comparative Study.* New York: Oxford University Press (for World Bank).

Cho, D. S. 1987. *The General Trading Company Concept and Strategy.* Lexington, Mass.: Lexington Books.

———, and M. E. Porter. 1986. "Changing Global Industry Leadership: The Case of Shipbuilding." In *Competition in Global Industries,* M. E. Porter (Ed.). Boston: Harvard Business School Press.

Cho, Y. J., and D. C. Cole. 1986. "The Role of the Financial Sector in Korea's Structural Adjustment." Mimeo, Korea Development Institute and World Bank, Washington, D.C.

Cho, Y. S. 1963. *Underdeveloped Areas with Special Reference to South Korean Agriculture.* Berkeley, Calif.: University of California Press.

Choi, J. J. 1983. "Interest Conflict and Political Control in South Korea: A Study of the Labor Unions in Manufacturing Industries, 1961–80." Dissertation, Political Science, University of Chicago.

Choi, M. H. 1960. "A Review of Korea's Land Reform." *Korean Quarterly* 2 (1):55–63.

Chou, T.-C. 1988. "The evolution of Market Structure in Taiwan." *Revista Internazionale di Scienze Economiche e Commerciali* 35 (2):171–94.

Chung, M. J. 1982. "Status of the Korean Shipbuilding Industry." Paper presented at International Forum on Industrial Planning and Trade Policies, Seoul, June.

Cole, D. C., and P. N. Lyman. 1971. *Korean Development: The Interplay of Politics and Economics.* Cambridge, Mass.: Harvard University Press.

———, and Y. C. Park. 1983. *Financial Development in Korea, 1945–1978.* Cambridge, Mass.: Harvard University Press (for Council on East Asian Studies, Harvard University).

Commission of the Churches on International Affairs. 1979. "Human Rights in the Republic of Korea." Background Information Occasional Publication 1, New York, N.Y.

Conroy, H. 1960. *The Japanese Squeeze of Korea: 1868–1910.* Philadelphia: University of Pennsylvania Press.

Corbo, V., and S.-W. Nam. 1986. "Controlling Inflation: Korea's Experience." Mimeo, Korea Development Institute and World Bank, Washington, D.C.

Council for Economic Planning and Development, Republic of China. Various years. *Taiwan Statistical Data Book.* Taipei: Council for Economic Planning and Development.

Cumings, B. 1981. *The Origins of the Korean War.* Princeton, N. J.: Princeton University Press.

Cumings, B. G. 1974. "Is Korea a Mass Society?" *Occasional Papers on Korea, No. 1.* Seattle: University of Washington Press.

Cusumano, M. A. 1985. *The Japanese Automobile Industry.* Cambridge, Mass.: Harvard University Press (for Council on East Asian Studies, Harvard University).

Daito, E. 1986. "Recruitment and Training of Middle Managers in Japan,

1900–1930." In *Development of Managerial Enterprise,* K. Kobayashi and H. Morikawa (Eds.). Tokyo: University of Tokyo Press.

Deane, P. 1965. *The First Industrial Revolution.* Cambridge, Mass.: Cambridge University Press.

Delehanty, D. E. 1968. *Nonproduction Workers in U.S. Manufacturing.* Amsterdam: North Holland Press.

Dickens, W. T. 1986. "Wages, Employment and the Threat of Collective Action by Workers." Working Paper No. 1856, National Bureau of Economic Research, Cambridge, Mass.

Dodge, H. W. 1971. "A History of U.S. Assistance to Korean Education, 1953–1966." Dissertation, George Washington University, Washington, D.C.

Dornbusch, R., and Y. C. Park. 1986. "The External Balance of Korea." Mimeo, Korea Development Institute and World Bank, Washington, D.C.

Duus, P. 1984. "The Economic Dimensions of Meiji Imperialism: The Case of Korea." In *The Japanese Colonial Empire, 1895–1945,* R. H. Myers and M. R. Peattie (Eds.). Princeton, N.J.: Princeton University Press.

Easterlin, R. A. 1981a. "Why Isn't the Whole World Developed?" *Journal of Economic History* 41:1–19.

———. 1981b. "A Note on the Evidence of History." In *Education and Economic Development,* C. A. Anderson and M. J. Bowman (Eds.). Chicago: Aldine.

Eckert, J. C. 1986. "The Colonial Origins of Korean Capitalism: The Koch'ang Kims and the Kyongsong Spinning and Weaving Company, 1876–1945." Dissertation, University of Washington, Seattle.

Economic Planning Board. 1962. *Economic Survey.* Seoul.

———. 1966. *Report on Mining and Manufacturing Survey.* Seoul.

———. 1985. *Report on Industrial Census,* Vol. 1, *1983.* Seoul.

———. Various years. *Major Statistics of Korean Economy.* Seoul.

Electronics. 1987. "Korea Aims for the Top in VLSI by 1991." April 2.

Ewing, G. O. 1973. "Labor Unions in Rapid Economic Development: Case of the Republic of Korea in the 1960s." Dissertation, University of Wisconsin, Madison.

Feder, G. 1986. "Growth in Semi-industrial Countries: A Statistical Analysis." In *Industrialization and Growth: A Comparative Study,* H. Chenery, S. Robinson, and M. Syrquin (Eds.). New York: Oxford University Press (for World Bank).

Fischer, D. H. 1970. *Historian's Fallacies.* New York: Harper and Row.

Fishlow, A. 1965. "Empty Economic Stages?" *Economic Journal* 75 (297):112–25.

Fortune. 1987. "The International 500." August.

Frank, A. G. 1969. "The Sociology of Development and the Underdevelopment of Sociology. In *Latin America: Underdevelopment or Revolution?,* J. Petras and M. Zeitlin (Eds.). New York: Fawcett.

Frank, C. R., K. S. Kim, and L. Westphal. 1975. *Foreign Trade Regimes and Economic Development: South Korea.* New York: National Bureau of Economic Research. (Distributed by Columbia University Press.)

Fukunishi, A., et al. 1980. "Competitive Relations between Japan and the Asian NICs in Materials Industries." In *Amazing Korea: Rapid Industrialization of Asian Countries and Japan's Response*, H. Omura (Ed.). Tokyo: NIRA.

Gerschenkron, A. 1962. *Economic Backwardness in Historical Perspective.* Cambridge, Mass.: Harvard University Press.

Gold, B. 1981. "On Size, Scale, and Returns: A Survey." *Journal of Economic Literature* 29:5–33.

Gorz, A. (Ed.). 1976. *The Division of Labour: The Labour Process and Class Struggle in Modern Capitalism.* Atlantic Highlands, N.J.: Humanities Press.

Government-General of Chosen. 1920–1921. *Annual Report on Reforms and Progress in Chosen, 1920–21.* Tokyo.

Grajdanzev, A. 1944. *Modern Korea.* New York: John Day (for Institute of Pacific Relations).

Great Britain, Committee on Industry and Trade. 1928. *Survey of Textile Industries.* London: Her Majesty's Stationery Office.

Grootaert, C. 1986. "The Labour Force Participation of Women in the Republic of Korea: Evolution and Policy Issues." Mimeo, World Bank, Washington, D.C.

Han, S. 1974. *The Failure of Democracy in South Korea.* Berkeley, Calif.: University of California Press.

Harbison, F. H., J. Maruhnic, and J. R. Resnick. 1970. *Quantitative Analyses of Modernization and Development.* Industrial Relations Section, Princeton University, Princeton, N.J.

Harvard Business School. 1985a. "Daewoo Group." Case Study 9-385-014. Harvard Business School Case Services, Boston.

———. 1985b. "Goldstar Co., Ltd." Case Study 9-385-264. Harvard Business School Case Services, Boston.

———. 1986a. "Business Groups in Developing Countries." Case Study 0-386-178. Harvard Business School Case Services, Boston.

———. 1986b. "Hyundai Heavy Industries and the Shipbuilding Industry." Case Study 9-385-212. Harvard Business School Case Services, Boston.

———. 1986c. "Korea's Computer Strategy." Case Study 9-685-070. Harvard Business School Case Services, Boston.

———. 1986d. "Samsung International, Inc." Case Study 0-686-123. Rev. 8/86. Harvard Business School Case Services, Boston.

Hattori, T. 1984. "The Relationship between Zaibatsu and Family Structure: The Korean Case." In *Family Business in the Era of Industrial Growth: Its Ownership and Management*, A. Okochi and S. Yasuoka (Eds.). Tokyo: University of Tokyo Press.

Hawtrey, R. G. 1937. *Capital and Employment.* London: Longmans.

Hayes, R. H. 1985. "Strategic Planning—Forward in Reverse?" *Harvard Business Review* November/December, pp. 111–19.

Henderson, W. O. 1954. *Britain and Industrial Europe, 1750–1870: Studies in British Influence on the Industrial Revolution in Western Europe.* 2nd ed. Leicester, England: Leicester University Press.

Hirschmeier, J., and T. Yui. 1981. *The Development of Japanese Business 1600–1980.* 2nd ed. London: George Allen.

Ho, S. 1980. "Small-Scale Enterprises in Korea and Taiwan." Working Paper No. 384, World Bank, Washington, D.C.

Ho, S. P.-S. 1984. "Colonialism and Development: Korea, Taiwan, and Kwantung." In *The Japanese Colonial Empire 1895–1945*, R. H. Myers and M. R. Peattie (Eds.). Princeton, N.J.: Princeton University Press.

Hong, W. 1975. *Factor Supply and Factor Intensity of Trade in Korea*. Seoul: Korea Development Institute.

———, and Y. C. Park. 1986. "Financing Export-oriented Growth in Korea." In *Pacific Growth and Financial Interdependence*, A. H. H. Tan and B. Kapur (Eds.). Sydney: Allen and Unwin.

Hubbard, G. E. 1938. *Eastern Industrialization and Its Effect on the West*. London: Oxford University Press (for Royal Institute of International Affairs).

Institute of Statistics. Various years. *Statistical Yearbook of Turkey*. Ankara: Institute of Statistics.

International Cooperation Agency, Fiscal Years 1954–1956. 1957. *U.S. Assistance Programs for Korea*. Audit Report to the Congress of the United States.

International Labor Office. 1986. *Yearbook of Labor Statistics*. Geneva: International Labor Office.

International Monetary Fund. Various years. *International Financial Statistics*. Washington, D.C.: International Monetary Fund.

Ito, S. 1984. "Ownership and Management of Indian Zaibatsu." In *Family Business in the Era of Industrial Growth: Its Ownership and Management*, A. Okochi and S. Yasuoka (Eds.). Tokyo: University of Tokyo Press.

Jacobs, N. 1985. *The Korean Road to Modernization and Development*. Urbana, Ill.: University of Illinois Press.

Johnson, C. 1982. *MITI and the Japanese Miracle: The Growth of Industrial Policy, 1925–1975*. Stanford, Calif.: Stanford University Press.

———. 1988. "The Japanese Political Economy: A Crisis in Theory." *Ethics and International Affairs* 2:79–98.

Jones, L., and I. Sakong. 1980. *Government, Business, and Entrepreneurship in Economic Development: The Korean Case*. Cambridge, Mass.: Harvard University Press (for Council on East Asian Studies, Harvard University).

Journal of Post Keynesian Economics. 1983. "Symposium: Kaldor's Growth Laws." 5:341–44.

Juhn, D. S. 1965. "Entrepreneurship in an Underdeveloped Economy: The Case of Korea, 1890–1940." Dissertation, George Washington University, Washington, D.C.

Jun, W. 1987. "The Experience of Technology Development in Korea: The Case of the Electronics Industry." Paper presented at Indian Seminar on Technology Development, sponsored by U.S. AID and Confederation of Engineering Industries of India. Korea Institute for Economics and Technology, April 27–May 1, Seoul.

Kaldor, N. 1967. *Strategic Factors in Economic Development*. Ithaca, N.Y.: Cornell University Press.

———. 1978. "Causes of the Slow Rate of Growth in the U.K." In *Essays in Economic Theory*. London: Duckworth.

Katz, D. F. 1986. "Efficiency Wage Theories: A Partial Evaluation." Working Paper No. 1906, National Bureau of Economic Research, Cambridge, Mass.

Keesing, D. B. 1967. "Outward-looking Policies and Economic Development." *Economic Journal* 77:303–20.

Kelley, M. E. 1986. "Programmable Automation and Skill Questions: Reinterpretation of the Cross-National Evidence." *Human Systems Management*, November.

Kemp, T. 1985. *Industrialization in Nineteenth-Century Europe.* London: Longmans.

Kim, C. I. E. 1962. "Japan's Rule in Korea (1905–1910): A Case Study." *Proceedings of the American Philosophical Society* 106.

Kim, C. J. 1982. "The Role of Technology in Economic Development: The Korean Case." In *Business Laws in Korea: Investments, Taxation, and Industrial Property.* Seoul: Pan-mun Book.

———. 1987. "The High Technology Industrial Drive of the Republic of Korea." B.S. Thesis, Massachusetts Institute of Technology, Boston.

Kim, C. K. 1981. "Industrial Policy and Small and Medium Industries in Korea." Working Paper No. 19, Korea International Economics Institute, Seoul.

———, and C. H. Lee. 1980. "Ancillary Firm Development in the Korean Automotive Industry." Korea International Economics Institute, Seoul.

Kim, E., and D. Mortimore. 1977. *Korea's Response to Japan: The Colonial Period 1910–1945.* Kalamazoo, Mich.: Western Michigan University Press.

Kim, H. 1971. "Land Use Policy in Korea: With Special Reference to the Oriental Development Company." Dissertation, University of Washington, Seattle.

Kim, H. H. 1980. *The Last Phase of the East Asian World Order: Korea, Japan, and the Chinese Empire, 1860–1882.* Berkeley, Calif.: University of California Press.

Kim, J. B. 1966. "The Korean Cotton Manufacturing Industry." Dissertation, University of California, Berkeley.

Kim, J. E. 1973. "An Analysis of the National Planning Process for Educational Development in the Republic of Korea, 1945–70." Dissertation, University of Pittsburgh.

Kim, J. W. 1983. "Subcontracting, Market Expansion and Subcontracting Activities Promotion—The Case of Korea's Machinery Industry." Working Paper 8305, Korea Development Institute, Seoul.

Kim, K.-D. 1976. "Political Factors in the Formation of the Entrepreneurial Elite in South Korea." *Asian Survey* 16 (5):465–77.

———. 1985. "The Distinctive Features of South Korea's Development." Mimeo, Department of Sociology, Seoul National University.

Kim, K. S. 1967. "An Appraisal of the High Interest Rate Strategy in Korea." Paper presented at Williams College, Williamstown, Mass.

———. 1985. "Industrial Policy and Industrialization in South Korea: 1961–1982." Lessons on Industrial Policy for Other Developing Countries, Working Paper 39, January, Kellogg Institute, University of Notre Dame, Notre Dame, Ind.

———, and M. Roemer. 1979. *Growth and Structural Transformation.* Harvard East Asian Monograph. Cambridge, Mass.: Harvard University Press.

Kim, K. Y. 1984. "American Technology and Korea's Technological Development." In *From Patron to Partners: The Development of U.S.-Korea Business and Trade Relations,* K. Moskowitz (Ed.). Lexington, Mass.: Lexington Books.

Kim, S. 1982a. "Contract Migration in the Republic of Korea." Working Paper MIG WP 4, International Labour Office, International Migration for Employment Branch, Geneva.

———. 1982b. "Employment, Wages and Manpower Policies in Korea: The Issues." Working Paper Series 82-04, Korea Development Institute, Seoul.

Kim, S. J. 1983. "Evaluation of and Reform Proposals for Promotion Policies in the Korean Machinery Industry." Working Paper Series 83-06, Korea Development Institute, Seoul.

Kim, S. K. 1987. "Business Concentration and Government Policy: A Study of the Phenomenon of Business Groups in Korea, 1945–1985." Dissertation, Harvard Business School, Boston.

Kim, Y. B. 1980. "The Growth and Structural Change of the Textile Industry." In *Macroeconomic and Industrial Development in Korea,* C. K. Park (Ed.). Vol. 3 of *Essays on the Korean Economy.* Seoul: Korea Development Institute.

Kindleberger, C. P. 1967. *Europe's Postwar Growth: The Role of Labor Supply.* Cambridge, Mass.: Harvard University Press.

Koh, S. J. 1966. *Stages of Industrial Development in Asia: A Comparative History of the Cotton Industry in Japan, India, China, and Korea.* Philadelphia: University of Pennsylvania Press.

Koo, B. Y. 1981. "Role of Foreign Direct Investment in Recent Korean Economic Growth." Working Paper No. 8104, Korea Development Institute, Seoul.

Korea Advanced Institute of Science. 1976. *Technological Behavior of the Petrochemical, Metallurgical and Electronics Industries in Korea.* Phase Three Report, Korean Science Technology Policy Instruments Project, Program in Science, Technology and Society, Seoul.

Korea Development Bank. 1984. *Industry in Korea.* Seoul: Korea Development Bank.

Korea Exchange Bank. 1980. "Adjustment of Korea's Heavy and Chemical Industry Investment." *Monthly Review* 14:1–21.

———. 1983. *The Korean Economy, Review and Prospects.* 5th ed. Seoul: Korea Exchange Bank.

Korea Institute for Educational Development. 1983. "Study on the Demand and Supply of Science and Engineering Manpower at Master's and Ph.D. Levels." Mimeo, Seoul.

Korea Institute for Industrial Economics and Technology. 1982. *The Heavy Machinery Industries of Korea: Problems and Prospects, Final Report.* Mimeo, Seoul.

Korea Shipbuilding Association. 1980. "A Seminar on the Technology and Productivity Improvements in Shipbuilding." Mimeo, Pusan.

Korea Traders Association. 1987. "How to Increase U.S. Exports to Korea.

Report of a Survey of Korean Business Executives." Seoul: Korea Traders Association.

Krueger, A. B., and L. H. Summers. 1986a. "Reflections on the Inter-industry Wage Structure." Discussion Paper No. 1252, Harvard Institute of Economic Research, Cambridge, Mass.

————. 1986b. "Efficiency Wages and the Wage Structure." Working Paper No. 1952, National Bureau of Economic Research, Cambridge, Mass.

Krueger, A. O. 1979. *The Developmental Role of the Foreign Sector and Aid.* Cambridge, Mass.: Harvard University Press.

Kublim, H. 1959. "The Evaluation of Japanese Colonialism." In *Comparative Studies in Society and History.* Vol. 2.

Kubo, Y., J. de Melo, and S. Robinson. 1986. "Trade Strategies and Growth Episodes." In *Industrialization and Growth,* H. Cherney, et al. (Eds.). New York: Oxford University Press (for World Bank).

Kuznets, S. 1966. *Modern Economic Growth.* New Haven, Conn.: Yale University Press.

Kwon, T.-h., et al. 1975. *The Population of Korea.* Seoul: Population and Development Studies Center, Seoul National University.

Lall, S. 1987. *Learning to Industrialize: The Acquisition of Technological Capability in India.* London: Macmillan.

Landes, D. S. 1969. *The Unbound Prometheus, Technological Change and Industrial Development in Western Europe from 1750 to the Present.* Cambridge, England: Cambridge University Press.

Lau, L. J. (Ed.). 1986. *Models of Development: A Comparative Study of Economic Growth in South Korea and Taiwan.* San Francisco: Institute for Contemporary Studies.

Lebergott, S. 1966. "Labor Force and Employment, 1800–1960." In *Output, Employment, and Productivity in the U.S. After 1800.* Vol. 30 of *Studies in Income and Wealth.* Proceedings of Conference on Research on Income and Wealth. New York: National Bureau of Economic Research.

Lee, C. S. 1963. *The Politics of Korean Nationalism.* Los Angeles: University of California Press.

Lee, H.-B. 1968. *Korea: Time, Change and Administration.* Honolulu: East-West Center Press.

Lee, H. K. 1936. *Land Utilization and Rural Economy in Korea.* Chicago: University of Chicago Press.

Lee, J. 1987. "Market Performance in an Open Developing Economy: Technical and Allocative Efficiencies of Korean Industries." *Journal of Industrial Economics* 35:81–96.

Lee, J. W. 1983. "Economic Development and Wage Inequality in South Korea." Dissertation, Harvard University, Cambridge, Mass.

Lee, K.-U., S. Urata, and I. Choi. 1986. "Recent Developments in Industrial Organizational Issues in Korea." Mimeo, Korea Development Institute and World Bank, Washington, D.C.

Lee, K.-W. 1983. "Human Resources Planning in the Republic of Korea: Improving Technical Education and Vocational Training." Staff Working Paper No. 554, World Bank, Washington, D.C.

Lee, Y. K., et al. (Eds.). 1971. *History of People Living in Korea under Japanese Occupation.* Seoul: Minjung Seokwan.

Leff, N. H. 1978. "Industrial Organization and Entrepreneurship in Developing Countries: The Economic Groups." *Economic Development and Cultural Change* 4:661–75.

———. 1979a. "Entrepreneurship and Economic Development: The Problem Revisited." *Journal of Economic Literature* 17:46–64.

———. 1979b. " 'Monopoly Capitalism' and Public Policy in Developing Countries." *Kyklos* 32 (4):718–38.

Leipziger, D. M. (Ed.). 1988. "Korea: Transition to Maturity." Special Issue, *World Development* 16 (1).

Levy, M. J. Jr. 1966. *Modernization and the Structure of Society.* Princeton, N.J.: Princeton University Press.

Lewis, W. A. 1954. "Economic Development with Unlimited Supplies of Labour." In *The Economics of Underdevelopment,* A. N. Agarwala and S. P. Singh (Eds.). London: Oxford University Press.

Lim, Y. 1981. *Government Policy and Private Enterprise: Korean Experience in Industrialization.* Korea Research Monograph No. 6, Institute of East Asian Studies, University of California, Berkeley.

Lindauer, D. L. 1984. "Labor Market Behavior in the Republic of Korea: An Analysis of Wages and Their Impact on the Economy." Staff Working Paper No. 641, World Bank, Washington, D.C.

Lindert, P., and J. G. Williamson. 1983. "English Workers' Living Standards during the Industrial Revolution: A New Look." *Economic History Review* 36:1–25.

Lipsey, R. E., and I. B. Kravis. 1985. "The Competitive Position of U.S. Manufacturing Firms." *Banca Nationale del Lavoro Quarterly Review* 153:127–54.

List, F. 1956. *National System of Political Economy.* Philadelphia: J. B. Lippincott.

Lloyd's Register of Shipping. Various years. *Shipping Economist.* London.

Lucas, R. E. B. 1986. "An Overview of the Labor Market in India." Development Research Department, Economics and Research Staff, Discussion Report No. DRD153, World Bank, Washington, D.C.

Luedde-Neurath, R. 1986. *Import Controls and Export-oriented Development: A Reassessment of the South Korean Case.* Boulder, Colo.: Westview.

Maddison, A. 1982. *Phases of Economic Development.* Oxford, England: Oxford University Press.

Maizels, A. 1963. *Industrial Growth and World Trade.* Cambridge, England: Cambridge University Press.

Mansfield, E., et al. 1971. *Research and Innovation in the Modern Corporation.* New York: W. W. Norton.

Marx, K., and F. Engles. 1961. *On Colonialism.* London: Lawrence and Wishart.

Maschke, E. 1969. "Outline of the History of German Cartels from 1873 to 1914." In *Essays in European History 1789–1914,* W. H. Crouzet, et al. (Eds.). New York: St. Martins.

Mason, E. S., et al. 1980. *The Economic and Social Modernization of the Republic of Korea.* Cambridge, Mass.: Harvard University Press (for Council on East Asian Studies, Harvard University).

Mathias, P. 1969. *The First Industrial Revolution.* New York: Charles Scribner.

McCraw, T. K. 1986. "Mercantilism and the Market: Antecedents of American Industrial Policy." In *The Politics of Industrial Policy,* C. E. Barfield and W. E. Schambra (Eds.). Washington, D.C.: American Enterprise Institute for Public Policy Research.

McGinn, H. F., et al. 1980. *Education and Development in Korea.* Cambridge, Mass.: Harvard University Press (for Council on East Asian Studies, Harvard University).

McHugh, J. 1980. *Alexander Holley and the Makers of Steel.* Baltimore, Md.: Johns Hopkins University Press.

McKenzie, F. A. 1920. *Korea's Fight for Freedom.* London: Simpkin, Marshall.

Melman, S. 1951. "The Rise of Administrative Overhead in the Manufacturing Industries in the United States 1899–1947." *Oxford Economic Papers* NS 3:62–112.

Minami, R. 1973. *The Turning Point in Economic Development: Japan's Experience.* Economic Research Series No. 14, Institute of Economic Research, Hitotsubashi University, Tokyo.

Ministry of Education. Various years. *Statistical Yearbook of Education.* Seoul: Ministry of Education.

———. Various years. *Educational Annals.* Seoul: Ministry of Education.

Ministry of Labor. Various years. *Yearbook of Labour Statistics.* Seoul: Ministry of Labor.

Ministry of Science and Technology. 1987. *Introduction to Science and Technology. The Republic of Korea.* Seoul: Ministry of Science and Technology.

———. Various years. *Handbook.* Seoul: Ministry of Science and Technology.

Mintzberg, H. 1979. *The Structuring of Organizations.* Englewood Cliffs, N.J: Prentice Hall.

Mitsubishi Economic Research Bureau. 1936. *Japanese Trade and Industry: Present and Future.* London: Macmillan.

Mitsubishi Research Institute. 1986. *Case Studies on the Trend of Japan-Korea International Division of Labor in the 1980s.* Tokyo: NIRA.

Mizoguchi, T. 1979. "Economic Growth of Korea under the Occupation: Background of Industrialization of Korea." *Journal of Economics* 20 (1):1–19.

Mody, A. 1986. "Recent Evolution of Microelectronics in Korea and Taiwan: An Institutional Approach to Comparative Advantage." Mimeo, AT&T Bell Laboratories, New Jersey.

Moore, B. Jr. 1966. *Social Origins of Dictatorship and Democracy.* Boston: Beacon Press.

Moskowitz, K. 1974. "The Creation of the Oriental Development Company: Japanese Illusions Meet Korean Reality." In *Occasional Papers on Korea,* No. 2, J. B. Pallais (Ed.). Joint Committee on Korean Studies of American Council of Learned Societies and Social Science Research Council, University of Washington, Seattle.

_____. 1979. "Current Assets: The Employees of Japanese Banks in Colonial Korea." Dissertation, Harvard University, Boston.

Mueller, W. F. 1982. "Conglomerates: A Nonindustry." In *The Structure of American Industry*, W. Adams (Ed.). 6th ed. New York: Macmillan.

Musgrave, P. W. 1967. *Technical Change in the Labour Force and Education: A Study of the British and German Iron and Steel Industries 1860–1964*. Oxford, England: Pergamon.

Myers, R. H., and M. R. Peattie (Eds.). 1984. *The Japanese Colonial Empire 1895–1945*. Princeton, N.J.: Princeton University Press.

Myint, H. 1964. *The Economics of the Developing Countries*. New York: Praeger.

Nahm, A. (Ed.). 1973. *Korea under Japanese Colonial Rule: Studies of the Policy and Techniques of Japanese Colonialism*. Kalamazoo, Mich.: Center for Korean Studies, Western Michigan University.

Nakagawa, K. 1986. "Government and Business in Japan: A Comparative Approach." In *Government and Business*, K. Nakagawa (Ed.). Tokyo: University of Tokyo Press.

Nakamura, J. I. 1974. "Incentives, Productivity Gaps, and Agricultural Growth Rates in Prewar Japan, Taiwan and Korea." In *Japan in Crisis*, B. S. Silberman and D. H. Harootunian (Eds.). Princeton, N.J: Princeton University Press.

Nam, S. W. 1980. "The Dynamics of Inflation." In *Macroeconomic and Industrial Development in Korea*, C. K. Park (Ed.). Vol. 3 of *Essays on the Korean Economy*. Seoul: Korea Development Institute.

Nath, S. K. 1962. "The Theory of Balanced Growth." In *Economic Policy for Development*, I. Livingstone (Ed.). Middlesex, England: Penguin.

Nelson, R. L. 1959. *Merger Movements in American Industry*. New York: National Bureau of Economic Research.

Nelson, R. R. 1981. "Research on Productivity Growth and Productivity Differences: Dead Ends and New Departures." *Journal of Economic Literature* 19:1029–64.

_____. 1987. "Innovation and Economic Development, Theoretical Retrospect and Prospect." In *Technology Generation in Latin American Manufacturing Industries*, J. M. Katz (Ed.). New York: St. Martin's.

_____, and S. G. Winter. 1982. *An Evolutionary Theory of Economic Change*. Cambridge, Mass.: Belknap.

New York Times. 1987. "Japan's Neighbors in Asia Benefit from Rise of Yen." August 24, p. 1A.

Noble, D. F. 1977. *America by Design: Science, Technology and the Rise of Corporate Capitalism*. Oxford, England: Oxford University Press.

Norton, R. D., and S. Y. Rhee. 1980. "A Macroeconomic Model of Inflation and Growth." In *Macroeconomic and Industrial Development in Korea*, C. K. Park (Ed.). Vol. 3 of *Essays on the Korean Economy*. Seoul: Korea Development Institute.

Ohkawa, K., and H. Rosovsky. 1973. *Japanese Economic Growth: Trend Acceleration in the Twentieth Century*. Stanford, Calif.: Stanford University Press.

Ohlin, G. 1967. *Population Control and Economic Development*. Paris: Development Centre of Organization for Economic Cooperation and Development.

Ohno, T. 1984. "How the Toyota Production System Was Created." In *The Anatomy of Japanese Business*, K. Sato and Y. Hoshino (Eds.). Armonk, N.Y: M. E. Sharpe.

Orchard, J. E. 1930. *Japan's Economic Position*. New York: McGraw-Hill.

Organization for Economic Cooperation and Development. 1970. *Inflation: The Present Problem*. Report by the Secretary General, Paris.

Osterman, P. (Ed.). 1984. *Internal Labor Markets*. Cambridge, Mass.: MIT Press.

Ozawa, T. 1974. *Japan's Technological Challenge to the West, 1950–1974: Motivation and Accomplishment*. Cambridge, Mass.: MIT Press.

PaineWebber. 1985. *POSCO: Korea's Emerging Steel Giant*. World Steel Dynamics Core Report, V, New York.

Paldam, M., and L. A. Riveros. 1987. "The Causal Role of Minimum Wages in Six Latin American Labor Markets." Report No. DRD270, Economics and Research Staff, Development Research Department, World Bank, Washington, D.C.

Pallais, J. B. 1975. *Politics and Policy in Traditional Korea*. Cambridge, Mass.: Harvard University Press.

———. 1986. *Human Rights in Korea*. Asia Watch Report, Washington, D.C.

Park, C. H. 1962. *Our Nation's Path: Ideology for Social Reconstruction*. Seoul: Dong-A.

———. 1963. *The Country, the Revolution and I*. Translated by L. Sinder. Seoul: No publisher.

Park, Y. C. 1985. "Korea's Experience with External Debt Management." In *International Debt and the Developing Countries*, G. Smith and J. Cuddington (Eds.). Baltimore, Md.: Johns Hopkins University Press.

Parker, W. N. 1984. *Europe, America, and the Wider World: Essays on the Economic History of Western Capitalism*. Vol. 1 of *Europe and the World Economy*. Cambridge, England: Cambridge University Press.

Patrick, H., and H. Rosovsky. 1976. "Japan's Economic Performance: An Overview." In *Asia's New Giant: How the Japanese Economy Works*, H. Patrick and H. Rosovsky (Eds.). Washington, D.C.: Brookings Institute.

Pearse, A. S. 1929. *The Cotton Industry of Japan and China*. Manchester, England: International Cotton Federation.

Piore, M. J., and C. F. Sabel. 1984. *The Second Industrial Divide*. New York: Basic Books.

Pohang Iron and Steel Co. Ltd. 1984. *POSCO: A Graphic History*. Pohang, South Korea: Pohang Iron and Steel Co. Ltd.

Psacharopoulos, G. 1985. "Returns to Education: A Further International Update and Implications." *Journal of Human Resources* 20:583–604.

Reeve, W. D. 1963. *The Republic of Korea: A Political and Economic Study*. London: Oxford University Press.

Reynolds, L. 1985. *Economic Growth in the Third World, 1850–1980*. New Haven, Conn.: Yale University Press.

Rhee, Y. W., B. Ross-Larson, and G. Pursell. 1984. *Korea's Competitive Edge: Managing the Entry into World Markets*. Baltimore, Md.: Johns Hopkins University Press.

Richardson, R., and B. Y. Kim. 1986. *The Structure of Labor Markets in LDCs:*

Overview for South Korea, 1953–1984. Discussion Paper, Report No. DRD162, Economics and Research Staff, Development Research Department, World Bank, Washington, D.C.

Rosenberg, N. 1972. *Technology and American Economic Growth.* New York: M. E. Sharpe.

———. 1976. *Perspectives on Technology.* Cambridge, England: Cambridge University Press.

Rostow, W. W. 1960. *The Stages of Economic Growth: A Non-Communist Manifesto.* Cambridge, England: Cambridge University Press.

Sabel, C. F. 1982. *Work and Politics.* Cambridge, England: Cambridge University Press.

———, and J. Zeitlin. 1985. "Historical Alternatives to Mass Production: Politics, Markets, and Technology in Nineteenth Century Industrialization." *Past and Present* 108:133–76.

Sachs, J. D. 1987. "Trade and Exchange Rate Policies in Growth-oriented Adjustment Programs." IMF-IBRD Symposium on Growth-oriented Adjustment Programs, Washington, D.C., February 25–27.

Samuel, R. H., and R. H. Thomas. 1949. *Education and Society in Modern Germany.* London: Rutledge & Kegan Paul.

Sanches-Albornoz, N. 1974. *The Population of Latin America: A History.* Berkeley, Calif.: University of California Press.

Scherer, F. M. 1986. "On the Current State of Knowledge in Industrial Organization." In *Mainstreams in Industrial Organization.* Book I. *Theory and International Aspects,* H. W. de Jong and W. G. Shepherd (Eds.). Dordrecht, Holland: Kluwer.

Schonberger, R. J. 1982. *Japanese Manufacturing Techniques.* New York: Free Press.

Schumpeter, J. A. 1938. *The Theory of Economic Development.* Cambridge, Mass.: Harvard University Press.

Scott, B. R. 1985. "National Strategies: Key to International Competition." In *U.S. Competitiveness in the World Economy,* B. R. Scott and G. C. Lodge (Eds.). Boston: Harvard Business School Press.

Shefter, M. 1986. "Trade Unions and Political Machines: The Organization and Disorganization of the American Working Class in the Late Nineteenth Century." In *Working-Class Formations: Nineteenth-Century Patterns in Western Europe and the United States,* I. Katznelson and A. R. Zolberg (Eds.). Princeton, N.J.: Princeton University Press.

Shepherd, W. G. 1986. "On the Core Concepts of Industrial Economics." In *Mainstreams in Industrial Organization.* Book I. *Theory and International Aspects,* H. W. de Jong and W. G. Shepherd (Eds.). Dordrecht, Holland: Kluwer.

Shiba, T. 1986. "A Comparative Study of the Managerial Structure of Two Japanese Shipbuilding Firms: Mitsubishi Shipbuilding and Engineering Co. and Kawasaki Dockyard Co., 1896–1927." In *Development of Managerial Enterprise,* K. Kobayashi and H. Morikawa (Eds.). Tokyo: University of Tokyo Press.

Shipping World and Shipbuilder. 1985. "South Korea." London, November.

Shoichi, F. 1970. "Capitalism, International Politics and the Emperor System." In *The Emergence of Imperial Japan: Self Defense or Calculated Aggression?*, M. Mayo (Ed.). Lexington, Mass.: D. C. Heath.

Shonfield, A. 1965. *Modern Capitalism: The Changing Balance of Public and Private Power*. London: Oxford University Press.

Short, R. P. 1984. "The Role of Public Enterprises: An International Comparison." In *Public Enterprise in Mixed Economies: Some Macroeconomic Aspects*, R. H. Floyd, O. S. Gray, and R. P. Short (Eds.). Washington, D.C.: International Monetary Fund.

Smith, A. D. (Ed.). 1967. *Wage Policy Issues in Economic Development*. London: Macmillan.

Sombart, W. 1933. *The History of the Economic Institution of Modern Europe*. New York: F. S. Crafts.

Souza, P. R. 1978. "Wage Disparities in the Urban Labour Market." *CEPAL Review*, January–June, pp. 199–224.

Spence, M. 1983. "Reviewing Contestable Markets and the Theory of Industry Structure." *Journal of Economic Literature* 21:981–90.

Standing, G. 1978. *Labour Force Participation and Development*. Geneva: International Development Office.

Statistics Bureau. Various years. *Japan Statistical Yearbook*. Tokyo: Statistics Bureau.

Stern, F. 1977. *Gold and Iron: Bismarck, Bleichroder and the Building of the German Empire*. New York: Knopf.

Stigler, G. 1951. "The Division of Labor Is Limited by the Extent of the Market." *Journal of Political Economy*, June.

Suh, S.-C. 1978. *Growth and Structural Change in the Korean Economy, 1919–1940*. Cambridge, Mass.: Harvard University Press.

Suh, S. M., and Y. H. S. Cheong. 1986. "Structural Adjustment and Social Welfare in Korea." Mimeo, Korea Development Institute and World Bank, Washington, D.C.

Sumiya, M. 1974. "The Emergence of Modern Japan." In *Workers and Employers in Japan*, K. Okochi, B. Karsh, and S. B. Levine (Eds.). Princeton, N.J.: Princeton University Press.

Taylor, A. J. 1972. *Laissez-faire and State Intervention in Britain*. London: Macmillan (for Economic History Society).

Tewksbury, D. G. 1950. *Source Materials on Korean Politics and Ideologies*. New York: Institute of Pacific Relations.

Thurow, L. C. 1987. "Economic Paradigms and Slow American Productivity Growth." Mimeo, Massachusetts Institute of Technology, Cambridge.

Toshiyuki, M., and Y. Yuzo. 1984. "Capital Formation in Taiwan and Korea." In *The Japanese Colonial Empire, 1895–1945*, R. H. Myers and M. R. Peattie (Eds.). Princeton, N.J: Princeton University Press.

Tsurumi, E. P. 1984. "Colonial Education in Korea and Taiwan." In *The Japanese Colonial Empire, 1895–1945*, R. H. Myers and M. R. Peattie (Eds.). Princeton, N.J.: Princeton University Press.

United Nations. 1960. *Patterns of Industrial Growth, 1938–58*. New York: U.N. Department of Economic and Social Affairs.

———. 1979. *The 1973 World Programme of International Statistics. Summary of Data from Selected Countries*. New York: United Nations.

————. 1982. *International Migration Policies and Programmes: A World Survey.* ST/ESK/SER.A/80. New York: United Nations.

————. Various years. *Statistical Yearbook.* New York: United Nations.

United States Department of Commerce. Various years. *Statistical Abstract of the United States.* Washington, D.C.: Government Printing Office.

United States Embassy. 1986. "Has the United States Been Negotiating Improved Korean Market Access for Japan?" Mimeo, Seoul.

United States House of Representatives. 1954. *Relief and Rehabilitation in Korea.* 83rd Congress, 2nd Session, House of Representatives 2574. Washington, D.C.: Government Printing Office.

Veblen, T. 1965. *Imperial Germany and Industrial Civilization. 1915.* New York: Viking.

Vogel, E. 1985. "Shipbuilding: High-Priority Basic Industry." *Comeback.* New York: Simon and Schuster.

Weems, B. B. 1964. *Reform, Rebellion and the Heavenly Way.* Tucson, Ariz.: University of Arizona Press.

Weems, C. N. Jr. 1954. *The Korean Reform and Independence Movement.* Dissertation, Columbia University, New York.

Westphal, L., and K. S. Kim. 1982. "Korea." In *Development Strategies in Semi-industrial Countries,* B. Balassa, et al. (Eds.). Baltimore, Md.: Johns Hopkins University Press.

————, L. Kim, and C. J. Dahlman. 1985. "Reflections on the Republic of Korea's Acquisition of Technological Capability." In *International Technology Transfer: Concepts, Measures, and Comparisons,* N. Rosenberg and C. Frischtak (Eds.). New York: Praeger.

Westphal, L. E. 1978. "The Republic of Korea's Experience with Export Led Industrial Development." *World Development* 6 (3):347–82.

Whang, I.-J. 1986. "Korea's Economic Management for Structural Adjustment in the 1980s." Korea Development Institute and World Bank, Washington, D.C.

Williamson, O. E. 1985. *The Economic Institutions of Capitalism.* New York: Free Press.

Woo, K. D. 1978. "Wages and Labor Productivity in the Cotton Spinning Industries of Japan, Korea and Taiwan." *Developing Economies* 16:182–98.

Woodruff, W. 1973. "The Emergence of an International Economy, 1700–1914." In *The Emergence of Industrial Societies.* Vol. 2 of *The Fontana Economic History of Europe,* C. M. Cipolla (Ed.). Fontana: Collins.

World Bank. 1987. *Korea: Managing the Industrial Transaction.* Vols. 1 and 2. Washington, D.C.: World Bank.

————. Various years. *World Development Report.* Washington, D.C.: World Bank.

Yamazawa, I. 1982. "Renewal of the Textile Industry in Developed Countries and World Textile Trade." *Hitotsubashi Journal of Economics* 24:25–42.

Yasuoka, S. 1984. "Introduction." In *Family Business in the Era of Industrial Growth: Its Ownership and Management,* S. Yasuoka (Ed.). Tokyo: University of Tokyo Press.

Yelle, L. F. 1979. "The Learning Curve: Historical Review and Comprehensive Survey." *Decision Sciences* 10:302–28.

Yonekawa, S. 1984. "University Graduates in Japanese Enterprises before the Second World War." *Business History* 26:193–218.

Yoo, J. H. 1983. "Korea's Experience and Prospects." In *Northeast Asia and the United States: Defense Partnerships and Trade Rivalries*, R. F. Kosobudo (Ed.). Chicago: Chicago Council on Foreign Relations.

Young-Hwa, K. 1986. "Education and Male-Female Earnings Inequality in the Structured Labor Market: A Case Study of Korea." Dissertation, Stanford University, Stanford, Calif.

Zymelman, M. 1980. *Occupational Structures of Industries*. Washington, D.C.: World Bank.

Korean and Japanese Works Cited

Ahn, B. J., et al. 1980. *Han'guk kŭndae minjok undongsa [The History of the Korean National Movements in Modern Ages]*. Seoul: Dol pegae.

Amsden, A. H. 1988. *Han'gukŭ; kyŏngjebalchŏn: Angjŏnggwa chaejojŏngch'aek [Wider Country Study, Republic of Korea]*. Seoul: Sĭsayŏngasa Publishers.

Cho, K. J. 1981. *Han'guk chabonjuŭi sŏngnip saron [Discourses on the Formative History of Korean Capitalism]*. Rev. ed. Seoul: Taewangsa.

Choi, H. J. 1986. "Han-Mi t'ongsang kkŏlkkŭnrŏun macharŭm" ["Korea–U.S. Trade: 'Troublesome Frictions' "]. *Tonga Ilbo [Dong-A Daily]*, December 16.

Choo, H. J. 1987. "Sodŭk punbae" ["Income Distribution"]. In *Han'guk kyŏngje ŭi iron kwa hyŏnsil [Theories and Facts of the Korean Economy]*, S. Cho, H. J. Choo, et al. (Eds.). Seoul: Seoul National University Press.

Chosŏn Ilbo [Cho-Sun Daily]. 1986. "Haeoe kŏnsŏl suju choeak" ["The 'Worst Overseas Construction Order' "]. July 25.

———. 1987. "Mi, sijang kaebang punya-byŏl hyŏpsang yogu" ["U.S. Asked Market-oriented Sector-Specific Negotiation"]. July 21.

Chungang Ilbo [Choong-Ang Daily]. 1986. "Ŭnhaeng poyu pusil ch'aekwŏn samnyŏn sihan chŏngni" ["Bad Debts of Commercial Banks To Be Cleared within Three Years"]. February 24.

Chungbu, H. 1976. *Che sach'a o-gaenyŏn kyŏngje kyehoek, 1977–81 [Government of the Republic of Korea, Economic Development Plan, 1977–1981]*. Seoul.

Chŭnggwon Kamdogwon [Securities Supervisory Board]. 1984. *Chabon sijang changgi palchŏn panghyang [Long-Term Development Plan for Securities Market]*. Seoul: Chŭnggwon Kamdogwon.

Donga Ilbo [Dong-A Daily]. 1986a. "Chejoŏp sŏlbi t'uja kyŏngjaeng" ["Competition for Capacity Expansion in Manufacturing Industry"]. March 3.

———. 1986b. "Kukche kyeyŏl sagae kiŏp chŏngni" ["Clearing of 4 Subsidiaries of Kook-Je ICC Group"]. June 27.

———. 1986c. "Chejoŏp kadongyul chilsipgu-nyŏn irae ch'oego" ["The Highest Operating Ratio of Manufacturing Industry since 1979"]. July 12.

———. 1986d. "Taegiŏp munŏbŏl hwakchang yojŏn" ["On-Going Expansion by Chaebol"]. July 28.

_____. 1986e. "Chŏnja ŏpkye ŭmji sŏ yangji toetta" ["Electronics Industry Turns from Dark to Bright Side"]. August 30.

_____. 1986f. "Chaebŏl kurup chikchŏp sangho ch'ulcha kŭmji" ["Ban on Chaebols' Cross-Investment"]. September 3.

_____. 1986g. "Chŏngni nŭn hajiman chŏngsanghwa ka munje" ["Impending Problem of Recovery after Rationalization"]. September 22.

_____. 1986h. "Chŏnja, sinbal tŭng ilbu ŏpchong illyŏk nan" ["Hard to Find Workers in Such Industries as Electronics, Shoe, Etc."]. December 18.

_____. 1987. "Taejol sirŏp k'ŭgye nŭnda" ["Unemployment of College Graduates Greatly Increases"]. July 15.

Federation of Korean Industries. 1984. "Sanŏp kisul kaebal chosa" ["Industrial Technology Development Survey"]. Seoul.

Han, G. E. 1973. *Han'guk sasang kwa kyoyuk [Korean Ideology and Education].* Seoul: Ilchogak.

Han, W. K. 1977. *Han'guk t'ongsa [The History of Korea].* Seoul: Ŭlyu Munhwasa.

Han'guk chŏlgang yŏnhap [Korea Steel Association]. 1980. *Ch'ŏlgang pogosŏ [Steel Report].* Seoul: Korea Steel Association, October.

Han'guk Ilbo [Han-Kook Daily]. 1986a. "Chaebŏl kyŏngjeryŏk chipchung man kasokhwa" ["Acceleration of Economic Concentration by Chaebol"]. November 16.

_____. 1986b. "Haeun ŏpkye i-dan'gye chŏngni ch'aksu" ["Start of Second Round Rationalization of Shipping Industry"]. December 4.

_____. 1986c. "Kŏnsŏl ŏpkye orhae haeoe sujuaek isipŏk talla nŏmchi mothal tŭt" ["The Overseas Construction Order of This Year Is Expected to Be Less Than $2 Billion"]. December 17.

_____. 1987. "Kiŏp sŏllip e obaek samsip il kŏllinda" ["It Takes 530 Days to Establish a Firm"]. August 6.

Han'guk Kyŏngje Sinmun [Korea Economic Daily]. 1987. "Muyŏk oe kŏrae hasun put'ŏ taep'ok chayuhwa" ["Large Scale Liberalization of Noncommodity Transactions"]. July 11.

Han'guk kyoyuksa yŏnguhoe [Association for Study of History of Education]. 1972. *Han'guk kyoyuksa [History of Korean Education].* Seoul: Education Publishers.

Han'guk Saengsansŏng Cent'a [Korea Productivity Center]. 1985. *Uri nara sanŏp ŭi saengsansŏng hyŏnhwang kwa apuro ŭi kwaje. [Situation of Productivity Level in Korea's Industry and Future Task].* Seoul: Korea Productivity Center.

Hattori, T. 1984. "Kodoseichoki ni akenu Sangyo no Keisei: Kankoku no Zirej, 1962, 78" [The Formation of Industrial Elites in the Era of Rapid Growth: The Case of Korea, 1962–78]. In *Hatten Tojyokoku no Business Leadership [Business Leadership in Developing Countries].* Tokyo: Asia Keizai Kenkyu zyo.

Kim, C. K., J. S. Yoo, and K. C. Whang. 1984. *Han'guk Taeman Ilbon ŭi Chejoŏp saengsangsŏng punsŏk [The Analysis of Manufacturing Productivity in Korea, Taiwan, and Japan].* Seoul: Hangyang University, Institute for Economic Research.

Kim, C.-L. 1964. "Pujŏng ch'ukchae ch'ŏri chŏnmalso" ["Report on the Reverse Policy toward Illicit Accumulation of Wealth"]. *Sindonya*, December.

Kim, D. G. 1986. "Chaejŏngŭi Kyŏngjiksŏnggwa hy'oyulsŏng" ["Inflexibility and Efficiency of Fiscal Policy"]. In *Han'guk kyŏngje samsip samjeŭi insik [Recognition of 33 Issues of the Korean Economy]*. Seoul: Taechakyo Ch'ulpanbu.

Kim, H. K. 1985. "Kyŏngje kaebal kwa kukka ŭi yŏkhal e kwanhan yongu" ["A Study of Economic Development and the Role of the Government]. In *Han'guk chabonjuŭi wa kukka [Korea Capitalism and Nation]*, J.-J. Choi (Ed.). Seoul: Han-Wool.

Kim, K. M. 1987. "Chujŏk: oehwa top'i" ["Investigation: Capital Flight"]. *Sin Tonga*, June.

Kim, S. 1976. *Nodong konggŭp kwa sirŏp kujo [Labor Force Behavior and Unemployment in Korea]*. Seoul: Korea Development Institute.

Kim, S. W. 1986. ["Shipbuilding Industry Endeavors to Lose Weight"]. In *Maeil Kyŏngje Sinmun [Daily Economic News]*, October 3.

Kim, Y. B. A. 1975. *Uri nara kyoyuk ŭi suyo hyŏngt'ae mit kyŏngje sŏngjang kiyŏdo (Demand Pattern and Contribution to Economic Development)*. Seoul: Korea Development Institute.

———. 1979b. *Han'guk ŭi kalla TV kongŏp [The Korean Color TV Industry]*. Seoul: Korea Development Institute.

Kim, Y. C., and E. B. Kong. 1983. *Kyoyuk ŭi kyŏngje palchŏn e taehan kiyŏ [Contribution of Education to Economic Development]*. Seoul: Korea Education Development Institute.

Kim, Y. H. 1970. *Han'guk nodong undongsa [History of Korea's Labor Movement]*. Seoul: Ilchogak.

Korea Advanced Institute of Science and Technology. 1985. *Chungso kiŏp ŭl t'onghan tae-Mi kisul hyŏmnyŏk pangan e kwanhan yongu [A Study on the Strategies for Importing U.S. Technologies through Small- and Medium-sized Firms by Enhancing Korea-U.S. Technological Cooperations)*. Seoul: KAIST.

———. 1986. *Uri nara kwahak kisul kaebal sisŭtem chŏngae kwajŏng kwa chŏnmang [A Study on the Science and Technology Development System in Korea and Its Future Direction]*. Seoul: KAIST.

Korea Development Institute. 1983. *80 nyŏndae nosa kwan'gye palchŏn wihan kandamehoe pogosŏ [Symposium Report on Korea's Management-Labor Relations in the 1980s]*. Seoul: Korea Development Institute.

Kwahak Kisulch'ŏ [Ministry of Science and Technology]. 1986. *Kwahak Kisul yŏngam [Science and Technology Yearbook]*. Seoul: Ministry of Science and Technology.

Kyŏngje Kihoekwŏn [Economic Planning Board. 1986. Kosīje 86-7 Ho, "1986 Hyŏndo Sijangch'ŏk saūpcha Ch'ijung" [Notification of 86-7, "Designation of Market-dominating Enterprises for the Year 1986"].

Lee, J. J. 1986. *Sanŏp yuhyŏng-byŏl kisul kaebal kwajŏng mit chŏngch'aek kwaje [The Process of Technology Development by Industry and Its Policy Implications]*. Seoul: Korea Economic Institute.

Lee, K. E. 1984. *Han'guk kyŏngje wa chungso kiŏp [The Korean Economy and Small and Medium Sized Firms]*. Seoul: Ka-Chi.

Lee, K. U. 1984. "Uri nara chejoŏp ŭi sijang kujo" ["Market Structure of

Korean Manufacturing Industry"]. In *Han'guk kaebal yŏn'gu [Korea Development Studies]*. Seoul: Korea Development Institute.

———, and J. K. Kim. 1981. *Han'guk chejoŏp ui sanŏp chipchung punsŏk [Analysis of Concentration of Korean Manufacturing Industry]*. Seoul: Korea Development Institute.

———, and Lee, J. H. 1985a. "Kiop kyorhap kwa kyŏngjeryŏk chipchung" [Corporate Mergers and Economic Concentration"]. In *Han'guk kaebal yŏngu [Korea Development Studies]*. Seoul: Korea Development Institute.

——— and S. S. Lee. 1985b. *Kiŏp kyŏrhap kwa kyŏngjeryŏk chipchung [Corporate Mergers and Economic Concentration]*. Seoul: Korea Development Institute.

Lee, T. Y. 1987. *Ŏpchong-byŏl yŏngu kaebal t'uja hyŏnhwang mit sanŏp kisul chiwon chedo chŏkchungsŏng kŏmt'o [R&D Investment by Industry and the Appropriateness of Korea's Technology Development]*. Seoul: Korea Institute for Economics and Technology.

Lim, J. C. 1986. "Imgŭm kwa nodong chukŏn" ["Wage and Working Conditions]. In *Han'guk kyŏngje samsipsam kwaje ŭi insik [Recognition of 33 Issues of the Korean Economy]*. Seoul: Seoul National University Press.

Maeil Kyŏngje Sinmun [Daily Economic News]. 1986a. "Samjung kosok ui haeoe kŏnsŏl" ["Overseas Construction among Three Problems"]. February 25.

———. 1986b. "Chadongch'a pup'um taegiŏp chamyŏbum: yumang ŏpchong pusang ddara" ["Boom of Large Firms' Entry to Automobile Parts Industry As the Industry Shows Bright Future"]. August 1.

———. 1986c. "Mi sŏbisŭ nongsanmul p'oham kaebang yogu" ["U.S. Asks to Open Service and Agriculture Market"]. August 12.

———. 1986d. "Mi yogu p'ummok chogi kaebang kŏmt'o" ["Earlier Import Liberalization Is under Consideration for Items that U.S. Asked to Liberalize"]. November 7.

———. 1986e. "Kuknae kiŏp haeoe t'uja kwŏnjang" ["The Korean Government Recommends Foreign Direct Investments by Korean Firms"]. November 20.

———. 1986f. "Han'guk, chungjangbi kiji-ro kakkwang" ["Korea Becomes Manufacturing Base for Heavy Machinery"]. November 22.

———. 1986g. "Kaehwagi matchŏn kigye kongŏp" ["Booming of Machinery Industry"]. December 2.

———. 1986h. "Taegiŏp haeoe t'uja kanghwa" ["Increase of Foreign Direct Investment by Large Firms"]. December 18.

———. 1987a. "Chosŏn sasa sŏnjong chŏnmunhwa" ["Four Shipbuilding Companies Agreed to Specialize in Type of Ship"]. July 18.

———. 1987b. "Mingan chudo kyŏngje silmyŏn twi-bat'ch'im" ["Support for Private-led Economy"]. July 22.

———. 1987c. "Chaebŏl ta hoesa ch'ulcha samjo sach'ŏnch'ilbaek sasipŏk" ["The Volume of Cross Investment by Chaebol Amounts to 3474 Billion Won"]. July 27.

———. 1987d. "Chosŭn suju segye ilwi" ["Shipbuilding Order, the Largest in the World"]. August 1.

Moon, P. Y. 1987. ["Agriculture and Rural Sector"]. In *Han'guk kyŏngje ŭi iron kwa hyŏnsil [Theories and Facts of the Korean Economy]*, S. Cho, H. J. Choo, et al. (Eds.). Seoul: Seoul National University Press.

Park, F. 1983. "Sanŭppyŏi imgŭm kyŏkch'ŭi t'ŭksŏnggwa byŏnhwa" ["Characteristics and Changes in Wage Differences Between Industries]. In *Han'guk kyŏngjeji [Korea Development Review]*, volume 5 (1), Spring.

Park, F. K. and S. I. Park. 1984. *Han'guk ŭi imgŭm kujo [Wage Structure in Korea]*. Seoul: Korea Development Institute.

Park, H. C. 1985. *Han'guk chabonjuŭi nodong munje [Korea's Capitalism and Labor Problems]*. Seoul: Dolbegai.

―――. 1986. *Han'guk kyŏngje kujoron [Study of the Structure of the Korean Economy]*. Seoul: Il-Wol-Seo-Gak.

Park, J. H. 1987. "Chaebŏl kurup chonghap yŏnsuwon sŏllip rŏsi," ["Rush in Establishment of Group-Level Training Center by Large Business Groups"]. In *Maeil Kyŏngje Sinmun [Daily Economic News]*, July 20.

Park, W. H. 1987. *Han-Il kisul punŏp ŭi saeroun chŏn'gae [New Technological Collaboration between Korea and Japan]*. Seoul: Korea Institute for Economics and Technology.

Raj, M-K. 1984. *Nodong kyŏngjehak [Labor Economics]*. Seoul: Kyungmoosa.

Seoul National University (College of Business Administration). 1985. *Han-'guk kiŏp ŭi hyŏnhwang kwa kwaje [Current Situation and Task to Be Done by Korean Firms]*. Seoul: College of Business Administration, Seoul National University.

Sobija Poho Danch'e Hyŏpŭihoe [Association of Organizations for Consumer Protection]. 1987. *Sobija poho chedo wa pihae kuje [Regulation for Consumer Protection and Recovery of Damage]*. Seoul: Association of Organizations for Consumer Protection.

Son, H. K. 1987. "Chip'yo ka malhanŭn pinbu kyŏkch'a ŭi silt'ae" ["The Realities of the Gap between the Poor and the Rich Revealed by Indicators"]. *Sin Tonga*, February.

Song, H. Y. 1987. "Pusil kiun pusil kiŏp chŏngni" ["Rationalization Aggravated More Firms]. In *Wŏlgan Chosŏn [Cho-Sun Monthly]*, July.

Song, Y. M. 1987. "Pusil kiŏp chŏngni ŭi naemak" ["Inside Story of Bailout of Failing Firms"]. In *Wŏlgan Chosŏn [Cho-Sun Monthly]*, July.

Suh, J. S. 1986. "Han yŏngnong hugyeja ŭi chukŭm kwa nongch'on hyŏnsil" ["Death of a Successor of Agricultural Business and the Present Condition of Rural Community"]. *Sin Tonga*, June.

Taehan Chubu Kŭllŏp Yŏnhaphoe [Association of Housewife Clubs, forthcoming). 1987. *Kobal sarye chip [Complaint Cases]*. Seoul: Association of Housewife Clubs.

Taehan Pangjik Hyŏphoe [Spinners and Weavers Association of Korea]. 1987. *Panghyŏp sasim-nyŏn sa [The 40-Year History of Spinners and Weavers Association of Korea]*. Seoul: Spinners and Weavers Association of Korea.

Yoon, J. I. and J. Y. Park. 1977. *Kyoyuk chaejŏng ŭi hyŏnhwang kwa munje kyoyuk pi punsŏk yŏngu [Present Situation and Problem of Education Budget]*. Seoul: Han'guk kyoyuk kaebalwon.

Yoon, W.-S. 1986. "Kyosa ŭi chiwi: chŏu-nun twitjŏn ch'ŏbŏl-ŭn minch'ŏp" ["Teacher's Status: Mistreatment"]. *Wŏlgan Chosŏn*, July.

Yun, S. C. 1982. *Kisul ch'ukchŏk-kwan iron [Theory of Technology Accumulation and Management]*. Seoul: Il-Shin-Sa.

Name Index

Subject Index

Steel industry in Korea (*continued*)
government favoritism in, 73
history of, 293
and import substitution, 155
minimills, 73, 301, 316n
Pohang Iron and Steel, 291–318. *See
also* Pohang Iron and Steel Company, Ltd.
shipbuilding dependent on, 274
wage difference for, 251
Students, Korean, vi, 52
vs. military/U.S., 42, 48
protests by, 42–43, 52, 148
Subcontracting, 161. *See also* Small-
and medium-size firms, Korean
by Hyundai Motors, 179, 180, 184–87
by Japanese firms, 183
in Korean industry, 183–84, 187–88
in late industrialization, 187
and POSCO "contracted-out" workers, 209–10, 314
Subsidies, 143–44, 146
to exporters in late industrializing
countries, 68
and ideal interest rate, 144
in late-industrializing countries, 8–9, 13
in market-augmenting paradigm, 150
Subsidies, Korean, v–vi, 143
in accumulation model, 63
and capital flight controls, 17–18
and diversification, 127–28
and exports, 66–68, 74, 78
for HHI, 276
and investment opportunities, 235
for POSCO, 297, 301
progress from, 155
Sunkyong group, 135
Synthetic fiber industry, 78

Taihan group, 15
Taiwan, v, vi, 140
agricultural labor force in, 203
diversified business groups in, 151
economic concentration in, 121, 122, 123
and education, 215
firm size and value-added in, 162
and government budgets, 88
government expenditures in, 93

and Japanese colonialism, 53
and Korea (income), 48
land reform in, 149
large-size firm in, 9
large and small firms in, 161–63
and late industrialization, 4, 11
and liberalization policy, 76–77
market-conformance pressures on, 143
as POSCO competitor, 301
reforms in, 141
state discipline in, 146–47
state management needed in, 148
subsidies in, 8, 143
and textiles, 249
trade coefficient of, 70, 72
vertical disintegration in, 245
wage increases in, 196
wages as advantage of, 143
as yacht competitor, 259
zaibatsu-like groups in, 115
Tariffs, Korean, 70, 145, 301
Taxation, in Korea, 18. *See also* Budgets, government
Technical assistance. *See* Technology
transfer
Technical expertise, and heavy-industry competition, 19
Technical training, Korea. *See* Training for Korean workers; Vocational training, in Korea
Technological capability, elements of, 173–74
Technology Development Promotion Act (1972), 328
Technology and technological change
of cement firm (Ssangyong), 265
Cheil Wool acquisition of, 237
in growth model, 110
and Japanese education, 220
and Korean/Japanese wage rise, 189
and range of firms, 160–61
as Schumpeterian discipline, 145
Technology transfer (technical assistance), 20, 329
business appreciation of, 22–23
in dynamic of late industrialization, 152, 153
by Germany vs. England, 21–22
imitation vs. apprenticeship in, 20
and late industrializing countries, 215
from POSCO to USX, 292